Trouble Showed the Way

Njahe

Trouble Showed the Way

Women, Men, and Trade

in the Nairobi Area,

1890–1990

Claire C. Robertson

Indiana University Press
Bloomington and Indianapolis

Published by
Indiana University Press
601 North Morton Street
Bloomington, IN 47404-3797 USA

http://www.indiana.edu/~iupress
telephone orders 800-842-6796
fax 812-855-7931

The paper used in this publication meets the minimum
requirements of American National Standard for Information
Sciences—Permanence of Paper for Printed Library
Materials, ANSI Z39.48-1984.

Manufactured in the United States of America

Library of Congress Cataloging-in-Publication Data

Robertson, Claire C., date
Trouble showed the way : women, men, and trade
in the Nairobi area, 1890–1990 / Claire C. Robertson.
p.   cm.
Includes bibliographical references and index.
ISBN 0-253-33360-1 (cl : alk. paper). —
ISBN 0-253-21151-4 (pbk. : alk. paper)
1. Women, Kikuyu—Commerce. 2. Women, Kikuyu—Economic conditions.
3. Women, Kikuyu—Social conditions. 4. Women, Kamba—Commerce.
5. Women, Kamba—Economic conditions. 6. Women, Kamba—Social conditions.
7. Beans—Economic aspects—Kenya—Nairobi. 8. Sex role—Kenya—Nairobi.
9. Nairobi (Kenya)—Commerce. 10. Nairobi (Kenya)—Economic conditions.
11. Nairobi (Kenya)—Social conditions.   I. Title.
DT433.545.K55R63   1997
338.9'0089'963954067625—dc21   97-40099

1   2   3   4   5   02   01   00   99   98   97

Contents

TABLES

Figures/Illustrations

ACKNOWLEDGMENTS AND DEDICATION

In trade there is always debt; my debts incurred while preparing this book are various and extensive. It could not have been completed without essential contributions from many persons across several continents. Foremost is my husband, Edward Robertson, whose patience and hard work are (always) appreciated. He and my sons not only suffered without complaint the household disorganization consequent upon the absorption of one of its managers in this project, but he also did much of the computer formatting of the manuscript. Gary Eubanks was infinitely patient, innovative, and cooperative about the vagaries of trying to press multidimensional people onto flat computer printout. Data entry was completed with accuracy, cheerfulness and dispatch by Valerie Rake, Rebecca Thomas and Anene Ejikeme, while Valerie Rake also put in painstaking hours on the bibliography. The financing of the above came from generous grants by my employer, the College of Humanities at The Ohio State University. The field research was supported by Fulbright, Ford Foundation and American Philosophical Society grants.

In Kenya "too many" people earned my everlasting gratitude. Godfrey Muriuki, eminent Kikuyu historian, helped in many ways, not least in vouching for my respectability for the purposes of getting research clearance; the Office of the President not only produced clearance but also its renewal in record time with a friendly face. At the Kenya National Archives, my second home for a year, Maina Keru and Richard Ambani were of inestimable help in honoring even the most exigent and obscure of requests, while Ministry of Agriculture personnel were cordial in facilitating access to relevant files. Local officials like Matthew Muigai at Kiambu and John Njora in Nairobi were cooperative and informative. My three research assistants, J.N.T., E.W.K., and R.W.C., were a delight as coworkers and friends; the ongoing help of J.N.T. has been especially appreciated. B.D., my best market mentor, unravelled mysteries and provided a sterling model. (Initials only are used here to prevent any negative consequences of their participation.) David Kang'ethe, transport expert extraordinaire, supplied complete reliability, unfailing good nature, courtesy, and good humor to the enterprise, as well as an athletic rescue. The several tape translators also put in yeoman's work on a tight schedule. Jill Stever completed a separate inquiry/survey regarding possible sources of loans for traders at short notice. Centro International para la Agricultura Tropicale (CIAT) bean experts Roger Kirkby and Louise Sperling rendered invaluable help by consultation and sample collection in Rwanda for purposes of comparison, while at Girton Colin Leakey shared his extensive knowledge of African beans and family hospitality.

Also at Cambridge Jeanne Fisher shared her home, her memories, her data and her photographs, some of which are reproduced here. John Lonsdale, whose knowledge regarding Kenya and its archival sources is unparallelled, provided a valuable exchange of insights, numerous contacts, and, with Moya Lonsdale, extensive hospitality, while Anne Darvall gave necessary help with Cambridge library resources. Elsewhere in England, Andrew Hake, Elspeth Huxley, Thomas and Patricia Askwith and Thomas and Nancy Colchester gave generously of their time, hospitality, and recollections. In Kenya and in the United States Celia Nyamweru was a patient listener and reader, and particularly helpful with contacts and insights.

In the U.S. and Canada wise feminist colleagues provided wonderful input, among them Luise White, Kathleen Staudt, and Jean Hay, who lent knowledgeable and willing ears to even the most fatuous of my fledgling East Africanist inquiries, halting more exiguous flights of fancy and correcting inaccuracies. Esther Njiro, Inge Brinkman, Cynthia Brantley, Eric Onstad, Dorothy McCormick, and Susan Watkins provided me with advance copies of essential manuscripts or helpful but hard to obtain sources. Surprised but instantly cooperative, Greet Kershaw, Paul Gepts, Herbert Werlin, Christopher Leo, and others responded informatively to phone queries. For careful reading and suggestions regarding the manuscript I am grateful to: Margaret Strobel, Gracia Clark, Patricia Stamp, Luise White, Kevin Cox, Jeanne Fisher, Celia Nyamweru, and Njuguna Mwangi. Also, the members of the Gracia Clark/Beverly Stoeltje African Women Seminar at Indiana University made excellent suggestions.

But most of all, the many hardworking citizens of Nairobi's markets made this study possible. Despite their difficult lives, they welcomed me, suffered the inconvenience of interviews without complaining, for the most part, and generally saw to it that I had what I needed. My admiration for their efforts has only grown with the absorption of the many facets of their lives presented in this book. I honor their dedication, intelligence, persistence, and spirit, and wish them well, while apologizing if anything I have presented here is not an accurate reflection of their situation. I have done my best here both to further their interests and shield them from any harm that might arise from their disclosure of information. To them this book is dedicated.

A NOTE ON CURRENCY AND MEASURES

Until about 1905 cowries and beads (called *ukuta* by Mackinder) were in widespread use in East Africa, at which point rupees, pice, and annas began rapidly to replace them. Barter, however, was also common, called *mali kwa mali* in Kiswahili, even in areas as close to Nairobi as Gatundu Market in the 1950s. For major purchases or bridewealth livestock were used in Central Kenya--sheep, goats and cattle. In the 1930s one cow was equivalent to ten sheep or goats, one bull to five sheep or goats. Beginning in 1921 a modified British currency system was adopted with a pound sterling equal to twenty shillings, and 100 cents to a shilling. One rupee equalled two shillings. In 1967 the sterling standard was abandoned. In 1971 one Kenyan pound was worth 1.167 British pounds or $2.80. In the mid-1970s seven to nine Kenyan shillings were worth U.S.$1, in 1987 about seventeen shillings. The value of the currency floated downward and was negatively affected by structural adjustment measures in the 1990s. Kenyan shillings are a hard currency but do not have much international trade; there are exchange restrictions regarding Tanzanian currency, in particular.

The chief grain measure used precolonially by caravans was the *kibaba*, equivalent to about 1.5 pounds or .75 kilogram. Calabash measures used widely until the 1970s came in four sizes detailed in Chapter II. Now two, one, half, and quarter kilogram metal margarine tins are used, shown in some of the photographs from Gikomba Market. A common large measure for produce is the *debe*, equivalent to about ten to fifteen kilograms.

Sources: Kenyatta, *Facing*, pp. 62-64; interview Githuka, Nairobi: 2 Nov. 1988; Mackinder, *Ascent*, pp. 102,139; White, *Comforts*, p. viii; Etherton, *Mathare Valley*, p. iv. All references have been abbreviated. Full citations may be found in the bibliography. Archival files used are cited first by call number. Unless otherwise specified, the numbers refer to files in the Kenya National Archives (KNA), also the repository for most of the government documents used.

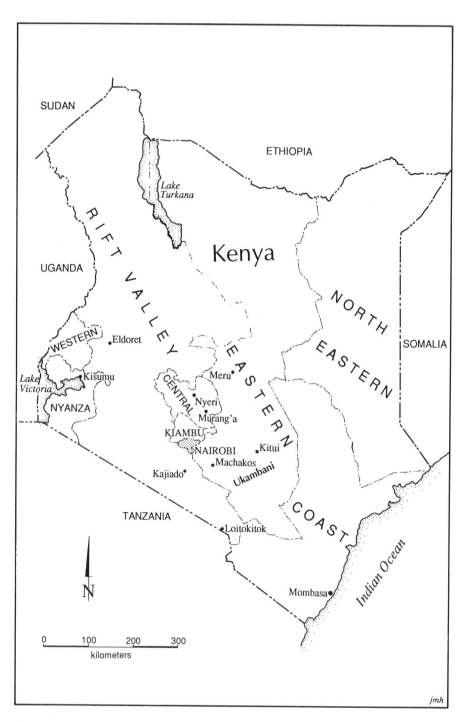

0.1 Map of Kenya with Locale of Study

Trouble Showed the Way

I

Introduction

African woman I want to praise you
the way you work in this world.
Oh bless you!
Translation of Kiswahili song composed by Elliot Ngubane[1]

Should the new markets of eastern and southern Africa develop lines of sex division in buying and selling comparable to those which characterize the markets of the western and central parts of the continent, it seems likely that not only the economic position of women, but their place in the social order in general may undergo change.

M. J. Herskovits[2]

Central Kenyan women traders and farmers were and are key actors in the development of the trading and market gardening system that feeds Nairobi. Their accomplishments represent an unheralded achievement that remains hidden partly because government persecution has pursued some of their activities. While women supported their families and took pride in their capabilities, their work was also essential to the transformation of the economy to fill the needs of the large Nairobi urban agglomeration to such effect that their lives--their relationship to their bodies, to relatives and children, and to other women involved in organizational attempts, were also transformed. Their efforts belong to the economic, social and cultural history of Africa as much as, for instance, those of Gold Coast cocoa farmers, but this history has been ignored, disclaimed or discounted as unimportant. And yet, their achievements were grand in sum, durable, transformational, and intentional. In effect, central Kenyan women reclaimed themselves by pursuing trade. This book chronicles those efforts, but also the ambivalent implications of some transformations for the women who furthered or instigated them. The increasingly convoluted world capitalist economy, race, class, ethnicity, and gender all were imbricated in the processes that caused their problems. However, they used links welded most solidly out of gender-shaped experiences in efforts to overcome the trouble that showed them the way to Nairobi.

The herstory of women traders stands at the intersection of gender, business, and labor history, with all the contradictions implicit in such a location. The view

---

[1] Performed by the Amubuto Male Chorus, "Soweto" album.

[2] "Introduction" to *Markets*, ed. Bohannan and Dalton, pp. xi-xii.

1

presented here is shaped by multidisciplinary lenses into a faceted invocation of the experiences of those in a city-in-the-making. Here we see the fundamental importance of women's work in creating a new world, but also how they overcame difficulties by using collective strength predicated upon the old world and delineated by the objectification imposed upon women by colonialism to mediate and transform the new situation. In so doing women offered a reconstruction of gender that has transformative value for the society. Contravening the stereotype of East African women as docile farmers, this history explores the symmetry of symbolic and material categories in making beans and other dried staples the focus of a commodity-based history of trade that foregrounds the heretofore submerged voices of those whom colonialists and tourists found/find invisible. If they were noticed, they were not wanted, like the beans in the maize fields of colonial agriculture officers promoting maize monoculture. Here I will argue that colonial experiences were key in the transformation of precolonial trade--in which women and men performed complementary roles--to a gender-segregated trade of ever increasing importance for women and men. The progressive segregation of trade by gender, as well as landlessness and urbanization of women in large numbers, then facilitated the contemporary situation in which women traders are more autonomous but still usually act in the collective interests of their families, whose composition has been redefined, and of their coworkers. These transformations brought new ideas of self-respect among women that are helping to engender societal reconstruction, but the gender segregation fostered by colonialism in the divide-and-conquer strategy that was effective in many realms of African life now threatens to overwhelm the survival capabilities of even the most determined.

This story of women traders, of the beans they trade/d, of the development of a food provisioning system, and of the changing construction of gender and male dominance, focuses on central Kenya, first on the Kikuyu, the largest ethnic group in Kenya who dominate among Nairobi area traders, and second on Kamba women, for whom Nairobi trade is more recent but rapidly increasing.[3] These traders are experiencing the full impact of an increasingly unified world economy in which some have been marginalized further and a few have expanded their businesses beyond Ukambani and Kikuyuland. They feed Nairobi, but they also now conduct much of the dried staples trade all over Kenya, an expansion of central Kenyan women's trade that will be documented here from the late nineteenth to the late twentieth century. While these traders now are mostly among the poor within a neocolonial economy whose comprador class claims for itself the right to perpetuate an increasingly

---

[3] Kikuyu can also be spelled Gikuyu; the Kikuyu language sound is between a hard 'g' and a 'k' sound in English. In English spelling the 'k' is less ambiguous and I have chosen therefore to use it here. Most censuses have listed Kikuyu as about 20% of Kenya's population, Kamba at about 12%. Kikuyu predominated among Nairobi's African population from its beginning. PC/CP 8/3/1 Census and Vital Statistics 1919-28; African Affairs Dept. *Annual Report* (hereafter abbreviated as AR) 1950: 65; Morgan, "Kikuyu," p. 62.

rapacious capitalism, at the same time they have utilized creatively the interstitial opportunities presented by small-scale businesses. To do so they grappled with per- vasive male dominance, which solidified with the impact of colonialism and changed its form to maximize its advantages. It did not, however, always succeed.

The goals of this study are multiple and intersecting; in delineating the history of women's trade in the Nairobi area I will stress its integration into the East African economy from the late nineteenth century to the present; illustrate the reciprocal effects of changes in trade and family structure; look at efforts at control of women and by women of their lives; outline the impact of discrimination and persecution by the Kenyan state in its various incarnations; and commend the pervasive independent reconstructive efforts undertaken by these working-class women. After examining the construction of gender in late nineteenth and early twentieth century central Kenya, I will carry out an ethnobotanical analysis of the symbolic centrality of some varieties of beans for Kikuyu women that shows the history of beans in Kenya to be a template for the history of women. As women were caught up in colonialism, marginalized, and devalued, so beans were displaced as a staple in favor of more profitable maize in a prototypical case of agricultural imperialism. Next, pieced together from varied sources is a tandem history of the women's dried staples trade in the Nairobi area and of attempts to control it. The history of Kenyan women's trade suggests that one answer to the long-standing but by now tedious debate over the dominance of local or foreign capital in the development of Kenyan capitalism can be found in this true grassroots commerce in exclusively local commodities by those whose existence has been neglected in previous studies.[4] That development, however, both preceded colonialism and proved to be of limited value for capital for- mation due to the impediments faced by women and their commitment to the collec- tive welfare. The changes in marital and organizational strategies for women facili- tated by involvement in trade are analyzed next, incising the theme of working-class women's increased autonomy that they have channelled into ever stronger collective efforts.

Theoretical Premises

At the core of this story is the struggle over control of women's labor. Male dominance, sometimes less exactly called patriarchy, is not a fixed phenomenon, but is situated historically and changes along with the society that encodes it. It was firmly embedded in Kikuyu and Kamba socioeconomic structure and British colonial thinking and cultural practices. The interaction of these structures in the colonial experience generated strong socioeconomic and political changes. Colonialism in

---

[4] This debate is best summarized in Leys, "Capitalists." Even Freeman, *City of Farmers*, p. 17, in an otherwise excellent recent study of Nairobi urban farmers, assumed that women played an insignificant role in Nairobi trade as in Dar es Salaam, following Bryceson, *Liberalizing*, p. 102.

central Kenya encountered relatively[5] unstratified societies and stratified them, using pre-existing lines of cleavage to produce class formation, which proceeded apace. Gender relations then became embedded in a web of conflicts--between older and younger Kikuyu men, between British-appointed Kikuyu authorities and anticolonial movements, and ultimately between the poor and the better off. In this respect the case of Nairobi area traders illustrates how, when economic and social interests coincide, colonialist and colonized men may cooperate in the attempt to control women. More often, however, their interests did not coincide and African men found their efforts to reconfigure gender and control women, which became an essential part of the nationalist movement, not supported by the British. Such efforts were a critical element in the objectification of women that segregated their interests from those of men. After independence controlling women became a core issue in nationmaking for male authorities, although the aspects of women's labor men wished to control changed. If, as I suggest, the desire to control women's labor lay at the root of many attempts to control women, the assertion of women's rights to control their own labor, and by extension their bodies, has both assured the survival of, and transformed, the peasant women's groups out of which the traders' groups arose. Together women sought solutions to their troubles and struggled for autonomy through their work.

Central Kenyan women to a great extent predicate their identities upon their work and have been roused to protest most when that work is impeded, exploited or distorted. Guy called "the continuous acquisition, creation, control, and appropriation of labour power ... the dynamic social principle upon which ... precapitalist societies were founded," and stressed women's productive labor in this regard.[6] Ngugi wa Thiong'o, preeminent Kenyan writer, stressed the importance of work to the extent of making it the defining feature of history, a belief that coheres with the experiences of these women. "History is ... about human struggle: first with nature as the material source of the wealth they create, food, clothing and shelter; and secondly, struggle with other humans over the control of that wealth. Labour, human labour, is the key link between the two struggles."[7] The intricate intertwining of work and identity, so presciently forecast by Simone de Beauvoir in her emphasis on transcendence through commitment to a life *projet*, is here recast into a working-class context.[8] If women's work has been the means for their exploitation, organization

---

[5] By comparison with many West African societies, which were highly stratified with centralized governments.

[6] Guy, "Analysing," p. 22. He differentiated controlling labor from controlling the product of labor, which he said characterized more developed economies, but male dominance assured control over the product of women's labor in many cases.

[7] Ngugi, *Moving*, p. 96. The correspondence to Marxist views is evident.

[8] De Beauvoir, *Second Sex*. I am also grateful to the freedwoman Sojourner Truth for this insight. Her most famous speech, "Ain't I a Woman?", stressed that she could work as hard or harder than a man without the chivalric allowances made that U.S. middle-class white women expected (in Schneir, *Feminism*, pp. 93-95).

around it has also centered their attempts at empowerment and the reformulation of their collective and individual identities.

If African working-class women construct themselves and are constructed on the basis of their work, elite women suffer from Western influence that has (since the Industrial Revolution) imposed notions of invisibility or impropriety upon women's work. The influence of nineteenth century European middle- and upper-class notions of women's domesticity in convincing the world that women historically were house-wives has been such that the importance and prevalence of women's work outside the home has been almost completely ignored until recently. In stressing the critical importance of women's labor for the creation and perpetuation of male dominance, I am countering a tendency to underestimate its centrality in venues ranging from con-temporary Western feminist theory to Kenyan government and development policies. Before industrialization there was little meaningful distinction between work inside and outside the home. A key motivation for male dominance was that women's labor was essential to survival and control over women's labor to male accumulation of surplus. The Engelian distinction between the productive and reproductive functions of labor that saw women's labor inside the home as unproductive because it did not generate profits for employers (surplus value) ignored the profits it generated by sup-plying related men with unpaid services. Lerner located the source of women's oppression in women's biological reproductive labor, although she led the way toward establishing that concepts of subordination originated in men's desire to con-trol women.[9] Sacks, Leacock and others, following Engels, linked the rise of private property with corporate kin control of ownership to the subordination of women that accompanied the rise of socioeconomic differentiation.[10] Edholm, Harris and Young extended the definition of reproductive labor to include socializing and maintaining the labor force.[11] They did not go far enough.

Following Kusterer, I will place women's "domestic" labor in the productive realm because it generated profits for men and formed an arena for struggle between women and men. Kusterer excoriated those Marxist political economists of the 1980s, who defeated the feminist attempt to place housewives and their work inside rather than outside the working class and the capitalist mode of production, as "tech-nically correct, theoretically sophisticated and also essentially incorrect and funda-mentally irrelevant." In his view they had ignored the feminist challenge to explain the subjugation of women as a necessary step toward ending it. He then emphasized the importance of women's unwaged work, saying that productive work takes place within the household, and attributed the Victorian Marxist underestimation of domes-tic work to "peculiarly male misunderstandings of the nature of production."

---

[9] Engels felt women would take a step toward liberation with employment outside the home; how-ever, he saw women's wage work as unfortunate and hoped to make it unnecessary by improving male earnings. Engels, *Origin*; *Condition*, pp. 170-78; Lerner, *Creation*, "Women."

[10] Sacks, *Sisters*; Leacock, *Myths*; Coontz and Henderson, "Property Forms," pp. 111-12.

[11] Edholm, Harris, and Young, "Conceptualising Women," pp. 101-30.

"Things once separated from nature by human labor [which fall within the Marxist definition of manufactured goods for whose production wages are paid] require constant continuing inputs of human labor to keep them from returning to nature [labor dismissed by Marxists as unproductive because unwaged and therefore not contributory to surplus value]," he said.[12] Women's unwaged labor within and without the home is therefore productive labor. Even in orthodox Marxist terms, it contributes to surplus value in allowing related male wage workers to work longer hours for more pay. Here I have tried to emphasize economic causality and process without the disadvantages of some variants of Marxist and neoclassical analysis by abandoning androcentrism, eschewing the assumption that only wage workers have agency and importance in forcing change, and emphasizing the vitality and instrumentality of those involved in petty commodity production and services that are not pre-capitalist holdovers but intimately connected to the uneven expansion of industrial capitalism.

Women's labor, moreover, is absolutely essential to the economy, even though usually unrecorded or underestimated in value. Without it the economy, and the society, could not function. Many have dismissed as trivial the usual reasons men give for beating their wives; indeed, the beating is condemned all the more for being done because dinner was not ready at the expected time. But the issue of women's provision of domestic services is not trivial for many men; it may make the difference between just getting by or having leisure time, surviving comfortably, with constant problems, or not at all. For most African families rural women's labor was/is the basis of survival, and there is no practical distinction between tasks done within and without the home. In central Kenya such labor produces/d and prepares/d most of the food and now is crucial for cash crop production.

Control over women's labor, whether waged or not, was/is therefore worth contesting, which is/was an inevitable result of women's urbanization. Coontz and Henderson emphasized the role of kin relations in the control of women's labor, saying that "the oppression of women provided a means of differential accumulation among men," while Hirschon stressed that "the differential capacity to recruit labour. . . is a crucial aspect of inequality in gender relationships," masked by an ideology of sharing within households.[13] Labor control is a critical resource essential to gender stratification and class formation; for instance, the majority of slaves held in Africa in the nineteenth century were women because they did most of the agricultural labor necessary to generate wealth.[14] We can, therefore, situate control over women's labor historically.

Looking at conflicts over women's labor and its products is of particular relevance to studying how women developed the local and long-distance dried staples

---

[12] Kusterer, "Demise," pp. 239-40, 242-44. While subscribing to patriarchy as the sole source of women's oppression, he located the end of that oppression where Engels did, in women's employment outside the home, thereby underrating its intrafamilial aspects and longevity.

[13] Coontz and Henderson, "Introduction," pp. 36-37; Hirschon, "Property," p. 7.

[14] Robertson and Berger, "Introduction"; Robertson and Klein, "Importance."

trade in the Nairobi area. Women's (and men's) labor in trade and agriculture was a key factor in the accumulation of wealth within households; the threat of losing control over that accumulation became a locus of conflict between men and women under colonialism. One consequence of colonialism's intentional class differentiation among Kenyan Africans was to raise the stakes regarding male control of women's labor. If land in and around Nairobi became contested terrain under colonialism, the object of quarrels between white settlers and Africans, governments of various kinds and traders of both sexes, so did the profits of trade and agriculture between women and men.

Markets were an emblematic site of conflict in Nairobi, where the contest over territory and profits converged. The many struggles that centered in the African markets involved not only turf wars between a hegemonic but schismatic upper class and a rambunctious underclass, but also increasingly factionalized petty commodity traders, differentiated through gender in their relationship to the means of production. This study problematizes the construct of undifferentiated petty commodity trade by illustrating how discrimination against women and an increasingly segregated gender division of labor gave women significantly less access than men had to critical resources like their own labor and that of others, capital and education. Countering the assumptions of those like Colin Leys, who failed to grasp the multiple indissoluble linkages between control over women's labor and class formation, this study illustrates the absolute necessity for any study of class formation to take gender, and gender constructs, into account.[15] It also rejects an overly economistic approach by looking at many facets of the lives of central Kenyan women traders as well as their work, giving life to the process of class formation in broaching symbolic material.

One of the themes in this study is dispossession, that dispossession that accompanies segregation for those disadvantaged by it. The systematic imposition of industrial capitalism on Kenya was motivated by the greed of ambitious and sometimes dispossessed Europeans seeking better fortunes elsewhere. They in turn dispossessed local peoples, among whom the Kikuyu and Kamba figured prominently, generating irredentism. The men wanted their prized possession back, the land (an overwhelming proportion of the land was male-controlled), but tried to expand their control where they could, over women and children, whose labor was essential to making the land profitable.[16] But sons left and women wanted their bodies back--to

---

[15] Leys, "African Capitalists," p. 27. Gerry and Birkbeck, "Petty Commodity Producer," have an excellent discussion of differentiation within petty commodity production, but do not include gender as a distinguishing variable.

[16] The Emergency measures of the 1950s further dispossessed many Kikuyu, in particular, and generated among families at Kawangware, a suburb of Nairobi, what Browne, "Kawangware," p. 76, has called an obsession with security regarding family, household, land and hunger which lasted into the 1980s. Kershaw, "Changing Roles," has the best discussion of the symbolic meanings of land for the construction of Kikuyu concepts of masculinity.

construct a world safe from predation, to control themselves, their labor, and their children, and to reconstruct a world with connections to, and consideration for, the natural world.

Poverty in Analysis

The world is a series of screens.[17]

Ancient philosophers debated the verities of existence and some became idealists; that is, they believed that there was no such thing as reality, only human perceptions of reality. Thus, they said that if a tree fell in a forest and no human heard it, then it made no sound. With the resurrection of idealism in some forms of postmodern analysis, we have had excellent and extremely useful insights on the subjects of voice, cultural process, and language, which have been especially fruitful for feminist analysis and inform my methodology and the treatment of my subject. Particularly useful also are what Shaw has called the "imbrication of power and knowledge such that power is implicated in all scholarship," and the nonlinear treatment of time so that the past not only shapes the future but the future reinvents the past and may redeem it.[18] However, these insights have not been as useful for the analysis of causality, so critical to African historians. Rerouting analysis back to the actions of the colonialists in Africa, to a concentration on written sources (logocentrism), removes the necessity for researchers to learn African languages or do significant fieldwork. The assumption has been that changing ideology will change policy, that racism, for instance, is sui generis and will stop when it has been deconstructed to illustrate its fallacies. The elitist Western bias is evident; the focus on media is common but understandable, given current media-manipulated and -saturated Euro-American societies, but dubious in other contexts. Moreover, the individualizing tendency within postmodernism leads away from acknowledging collective process and agency, foreswearing collective labels in favor of nuanced ambiguity, thus weakening possibilities for collective action.[19] While misuse of deconstruction can sometimes be blamed for such faults, we may still be left with flaccidity in causal analysis, especially when processual change is involved, and a theoretical vacuum.

---

[17] DC/MKS 10B/13/1 *Muig.* I, 6 (Oct. 1928): 6. A literal meaning is any high ridge obscures the country beyond, signifying that all knowledge is parochial.

[18] Shaw, *Colonial Inscriptions*, p. 17.

[19] Eisenstein, *Color*, pp. 208-209; Christian, "Race," pp. 73-74; Duchen, *Feminism*, pp. 102-103. The value of current research that concentrates on culture as a process, power relations involving gender and ethnicity in particular, constructions of gender and ethnicity, and multiple and competing identities of nation, ethnicity, gender, race, class, sexual preference molded "historically and discursively," is incontrovertible, but its insights do not derive exclusively from postmodern approaches. Moghadam, "Introduction," pp. 4-5, 10, 22, offers an excellent example of absorption of new directions in research but theoretical poverty. See also Brown, "Finding," for an innovative deconstruction of the state, but problematical solutions for its defects (further deconstruction). Scott, "Gender," pp. 17-19, has a useful critique of the limitations of both liberal and Marxist feminist approaches to gender.

When a tree falls the noise it makes is perhaps the least important of its attributes; a lot of hidden and overt damage may be done to other trees, animals, and occasionally humans. The end result may provide homes for other animals and replenish the environment, which consists of all aspects of the world, not just human perceptions. While attempting to change perceptions about working-class women among elites is necessary and laudable, even success in that regard will not necessarily improve their lot, especially when it is in the economic interests of the elite to keep those women poor. Questions of class and economic justice, as Moghadam pointed out, are still fundamental.[20] The shift away from such issues is detrimental to most of the world's women, who are also most of the world's poor. Poverty, whatever else it might be conceptually, is a material condition requiring material solutions. Concentrating exclusively on the construction of knowledge, however well done, may deflect attention from underlying causes and serve the purposes of those who wish to preserve exploitative relations. The construction of gender changes with economic shifts, and women's changing economic roles can change how they view themselves. Similarly, forms of male dominance and patriarchal ideology, like forms of racism and discrimination, mutate based on the changing needs of men and the dominant classes to keep control over those who have been subordinated in order to pursue economic and political goals. To some extent I want to challenge the distinction between materialist and cultural theories and argue that the cultural is material, the material embedded in the cultural and vice versa. Discourse has incontrovertibly material effects and material conditions have clear consequences for discourse.

Of Voice, Method and Agency: Reconstructing the Silences

One of the goals of this study is to delineate changes in gender construction consequent upon incorporation into a changing world capitalist economy and changes in women's economic roles. Glazer has defined the ethics of feminist scholarship as follows: "Feminist scholarship ... has an obligation to present a nonfatalistic view of the social world that emphasizes how we can collectively change our social world and build a better human society."[21] This study is fundamentally imbued with the necessity to take on issues of importance to women, both practical, local, culturally constructed interests and "strategic gender interests," to use Molyneux's term: change of the gender division of labor, alleviation of the burden of domestic labor and childcare, removal of gender discrimination, political equality, women achieving control over their own bodies, and reduction of male violence against women. Above all, following Mohanty's prescriptions, I view the women in this study as subjects, not objects, universal victims or automatic sisters. I have attempted here to present them as they present themselves, to give priority to what

---

[20] Moghadam, "Women," p. 4.

[21] Glazer, "Questioning," p. 304. See also Mazumdar, "Education," p. 41, on the necessity to promote "positive, dynamic, participatory images of women."

they wished to convey, while situating the women's experiences historically and culturally. I am trying to reconstruct a multivocal narrative to fill the silences of male dominant colonial and postcolonial documents, rather than to deconstruct one.[22]

At the same time, it would be unethical to deny my own agenda in studying Nairobi market women. I pursued academic, theoretical, and long-term economic interests in Nairobi by comparing/contrasting the experiences of Nairobi traders with those of Accra (Ghana) market women, taking into account cultural, socioeconomic and historical differences.[23] Another goal, however, was to improve the women's lives if necessary or possible. The best that can be said of this (and any other such) project is that enlightened self-interest mandated making a positive difference for the women by discovering and writing their history using resources inaccessible to the uneducated and thereby attempting to make those resources available to them; by exploring alternative explanations and methods that include women; and by providing data useful both for women's empowerment economically and psychologically and for governments and aid agencies to design policies beneficial to these women and the economy as a whole. There are, however, limits to accomplishing the latter goal, since the results are likely to be ignored by policymakers intent on serving elite interests rather than alleviating women's poverty. The assumption that women bear preeminent responsibility for solving the problems of the world is yet another gender construct that helps to defeat women. But we can try to help a little; more strongly, we must try, and our efforts should extend beyond our own backyards.

Feminist scholars have been wrestling with notions of voice, that is, the legitimacy and authenticity of the speaker/observer/researcher, especially in dealing with cultures other than one's own. The usage of voice is an ethical issue that needs to be faced directly by all scholars, but particularly by those who are dealing with actual voices--in fieldwork. Here I delineate the imperatives and perils of the intercalary voice in explicating the methods used in this study. What are the characteristics of the intercalary voice? It is historically situated in time and space, located specifically in socioeconomic structure. It tries to be faithful to the sources while recognizing the possible impact of the researcher on the narratives provided to her/him, to be nonintrusive in terms of changing the actions of the subjects of the study. It is as meticulous as possible in expression--with cross-checks on translations and consideration of alternative interpretations. Lastly, it tries to avoid harm and provide help defined by the subjects of the study. The intercalary voice concerns actual voices more than written or cinematic texts.

Self-reflexivity, analyzing one's self in relation to one's own culture and that in which one is doing research, is one of the silences in the explanation of methodology given by researchers on Kenya, and yet the colonial past and heritage of most of the

---

[22] Molyneux, "Mobilization," pp. 232-35, 248; Mohanty, "Western Eyes," pp. 64-66, 82. Ironically, the silences are fewer regarding beans than women.

[23] Robertson, *Bowl*.

peoples involved are clearly relevant. Race, class, gender, and nationality are particularly relevant categories here that demand a self-analysis to heighten awareness and critical facility. Much Kenyan history has been written by British historians of varying political persuasions who are middle class, white and male. I am neither British nor male, but I am middle class and white, categories very relevant for Nairobi colonial history. I was born and have lived much of my life in the midwestern United States, where race has been the defining characteristic of "otherness" for much of our history. U.S. colonial history involved the anti-British sentiment of the Revolution (taxation without representation was a reality in both Boston and Nairobi), but also the slavery of Africans as well as the dispossession of Native Americans, whose continuing disenfranchisement without compensation dwarfs the Kenyan white settler enterprise in importance. My critique of these aspects of the American past motivates me to try to restore, in whatever ways that lie within my capabilities, the history of those who have been disenfranchised. I am concerned preeminently with the efforts of women to define themselves as fully valiant and valuable human beings in the face of determined mental and physical assaults. To try to understand the experiences of those with whom I worked on this research required leaps of the imagination combined with an enormous effort to appreciate unfamiliar meanings. This understanding was impaired by language barriers, since the form of Kiswahili I learned was neither used in Nairobi nor spoken much of the time by the traders, who used mainly their first languages, Kikuyu, Kikamba, Sheng (a Nairobi language), Luo or others of the many Kenyan languages. I was therefore fortunate to have several excellent female research assistants to interpret when needed. It is past time, then, to consider the setting of this study and the traders whose story it is.

The Setting

Nairobi is a way of life.[24]

In the eighteenth century northern Bantu Kikuyu farmers, who traced their origins to the Mount Kenya (Kirinyaga) area, moved south into the higher elevations (1200 to 1800 meters) of what is now the Kiambu district edging Nairobi and acquired land rights through agreements involving payments of livestock to the indigenous Ndorobo (Athi) people or to the Maasai. Meanwhile, to the east Kamba farmers had occupied most of their current area of settlement called Ukambani by 1750, and Kamba, Maasai and Kikuyu married, raided, and traded with each other, many Kikuyu men participating in a pastoralist economy in this frontier area.[25] Kikuyu *mbari* (clans) gradually imposed their agricultural system on fertile country with about 100 centimeters of rainfall a year divided into the long and short rains yielding two growing seasons. The temperature range of 8 to 32^C. at Kiambu made

---

[24] To protect confidentiality survey informants will be cited by number, location of interview and date. Interview 185 Gikomba: 26 Feb. 1988. Names given are typical but not actual.

[25] Muriuki, *History*, p. 29; interview F Wangige: 27 June 1988; McVicar, "Twilight," p. 3; Dundas, "Notes," p. 138n.; Tate, "Native Law," p. 233, 236; Muriuki, *History*, p. vii; Jackson, "Family," p. 196.

for a relatively cool environment so near the equator at this intersection of two ecological zones, forest and savanna. At a lower elevation with hotter temperatures and
poorer soil, Ukambani suffered frequent droughts and famines, causing migrations
and more dependence on trade as a livelihood for men.[26]

In 1888 the Imperial British East African Company (IBEAC) assigned Frederick Lugard to establish a fort and trading station at Dagoretti in Kiambu on the southern fringe of Kikuyu country. Another such station was established in 1889 at
Masaku, or Machakos, in Ukambani.[27] The European incursion further west into the
place they called Nairobi (Maasai=place of cold water, Nkare Nairobi) followed
upon increasing caravan trade, documented in Chapter III. Subsequently, John
Boyes, sometime adventurer, was stunned by the rapid development of Nairobi on a
site that earlier teemed with game at the edge of a 160-kilometer-wide plain,

> a splendid grazing country, with magnificent forests and beautiful woodland
> scenery, making a very pleasant change from the bare landscape of the last few
> marches. What is now known as Nairobi was then practically a swamp, and from
> the nature of the surrounding country I should never have imagined that it would be
> chosen as the site for the future capital of British East Africa.[28]

Despite the vagaries of intergroup relations, marred by increasingly alienating
misbehavior by members of caravans who provisioned themselves in the area in the
late nineteenth century, the destruction of Lugard's fort, "pacification" campaigns
against the Kikuyu, plague epidemics, an unpleasant immediate environment involving spongy black cotton soil on the north side of the river, as well as an argument
over its siting, Nairobi prospered. It grew from a small IBEAC tent camp for the
construction of the Uganda railway in 1899 to a town of some 6000 inhabitants in
1902.[29] From the beginning there were housing and sanitary problems, graphically
described by a medical officer in 1902, whose racism and ethnocentrism were typical
and persistent among the Europeans in Kenya. They were expressed in successful
efforts to segregate the town, despite lip service to the contrary.[30]

> Such was Nairobi in January, 1902--a town of mushroom growth, undrained, insan-
> itary and foul, sheltering some 5000-6000 Inhabitants mostly of alien extraction
> who bringing with them their caste prejudices, oriental vices, and inherent love of
> filth, darkness and overcrowding, attracted the Native in numbers who quickly ac-

---

[26] White et al., *Nairobi*, p. 23; Morgan, "Kikuyu," p. 57; Wisner, "Man-Made Famine," pp. 3ff. Kershaw, *Mau Mau*, pp. 21, 29, defined ethnicity as dependent on mode of production at this time, pastoralists joining the Maasai, hunters and gatherers the Ndorobo, and farmers the Kikuyu and Kamba.

[27] Halleman and Morgan, "City," p. 100; Munro, *Colonial Rule*, p. 33.

[28] Boyes, *King*, pp. 47-48, 308.

[29] White et al., *Nairobi*, pp. 11-15; PC/CP 4/2/1 Ukamba Province AR 1920-21: 4; DC/NBI 1/1/1
Nairobi Political Record Book: 1-2; PC/CP 4/4/1 Nairobi AR 1941: 6.

[30] The 1906 Simpson report recommended segregation and the British government rejected it.
Etherton, *Mathare Valley*, p. 2.

quired all the vices and immorality his Eastern superiors could teach him, which he practiced with such terrible results to himself and the community at large.[31]

The railway officials refused to move the town away from the swamp, although it was viewed as unhealthy and contributed to endemic malaria; instead, Europeans chose to live well away from it, while railway workers were confined to the Landhies area barracks near the river. The bazaar housed many Indians and Africans in poorly constructed housing. European commercial firms moved in south of the river, while various groups, local and immigrant, established dispersed villages in the nearby countryside. Nairobi's earliest market gardens were small swampy riverain plots leased from Europeans by Asians, who also rented rooms for brothels near the bazaar. Eventually the intervening countryside was occupied and the whole agglomeration took on impressive size, becoming the administrative headquarters of the colony in 1905 and its capital in 1907.[32] By 1908 Nairobi had cars, trains, banks and clubs, and by World War I commercial European Nairobi had a full range of amenities like electricity, water purification, and permanent stone buildings.[33]

International links grew; British East Africa was first an imperial stopover on the way to India, but subsequently connected more to South Africa, whence many settlers and administrators drew their experience. By World War I Kenya's status as a white settler colony was well established through European immigration and local land alienation, and confirmed in the 1920s by absorption of even more Kikuyu and Maasai land; ultimately half of Kenya's arable land was taken, with local Africans assigned to "tribes" and "tribes" assigned to reserves.[34] White settlers viewed Nairobi as a European town, even though its African population always outnumbered all others. The proportion of Africans in the population hovered at around 60 to 70% until independence in 1963 and went up to 80% or more after, when the total population exceeded 509,000 in 1969, 1,200,000 in 1987.[35] The population of what is now Kiambu District also grew from 110,500 in 1926 to 475,600 in 1969.[36] Kabete, the area of Kiambu nearest to Nairobi and the site of the rural markets included in this study, soon became intertwined with the town with much daily commuting, which

---

[31] Ministry of Health 1/6019 Radford, "Bubonic Plague," pp. 7-8. Some 32,000 East Indians were brought in to build the railroad, joining crews of several thousand Africans. Halleman and Morgan, "City," p. 100.

[32] White et al., *Nairobi*, pp. 11-15; PC/CP 4/2/1 Nairobi AR 1909-10: 1; DC/NBI 1/1/1 Nairobi Political Record Book; PC/CP 4/2/1 Report on Nairobi Township 1909: 19; Smart, *History*, pp. 21, 27-29.

[33] Boyes, *King*, p. 308; PC/CP 4/2/1 Ukamba Province AR 1906-07: 9; Smart, *History*, p. 31.

[34] Hake, *African Metropolis*, pp. 24-26; Kanogo, "Women," p. 14.

[35] Obudho, "Perspective," pp. 6-8; Censuses 1911, 1948, 1962, 1969, 1979; Masaviru, "Population Trends," pp. 64-67; White et al., *Nairobi*, pp. 42-43; PC/CP 4/2/1 Ukamba Province AR 1911: 31; DC/KBU 1/14 Ukamba Province AR 1920-21: 13; LG 2/39 Nairobi Municipal Council (NMC) AR 1948: 5; LG 3/2959 Nairobi City Council (NCC) Social Services and Housing Report 1960: 18; Urban Food and Fuel Report 1987: 1.

[36] Ministry of Economic Planning and Development, Kiambu District Development Plan 1979-1983: 4.

only increased with improvements in transportation. Land alienation by white settlers made it into a patchwork of white-owned plantations and Kikuyu farms.[37]

In Nairobi discrimination proceeded apace. Pass laws for Africans began in
1901, and the presumption of the illegitimacy of Africans' presence in Nairobi was
maintained and expressed in various laws like the 1922 Vagrancy Ordinance, whose
impact on traders will be explored in Chapters IV and V. From 1902 on Africans
were regularly picked off Nairobi's streets and "repatriated" to the Reserves, officially established by 1926. The Reserves became progressively segregated, dividing
old people, women and children from young men when the latter were drafted for
work or the military (Kiambu was probably Africa's largest supplier of conscripts per
head in both world wars). Men crowded into Nairobi in search of cash to pay taxes,
but most women stayed in rural areas. Municipal revenue was overwhelmingly generated by poll and/or hut taxes on Africans, who under colonialism received few benefits in terms of housing or services in return (between 1932 and 1947 only 1 to 2%
of revenue was spent on services for Africans).[38] In 1938 differential living standards
were evident in the lower infant mortality rate for Europeans compared to other
groups: 90.9 per thousand births for Europeans, 262.4 for Asians and 266.6 for
Africans.[39]

Nairobi's chaotic growth always outran any ex post facto plans devised by a
procession of city governments,[40] which had an impact on traders through regulations and variations in their enforcement. Government personnel incorporated
Africans only gradually and in subordinate positions until the approach of independence in 1963. Provision of basic infrastructure was always uneven, with the African
population bearing the chief brunt of financial shortfalls. The most critical problem
all Nairobi administrations faced was the poverty of many Nairobi people and therefore housing; most of the growing population could neither afford to pay high rents
for the scarce available housing nor to construct anything but makeshift housing.[41]
To begin with African housing was not regarded as the responsibility of the colonial
municipal government except to prevent self-help efforts by Africans. There was
neither the motivation nor the wherewithal to deal meaningfully with urban housing

---

[37] ARC(MAA) 2/3/1 VIA Municipal Native Affairs Dept. AR 1938:7; KNA, Ogilvie, *Housing*, p.
13.

[38] PC/CP 4/4/3 Nairobi AR 1947: 6; Parker, "Aspects," pp. 261, 196; van Zwanenberg and King,
Economic History, pp. 270, 268.

[39] Africans in Nairobi also had a lower birth rate than other groups: 12 per 1000 compared to 13.5
for Europeans and 24.9 for Asians (those who had the most normal sex ratio had the highest birth rate).
Kuczynski, *Demographic Survey* II: 184.

[40] For instance, the 1948 Nairobi Master Plan projected a population of 270,000 in 1975 instead of
over 650,000, which made it the largest East African city. Its projected population by the year 2000 is 2.3
million, while the proportion of Kenya's population that is urban rose from under 10% in 1969 to 15% in
1986, with a projection of over 25% in 2000. Manasseh, "Problems," p. 20; Cummings, "Migration," p.
159; McCormick, "Enterprise," p. 97; KNA, "Case Study," p. 6.

[41] Van Zwanenberg, *Capitalism*, p. 1.

due to the skewed tax burden (taxing those who had less more and those with more less).[42] As the town grew politics became an increasingly complex affair as administrators intermarried and sided with settlers, fought or sided with missionaries, or pursued policies they told themselves protected the interests of Africans.[43] Kiambu's governance also became more complicated; more than one administrator found Kiambu District to be "unworkable" due to the necessity of pacifying the small white population while the much larger African population was neglected.[44] In both Nairobi and Kiambu infrastructure was differentially provided to Europeans, but because Kiambu was divided up so eccentrically,[45] some Africans did have roads that were useful and government-maintained.

The Legislative Council established for the colony in 1906 was composed of Europeans only, became elective in 1919 and added Asian representation on a token basis in 1924. The Nairobi Municipal Council mirrored these compositional changes with Asian representation added in 1917, at which point there was still no place in Nairobi where Africans were allowed to live independently of their employment.[46] In 1919 permission was given to establish a "native location" and the first of many town planning efforts was undertaken.[47] African representation in rural areas was inaugurated in 1925 by the establishment of Local Native Councils composed of chiefs and subchiefs (all male), who were appointed by the British administration. The Kikuyu and Kamba had direct, not indirect rule; their newly imposed chiefs had arbitrary powers non-existent in the old acephalous systems.[48] Given the lack of African representation, it is not surprising that the 1920s saw the first large scale demolition of "unauthorized settlements," three of Nairobi's eight villages. Such demolitions, which became habitual, always removed more housing than was supplied by the government.[49]

---

[42] Maxon, *Ainsworth*, pp. 109-10; White et al., *Nairobi*, p. 17; Halleman and Morgan, "City," p. 100.

[43] The "paramountcy" of African interests in Kenya was proclaimed by a government White Paper in 1923 and a 1930 Memorandum on Native Policy in East Africa, but from 1903 on the idea of a White Highlands progressively dominated until events after World War II forced its abandonment. Werlin, *Governing*, pp. 39-40.

[44] This was C. W. Hobley's term. PC/CP 4/2/1 Ukamba Province AR 1911: 4.

[45] For instance, as a reward for loyalty Chief Kinyanjui (see Chapter III) was allowed to keep land at Kawangware despite continual surrounding European encroachment. Browne, "Kawangware," p. 30.

[46] Werlin, "Governing," pp. 40-43; DC/KBU 1/11 Ukamba Province AR 1917-18: 17. Both Smart, *History*, p. 53, and White et al., *Nairobi*, p. 17, appear to be incorrect in assigning initial Asian representation to 1924-25.

[47] DC/KBU 1/13 Ukamba Province AR 1919-20: 21, 23.

[48] Pedersen, "National Bodies," p. 647, incorrectly called this system indirect rule. By 1920-21 the administration claimed chiefship to be hereditary. PC/CP 4/1/2 Kikuyu Province AR 1925: 5-7; DC/KBU Kiambu AR 1920-21: 4; Jackson, "Family," p. 197; Munro, *Colonial Rule*, p. 29.

[49] Native Affairs Dept. AR 1923: 17.

The many problems that challenged urban order led the Feetham Commission to recommend the appointment of a Municipal Native Affairs Officer for Nairobi in 1928, so that the Municipality would "accept responsibility for native affairs within its boundaries"; the administration was forced to acknowledge the African urban presence. Typically, this was not done until 1930, given the low priority placed on "native affairs" in the "white man's country." In 1939 a Native Advisory Council was established in order to improve tax collection, but housing efforts fell steadily further behind population growth.[50] The 9000 housing units built for Africans during World War II to assuage protests did not satisfy the huge demand that had built up before the war, much less the needs generated by the war-induced influx.[51] One official remarked drily, "in towns natives are theoretically expected to be celibate," but more and more women were coming to town and crowding into government medical and police lines, in particular, some of the "worst slums in Nairobi."[52] African Americans stationed at Eastleigh Aerodrome, outraged by conditions, launched an armed attack on the Eastleigh police station in 1942, while Nairobi Africans suffered discriminatory food rationing, the destruction of maize grown on open land, film censorship, early morning mass roundups with challenges to show tax receipts, and grossly inadequate health facilities.[53] In the face of such problems the first African, Eliud Mathu, was appointed to the colony's Legislative Council in 1944, and two African councilors were appointed to the Nairobi Municipal Council. Their attitudes were condemned as "racial" by administrators because they insisted that Africans, as well as Europeans, have individual burials.[54] On one occasion T. G. Askwith, the Municipal Native Affairs Officer, was applauded by the Native Advisory Council after apologizing for making a decision without consulting them; no British official had ever admitted any error to them previously. One of the chief goals of both African and British administrators was to prevent "the drift to the towns of women and girls,"[55] an aspect that will be explored in Chapters III and IV.

---

[50] LG 3/3207 Nairobi Municipal Native Affairs Dept AR 1939: 39; Nairobi Municipal Council AR 1939: 1; MAA 7/491 Memorandum 5 Sept. 1945 Provincial Commissioner Central Province to Colonial Secretary Nairobi.

[51] Nairobi Municipal Native Affairs Dept. AR 1938: 1-2. At Pumwani 492 people were found sleeping in houses with a capacity for 163. MAA 8/22.

[52] MAA 8/22 Memo. on African Housing 20 Nov. 1947, Municipal African Affairs Officer T. G. Askwith to Chief Native Commissioner Nairobi; ARC (MAA) 2/3/8II Nairobi Municipal Native Affairs AR 1940: 15; PC/CP 4/4/1 Nairobi AR 1941: 6; Nairobi District AR 1941: 4; ARC (MAA) 2/3/8 III Nairobi Municipal Native Affairs AR 1941: 19.

[53] ARC (MAA) 2/3/8 IV Nairobi AR 1942: 7; CS 1/14/11 Nairobi Native Advisory Council minutes 16 Dec. 1944: 3; 21 Feb. 1945: 2; 2-3 Aug. 1945: 2; 18-19 June 1945: 2; White et al., *Nairobi*, pp. 33-34.

[54] PC/CP 4/4/2 Nairobi District AR 1944: 2; PC/CP 4/473 Nairobi AR 1946: 5.

[55] Interview Askwith 13 Oct. 1992; MAA 7/491 T. G. Askwith, report 22 Aug. 1945: 3; memo. 14 Sept. 1945 to the Chief Native Commissioner.

The end of the war and attendant ructions in Nairobi (see Chapter V) brought increased attention to African governance by British officials in the form of the establishment of an appointive African Affairs Committee for the colony, which dealt with issues such as overstocking, individual land titles for Africans, limitations on the amount of bridewealth, urbanization, housing, taxation, and health facilities. Nairobi Africans were disproportionately represented with nineteen out of twenty-eight members. Interestingly, it had two places reserved for women.[56] In 1949 Nairobi received a royal charter as a city and a British apologist not only resolutely ignored how the majority of Nairobi's population was faring, but also chose to forget the existence of memory among Africans. "So, in the knowledge of its new importance, with a little feigned insouciance, gay, polyglot, industrious, expanding Nairobi stepped out of 1949 into its Charter Year to gather to itself, in the words of the pioneers, the 'first traditions of a land which has no memory yet.'"[57]

The memory it had was to make it increasingly ungovernable in the 1950s and 1960s with the Mau Mau Emergency and the hawker wars described in Chapters IV and VII. New housing estates were given names of African Advisory Council members assassinated in the 1952-60 Emergency (see Chapter IV). Africans sought their own solutions to employment in small-scale self-employment, and to housing by shifts ranging from construction of small European-style homes, to thatched round huts and paper shacks, the latter becoming increasingly common with the burgeoning of vast peri-urban slums in eastern Nairobi from the 1960s on.

The first African elections were held in Nairobi in March 1957, but only a small minority of Africans were registered voters. As late as 1961 to 1963 Europeans in Nairobi paid disproportionately low taxes and Africans had very poor city services.[58] Only with independence in 1963 did African representation become proportional to their numbers; Africanization of Nairobi government proceeded rapidly from 1962 on. In 1963 Kenya adopted a parliamentary government with strong powers vested in the president, Jomo Kenyatta. It was a de facto one party (KANU) state from late 1969 to 1982 (Kenyatta died in 1978), a legal one from 1982 to 1991. If

---

[56] MAA 6/38 minutes Native Affairs Committee 1948-52. The membership was a curious amalgam of categories: six from Central Province (Kikuyu or Kamba), three from Nyanza (Luo), one from Coast, one Ugandan, one Nubian (Nairobi), three Muslims, six village committee members, one Kenya African Union representative, two houseboys, one Nandi/Kipsigis, one sports, three trade, two women, six ex-officio African employees of the Municipal African Affairs Department and the headman of Pumwani, and the two African councilors from the Nairobi Municipal Council. Parker, "Aspects," p. 177.

[57] Smart, *History*, p. 104; LG 2/39 Nairobi Municipal Council African Affairs AR 1949: 69. The activist Kenya African Union (KAU, successor to the Kikuyu Central Association, KCA) asked Africans to boycott the celebration of Nairobi's charter year. Kershaw, *Mau Mau*, p. 230.

[58] LG 3/2959 NCC AR 1959: 14; African Affairs Dept. AR 1957: 105. Interview Hakes 12 Oct. 1992. The Reverend Andrew Hake was a Church of Scotland missionary who not only wrote an excellent book about Nairobi but also served on the Nairobi City Council (NCC) from 1961 to 1953. Jean Hake was the first social worker appointed to work with Nairobi Africans in the 1950s. AA 13/1/8/9 Nairobi AR 1962: 2.

colonialists concentrated services on Europeans, postindependence politicians routinely privileged economically rather than racially segregated neighborhoods. As Tiwari put it, the three Nairobis, Asian, African and European, merged into one racially, but resegregated "in the process of exchanging social for economic characteristics."[59] The brunt of the vast population growth has been borne by areas like Mathare Valley, one of the few areas of self-help housing that the Nairobi City Council has allowed to stand relatively unimpeded, which grew from a population of 19,436 in 1969 to over 100,000 in 1979. In 1960 only 6% of Nairobi's population was in squatter settlements, in 1980, 40%. Population densities varied wildly from one neighborhood to the next. Karen and Langata, areas with multi-acre elite compounds and houses, had fewer than 500 persons per square kilometer in 1979, while eastern Nairobi areas like Mbotela, Pumwani, Maringo and Mathare had over 20,000 in 1969 and 30,000 in 1979. The population density in peri-urban areas to the west like Kangemi, Kawangware, Uthiru, and Kibera varied between 1200 and 8500 per square kilometer in 1979.[60]

Post-independence policies that affected traders shifted constantly, as documented in Chapters V and VII, but often reflected the same preoccupations as those of the colonial government. In the new government no places were reserved for women and their representation was minimal.[61] In 1983 the elected Nairobi City Council was replaced by the appointed Nairobi City Commission, but mismanagement and lack of investment in infrastructure continued, and appointed officials often had had very limited experience with Nairobi. When a strong Kikuyu mayor was elected in 1992 along with opposition party Nairobi members of parliament, the power of mayors was immediately circumscribed.[62] If before independence the vast majority of Nairobi's population was disenfranchised, afterward the shifting population of Nairobi women traders fit most nearly into this category, but never willingly.

The Markets, the Surveys, and the Samples

Linking together the vast present-day complex of Nairobi and Kiambu economically and socially is an ever expanding market system. In order to look at the urban-rural connections of traders, I chose a varied sample of urban, suburban and rural markets that occupies a wedge with its furthest eastern point at Gikomba and Shauri Moyo, two markets near the Nairobi River in eastern old Nairobi, its northernmost point at Kiambu Town market, and its western extremity at Limuru market. Figures I.1a and I.1b show their location. There were many types of markets in the sample: legal and illegal; large, small and middling in size; muddy, grassy or paved; new or old; indoor and outdoor; periodic (meeting twice weekly) or daily. Gikomba

[59] Tiwari, "Aspects," p. 60.

[60] Chege, "Tale," pp. 74-88; Masaviru, "Trends," pp. 67-71; Obudho, "Perspective," p. 6.

[61] Despite the strengths of such long-term elected members of Parliament (MPs) as Grace Ogot.

[62] Stren et al., "Coping," pp. 185, 199.

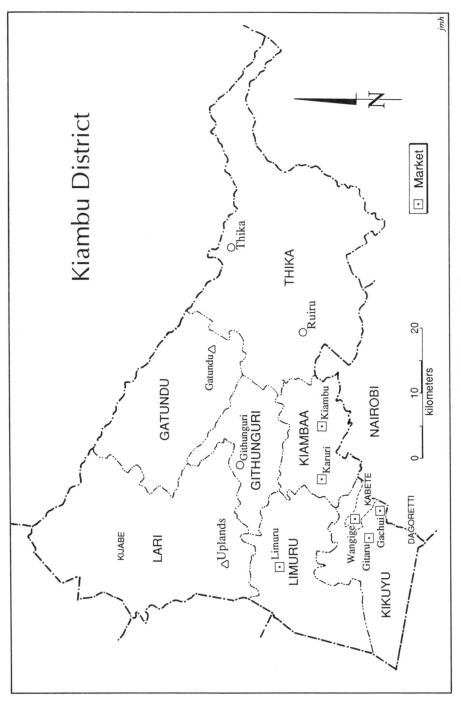

I.1a Markets in Sample, Kiambu

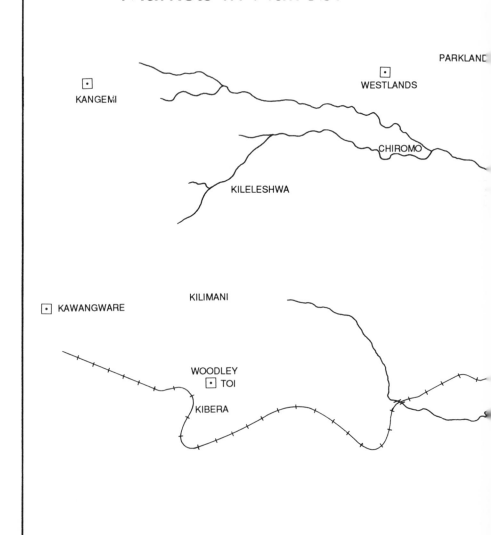

Markets in Nairobi

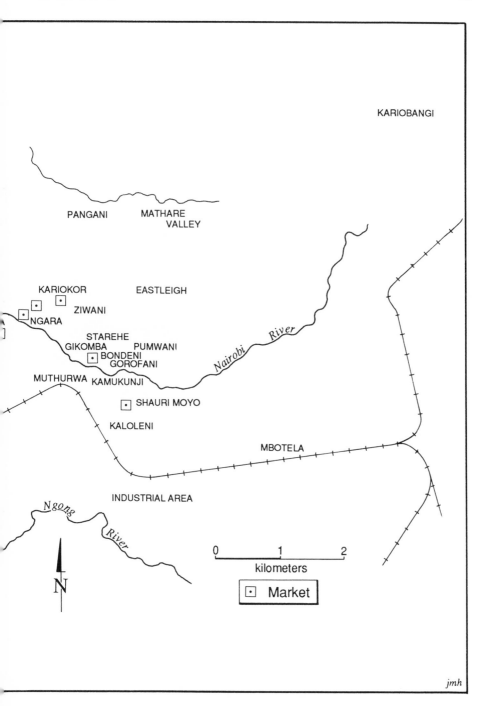

I.1b Markets in Sample, Nairobi

represents all types--in 1987-88 it was a very large (1800 sellers), permanent, legal and illegal market (depending on whether indoor or outdoor), which met daily for the mostly urban-resident sellers, twice weekly for some 300 of them who sold in one area on Mondays and Thursdays and came from distant towns. Next in size were several large suburban markets; Kawangware and Kiambu Town markets were very crowded on their market days. Medium-sized markets were well represented by relatively peaceful and spacious rural markets such as Karuri or Gitaru on grassy or muddy slopes with sellers strung out by commodity, edged by small shops. At the other end of the spectrum were a nascent market in a purposefully obscure illegal location bordering a large squatter settlement, and the few people selling out of sheds at Gachui, a moribund legal market on the outskirts of Nairobi. Most of the markets surveyed included a full range of commodities for sale retail or wholesale, but one was an illegal wholesaling depot and another a retail street market for dried staples. The endlessly fascinating variety of peoples, processes (manufacturing takes place in many markets), and products in and around markets formed one motivation for continuing to explore market trade beyond my initial research in Ghana.

Before surveying a market my research assistants and I sought the permission of the relevant legal or de facto authorities, given in all cases. We began by conducting a census of all of the sellers in sixteen markets that yielded information about approximately 6000 male and female traders, of whom two-thirds were female. At each market we then conducted a sample survey, called the short survey here. Because dried beans, in particular, were sold exclusively by women, a facet I particularly wanted to explore, we intentionally oversampled the dried staples sellers by selecting one out of three instead of one out of six in this random sample, which included over a thousand sellers of both sexes. The census and short survey took respectively two to five or fifteen to thirty minutes with each individual. Depending on the size of the market and its periodicity, we spent one to ninety days in it and absorbed much information by participant observation as well. In order to secure more detailed histories we selected from the large sample fifty-six female dried staples sellers with whom to do long interviews. This nonrandom selection favored those who were particularly helpful and aimed at equal numbers by age cohort. These interviews were recorded in my "office," as the traders called it, my car parked next to the market. Most markets had no place to sit comfortably except traders' nests carved economically from their tiny allotted spaces, where noise and constant interruptions made recording impossible. After securing permission, I took notes and recorded long interviews, which were transcribed, translated and explicated by first language Kikuyu or Kamba female or male University of Nairobi linguistics students.

In some markets we became popular with sellers clamoring to be interviewed; at others we were regarded with high suspicion as possible government spies or journalists. Nonetheless, the cooperation rate was phenomenal; very few traders refused to be interviewed. Informants doing long interviews were compensated for their time and consequent loss of sales. Three women research assistants helped in all, two of whom conducted censuses and short surveys independently after initial training. One was my constant companion and mentor, whose patience and imperturbability lasted through rat hunts, shocking revelations, theft and controversy, and facilitated interpreting complicated interviews.

After mornings spent interviewing, afternoons involved archival research in one of nine libraries in Nairobi, especially the Kenya National Archives and the Ministry of Agriculture library. The various libraries at the University of Nairobi (History, Institutes for Development Studies and African Studies, Geography, Law, Architecture, and Population Studies) yielded rich rewards in the form of a number of well-researched theses, dissertations and papers. In addition to the surveys we conducted interviews with selected individuals such as retired traders, market officials, and government functionaries, who were in a position to give useful information, sometimes at their homes. The Nairobi area fieldwork took place in 1987-88 over a period of fourteen months. In 1992 I went to England to interview former colonial officers and their wives, who often knew more than their husbands did on relevant subjects, and various experts, with particular attention to the 1940s and bean development. In this study each chapter represents a different amalgam of disciplines, methods, sources and approaches.

It is extremely difficult to situate this population historically because of the paucity of records enumerating traders in Nairobi. Hake noted that traders and prostitutes were viewed as surplus undesirables in Nairobi by colonial authorities,[63] who were never interested in surveying them. Segregation and white racism generated ignorance and promoted false assumptions of nullity for African experience: no history, settled agriculture or personalities. The European population was surveyed minutely but the Africans largely ignored. Even after independence plans for Nairobi routinely ignored commercial development, especially small business; a 1974 study of Nairobi commerce neglected to mention either markets or traders.[64] There were also the problems of gender and class discrimination. When Jeanne Fisher went to Kikuyuland in 1950 with the innovative goal of investigating women's roles, she found that Kikuyu women would not talk freely to males or to females in the presence of males, of whatever race.[65] European observers' knowledge of African life was biased irrevocably by self-imposed barriers of race, class, and gender; only "a few leading Africans" ever socialized with Europeans on a semi-equal basis, and that was after World War II.[66] These did not include women. Also, with the exception of those whose specific focus is gender who are cited throughout this study,

---

[63] Hake, *Metropolis*, p. 24.

[64] Huxley, *Lizard*, pp. 116-17; Kuczynski, *Survey*, p. 156; White et al., *Nairobi*, pp. 20-21; Manasseh, "Problems," pp. 25-27a; NCC General Purposes Committee Nairobi Urban Study Sub-Committee minutes, 14 Jan., 10 May 1974.

[65] Interview 14 Oct. 1992. The predominance of women in many markets creates a fairly free space for them. Kershaw (interview 4 Aug. 1994) made the same claim regarding Kikuyu men talking to her in the 1950s.

[66] DC/KBU 1/40 Kiambu AR 1949: 2-3.

many contemporary researchers interested in the Kenyan economy and class formation have ignored gender.

These problems then fed into the common contemporary tendency by Western
economists to overlook the self-employed and those working in small businesses
when collecting statistics, both because of the difficulty of doing so and the assumption of their unimportance. Even the pathbreaking 1972 International Labour
Organization (ILO) study of Kenya's informal sector, which was largely responsible
for establishing the respectability of small enterprises as a subject for study and tool
for development,[67] neither paid much attention to traders nor attempted to generate
data about them. Both colonial and independent governments assiduously collected
data about wage workers in Nairobi, "the stable urban worker" (mostly male), but
deplored and tried to evict from Nairobi the more tenuous self-employed.[68] In agriculture, where women's unwaged labor increasingly predominated, studies routinely
underestimated their contribution.[69] After the recognition of the importance of what
was called the informal sector, attention still focused on male workers in it, a subject
taken up in Chapter V.[70] House's 1977 survey of Nairobi's informal sector purposefully excluded "the vast majority of sidewalk hawkers of vegetables" who were
women, while Ross and Hake did not do statistical breakdowns by sex.[71] Here I have
chosen not to use the term *informal sector* except when used by others, despite its
ubiquity. It suffers from vague and shifting definitions and false assumptions cri-
tiqued elsewhere in detail.[72] I will use the term *underground economy* if illegal

---

[67] ILO, *Employment*, p. 59, stated "The worst of all possible circumstances from the point of view
of seeking work is to be young, uneducated and female," and noted the arbitrariness of distinguishing economic from non-economic activities of women in rural areas because all were economic (p. 4).

[68] ARC (MAA) 2/3/8 III Nairobi Municipal Native Affairs Dept. AR 1941: 7. Sources that pay particular attention to female wage workers are Stichter, "Women"; Leitner, *Workers*; and Butterfield, "Wom-
en."

[69] Anker and Knowles, *Population Growth*, p. 190; Thadani, "Social Relations," p. 32. Kathleen
Staudt has documented the practice of ignoring women's agricultural work worldwide and in Kenya, and
its consequences in a number of works.

[70] Studies which fall into this category include: Westley, *Informal Sector*; Dondo et al., *Mobilization*; Collier and Lal, *Labour*; Child, "Entrepreneurship"; Child and Kempe, *Small-Scale Enterprise*; King,
African Artisan; Elkan, Ryan, and Mukui, "Economics"; Marris and Somerset, *African Businessmen*;
Ng'ethe and Wahome, "Rural Informal Sector." ILO, *Employment*, p. 547, was also not particularly concerned about women and recommended that women's wages should be equalized if they were heads of
households only. White et al., *Nairobi*, p. 8, stated that since urban African women did not work [!], efforts were needed to "occupy the woman productively in home crafts or in domestic employment."

[71] House, "Nairobi's Informal Sector," pp. 359-60; Hake, *Metropolis*; Ross, *Grass Roots*.

[72] Bromley, "Informal Sector," pp. 1033-34; McGee, "Mass Markets," p. 208; Robertson, *Bowl*, pp.
3-7. The ILO definition (ILO, *Employment*, p. 6) is probably most neutral and includes: ease of entry, reliance on indigenous resources, small scale of operation, use of labor intensive and adapted technology,
and skills acquired outside the formal school system. But it also is problematical since it adds family
ownership of enterprises, not a necessary characteristic, and the assumption restated by Macharia ("Integrating," p. 163) that the businesses serve unregulated and competitive markets. But police persecution
and maize control are regulations that impose costs on traders.

activities are involved and otherwise define precisely the kinds of economic activities to which I am referring.

What do we know, then, about the numbers of people engaged in trade in Nairobi, women in particular? In 1949 Mary Parker said in a study of labor in Nairobi that the number of small traders had increased steadily in the 1940s from about 2000 in 1941 (among whom 500 were mobile hawkers). They were estimated to be 6 to 10% of Nairobi's labor force. The next estimate relevant to this study came from Eastern Province (includes Ukambani) in the 1960s, where Mbithi and Chege found that in response to a famine 35% of women household members were trading and 18% of men. In 1969 Livingstone estimated that the informal sector accounted for 28 to 33% of African urban employment, while the ILO report substantially agreed with that estimate and placed 30,000 people in Nairobi's informal sector.[73] Nelson in 1974 surveyed shop ownership in Mathare Valley II and III and found that 20% of the shops belonged to women, many of whom sold vegetables. The 1975 Survey of the Urban Informal Sector put out by the Central Bureau of Statistics estimated its total size at 74,000 persons in eleven Kenyan municipalities, 21,500 in Nairobi, with 14,500 of those involved in trade, or 67.3%. Subsequent estimates were, significantly, incorporated into government reports on unemployment. The urban informal sector as a whole was said to have grown from employing 125,000 persons in 1976 to 181,000 in 1982, or 3% of total Kenyan employment. Of these 70.8% were employed in wholesale and retail trade or restaurants in 1977, 70.7% in 1982, making trade easily the most important single source of employment.[74]

Only in the 1980s did serious attempts to look at Nairobi women's trading activities begin, with a small survey by Adagala and Bifani and larger ones by Mitullah and myself, while Onstad did a study of male hawkers' organizations. In 1984 the Nairobi City Commission estimated that there were 30,000 hawkers in Nairobi, of whom only 5000 were licensed.[75] The markets we surveyed (seventeen in all) were perhaps a fifth of those within a circle covering about a thirty kilometer area centering in Nairobi, albeit many of the largest. In 1987-88 by this estimate there were perhaps 30,000 traders in the whole area in markets, plus an unknown number on the streets, of whom approximately two-thirds were female. Streetsellers were the focus of Mitullah's study, while market-based traders predominated in mine. These surveys form the largest data base for studying Nairobi area traders in the

---

[73] Parker, "Aspects," pp. 19, 21; Mbithi and Chege, "Linkage," p. 45; Livingstone, *Development* 6: 3; ILO, *Employment*, p. 224.

[74] Nelson, "Division," p. 285; Ogundo, "Data Collection," pp. 83-84; Kenya Report on Unemployment 1982/3: 27, 212-16, 259.

[75] Adagala and Bifani, *Self-Employed Women*; Onstad, "Street Life"; Mitullah, "Hawking," pp. 16-17.

1980s and the only one for those in rural markets.[76] This study embodies the only work specifically concerned with trade in a commodity dominated by women, dried beans, although it bears comparison with Bryceson's study of Tanzania's food trade and Pala Okeyo's small survey of Luo women traders in Western Kenya.[77] Because many men were present in the markets and included in the surveys it also illuminates gender differences in trade to a greater extent than most previous work.[78] The tables below give the general characteristics of the censused population, while large and small sample survey results are conveyed throughout the study where appropriate.

I.1. Number,* Location, and Gender of Traders/Business Owners in
Selected Nairobi Area Markets, 1987-1988

Name/Location of Market	Total Number of Sellers	Percent Female	Percent Male
Periodicity=daily(D) twice a week(P)			
Urban			
Gikomba (D/P)	1764	49.8	50.2
Kariakor (D)	251	43.9	56.1
Shauri Moyo (D)	272	44.8	55.2
Suburban			
Gachui (D)	30	86.7	13.3
Kangemi (P)	318	72.7	27.3
Kawangware (D/P)	616	75.3	24.7
Westlands (D)	113	40.0	60.0
Rural			
Gitaru (P)	150	89.3	10.7
Karuri (P)	192	82.1	17.9
Wangige (P)	424	80.1	19.9
Small town			
Kiambu (D/P)	617	86.4	13.6

*Numbers reflect all those selling inside and immediately outside the markets. Hawkers (mobile sellers) are underrepresented.

---

[76] Adagala and Bifani, *Self-Employed Women*, had a sample size of 49 women drawn widely from markets dispersed over eastern and central Nairobi, with some good qualitative analysis.

[77] Bryceson, "Liberalizing"; Pala Okeyo, "Women." See also Bryceson, *Food Insecurity*.

[78] Most studies of African traders have a West African focus and reflect the overwhelmingly female presence in the markets there.

In Table I.1 several small illegal markets are omitted because of their vulnerability to harassment, but they are included anonymously in the sample characteristics. One legal market, Ngara, is omitted because of irregularities in our initial experiment with the census. The census was conducted on a succession of market days when numbers of traders fluctuated. In most markets the personnel changed by about 10% daily, but in rural markets the percentage was higher due to farming activities. Overall, 67% of the traders were female. Women sellers outnumbered men in rural markets, but were somewhat outnumbered by men in the most urban markets, while at Westlands, the only upscale neighborhood market included, men outnumbered women three to two. Most (81.4%) traders were owner/operators with no family help or employees.

The ethnicity of the business owners is illustrated in Table I.2 by location of market as categorized in Table I.1. Nairobi's cosmopolitan nature is evident in the heterogeneity of the urban markets (the proportion of Kamba would have been even higher if one illegal market had been included), whereas both suburban and rural markets and Kiambu Town market are overwhelmingly Kikuyu. In this case ethnicity stands as a proxy for region of origin, since less than 4% of the urban traders were born in Nairobi, and even fewer of the others. Most sellers patronize local markets, especially in rural areas where women are more likely to be farming. While the rural/urban differences among those censused form a good introduction to the characteristics of the traders, the most stunning differences among them were gender-based, which will be explored in Chapters IV and V. Those material differences have direct relevance for the consideration of the changing construction of gender that frames this study.

I.2. Ethnicity of Business Owners by Type of Market Location, 1987-1988

Ethnicity by %: Location:	Kikuyu	Kamba	Luo	Luhya	Embu/ Meru	Maasai	Swahili	Other
Urban (N=2287)	48.5	27.2	13.1	6.9	1.6	1.0	1.0	2.4
Suburban* (N=1137)	85.7	2.8	2.2	5.6	.5	.5	.5	2.7
Rural (N=766)	97.3	1.1	.4	.1	.1	0.0	0.0	.9
Small town (N=617)	96.9	1.2	.3	.9	.5	0.0	.2	0.0

*Includes one illegal market not listed in Table I.2.

"If it wasn't for women the world would have been great!"[79]: The Changing Construction of Kikuyu Womanhood

The reconstruction of the gender system in central Kenyan society fostered by Kikuyu and Kamba urban residence and women's involvement in trade has certain historical continuities supported by widely held societal beliefs that differentiated the genders; the available evidence points to a great deal of male dominance. Ideology regarding women legitimates, perpetuates and is created by socioeconomic structure, and changes along with it. It is customary in studies of twentieth century change to establish a baseline for African societies, usually defined somewhat cavalierly as the precolonial period, or even more simply called "traditional." This may be due to lack of written sources for precolonial times and reliance upon late nineteenth century memories of twentieth century people, or in older studies to the assumption that societies did not change much before colonialism. This assumption rejected, the problem of sources remains. For Kikuyu and Kamba society there was no mid-nineteenth century traveller curious enough about local ways to record the languages or the social systems with thoroughness and publish the results. For the late nineteenth century there are mainly oral sources collected in the second half of the twentieth century and several ethnographies by the Routledges, Kenyatta, Kershaw, and Louis Leakey, which attempted to reconstruct precolonial culture. In what follows I have been as faithful as possible to chronology, not pushing back in time sources that cannot reliably be attributed to the nineteenth century, for instance. I am hesitant to assign chronology to proverbs or folktales because they are reinvented to serve the purposes of each generation, but I have employed them in examining ideological constructs, which seem to have a longer half-life than material conditions.

The evidence from the late nineteenth and early twentieth centuries regarding the place of Kikuyu women in conceptual categories is fairly unambiguous, but does not necessarily represent what came before. Embedded in a patrilineal, patrilocal, polygynous matrix, women were regarded by men as property. While this does not necessarily mean that they regarded themselves as property, men's categories appear to have dominated the societal ideology, which established oppositions devaluing women and justifying differences in wealth.[80] Even forms of wealth were differentiated with men having superior access to livestock, which were rated as most important and used as a form of currency. Shaw described colonial discourse about Kikuyu women as presenting conflicting views of female power and male dominance.[81] Ambivalence in sources from the colonial period on the topic may have reflected a contested precolonial situation to some extent, but the discourse of male dominance was superordinate, perhaps reflecting an increase in the reality of male dominance in the late nineteenth century, as I will argue in Chapter III.

---

[79] Likimani, *Passbook*, p. 123, attributes this line to a male character.

[80] "Patriarchal ideology is absolutely dependent on the construction of a fundamental male-female opposition." Winter, *Subjects*, p. 10.

[81] *Colonial Inscriptions*, p. 28.

Kikuyu myths of origin, derived from Kenyatta's 1930s' account, spoke of descent from Gikuyu and Muumbi, the first people, who begat nine daughters, the founders of nine clans.

> It is said that while holding superior position in the community the women became domineering and ruthless fighters. They also practised polyandry... through sexual jealousy many men were put to death for committing adultery or other minor offences... [T]he men were subjected to all kinds of humiliation and injustice [so they] planned a revolt by getting all the women pregnant at once... [T]he brave women were almost paralysed by the condition in which they were. The men triumphed, took over the leadership in the community and became the heads of their families instead of the women. Immediately steps were taken to abolish the system of polyandry and to establish the system of polygamy.

The name of the group was changed from Muumbi to Kikuyu but the women threatened to kill all the boys and not bear any more children if the clan names were changed, so they were kept.[82]

Beyond providing justification for an oppressive patrilinearity, this myth established women as a threat to civilization, who would kill their own sons to maintain prestige, and who required male control of their sexuality through marriage. Marriage is given primacy as a key societal institution. Kenyatta later stated that the myth showed that women claimed only the privileges not the responsibilities of leadership, and that it represented only the men's viewpoint. He added that men had introduced chiefship and that there was no record of women's views. Elaborating on this myth, he told of women killing animals slowly with wooden knives, so that the animals fled and never returned; men never killed their animals so they remained domesticated and God [Mogai] gave men iron and the power to forge better knives.[83] Here Kenyatta furthered the oppositional view of men and women; men represented civilization, power, skill and wealth counted in livestock while women were associated with wildness, cruelty and irrationality, conforming to categories well analyzed by Cixous and Ortner.[84] Is it accidental that glorious myths about the daughters of Muumbi are rare, although they were the putative founders of the race?

There are also folktales collected by female and male recorders which, when taken together, offer much evidence about the social construction of gender. These attempts to reconstruct old folktales come from Kikuyu sources for the most part but a few are Kamba in origin. Although they derive mainly from female storytellers, they still present a fairly uniform view of women imbued with male dominant

[82] Kenyatta, *Facing*, pp. 6-9. Later Kenyatta recounted a myth concerning the dethroning of the autocratic King Gikuyu, grandson of Gikuyu, in favor of democratic forms (pp. 179-80).

[83] Kenyatta, *People*, pp. 7,11; *Facing*, pp. 69-70.

[84] Kamau, "Rooms," p. 115, further elaborated a tripartite categorization for central Kenyan cultures based on urban space in 1970s Nairobi, which associated women with unclean, raw, hidden, and otherwise negative qualities, although some neutral space was allowed. Cixous, "Laugh"; Ortner, "Female." The critique of bipolar characterizations, as in MacCormack and Strathern, *Nature*, is well-taken.

ideology, resurrected here in that some are intended to be read to children.[85] Many have heroines with the following characteristics: young, kind, gentle, hardworking, helpful, passive, obedient to male authority, self-sacrificing, ignorant and resourceful in escaping evil but unwilling to kill to do so.[86] In a prototypical tale repeated in most collections a young girl is expected to sacrifice herself to save her village. As she is drowning she appeals for help to her relatives and friends, enumerated carefully in order of importance; none helps her so she dies. Bad women are represented as jealous, vengeful, evil, willful, spiteful, lazy, vain, beautiful, and overly picky or disobedient, especially in the matter of choosing a husband from among the choices given by her parents. Older women are presented far less frequently and when they are as ignorant, overly possessive of their daughters, and above all, foolish.[87] In one song a line is, "I am not taught by women with breasts, from whom we might drink and become foolish."[88] Kenyatta and others placed strong emphasis on Kikuyu reverence for motherhood, but the folktales undermine that with an attitude bordering on contempt. Young girls save their mothers' lives; older women at best are helpless and ignorant, at worst evil stepmothers.[89] In one tale a peasant trickster full of unpleasant characteristics, an unusual male portrayal in this context, gets disgusted with his wife's foolishness and searches the world over for a new spouse. Having surveyed a wide selection, including a queen whom he also finds gullible, he returns home concluding, "all women are pleasant fools."[90] The portrayals of men contrast sharply with those of women. Most are presented as brave, ambitious, wise, wealthy or becoming so, and fiercely protective of their land, women and children. The male role as provider is stressed here and in other sources as a key part of the ideal. Men's role as provider, in turn, rested ultimately on their power to allocate land. By this rubric those who had no power to dispose of land, like women, were seen as expendable.[91]

Disobedient girls or women are punished by being eaten by ogres or hyenas, or chopped up with knives. If necessary, girls are supposed to sacrifice their lives for

---

[85] The works of Charity Waciuma, in particular.

[86] Kabira, "Storytellers," pp. 68-70, cited a rare exception, a story told by Wanjira wa Rukunya of a girl who showed exemplary knowledge of foods.

[87] Njau and Mulaki, *Women Heroes*, pp. 99-121; Adagala and Kabira, *Oral Narratives*, pp. 11-51; Kabira and Mutahi, *Gikuyu Oral Literature*, pp. 63-100; Mwangi, *Kikuyu Folktales*, pp. 72-112; Njururi, *Tales*, pp. 5-15, 63-67, 90-93.

[88] Kabira and Mutahi, *Oral Literature*, p. 166.

[89] Kenyatta, *Facing*, pp. 9-10; Cagnolo, *Akikuyu*, p. 59; Kabira, "Storytellers," p. 68.

[90] Njururi, *Tales*, pp. 103-10.

[91] Browne, "Kawangware," pp. 69, 57; Berman and Lonsdale, *Unhappy Valley* II: 380-83. For a contrasting interpretation of the construction of gender in precolonial Kikuyu society see Shaw, *Colonial Inscriptions*, pp. 48ff., who uses two versions of one tale to stress women's and men's interdependence. But interdependence does not exclude dominance by one over another and may even foster the desire for control, an observation that also applies to Kershaw's (*Mau Mau*, p. 21) emphasis on the complementary roles of men and women.

the benefit of the community. Although Muriuki stated that the killing of women and children and the rape or seduction of women prisoners of war were strictly forbidden, the tales sanction the killing of women for various reasons.[92] Like Grimm's fairy-tales, the tales are cautionary, used to get children to behave; their messages for both boys and girls were explicit regarding violence against women. Their didactic nature is echoed in at least one later collection of short stories which replays the same themes in contemporary dress.[93]

Proverbs convey additional meanings regarding gender and women that fill in around those drawn from myths and tales. The random selection given below comes from several sources, in each case translated by the recorder.

A young man is a piece of God.
A plant loses its bloom as soon as it bears fruit.
Old bees yield no honey (told by and to old women).
Beauty is not eaten.
Long live my mother and her ugliness.
Never cast a slight at those who dish out your food.
A barren woman is like a barren cow; she adds nothing to the worth of her
    father's clan.
War is not porridge.
Women's strife has no consequences.
One returns to the old wife when the young wife dies.
The woman who has children does not desert her home.
The she-goat that gives birth to six kids feeds them too.
The man comes out of childhood but the woman never outgrows womanhood.
A rich man's old age has no bad smell.[94]

Here women are at best faithful providers of food, at worst ugly, potentially faithless, childlike, and unimportant. Men are presented as next to God in importance, involved in important pursuits ("war is not porridge"), wise in maturity, and affirmed by wealth.[95]

The view of women as inconsequential also is evident in concepts of evil. With the Kikuyu, ogres (usually seen as cannibalistic with female victims) and witches were usually male; women were even denied an equal power to do evil.

---

[92] Muriuki, *History*, p. 125.

[93] Njau, *Market Literature*. All of these stories are, of course, open to other interpretations, but the content that sanctions violence against women has unities it would be irresponsible to ignore, in my view.

[94] Huxley, *Red Strangers*, pp. 4, 40, 240; Barra, *1000 Kikuyu Proverbs*, pp. 24, 40, 47-48, 60, 111, 116, 123, 109; DC/MKS 10B 13/1 *Muig.* (July 1928): 3. The last proverb given here serves as a main theme in Ngugi wa Thiong'o's *Devil on the Cross*.

[95] Berman and Lonsdale, *Unhappy Valley*, p. 342, interpreted this proverb as saying that porridge was more important, but war is the subject of the sentence.

Kamba women, however, were frequently accused of witchcraft and had considerable ritual power.[96] Smithing, a male occupation for both peoples, was particularly associated with the power to bewitch. In a group of 115 witchcraft cases from Kikuyuland tried in the District Commissioner's courts between 1946 and 1950 only 8% had women defendants.[97] A woman's ritual power rested mainly on her role as mother and provider but was negative to a large extent; an old woman could curse someone by stripping herself naked, one of the tactics employed in the Thuku demonstration to be discussed shortly.[98] But such beliefs can be modified; in Nairobi before World War II prostitutes were believed to lure men to their deaths, their menstrual blood being instrumental to that end.[99] Women's ownership of property in Pumwani may have contributed to men's rising belief in women's power to do evil.

Old Kikuyu customs surrounding death and birth reflected class and gender differences. The bodies of poor people, especially those who died from violence or a sudden onset of sickness attributed to witchcraft, were thrown out to be disposed of by predators.[100] Wealthy men, however, were buried with pomp and circumstance, and a respected woman elder might also have received burial.[101] The inferiority of left as compared to right was expressed by women being buried lying on their left side and men on their right.[102] When a child was born the mother screamed five times for a boy and four times for a girl, while the father cut five pieces of sugar cane for a boy and four for a girl. The scraps of cane left over after consumption by the mother and child were buried to the right of the hut entrance for a boy and to the left for a girl. The mother's seclusion after birth was supposed to be five days for a boy and four for a girl. Brave boys were praised with a special chant, not brave girls.[103]

Kikuyu avoidance customs convey the full meaning of the symbolic opposition between women and men and its consequences. Menstruating women were not supposed to cook grain or place food in the courtyard of a homestead, although they

---

[96] Kenyatta, *Facing*, pp. 288ff.; Beecher, *Kikuyu*, p. 22, claimed that the Kikuyu had no women witches but that the Kamba did. Lindblom, *Akamba*, pp. 257, 301, 448. Kershaw, *Mau Mau*, pp. 32, 195, however, said that Kiambu women could be witches and that they were not allowed to take oathes until after 1933.

[97] MAA 7/835 Witchcraft Cases, 1946-50. I have chosen to use this anglicized version to refer to Kikuyu country, as opposed to Kikuyu by itself, in order to avoid confusion with Kikuyu Province, Kikuyu District, or Kikuyu Location, all terms used now or historically to refer to portions of Kikuyuland.

[98] Likimani, *Passbook*, p. 71; Kenyatta, *Facing*, pp. 273ff.

[99] White, "Fluids." Menstrual blood is/was viewed as polluting in many societies. Delaney, Lupton and Toth, *Curse*.

[100] Beech, "Suicide," p. 56; Mwangi, *Folktales*, pp. 120, 130; Mackinder, *Ascent*, p. 143. It was impossible to determine for much of this material how old the custom was.

[101] Routledges, *People*, p. 139; Middleton and Kershaw, *Central Tribes*, p. 60. By 1950 burial was the norm for everyone. Interview Fisher: 14 Oct. 1992.

[102] Kenyatta, *Facing*, p. 94. Left-handedness was associated with bad luck, as in many cultures.

[103] Routledges, *People*, p. 147; Cagnolo, *Akikuyu*, p. 64; Middleton and Kershaw, *Central Tribes*, pp. 54-55; Likimani, *Passbook*, p. 191.

could work in the fields. Sexual intercourse was forbidden during menstruation because it was polluting to men.[104] Ideas of pollution as well as status placed prohibitions on women and children viewing certain religious rites performed by men; men had to escort them to sacred places. A whole host of prohibitions surrounded eating. Women were not permitted to see men eat meat and were only permitted to eat meat themselves on rare occasions if at all. Husbands and elders were to be served first separately from women and children.[105]

Blood compensation for murder was paid to the elders of the clan to which the victim belonged, 100 goats for a man and thirty for a woman.[106] Premarital pregnancy resulting in death,[107] adultery, rape and other assaults on a woman were treated as property violations requiring compensation to the husband or father of the woman. If a man murdered his wife he was destroying his own property and there was no fine. Women could not appear as litigants before the council of elders, the *kiama*; they were jural minors because they were not allowed to take the oaths essential to establishing the credibility of a witness or a litigant.[108] Women and girls were regularly seized in raids or used as pawns for debt, as shown in Chapter III.

The ideology embodied in myths of origin, folktales, proverbs and customs reflected a reality in which women existed as 'other,' as de Beauvoir put it, in a kind of limbic state between their fathers' lineages, to which they belonged only until marriage, and their husbands' lineages, in which they were perpetual strangers.[109] At marriage a woman took her husband's name to indicate her affiliation, whereas a man kept his father's name as his second name. It is no wonder, then, that many observers took women to be a form of property purchased by bridewealth, and passed on at the husband's death to a younger brother. Presley called the undervaluing of women the "legal fiction that women's lives were not as valuable as men's ...," and Kikuyu society nonegalitarian before colonialism, while Muriuki said it was "patriarchal, uncentralized and highly egalitarian." Kershaw had the most balanced view: "Society was undoubtedly stratified, but the social and economic requirements for mobility [land

---

[104] Presley, "Transformation," p. 38; Leakey, *Southern Kikuyu* II: 787.

[105] Routledges, *People*, pp. 232, 235; Tate, "Native Law," p. 243; Browne, "Kawangware," pp. 246-47, has a list of specific parts that women were allowed to eat at ceremonies including the stomach muscles, a portion of the rear leg and the front legs, prescriptions from 1980. Similarly, ceremonial beer-drinking surrounding marriages, which after all intimately determined women's fate, only marginally included women, who received only one-fourth of the beer in the only ceremony including them. Leakey, *Southern Kikuyu* II: 764; Cagnolo, *Akikuyu*, p. 208.

[106] PC/CP 6/4/4 Memo. Assistant District Commissioner Kiambu to D.C. Kiambu: 19 June 1922; Boyes, *King*, p. 307; Muriuki, *History*, p. 131.

[107] Compensation for this crime was a subject of discussion through 1960; PC/CENT 2/1/4 minutes Kiambu LNC 20 Sept. 1926; LG 3/2701-2 minutes Kiambu ADC 19 Jan. 1959, 5 Jan. 1960.

[108] Tate, "Native Law," p. 242; PC/CP 1/4/2 Dundas, "Notes on Kikuyu Law," 24 Oct. 1912, included in Kikuyu District Political Record Book II 1912-13. Muriuki, *History*, p. 130.

[109] Fisher, *Anatomy*, p. 9. de Beauvoir, *Second Sex*.

and labor control] were available to all males."[110] Gender differences continue, then, even in scholarly evaluations.

This situation had many real consequences for women in the early twentieth century. The few women chiefs appointed by the colonial government were highly resented by the men. Boys rather than girls were more likely to be taken to European hospitals for care or sent to school.[111] Women were far more likely to commit suicide than men, an eventuality associated in many cultures with wifebeating and the status of women as property. That such a suicide placed a curse on the husband's lineage in no way mitigated the consequences for the woman, who might have been seeking revenge for abuse or other offenses. Boys were preferred over girls as infants, and women were valued above all for their childbearing capacity.[112] Kenyatta stated that a girl was taught,

> she will be married and bring wealth to her family so that a poor brother can find the guarantee necessary for marriage. She will bear many children, bring honor to her family and to the tribe, and she will provide food for the poor relation ... She is taught to behave like a gentlewoman, not to raise her eyes or voice talking to men in public, not to bathe in the open, not to eat in the presence of men other than those of her own age or kinsfolk,

and to obey her husband and parents and care for her husband's property. This teaching was particularly important because, although fathers were to teach skills to boys, mothers were felt to be responsible for teaching both skills to daughters and customs and history to children of both genders.[113] Women's work in providing and preparing food was seen as fundamental, an aspect Shaw used to argue for women's empowerment in precolonial times by linking it to control over food distribution.[114] However, what is necessary is not always valued or endowed with authority, just as having agency does not necessarily mean winning.

While Kenyatta had his own nationalist agenda that involved inventing the docile "traditional" (but not oppressed) woman, he surely reflected something of the reality of the 1930s. Embedded in male dominant construction of female gender in Kikuyu society was a strong notion of women, especially wives, as male property and therefore appropriate objects for abuse on occasion. Perhaps most illustrative of the situation was his commentary on a rape case translated into Kikuyu for the benefit of readers of *Muigwithania* in 1928. The case involved a Boer settler who ordered two of his African workers to rape a woman walking on his farm. One of them did

---

[110] Routledges, *People*, p. 143; Presley, "Transformation," pp. 59, 62; Muriuki, *History*, p. 110; Kershaw, "Roles," p. 182.

[111] Muriuki, *History*, p. 133; Huxley, *Lizard*, p. 125; DC/KBU 1/9 Kiambu AR 1915-16: 36.

[112] Beech, "Suicide," p. 57; Levinson, *Violence*, p. 51; interview Kershaw 4 Aug. 1994; Cagnolo, *Akikuyu*, pp. 59-62.

[113] Kenyatta, *Facing*, pp. 103-105, 93-94, 97.

[114] Shaw, *Colonial Inscriptions*, p. 29 (see also Clark [Shaw], "Land"). Her contention is supported by citing Leakey and Kenyatta rather than independent oral sources (pp. 44ff.). Control over food distribution is dealt with extensively in Chapter III.

and was sentenced to three years in jail and twenty-four lashes. Kenyatta thought that people ought to know that the settlers considered rape a bad crime which could bring capital punishment. He said, "it is not good for a man to throw away his life for a profitless thing like that."[115] He marveled at such a severe punishment for what in the eyes of customary law was a property crime only, and no crime if the man was married to the woman.[116] Likewise, Kamba men viewed wives as property; Lindblom observed in the early 1900s that men's jealousy regarding wives' infidelity was connected not so much to sexual possessiveness, which the expected loan of wives to visiting age-mates discouraged in any case, as to the violation of property rights. Although he strongly believed that Kamba women had a certain power, he still stressed the instrumentality for men of controlling wives' labor, saying, "On the whole, the Kamba woman goes through life calmly and quietly, doing her duty and suitably subservient to her husband."[117]

And yet women were not completely powerless victims by any means; Lindblom in the same paragraph segued immediately into a discussion of ways that women in groups could influence male behavior, including public demonstrations involving property damage, ridicule and abuse. A key incident of the 1920s forms an appropriate starting point for a discussion of changing notions of gender in Kikuyu society. The 1922 Thuku protest was one of Nairobi's first mass demonstrations and constitutes critical evidence of the nature of Kikuyu women's political influence in the 1920s. Nairobi housing and employment problems contributed to nascent Kikuyu militancy in the form of the Young Kikuyu Association (later renamed the East Africa Association [EAA]), founded by Harry Thuku in 1921, but so did the routine use of forced labor (mostly of women) in rural areas.[118] Harry Thuku, a mission-educated government clerk from Kiambu, had been arrested on 14 March 1922 for his role in expressing labor grievances (including those of women coffeepickers, which caused him to be dubbed the "chief of women"), and incarcerated in the Nairobi police station on Government Road (now Harry Thuku Road). As a consequence the EAA organized a strike and on 16 March a large crowd (seven or eight thousand people) gathered in front of the police station, observed by Europeans on the verandah of the Norfolk Hotel across the way. The male leaders were persuaded by the Colonial Secretary to try to disperse the crowd, but failed amid accusations that they had been bribed. Accounts of the incident largely agree that the African women in the crowd then took over its leadership by taunting the men.

[115] DC/MKS 10B 13/1 *Muigwithania* Oct. 1928: 12. Henceforth referred to as *Muig.* Kenyatta was editor of this organ of the KCA (see Thuku below).

[116] One of the recent consequences in the U.S. of recognizing women as legal adults and not male property has been the criminalizing of marital rape.

[117] Lindblom, *Akamba*, pp. 557, 79-81, 180.

[118] Wipper, "Kikuyu Women," p. 320; Bujra, "Entrepreneurs," pp. 222-23; DC/KBU 1/14 Kikuyu District AR 1920-21: 10.

The most detailed account came from Job Muchuchu, a founder of the EAA and afterward secretary of the Kikuyu Central Association (see Chapter III). According to Muchuchu, the most prominent woman, Mary Muthoni Nyanjiru,

> leapt to her feet, pulled her dress right up over her shoulders and shouted to the men: "You take my dress and give me your trousers. You men are cowards. What are you waiting for? Our leader is in there. Let's get him." The hundreds of women trilled their *ngemi* [ululation] in approbation and from that moment on trouble was probably inevitable. Mary and the others pushed on until the bayonets of the [soldiers'] rifles were pricking at their throats, and then the firing started. Mary was one of the first to die ... [T]he European settlers sitting drinking on the verandah of the Norfolk Hotel joined in the shooting and it is said that they were responsible for most of the deaths over there. One of our people employed at the mortuary told us that 56 bodies were brought in, although the government said only 21 were killed.[119]

This story has assumed a sanctified place in nationalist mythology as part of the construction of the nationalist woman (and man). Thuku commented, "The death of the woman Mary showed that women were in the forefront of Kenya's fight for freedom." As a consequence of the protest tax hikes as a means of coercion to fill labor needs were abandoned.[120] Taxes, of course, were not, and "Africans [males] ... paid both their direct taxes and their duties on imported consumer goods as much by selling their wives' domestic produce as by wage employment for whites."[121]

The importance of this incident for this analysis rests with the women's exhortations to the men; they used a form of curse that is widespread in Africa, called *guturamira ng'ania* in Kikuyu, which entails displaying the buttocks and genitalia to men who are misbehaving. The power of the curse lies in the reference to motherhood, women's reproductive powers; men are threatened with repudiation by their mothers and with their own infertility/impotence. The intended audience in this case was *not* the authorities inside holding Thuku, but the Kikuyu male leaders and participants in the protest, whose enthusiasm was flagging in the face of threatened force majeure. Despite assertions that women were an independent political force, which Wipper and others have made in analyzing such incidents, this case indicates the contingent nature of their influence; the women were trying to force the men to play their proper role in making the protest successful. Women's political influence was exercised indirectly through symbolic action, a ritual of protest using an accepted vocabulary not understood by the Europeans but very potent for the Africans present. This incident serves as a baseline for considering change in urban women's perceptions of their own power, which has been influenced considerably by their

---

[119] Quoted in Rosberg and Nottingham, *Myth*, pp. 51-52. Spencer, *Kenya African Union*, p. 53n.52, disputes this story based on the evidence of an African woman participant.

[120] Wipper, "Women," pp. 315-16; Thuku, *Autobiography*, p. 33. A fuller analysis of Kikuyu women's political authority is in Chapters III and VIII.

[121] Lonsdale, "Depression," p. 99.

subsequent experience with trade. Wipper has suggested that the women leaders of the Harry Thuku protest were drawn from among the population of Kikuyu prostitutes in Nairobi. However, Bujra noted that Nairobi women beerbrewers were unhappy about the forbidding of their livelihood that accompanied the establishment of a municipal brewery in 1921. Beerbrewing provided a lucrative source of income and was one of the few occupations open to Nairobi women.[122] Mary Muthoni Nyanjiru might have been a prostitute or a beerbrewer; she might also have been one of the many women who in the 1920s went to Nairobi to trade, and she might have been all of the above. What is crucial is that her work brought her to the fateful event. Here I will historicize central Kenyan women's work in trade and assess its possibilities as a liberatory mechanism with respect to changes in women's self-perceptions.

* * * * *

In keeping with a multidisciplinary approach and nonlinear use of time, the organization of this study effects a compromise between thematic and chronological considerations, an unconventional solution that grew conceptually and organically from the data. If control over women's labor and the reconstruction of gender are major topics of the study, its framing structure is the template formed by the processes undergone by certain beans presented in Chapter II, which begins with an analysis of the symbolic meanings and material realities of beans in Kikuyu culture and then looks at the history of beans and dried staples as an example of agricultural imperialism. Beans serve as a multivalent symbol for women; the process of their material and symbolic marginalization as a crop is an index for the peripheralization of women and their dried staples trade, with segregation and subordination as dominant motifs. Chapters III through V give an extended history of women's trade from the 1890s to the 1980s, carrying through the comparison not only of men's and women's trade as they evolved at a different pace, but also of maize and beans. Particular attention is devoted to efforts at different levels to control that trade. This Kenyan history mandates strong attention to the control efforts that did so much to shape the conditions of trade, efforts in which race, class and ethnicity, as well as gender, are imbricated. Chapters VI and VII return to thematic organization while elaborating respectively a history of change in marital patterns and of women's collective organizing efforts connected to their changing role in trade. The seams of these diverse topics will be joined together into a Kenyan women's cloth that unites at once the material and the symbolic, the objective and the subjective, and creates a history dedicated to illuminating, respecting and transcending our and their differences.

---

[122] Wipper, "Kikuyu Women," p. 320; Bujra, "Entrpreneurs," pp. 222-23; DC/KBU 1/14 Kikuyu District AR 1920-21: 10.

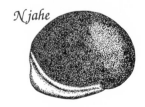

Njahe

II

From Njahe to Nyayo:
Beans and the Evolution of Agricultural
Imperialism in Kenya

Beans are intimately associated with women in central Kenya.[1] The symbolism associated with *njahe*, a variety especially important for the Kikuyu, was no less important than the trade in beans. Dried beans are a women's crop, a women's trade commodity, and preeminently a women's food. The study of beans and their trade turned out to be subversive of established orthodoxies in some ways and requires serious attention to women. Moreover, beans serve as symbolic articulators of women's labor in both their expropriation and their connection to the soil. In this chapter I will describe the history of beans as a crop, in which women struggled to control their own produce as a part of resistance to the impact of agricultural imperialism, defined as the expropriation of land, labor, profits, and plant genetic materials, and the imposition of alien priorities upon farmers in central Kenya.[2] Women have asserted themselves in the matter of crop choice and in so doing foiled some ill-judged export attempts and fostered multi-purpose hardy crops suited to Kenyan conditions. They have also, however, yielded to agricultural imperialism under the pressure of preferential pricing and high labor demands to the detriment of their diet and wellbeing. Given the limitations of the data, I will pay most attention to Kikuyu

---

[1] An extended version of this chapter is available in Robertson, "Black."

[2] To be distinguished from Crosby's term, ecological imperialism, which refers to an unplanned spread of Europeans and their plants into new temperate areas. Crosby, *Ecological Imperialism*.

beans and symbolic systems, but include information about the Kamba where available. The fullest picture was gained by combining oral, linguistic, secondary and archival sources.

Beans are ubiquitous in Africa; West Africa produces approximately 90% of the world's cowpeas. Kenya is Africa's largest producer of common beans (*Phaseolus vulgaris*). Beans are the second most important food crop in Kenya after maize, and had a similar status in Tanzania before colonial-induced changes. Rwanda, before its current devastation, specialized in producing a vast quantity of new varieties of *Phaseolus* beans intended to suit differing ecological conditions, while Tanzania has a thriving seed bean industry.[3] And yet, beans are as much taken for granted as women and their labor are, a fate commensurate with their status as a women's crop among the Kikuyu, Kamba, and other peoples. This chapter will not only describe the history and significance of beans among Kikuyu and Kamba in the Nairobi area, but also set beans in the context of other staple crops in the twentieth century. It documents a prototypical case of agricultural imperialism, wherein indigenous or indigenized crops are subordinated to imposed ones, even more rapidly in the hands of economic innovators like the southern Kikuyu, who were most intimately exposed to white settler colonialism under the British. Beyond the material issues documented here is the symbolic assertion of white over dark that Europeans applied not only to skin color but also to food preferences in beans and maize. The resultant market considerations were imposed on the Kenyan African population regardless of their own tastes. Purification campaigns aimed at segregating not only crops from each other but also different varieties of the same crops, mimicking the progressive segregation of women from men and the "races" or "tribes" from each other. Government policy concerning beans also moved from the dominance of local settler and agricultural officer interests before World War II to more subservience to the interests of the British metropolitan government after the war, and more subordination to the efforts of multinational corporations after independence.[4] After looking at the symbolic meanings of certain beans, this chapter will document the transition from beans to maize as a chief staple in central Kenya, the introduction of new bean varieties and government policies furthering exports that included purification campaigns, along with women's resistance to ill-judged export efforts, and the negative impact on the local diet of those policies.

Gender and the Symbolism of Beans among the Kikuyu

In English the term beans is undifferentiated, applied to a variety of edible seeds. In Kikuyu and Kikamba *mboco*, or *mboso*, are generic terms for the beans Europeans normally use, which mostly fall into the category of *Phaseolus vulgaris*,

---

[3] Michigan State Univ. Bean/Cowpea CRP, *Highlights*, p. 1; Bryceson, *Food Insecurity*, pp. 104, 19; Grisley, "Observations."

[4] Smith, "Overview," p. 111.

called *maharagwe* in Kiswahili. *Phaseolus vulgaris* are not indigenous to Africa. If we want to understand the history of beans in central Kenya we must begin with the indigenous varieties, termed *njahe* in Kikuyu, *nzahi* in Kikamba (*Lablab niger*, *Dolichos lablab*, or lablab beans), and *njugu* (*Cajanus cajan*, or pigeon peas).[5] Although Anglophones would classify *njahe* as beans, for Kikuyu they occupy a privileged category of their own. *Njahe* are small round black beans with a white cap on them. They have special significance for the Kikuyu and are intimately associated with women, especially women's reproductive functions. If all beans that are dried are grown by women, *njahe* are unique in their ceremonial usage and symbolism. Moreover, they are perhaps the only Kenyan crop associated uniquely with the Kikuyu, called "Kikuyu beans" by Leakey; it is often said that no one else eats them. The Kamba, however, did so, although they did not have the same ritual and symbolic associations as for the Kikuyu.[6]

The significance of *njahe* can be seen in their religious associations, usage and linguistic evidence. One of the best clues to their importance is the term Kianjahe (Kirima kia njahe, or Kilimambogo) applied to Ol Donyo Sabuk (the Maasai term now in common usage), a mountain considered to be the second most important dwelling place of God (*Ngai*) in Kikuyu indigenous religion. On the lower elevations of the mountain a special variety of *njahe* grew called *njahe cia Ngai* or *njahe cia ngoma*, the *njahe* of God or of the departed spirits. *Njahe* can be considered to be the closest Kikuyu approximation to a sacred food, also regarded as the most tempting food.[7] As in many religions, fertility enhancers are associated with the divine. The most important rains, the long rains which are essential for fertility, are called *mbura ya njahe*. *Njahe* have a longer growing season than most millets and maizes and so are grown during the long rains,[8] but the association of *njahe* with fertility goes beyond this elementary one to assume a special meaning for women.

At each critical transitional stage in women's reproductive lives they are given *njahe* as a special food considered to be most nourishing. Kenyatta tells us that, before the bloodletting associated with clitoridectomy at initiation, girls were given *njahe* and *ngima ya ogembe*, "a stiff porridge made of a small kind of grain [millet] ground into flour and mixed with water and oil." During marriage negotiations *njahe cia athoni* [Kikuyu=of the in-laws], a special dish prepared with bananas mixed with *njahe*, was consumed. During pregnancy and especially after childbirth for nursing women were given *njahe,* whose leaves were also consumed by women.[9] Kenyatta

---

[5] Lindblom, *Akamba*, p. 505. The pigeon pea is usually given an African origin, while lablab beans are sometimes given an Asian origin. Greenway, "Origins," p. 179; Juma, *Gene Hunters*, p. 17.

[6] Porter, *Food*, p. 35; Lindblom, *Akamba*, p. 505.

[7] L. Leakey, *Southern Kikuyu* III: 1077-78; Kabira and Mutahi, *Literature*, p. 97.

[8] Porter, *Food*, p. 35.

[9] Kenyatta, *Facing*, pp. 130-31; Porter, *Food*, p. 35. In contrast, Kamba women had many food restrictions during pregnancy such that their diet became mainly milk and sorghum or millet flour porridge; neither bananas nor their usual version of *irio* (Kikamba=isio) were allowed, one consequence being that some ate the common famine supplement, red earth. Lindblom, *Akamba*, p. 29.

called *njahe* "a very nourishing kind of bean used mostly to feed women after child-birth." A beanseller in 1988 joked that how many *njahe* she sold "depends on the birth rate of the Kikuyu."[10] Louis Leakey described *njahe* as an essential dish used as part of a ceremony to cure women of excessive menstrual bleeding, while Elspeth Huxley described black beans being used as instruments for divination in the 1930s.[11] Kikuyu men were not supposed to eat *njahe* unaccompanied by other food. *Njahe*, then, have a particular symbolic association with the fertility of women. Women past menopause, female elders, also have a special dish, but it is millet gruel, *ucuru wa mwere*. Moreover, this fertility was considered to be an essential foundation for a sense of Kikuyu identity. Indeed, knowledge about beans was considered to be an indicator of female identity; Jeanne Fisher described being tested about this knowledge by an elderly woman who wished to determine her degree of acceptability as a researcher on women's culture.[12]

The importance of beans, *njahe* in particular, comes out also in the use of metaphor and emphasis in twentieth-century language. It is present in *Muigwithania*, in complaints regarding Kiambu hospital food for pregnant women in the Kiambu Local Native Council (LNC) minutes, and in halcyon views of the past or an idealized future. Male age-set initiates in 1914 made up a song referring to the desirability of emigration to the Rift Valley, "I cannot continue to eat maize only, when there is a surplus of *njugu* at Njoro."[13] *Njahe* even had Kikuyu nationalist implications as their most important dish; in 1930 women involved in the Muumbi Central Association, a response to exclusion of women from membership in the Kikuyu Central Association, prepared them as part of their ceremonies of organization, and again when they joined with the men in 1933.[14] Ngugi wa Thiong'o composed a song attributed to the 1950s freedom fighters in *Devil on the Cross*, which made a bean a symbol of all food and of the loving qualities of women and children.

> Great love I found there
> Among women and children,
> A bean fell to the ground--
> We split it among ourselves.

In response the loyalist Homeguards sang,

---

[10] Leakey, *Southern Kikuyu* I: 265; Kenyatta, *Facing*, p. 57; interview Blundell 10 Sept. 1988; Kenya Native Affairs Dept. AR 1946: 64; interview 803 Kiambu: 11 Oct. 1988.

[11] Leakey, *Southern Kikuyu* III: 1172-74. Huxley, *Strangers*, p. 10, said that they came from the *mubage* bush and were shiny. She also described (p. 117) a game called *giuthi*, a form of wari, played with beans. For the Kamba certain beans may also have had special significance as ingredients in powerful medicines for which they were famous. Ndeti, *Elements*, p. 125.

[12] Fisher, *Anatomy*, pp. 99, 80; interview 14 Oct. 1992.

[13] DC/MKS/10B/13/1: *Muig.* I, 9 (Feb. 1929): 3-4; PC/CENT 2/1/13, 22-25 Oct. 1946; Kanogo, *Squatters*, pp. 23-24.

[14] Presley, *Kikuyu Women*, p. 118.

Self-love and the love of selling out
Among the traitors of the land.
The bean we steal from the people--
We struggle to see who can grab it all.

In 1988 a letter to the Nairobi *Daily Nation* spelled out for one nostalgic man the characteristics of an idealized past: "your stomach was tight then, with a mixture of *matoke* [bananas] mashed with *njahi* ... , sweet potatoes, and washed down with unboiled cow milk."[15]

Njahe and *njugu*, then, have a very special significance for Kikuyu; they are associated with fertility, spiritual and national nourishment, healthiness and women. This perception is a logical one. Beans have a higher protein content than all grains, and supply a necessary complement to millet or maize as staples. *Njahe* not only take a longer time to grow than most cereals, but also a longer time to cook than all grains, thus requiring nurturant attention from the women cooks and farmers. The cooking of vegetables is ascribed to women as a task almost universally and with the Kikuyu; the association of beans with women's fertility and childrearing functions is therefore appropriate.[16] The divine associations, the references to a halcyon past and the fundamental nurturant function of *njahe* make them the symbol of Kikuyu well-being par excellence, deemed, along with *njugu,* "foods of respect."[17]

The Transition from Beans to Maize

However, *njahe* in present-day Kenya are insignificant in the diet of most Kikuyu. Beans in general are widely recognized as being the second most important food crop after maize, but those beans are overwhelmingly of the *Phaseolus vulgaris* type. Most Kenyan beans now resemble closely those found in the Americas and Europe. The first questions to be answered then become: how did Kikuyu adopt *Phaseolus vulgaris* almost to the exclusion of *njahe,* and how did maize overtake beans and millet as the chief Kikuyu staple? Both answers derive from looking at the peripatetic activities of Kikuyu farmers, who played a significant role in the diffusion of new plants, and of British colonialists in the guise of the Kenya Agriculture Department.

The genetic history of *Phaseolus* beans indicates that they were first domesticated in Latin America in several locations at least 7000 years ago. *Phaseolus* beans were probably introduced into East Africa by Portuguese traders on the coast in the

---

[15] Ngugi, *Devil*, p. 39; *Daily Nation*, 10 June 1988: 7.

[16] The symbolic significance of women's cooking is a growing source of interest among feminist anthropologists. See Clark, "Money"; Guyer, "Raw, Cooked and Half-Baked," a critique of Levi-Strauss' incomplete analysis. In Tanganyika during World War II conscripted male laborers threw away beans rather than cook them. This may not have been solely due to the length of time involved but also to the symbolism. Matheson and Bovill, *Agriculture*, p. 168.

[17] Fisher, *Anatomy*, p. 80. Similarly, maize among Andean and Aztec peoples is used as a metaphor for food. Without it there is hunger. Sandstrom, *Corn*, pp. 132, 194; Harrison, *Signs*, p. 172.

sixteenth century and may have come into Kikuyu country in the seventeenth century.[18] Late nineteenth century Kikuyuland supplied caravans with thousands of kilograms of beans and maize and millet in lesser amounts.[19] In contemporary Kenya, however, the most popular varieties of *Phaseolus* grown and consumed derive from colonial and post-independence-introduced cultivars in the twentieth century.[20] The overwhelming dominance of the market for beans by these cultivars deserves an explanation, which comes out of the same processes responsible for the dominance of maize.

Africa and North America share the characteristic of having been the source of very few of the most common food crops of the twentieth century. One explanation for this phenomenon is the imposition of settler dominance on both continents as one manifestation of agricultural imperialism, which I am distinguishing from the earlier spread by African farmers (often women) of plants useful to them. Africa as a consequence has what Kloppenburg calls a dependency index (dependence on non-indigenous crops) of 87.7%, exceeded by North America and Australia at 100%, the Mediterranean at 98.2%.[21] We can therefore expect that Kenya with its history of white settler dominance and the temperate highlands allowing cultivation of some European crops would fit this dependency pattern very well. Here I will look at the changing relationship of maize to beans and the introduction of new varieties of beans during the twentieth century.[22]

When the British founded Nairobi, beans of various types were the chief staple of the Kikuyu along with millet and some maize.[23] In 1899 Mackinder listed Kikuyu staple foods in order of importance as beans, maize, Kaffir corn (durra), castor oil and sweet potatoes. A number of early sources also indicated the importance of sweet potatoes, which one colonial officer still found to be the most important food crop in 1937. In some areas further north, Meru, for instance, beans remained the chief staple well into the colonial period, while they spread into areas such as the

---

[18] Kaplans, "Phaseolus," p. 129. Columbus on his second return voyage to Spain in 1494 took maize and other seeds along, and Jacques Cartier took *Phaseolus* seeds to France from Canada in 1535. Brockway, *Science*, pp. 38, 43. Africans took cowpeas to New England by the 1660s and millet by the 1730s. Juma, *Hunters*, pp. 53, 182, 190; Njugunah et al., "Bean Production," p. 35; Adams and Martin, "Genetic Structure," p. 357.

[19] Lugard, *Rise*, p. 305; Rogers, "British and Kikuyu," p. 262; Mackinder, *Ascent*, p. 95, however, was chiefly supplied with the indigenized variety of maize and fed his porters *posho* (cornmeal). It is not clear from his account if his Swahili caravan masters demanded maize in their forcible extractions of food from a famine-stricken population in 1899.

[20] Pers. comm. Gepts 25 June 1992; Gepts and Bliss, "Pathways," p. 102; interview C. Leakey 15 Oct. 1992.

[21] Ferguson and Sprecher, "Women," p. 2; Kloppenburg, *Seed*, pp. 48, 182.

[22] For an earlier version of this chapter with a fuller account and more technical information about different varieties of beans and their popularity see Robertson, "Black."

[23] Miracle, *Maize*, p. 99; Lugard, *Rise*, p. 305; Chanler, *Travels*, p. 105; Morgan, "Kikuyu," p. 61.

coast as a new food.[24] Up to the present beans have remained the chief source of protein for the majority of the Kenyan population, second only to maize as a staple, especially in Central Province.[25] So what explains the transition to maize as the chief staple?

The speed of the transition to maize is most striking in the Kikuyu area, which felt the maximum impact of the colonial presence in terms of both land alienation and urbanization. The most common Kikuyu staple dish, *githeri,* was originally mainly *njahe* boiled along with papyrus salt and eaten unmashed; now it is mainly maize along with some *Phaseolus* beans. *Irio,* the most common Nairobi staple dish, was mainly mashed *Phaseolus* beans; now it is more often mashed English potatoes with maize, bananas and some beans, despite occasional efforts to maintain the high bean content.[26] How and when did this transition take place, and above all, why?

Maize dominance was a matter of British colonial policy, which used economics as the engine to force change, but these policies had both intentional and unintentional consequences that led to the same end. The intentional policies concerned cheap food supplies. Since Nairobi was founded as a railroad camp for the British East African railway workers, even before settlers came wishing to take advantage of cheap African labor the IBEAC had to feed its workers. The cheapest food to the knowledge of management was *posho,* which was already used widely in South Africa. Many Kenyan settlers came from South Africa and expected to continue the same labor policies, including rations. Indeed, production for the South African export market became a consideration early on.[27] There were advantages for growers in that maize has a shorter growing season than either sorghum or wheat and produces more calories per acre than any other staple except potatoes and cassava.[28] There was also the desire of early administrators to produce profitable cash crops that discriminated against food crops. John Ainsworth founded the East African Agriculture and Horticulture Society (EAAHS) in 1901 with the aim of promoting cash crops and pushed the growing of sisal, cotton and coffee while ignoring food crops.

---

[24] Mackinder, *Ascent,* p. 99; Thomson, *Through Masai Land,* p. 177; MacDonald, *Soldiering,* p. 109; DC/KBU 1/28 Kiambu AR 1937: 29; South Kikuyu Agriculture AR 1928: 315, 328.

[25] Bean 4/XV, Report to Provincial Directors of Agriculture 21 Jan. 1972: 1; Kenya Central Bureau of Statistics, *Integrated Rural Survey 1976-79*: 111-13; Jones, *Marketing,* p. 73. *Phaseolus vulgaris* have an average protein content of 22.3% compared to wheat, the best of the cereal grains at 12.3%, millet at 10%, and maize at 8.9%. Hidalgo, Song and Gepts, *Species,* p. 5.

[26] L. Leakey, *Southern Kikuyu* I: 265-66. The Nairobi *Daily Nation* reported on 12 June 1971, that local kiosk restaurants might have to stop serving *irio* because of a bean shortage making it difficult to achieve the desirable 50% bean content.

[27] Miracle, *Maize,* p. 23; Smart, *History,* p. 21; DC/CP 1/8/1 Nairobi Political Record Book 1899-1915: 67.

[28] Crosby, *Exchange,* pp. 197, 171. Maize was also probably introduced to Africa by the Portuguese in the fifteenth century, but new varieties were introduced in East Africa between 1863 and 1880 and grown widely by 1900, serving as cheap food for caravans. Miracle, *Maize,* pp. 137, 96-99. It seems, however, to have been more common in Ukambani than in Kikuyuland. The other crop that became of particular importance in the early colonial period was English potatoes.

Although the EAAHS collapsed, he saw to it that no more prizes were awarded at agricultural shows for English potatoes, beans or maize.[29]

The change in the relative positions of maize and beans, the growing importance of potatoes, and the decline in millet are shown in the railway shipping figures in Table II.1, which cover produce coming from settler farms and some African production. Until World War I most food crops were produced by Africans; settler farms only began large scale food crop production in the 1920s, often by "squatters." While the quantity of beans shipped doubled from 1903 to 1919, the amount of maize multiplied by seven. These figures, however, understate the magnitude of the change that was taking place. Miracle found that while in 1903 most maize was imported, by 1905 maize was displacing millets and sorghums in the diet and by 1910 maize production "took off," helped along by the government's granting preferential rail rates for its shipment.[30] The 1915-16 Dagoretti Annual Report listed the staple crops grown by Africans in order of importance: maize, beans, potatoes, sweet potatoes, and millets. By 1922 maize was the staple food for much of East Africa, and daily rations of two pounds of *posho* were given to all labor. In the same year the Bowring Commission recommended that Kenya concentrate on growing

II.1. Rail Produce Shipped from Ukambani Province, 1903-1919, in tons

Commodity: Year	Beans	Maize	Millet	English potatoes[†]	Various grains
1903/4	222	312	124	959	123
1904/5		535	166	1162	n.a.
1905/6	854	510	186	1031	120
1906/7	1083	407	93	1524	165
1907/8	434	1623	126	1138	547
1908/9	105	1067	49	288	133
1909/10	598	724	171	1109	1
1914/15	872	7579	98	2119	879
1915/16	2254	16,596	102	3427	670
1916/17	1035	2104	122	203	139
1917/18	282	2290	57	290	263
1918/19	480	2236	84	201	234

Sources: PC/CP 4/2/1 Ukamba ARs 1906-7: 6; 1907-8: Appendix p. 19; DC/KBU/1/1 Kiambu AR 1909-10: 10; Ukamba ARs 1914-15: 76a; 1915-16: 34a; 1916-17: 44a; 1917-18: 48a; 1918-19: 43.

[†] The 1912-13 Ukamba AR noted (p. 66) that Indian traders were doing an "enormous" trade in potatoes, with over 2000 tons sent from Limuru alone, apparently by routes other than the railroad.

---

[29] DC/KBU 1/5 Dagoretti AR 1913-14: 3; Kitching, *Class*, pp. 29, 67; Maxon, *Ainsworth*, pp. 124-26.

[30] Miracle, *Maize*, pp. 28, 137-39; Ukamba AR 1910: 23.

maize, perpetuating the myth of the inexhaustible fertility of African soil.[31] The
number of acres planted in maize then rose every year except from 1930 to 1942,
although the chief locale of maize production in Kenya shifted from the immediate
environs of Nairobi to Nyanza by the 1950s.[32]

The unintentional consequences of various policies constraining women's
labor furthered maize production and were masked by folkloric explanations used by
colonial administrators and settlers. Maize required less weeding than millet for
women, but the common explanation given for the displacement of millet was the
bird-scaring story as follows (which could also be called the dumb birds hypothesis).
Schoolboys were no longer available to scare birds away from millet, so farmers
grew maize instead. There are many problems with this story: schooling did not
become common until after World War II but the conversion to maize largely preceded it and even World War I in Kiambu; girls also were sent to scare birds but not
to school in significant numbers; and birds do attack maize, albeit not so severely.
The explanation regarding women's labor is better founded. The critical factor of
women's labor in Kenyan agriculture has often been ignored, but its universality
makes any change in it more likely to have the kind of broad impact that the shift
from millet to maize entailed. Kershaw also noted that millet was more labor intensive, requiring heavy weeding and monoculture.[33]

During the 1930s Kiambu only sporadically exported beans, which were omitted from official export statistics during World War II.[34] In 1936 the Kiambu Assistant Agriculture Officer commented, "It is apparant [*sic*] that this Reserve is the market garden of Kenya, vegetables are sent to all parts, as far as Uganda and Tanganyika, and we are now extending the industry to the more backward locations in
the North." The profits to growers from fresh vegetable production in 1942, inflated
by the military presence, were reported to be £120,000 with rapid expansion
underway.[35] In 1947 the people of Kiambu were reported to be growing cash crops
and purchasing food crops; by the 1950s Kiambu was moving into flower and fruit
production for export by multinational corporations, and such exotics as rhubarb
were being produced for sale.[36] Air transport of fresh agricultural produce to Europe

[31] DC/KBU 1/9 Kiambu AR 1922: 45; Cone and Lipscomb, *History*, p. 70; Hill, *Cream Country*, p.
16. Europeans were often disappointed when luxuriant tropical foliage gave way to eroded friable soil in
the face of methods used on heavy European soils.

[32] Miracle, *Maize*, p. 142; Cone and Lipscomb, *History*, p. 42; DC/KBU/1/1 Kiambu AR 1909-10:
6; Dept. of Agriculture AR 1958, I: 12.

[33] Interviews, 1992: Fisher 14 Oct.; Colchester 19 Oct.; Askwith 13 Oct.; Huxley 12 Oct; Kershaw,
Mau Mau, pp. 144-45.

[34] DC/KBU 1/27, 23, 24 Kiambu Annual Reports 1930: 8; 1931: 27; 1934: 16; Agr 4/114 Central
Province Agriculture AR 1936: 12; DC/KBU/1/29 Kiambu AR 1938: 32; 1939: 25.

[35] Agr 4/114 Kiambu Agriculture AR 1936: 8; Dept. of Agriculture AR 1942: 4.

[36] Native Affairs Dept. AR 1946-47: 65; DC/KBU/1/45 Kiambu District AR 1955: Appendix III;
Agr 4/440 Safari Diary 25 Nov. 1936.

began in 1958.[37] In 1960 when the Kiambu District Agriculture Marketing Officer offered five bags of Madagascar butter beans for seeds to the Kiambu District Agriculture Officer for free distribution to farmers and guaranteed purchase of the crop by the Produce Board, the reply was, "I have very few people who are interested with beans planting."[38] From 1970 to 1988 the area being cultivated in beans almost tripled and for maize only doubled, *but* the area in maize in 1988 was still double that in beans. Maize is the staple now grown along with beans for consumption on most farms.[39] Kiambu has been completely incorporated into the world market, not only for coffee and tea, but also for flowers and fruit. While still essential to the local diet, dried beans are of little interest now as a cash crop.

The Introduction of New Bean Varieties

Kenya, whose white settlers were lured by the agricultural potential of a benign climate in the highlands, had a strong Agriculture Department established in 1903. If within ten years or so of the establishment of the colony maize could supplant millets and beans as staples, this was in no small measure due to increased market interventions by the colonial government. There were also, however, important introductions of new varieties of maize and beans, some of which were enforced. Natal Flat White maize came in 1902 from South Africa and was crossed with an American variety, Hickory King, which arrived in 1907, to become Kenya White.[40] These varieties, which have less food value (a lower lysine content), replaced the indigenized yellow and purple maize. Less well known is the history of the introduction of new bean varieties, as well as of experimentation with beans, given lower priority than maize and wheat by the British. Agricultural experimentation in Britain has a long history; colonialism made it into a worldwide governmental enterprise, as Brockway documented.[41] It connected Kenyan agriculture to a multinational corporate network involved in testing the commercial viability of various crops. If the strength of Kenya's Agriculture Department was unusual for Africa due to its initial orientation toward improving the settler economy, its interventions ultimately focused on African agriculture. Even when crops or seeds were not purposefully introduced to African farmers, it was difficult to prevent their dissemination.[42] British

---

[37] Dept. of Agriculture AR 1958, I: 34.

[38] DAO/KBU/1/1/218 corres. 17, 25 Feb. 1960.

[39] Ministry of Planning and Development, *Agriculture and Livestock Data Compendium* (June 1989): 39; AA 13/1/8/9 Nairobi AR 1954: 19; Ministry of Finance and Economic Planning, *Situation Analysis* I: 30-31, confirmed the contemporary ubiquity of bean cultivation but did not bother to show the area on its crop map, while highlighting maize.

[40] European preferences leaned heavily toward white maize (manifested later in rejection of U.S. yellow maize offered as aid after World War II as unfit for human consumption).

[41] Interview Blundell 10 Sept. 1988; Hill, *Cream Country*, p. 3; Dept. of Agriculture AR 1962 II: 54; Brockway, *Science*.

[42] Kitching, *Class*, p. 30, and Sorrenson, *Origins*, p. 156, tell of Kikuyu getting potato stock illicitly from Fort Hall, but Miracle, *Maize*, p. 26, says that the British administration forced the Kikuyu to grow potatoes from 1901 to 1905. Unfortunately, the precolonial and early colonial history of bean seed intro-

experimentation involved most crops known to Europeans as well as a number derived from other colonies.[43]

By 1904 white settlers had introduced such bean varieties as Canadian Wonder, Scarlet Runner, French Cocus (rose coco), and California butter beans (limas). Various groups of missionaries cultivated European-type crops and introduced seeds of many types, as did colonial officers not involved with the Agriculture Department.[44] The agricultural research stations established around the country in the 1920s undertook a number of trials of different varieties of beans. By 1926 red, red and white, and white kidney beans (probably Canadian Wonder) were most common in the markets among the different types of beans and were "prominently shown at nearly every stall." In the 1930s there was more testing of different varieties than later in the colonial period. In 1931, for instance, thirty-seven indigenous legumes were being observed at Scott Agriculture Laboratories to determine their possible export value. In 1933, a boom year, twenty-four varieties of *Phaseolus vulgaris* were tested, seven varieties of peas, and several of soy beans, *njahe* and grams. In 1934 twenty Indian varieties of *njahe* were tested, indicating efforts to develop plants that were compatible with local ones. The names of the tested bean varieties and other information indicate their cosmopolitan origin, deriving from Japan, China, Turkey, Tanganyika, Uganda, India, Mauritius, Madagascar, Holland, Belgium, Canada, France, Illinois, Idaho, Michigan, Peru, Mexico, Rumania, South Africa, and Meru.[45]

Wide experimentation seems to have stopped in the mid-1930s, however, when agriculture officers decided that, since imported varieties had not generally done well but had "leaked" from seed farms to African farmers with the unfortunate result of mixing with rose coco, it would be best to stop such trials.[46] In the 1940s and 1950s testing was confined more narrowly to imported varieties. The East African

---

duction by Africans appears to be lost; in the early 1960s Miracle failed in efforts to collect any useful information on the subject, although he noticed that people were always looking for new seeds to try. Pers. comm. 2 Oct. 1992; *Maize*, p. 28. Little information about African seed introduction came from my interviews, although I was told that women at Ndeiya in Kiambu introduced coriander and chickpeas in the 1950s, which they may have gotten from Mwea in Kirinyaga where contacts with Kamba were common. Ukambani is now the primary area for chickpea and coriander production. A woman at Ngara asked me to supply her with a new variety of popcorn to test.

[43] Kudzu, for example, was tried in 1931, but happily failed. Dept. of Agriculture AR 1931: 155; Agr 4/239 28 June 1949 Senior Agriculture Officer Pasture Research to Agriculture Officer Machakos.

[44] Miracle, *Maize*, p. 28; interview C. Leakey 15 Oct. 1992. In 1899 Canon Leakey, a CMS missionary, introduced apples, plums and strawberries at Kabete; another missionary imported fruit trees, and a railway engineer at Nairobi started a European-type vegetable garden. Mackinder, *Ascent*, pp. 90, 96. Agricultural innovations introduced by missionaries need systematic documentation by region, which goes beyond the scope of this project.

[45] Procter, "Market," p. 16; Dept. of Agriculture ARs 1931: 67; 1933: 64, 94; 1934, I: 64. All names are found in the Agriculture Department's annual reports between 1929 and 1973.

[46] Agr.4/319 corres. 29 Jan. and Feb. 1935 Senior Plant Breeder and Experimentalist to Agriculture Officers Nyeri, Kisumu, Kibaroni, Njoro, reply 2 Feb. 1935, from W.G. Leckie, Central Province Senior Agriculture Officer.

Agriculture and Forestry Research Organization was set up in the late 1950s to coordinate regional research, including a bean breeding program that was one of the best efforts in these years to develop better local food crops.[47] All along, however, the chief goal was to find plants with export value. Government testing declined drastically after the early 1970s. Attempts to pool genetic resources for bean breeding among East African countries broke down with the collapse of the East African Community in 1977, and the largest seed bank in Kenya had its stored genetic materials destroyed by equipment failure in 1983. Bean breeding in Kenya has normally used more local materials than are used for maize or other pulses, but at least one major foreign assistance project conformed exactly to Kloppenburg's description of agricultural imperialism.[48] At present most testing is done in conjunction either with foreign aid agencies, especially the predecessors of the U.S. Agency for International Development (USAID, whose involvement increased strongly in the 1950s), or with private companies (for *Phaseolus* primarily with Dutch companies at the Thika research station outside Nairobi). However, the Crop Science Department of the University of Nairobi was testing irradiated beans and selling seeds in 1988.[49]

Consonant with the testing, new bean varieties were introduced by the government. Most beans sold now in Nairobi belong to four popular varieties of *Phaseolus vulgaris* (*nyayo*, rose coco, red kidney and pinto), all introduced by the Kenyan Agriculture Department under late colonialism or after independence.[50] Most popular is *nyayo*, named after President Moi because of its introduction from Uganda at the time of his accession to office, and developed under a government beanbreeding program there.[51] There was very little indication from women in rural markets that they were experimenting with breeding or growing new varieties. A singular exception was a seller/farmer at Gitaru Market who was, also exceptionally, selling mixed beans. She told us that because she had little land she needed to vary her crops to minimize her risk and therefore was trying out any new variety she found. Among her mixed beans were several rare varieties, some with old origins. She had brought zebra beans back from Tanzania to try out after visiting a friend, and some of the

---

[47] Pers. comm. C. Leakey 13 Nov. 1992.

[48] Juma, *Hunters*, p. 184; Kloppenburg, *Seed*. The project involved collaboration between a U.S. university and the University of Nairobi to develop new varieties that withstood environmental stress and had improved yield. The research was done in the U.S. only. When germplasm was exchanged the Americans obtained access to a valuable resource that they were more likely to be able to maximize than the Kenyans were. Kenyans were trained in the U.S., thus distancing them and the U.S. researchers from local knowledge and practices. The research was carried out independently of that sponsored by the Dutch, so pooling of knowledge was limited. Michigan State Univ. Bean/Cowpea CRP AR 1983: 86-87.

[49] Agr 4/239 Agriculture Officer Horticulture to Assistant Agriculture Officer Embu, 15 May 1953; Kiambu Agriculture AR 1962: 3; *Daily Nation* 27 May 1988: 14.

[50] Suttie asserted incorrectly in 1970, "Review," p. 373, that all major food crops had been introduced fifty or more years previously.

[51] Interviews Kirkby 18 July 1988; C. Leakey 15 Oct. 1992. Colin Leakey bred *nyayo*'s progenitors in Uganda with Samwere Mukasa at Kawanda Research Station in the 1960s.

other ones she picked out of odd ones from her grandmother's harvest. Her grand-mother, who had ten acres, had planted pure stands of kidney and rose coco beans.[52] There exist, then, the possibilities for experimentation, but the experimenters seem rare.

The dominant role of the government in providing new varieties was under-stood by many and even applauded on occasion, although some understood the dam-aging reduction in biodiversity. For example, a ninety-two-year-old woman at Wangige played on the word *nyayo*, President Moi's nickname meaning footsteps in Kiswahili (he followed in Kenyatta's). "[The old varieties] went with *nyayo* [com-ing]. They are all gone. Even vines for Kikuyu sweet potatoes, they are all gone. *Nyayo* has taken everything. Everything that he brings we take and ignore all of ours, even bananas." A fifty-two-year-old woman beanseller at Wangige said, "The new varieties like rose coco and *nyayo* come through the big farmers. We are taught these things by the Agriculture Department and then we sell them so they must spread all over." Another sixty-two-year-old woman at Ngara bean market boasted of new agricultural techniques, "We are going European!"[53] The fifteen commonly mar-keted (and grown) named Kenyan varieties are sparse in number compared to the 400 observed in Rwanda and the 188 varieties in Malawi.[54]

Among the women farmers preferences for growing one variety of beans over another depend on many factors. Desirable qualities were, in no particular order, high yield, short length to maturity, short cooking time, drought and moisture resis-tance, red color, texture when cooked, taste, labor intensity of cultivation, and marketability.[55] The imparting of red color to the food when cooked is an aesthetic preference that has endured with the Kikuyu.[56] Short cooking time is especially important if fuel is scarce, and the frequent droughts make drought-resistant beans more popular, especially in Ukambani. In the highlands moisture-resistant beans are useful; many beans will not tolerate too much rain (the most frequent complaint about bean yields in government agricultural reports from Kiambu was that the beans rotted before they could be harvested). Most beansellers knew which varieties did

---

[52] Interview 728 Gitaru: 3 Aug. 1988. There was no evidence of intentional crossbreeding by hand pollination, which is usually necessary to achieve the development of alternate strains. Gepts, "Evidence," p. 33; interview C. Leakey 15 Oct. 1992.

[53] Interviews A Wangige: 9 June 1988; 453 Wangige: 6 June 1988; 59 Ngara Bean: 25 Oct. 1987.

[54] Interview Voss 30 July 1988; Ferguson and Sprecher, "Women," p. 10. Fifteen varieties are de-tailed in Robertson, "Black."

[55] Ferguson and Sprecher, "Component Breeding," p. 3, found in Malawi that the following charac-teristics largely determined farmers' bean preferences in this order: yield, taste, cooking time, marketabil-ity, growing time (length to maturity), health-related issues, insect and disease resistance, and ability to withstand environmental stresses.

[56] DC/KBU 1/1 Kiambu AR 1907-08: 2-3; 1/3 Kiambu Quarterly Report Apr.-June, 1911: 14; 1/4 Dagoretti Handing Over Report 1912-13: 11; PC/CP 4/2/1 Ukamba AR 1914-15: 14; DAO/KBU 1/1/218 Deputy Director Plant Industry to Agriculture Officer Central Province 9 May 1934. C. Leakey, "Im-provement," p. 100, assumed that a preference for pale-colored beans was universal.

well in different areas and conditions and which yielded the most. But this knowledge, if anything, would promote experimental practices like those of the Gitaru bean farmer, and such experimentation was rare. Why?

The Development of Exports and Purification Campaigns

Before colonialism farmers normally intercropped maize or millet and beans, thus assuring better soil fertility and reducing weeding time and pest and disease losses. They also grew mixed beans. There is weak evidence that Kikuyu farmers might have grown pure stands,[57] but more indicators that intercropping was the rule for both Kamba and Kikuyu, a practice that still dominates on small Nairobi plots where urbanites grow food to supplement their budgets.[58] Louis Leakey in the 1930s described intercropping and deplored the thinking that led to attempts to change these practices.

> When a piece of ground has been cleared and hoed and prepared for planting a number of different crops are planted all mixed up on one and the same patch. No attempt is made to segregate the different crops, and no attempt is made to plant in lines. This to the white man appears to be very crude and unscientific. I have heard it argued again and again that if a Kikuyu would only divide up the plot of ground that he happens to have available, and would plant his maize in one part of it, his beans in another and his sweet potatoes in another and so on, he would get a bigger yield of each of these crops, and, moreover, a better one. But would he?

He then carefully described the symbiotic properties of the various crops whose intercropping assured soil preservation and food crops all year round. Consumer preferences in many areas, in fact, still tend toward mixed beans. Closer to Nairobi there seem to be fewer mixed beans for sale. Kikuyu women farmers, like the grandmother of the woman at Gitaru, seem to be more interested in growing pure stands. Have Nairobi taste buds somehow also been purified along with plant genetic diversity in the area? A trader at Kangemi Market in 1988 was sorting beans, an unusual event since most are grown in pure stands, and told us that she had to do it because people would not buy them mixed, thus ascribing the change to popular taste.[59]

However, the growing of beans in the Nairobi area has been severely affected by two factors: the colonial presence forcing the growth and sale of cash crops (or wage labor) to pay taxes and, after independence, continued similar taxation policies along with the need to pay school fees. The two most common explanations given

---

[57] The 1904 report of the Kenya Director of Agriculture stated, "The Wakikuyu near Fort Hall [Murang'a] are very regular cultivators, the crops usually being planted unmixed in straight rows, which is very uncommon." He went on to say that *Phaseolus* were becoming an important crop. Cited in Cone and Lipscomb, *History*, p. 42.

[58] Freeman, *City*, p. 88. Maize is the most common crop grown by such farmers, *Phaseolus* beans a distant second.

[59] L. Leakey, *Contrasts*, pp. 118-23; Voss, "Management"; Juma, *Hunters*, p. 190; interview 663 Kangemi: 21 July 1988.

by women for the adoption of new varieties were marketability and yield, both of which were directly connected to profitability. Colonial campaigns were very specific regarding the conversion of crops previously grown only for consumption to cash crops; African farmers were to raise yields by planting pure stands of maize and beans and only one variety of beans was to be grown in a field, even in a whole area. Spurred by the Depression, the Kenya Agriculture Department in the 1930s implemented policies intended to raise revenue by taxing Africans. In 1936, W. G. Leckie, the Central Province Senior Agriculture Officer, wrote to his subordinates at Machakos, Fort Hall, Meru and Embu saying that the world market could absorb about 200 to 300,000 ninety-kilo bags of beans yearly, which would "go a long way toward finding taxes."[60]

Purification campaigns were undertaken for several reasons: to develop exports to European canning companies and finicky European consumers, and to raise yields (most agricultural testing was short term and so did not catch long-term soil depletion as a result of maize monoculture, ameliorated by growing beans, which are nitrogen fixatives). The colonial administration sought to impose on Kenya the British model of agriculture, including an approved list of crops to be grown to the exclusion of all others. The chief vehicles for this imposition were the price controls and produce inspection described in Chapter III, which began in the 1930s. In May 1936 compulsory inspection of marketed beans began in Kiambu with the goal of eliminating the sale of mixed beans. In December 1936 the Central Tender Board, which dealt with supplies of inspected produce, agreed upon the advice of the chief produce inspector to take tenders only for pure varieties.[61]

In 1934 initial efforts were made to enforce a policy of one-variety-only-per-location, but it was the advent of inspection which spurred and hardened the campaign, which was further limited to three varieties instead of four for Central Province. In 1935 Kiambu African farmers, along with those in Fort Hall, South Nyeri, and part of Embu, were told to grow rose coco beans only. In the same year compulsory inspection of wattle was instituted and voluntary inspection of maize, beans, peas, and potatoes in South Nyeri, Fort Hall, Embu and Meru. Spranger, the Kiambu Agriculture Officer, wrote to his superior, "My idea is to flood Chief Josiah's location [with rose coco seeds]. Natives receiving an issue will agree in future to plant only the variety issued." People in Embu and Meru got Boston beans, and those at Thika Canadian Wonder. Seeds for other varieties were sold off as mixed beans.[62]

---

[60] The standard bag size is 200 pounds, or ninety kilograms. Agr 4/319, 29 Jan. 1936.

[61] Interview Bliss 25 June, 1992; Agr 4/114 Kiambu Agriculture AR 1936: 5; Agr 4/319 Deputy Director Produce Inspection to Agriculture Officer Nyeri 21 Dec. 1936.

[62] Agr 4/334 Leckie, Agriculture Officer Central Province, "Report on Produce Inspection, 1935," p. 1; DAO/KBU 1/1/257 Agriculture Officer Kiambu to Agriculture Officer Central Province 13 Aug. 1935; Agr 4/319 Senior Agriculture Officer Central Province to Actg. Deputy Director of Agriculture Nairobi, Sept. 1938; Agr 4/319 Agriculture Officer Meru to Agriculture Officer Central Province 15 Sept. 1936.

The impact of inspection and the marketing of pure varieties was immediate and began before compulsory inspection was instituted. People began sorting beans into types before selling them in order to get a better price.[63] According to Leckie, before inspection began the average sample of "native beans" contained six different varieties and therefore had no world market, bringing an average price of 4/50 shillings per bag. After inspection began they could export the pure varieties, which brought a rise in the price to Sh.8/50 per bag or even 13/50. For the same reason maize prices went from Sh.2/70 to Sh.5 per bag in October 1936, with the first (he believed) African farmers' exports due to improved quality.[64] Geoffrey Mwaura Ngoima, a smallholder at the Church of Scotland Mission at Kikuyu, wrote to the Kiambu Assistant Agriculture Officer in March 1937 saying that he had thirty bags of pure rose coco for sale for which he would like to receive more than Sh.9/50 per bag. He sold them at Sh.11/50 or 12, in fact.[65] The Kenya Farmers Association, which represented European large-scale farmers, was still willing to buy mixed beans to use for rations, although at three-fourths of the price of export grade. By 1943 the Central Province Senior Agriculture Officer was boasting to the Nairobi Produce Controller, "We have no mixed beans in Central Province," and claimed that due to food shortages producers were eating more of them, instead of just selling them. In 1950 Fisher observed only pure varieties being sold in markets in Murang'a and Kiambu.[66]

The advent of controls allowed the colonial administration to embark upon systematic orientation of the bean market toward exports, despite local preferences. Farmers growing beans then became subject to the whims of a capricious international market as well as a dictatorial local government in an area which previously had preserved some autonomy from governmental interference. Administrators sometimes made mistakes in calculating future prices and demand, leaving farmers to absorb the loss. For instance, in 1939 the European canning potential for Boston beans caused an effort to get farmers to raise them--seed distribution and a promise of a premium price. But in the end they brought Sh.1 per bag less than rose coco, and furthermore were not appealing for local consumption.[67] In 1950 in Murang'a and Kiambu, Fisher observed no white beans being eaten, so the earlier campaign

---

[63] Agr 4/334 Leckie, "Report," p. 4; Assistant Agriculture Officer Embu to Agriculture Officer Central Province 20 July 1936. Huxley, *Strangers*, p. 378, described women being forced to begin sorting beans in the 1930s because of inspection.

[64] Agr 4/114 memo to Deputy Director Produce Inspection 20 Apr. 1937. White settler farmers regularly sold African-grown maize as European-grown to secure a better price, and African-grown beans were exported before World War I.

[65] DAO/KBU 1/1/218 corres. 13, 18, 30 Mar. 1937.

[66] DAO/KBU 1/1/218 Sr. Agriculture Officer Central Province to Agriculture Officers Central Province 3 Sept. 1937; Agr 4/527 corres. 4 Oct. 1943; interview Fisher 14 Oct. 1992.

[67] Agr 4/574 Agriculture Officer Embu to Senior Agriculture Officer Central Province 3 Feb. 1939. Agri 4/527 D.C. Embu to Provincial Commissioner Central Province 9 Feb. 1939.

clearly had not introduced them to local usage. Many of the beans exhibited high susceptibility to disease, a major problem associated with monoculture.[68]

In the 1940s the purification campaigns continued and spread to more remote areas.[69] The most major development, however, was the privileging of maize to an even greater extent in price policies in order to feed the military and the growing Nairobi population as cheaply as possible. The colonial government was never monolithic, however, and some agriculture officers were highly offended by the consequent "maize mining," which undermined their soil conservation efforts. In one case the battle was fought in defense of *njahe.* At the end of 1947, after receiving complaints from Central Province Agriculture Officers, A. C. M. Mullins, the Provincial Commissioner, sent a long and heated letter to the Honorable Member for Agriculture and Natural Resources at Nairobi protesting the addition of *njahe* to the controlled produce price list. His comments went right to the heart of the issue.

> To control these leguminous crops and to fix their price below the current market price will most certainly lead to black marketing, a reduction in soil fertility and a considerable increase in maize mining which we have been at such pains to discourage. [It will] nullify all our efforts ... and constitute a most serious blow at the good faith of the Government and our policy of conserving the soil and adopting proper agricultural methods. It seems we must abandon this [conservation] policy and admit that the economic interest of a particular section must override the general aim of conserving the land. It is now more advantageous to grow maize than Njahi and so we have no moral grounds for encouraging the production of a leguminous crop which helps the soil, but must allow maize mining... I fear my criticisms are somewhat outspoken, but I make no apology. Maize, an exotic crop, has done nearly as much as the goat to ruin the land in this Province.[70]

Njahe had developed an export market to India fetching the Meru producers Sh.45 to 50 per bag. Its properties as a drought-resistant ground cover and fodder for animals were also appreciated. This exchange signalled the beginning of an on-again-off-again policy regarding placing *njahe* on the controlled price list, but the damage appears to have been done. From 1915, when *njahe* were "still largely grown," to the

---

[68] In 1959 Boston beans were also being encouraged, despite poor local demand. Interview Fisher 14 Oct. 1992; DAO/KBU 1/1/218 Genl. Mgr. Central Province Marketing Board to Central Province Agriculture, Marketing, and Storage Officers, District Commissioners, 3 Nov. 1959; interview C. Leakey 21 Oct. 1992.

[69] Agr 4/514 Assistant Agriculture Officer Meru to Meru Traders 15 July 1941; Agr 4/527 same to Senior Agriculture Officer Nyeri 8 Oct. 1942.

[70] Agr 4/409 31 Dec. 1947. Even those not partial to *njahe* complained about maize mining. In June 1950 the Acting Provincial Agriculture Officer for Central Province claimed that a "grain shortage is likely, very largely due to the imbecile insistence on maize as a staple grain crop." Agr 4/510. This material contradicts Anderson's assertion, "Depression," p. 324, that soil conservation efforts at this level were simply a mask for the issue of the sanctity of the White Highlands.

present, the cultivation of *njahe* went from being almost universal in central Kenya to being confined mainly to Meru.[71]

If the 1930s saw a fair amount of experimentation with introducing different bean varieties, that situation reflected the interwar concentration on making each colony self-sufficient, which allowed for a fair amount of local autonomy. But from the 1940s through the early 1970s new bean varieties were introduced with the over-riding aim of chasing the export market--to achieve British independence from U.S. imports and then after independence to further the purposes of multinational corporations.[72] The low prices for beans other than approved varieties of white Boston or Michigan pea beans, rose coco and Canadian Wonder, discouraged those interested in selling their surplus from growing new varieties.[73] A number of experiments were tried, most of which failed because the beans in question could not be eaten. Beans have always been chiefly a small producer crop in Kenya.[74] Women, the majority of producers, needed to feed their families and could not afford crops which did not satisfy both subsistence and market needs. Persistent problems with storage made holding beans for six months or longer difficult. White beans' appeal to the export market was not matched locally; they often brought lower prices and families could not risk having a large inedible surplus. The longer beans are stored the more they are subject to insect damage and the harder they become, causing cooking time to lengthen. Table II.2 summarizes the export experiments which largely failed, sometimes for reasons extraneous to Kenya, sometimes because of organizational difficulties within Kenya. The Mexico 142 effort was the strongest; in 1975 11% of the bean acreage in Kenya was devoted to this variety, which was the only one purchased by the Maize Produce Board in Central Province in 1974.[75] But food preferences, poor pricing policy, and susceptibility to insects and disease caused even this effort to fail.

The arbitrariness of a market increasingly dependent upon export and private companies often frustrated agricultural officers, a frustration best expressed in 1934 by Leckie in communication with Messrs. Gibson and Co. "It is quite impossible for this Department to make headway in the Reserves if one year you advise us not to

---

[71] Agr 4/409 Sr. Agriculture Officer Central Province to Director of Agriculture Nairobi 12 Dec. 1947; Agr 4/239 Sr. Agriculture Officer Pasture Research to Agriculture Officer Machakos 28 June 1949; DC/KBU/1/9 Kiambu AR 1915-16: 42.

[72] Cowen and Westcott, "Policy," pp. 20-21, 43, 58-59.

[73] Agr 4/239 Agriculture Officer Embu to Provincial Agriculture Officer Central Province 7, 26 Feb. 1952.

[74] Casley and Marchant, "Smallholder Marketing," Sec.1.12, pointed out that in 1974-75 95% of Kenya's smallholders were growing maize, 98% beans, the highest proportion for any crop.

[75] Schonherr and Mbugua, "Bean Production," pp. 9, 12; C. Leakey, "Report"; interview 15 Oct. 1992.

II.2. Bean Variety Export Efforts by Year and Reasons for Failure, 1933-1992

Variety	Years	Reason Export Campaign Failed
White haricot called in Kikuyu *ketho*	1933-1952	"Steamed black eye ... gives a most unsightly effect to the finished canned product." White.
Michigan pea	1956-1958	Price too low, competition from Michigan, Heinz Corporation unwilling to buy due to problems with bruchid beetle infestation. White.
Boston	1939-1945	Long cooking time, problems with insect infestation, too dry, different flavor from European variety, tough skins, seed shortage. White.
Mexico 142	1963-1979	Samples too dry, insect-infested, intermittent availability of seed, low prices announced at harvest, not planting. Extreme rust susceptibility. White.
Velvet	1969-1973	Competition with synthetic form of L-Dopa used to treat Parkinson's disease. Synthetic cheaper to produce and as effective.
Canadian Wonder	1989-1992	Do not retain redness when cooked. Misrepresented to buyers as Dark Red Kidney (Montcalm, Charlevoix). Insufficiently red.

Sources: White haricot: Agr 4/239 Produce Controller to Director of Agriculture Nairobi 19 June 1933.

Michigan pea: Agr 4/239 corres. Acting Provincial Agriculture Officer Central Province with District Agriculture Officers 5, 11, 24 July 1956; Purchasing Dept. H.J. Heinz Co. to Kenya Canners 29 Aug. 1958.

Boston: Ministry of Agriculture Files Bean 4/XV corres. among Purchasing Division Manager H.J. Heinz, General Manager Maize Produce Board, and Permanent Secretary Ministry of Agriculture, June 1973.

Mexico 142: Dept. of Agriculture AR 1967, I: 18; Ministry of Agriculture Files Bean 1/II, 4/XV corres. among H. J. Heinz, Ministry of Agriculture, and Cereals Marketing Board officials 12 Nov. 1972 to 26 Mar. 1974. DAO/KBU 1/1/93 minutes Central Province Marketing Advisory Committee 4 Dec. 1956: 3. Pers. comm. C. Leakey 13 Nov. 1992.

Velvet: Ministry of Agriculture Files Bean 1/II, Bean 4/XV corres. Provincial Crops Officer Coast Province to Head, Economic Planning Division, Ministry of Agriculture 30 Dec. 1971; memo. Officer Economic Planning Division to Head of Division 19 Jan. 1972. Velvet beans are not normally used for food.

Canadian Wonder: Pers. comm. C. Leakey 13 Nov. 1992.

grow Canadian and the very next year offer for Canadian Wonder only."[76] The experience with soy beans encapsulates this bean history. Soy beans were of perpetual interest to the government, both for their export potential and their possible domestic use for fodder and oil. Some even saw them as being of strategic use during World War II.[77] Despite the failure of much of their testing, efforts to develop viable strains for Kenya continue to the present, and some are grown in Western Kenya, where

---

[76] Agr 4/319 Agriculture Officer Central Province to Messrs.Gibson & Co., 28 Sept. 1934.

[77] The success of the Nazi Polish campaign was attributed partly to the use of soy food products, as was the survival of POWs in the Hong Kong jail. DAO/KBU 1/1/218 *British Medical Journal* 23 Aug. 1941; Agr 4/239 Acting Provincial Agriculture Officer Central Province to J.J. Peterson, 19 Oct. 1950.

women's groups were organized to grow them and green beans. The soy beans did well but the private company promoting them lost interest and did not purchase their production, leaving the women with an uncookable surplus.[78] Aside from their poor showing as a crop, other factors made them unpopular and especially unsuitable as a women's crop: a bitter taste, long cooking time, pale color, and the necessity to inoculate the soil before planting them, a capital input difficult for small farmers.[79]

Although exports are still of interest to the Kenyan government, the Africanization of the Kenya Ministry of Agriculture has changed its policy regarding beans. The last big government-sponsored export drive for dried beans was the failed Mexico 142 effort.[80] The change began in 1970 when the General Manager of the Maize and Produce Board banned exports of certain beans (rose coco, Canadian Wonder and mixed) due to insufficient supplies, while allowing the export of Mexico 142, limas and white haricots, "as they are not normally consumed locally," much to the consternation of many buyers. An April 1973 memo by the Head of the Crop Development Division of the Ministry of Agriculture to all Agriculture officers proposed to include food beans in research efforts, while directing District officers to survey them and their popularity. In 1974 J. M. Kabuga, Eastern Province Crops Officer, wrote to the head of the Division that prices should be raised on food beans to encourage production. In 1976 S. K. Njugunah, research officer at Thika, discontinued research on white haricots for canning such as Mexico 142 and Boston and increased efforts on "local food beans."[81] In 1988 Kabuga, as former head of the Industrial Crops Division of the Ministry of Agriculture, said that dried beans were no longer being pushed for export, but rather exported only if there was a surplus, an opinion concurred in by an official at the Maize and Cereals Board. An Industrial Crops officer stressed that the Thika research station was involved in promoting high yield bean varieties and that intercropping was encouraged.[82] The chief bean export crop was green beans, while the only dried bean encouraged by research and seed distribution was soy, where interest focused on domestic uses rather than export value.

---

[78] Their testing probably began in the late 1920s. Dept. of Agriculture AR 1929: 588-589; Auckland, "Soya Bean," pp. 135, 150; Agr 4/527 Agriculture Officer Plant Breeding Station Njoro to Director of Agriculture Nairobi 14 May 1940; interview Were, Head, Crop Production, Ministry of Agriculture, 13 July 1988; *Daily Nation* 29 June 1988: 19.

[79] Brown, *Policy*, pp. 9, 87; Agr 4/114 Central Province Agriculture AR 1937: 12; Agr 4/319 Acting Director of Agriculture to Agriculture Officer Central Province 17 Sept. 1937; Ministry of Agriculture File Bean 5/VII Crop Development Officer to Permanent Secretary of Agriculture 8 Nov. 1968; Head, Crop Production Development, to Director of Agriculture 7 Sept. 1972; interview Njugunah 29 Sept. 1988.

[80] Ministry of Agriculture File Bean 1/II Chief Agriculturalist to Kenya Farmers Association and Assistant Directors of Agriculture, all provinces 24 Jan. 1964.

[81] Ministry of Agriculture Files Bean 1/II Chief Agriculturalist to Kenya Farmers Association and Assistant Directors of Agriculture, all provinces, 24 Jan. 1964; corres. 16 Sept. 1970, Oct. 1970; Bean 4/XV 7 Oct. 1974; Bean 1/II S.K. Njugunah, Thika National Horticultural Research Station, to Chief, Crop Production Division, Ministry of Agriculture 6 Mar. 1979.

[82] Interviews 1988 in Nairobi: Were 13 July; Migunda 10 Aug.; Odok 13 July.

The export of green beans to Europe began in the late 1940s and grew in importance as air transport became more efficient. Green (also called French) beans and peas are an important part of the growing export market gardening industry dominated by male growers using female labor.[83] As one future of the bean industry they represent the contradiction between local and international relations, the triumph of hierarchy, and the fulfillment of agricultural imperialism. Kenyan green beans are usually picked long before maturity. In contrast, dried beans represent lateral connections, more democratic tendencies, and the potential fertility of maturity.

The special status of beans as a women's crop important in the diet of most Kenyans make those that are readily consumable most popular and therefore most marketable. Farmers and consumers are quite willing to take up new varieties, as the enduring success of *nyayo* and rose coco beans has shown,[84] so long as they have such desirable characteristics as high yield, red color, marketability, and a short cooking time, in particular. Higher digestibility reinforced *nyayo's* popularity, for instance. An exception that eventually proved the rule was what Wisner called the "rare success story" involving Kamba farmers moving into Karaba in the 1960s and 1970s and growing coriander and grams of various kinds to sell to traders.[85] Kamba women traders now dominate the sale of these commodities to Asians in Nairobi, so that it is a form of market gardening. Marketability for women usually refers to local markets, not to the marketing board, meaning that local tastes prevailed. Coriander has now entered the local diet in the form of cilantro (called *dania* from Hindi). Export campaigns for dried beans have almost stopped; most are consumed locally by a burgeoning population. Thus, efforts to develop exports need to be congruent with those to develop food crops, rather than mutually exclusive.[86] Moreover, the focus on the European white bean market did Kenya a disservice; red beans have a good market in Latin America and an increasing one in North America. But red Canadian Wonder beans lose their color in cooking and the export market demands beans which retain their redness. This confusion undermined recent private-sector Kenyan bean export efforts in which Canadian Wonder were sold as Dark Red Kidney beans; when buyers discovered the defect Kenyan beans developed a bad reputation which will be difficult to overcome. Meanwhile, the red retaining varieties were not introduced to Kenya. Pinto beans, which are the largest growing world seller due

---

[83] Interviews Were 13 July 1988; Migunda, Operations Director, Maize and Cereals Produce Board 10 Aug. 1988; Odok 13 July 1988; MA/12/80 Kiambu AR 1949: 45. For a case study of this industry in one Murang'a district see Thomas-Slayter and Rocheleau, *Gender,* pp. 93-94.

[84] Juma, *Hunters,* p. 190; van Rheenen, "Diversity," p. 453.

[85] Wisner, "Man-Made Famine," p. 25, 20. He described the disastrous effects on the Kamba pigeon pea crop of efforts to introduce cotton as a cash crop in the 1960s; the high demands on women's labor in weeding it interfered greatly with the pigeon pea harvest.

[86] In this context the usual technocratic explanation for failure to develop bean exports seems limited. Schluter, "Constraints," p. 10, claimed that poor quality determined the lack of an export market from 1971 to 1981, which he attributed to "the absence of strong vertical linkages in the information chain from the world market back to the research and extension system." Interview 585 Kawangware: 7 June 1988.

largely to their use by Taco Bell (Pepsico) for refried beans, also sell well in Nairobi. They may present a better export opportunity. However, making food crops into cash crops under current conditions may indicate increased economic stress rather than expendable surpluses.[87]

Changes in Diet

The consequences of seed introduction, preferential pricing, and purification campaigns can be seen in dietary changes, which varied/s by socioeconomic status as well as over time. Summing up the chronology of the introduction of different varieties of beans and other crops important to the Kikuyu diet now is Table II.3, which combines seed introduction information from the colonial records with the material given by informants. It shows that the contemporary Kikuyu diet, while quite sufficient in general, has declined in quality from precolonial standards due to a decrease in variety, especially in consumption of Vitamin A-rich green leaves and the use of white instead of yellow maize.

Like many peoples, the Kikuyu had specific gender distinctions in dietary matters. In general, they valued foodstuffs according to the feeling of fullness given, in 1950 ranking maize, dwarf beans (*Phaseolus*) and *njahe*, bananas, sweet potatoes and millet or maize gruel high. Men ate roasted tubers such as sweet potatoes, yams and cassava, and maize and millet, while women ate boiled tubers, legumes, plantain, green leaves and edible earth. The food viewed as most choice went to men. Women's diet was thought to be predominantly vegetarian; men's included more meat,[88] meaning that beans were particularly important in women's diet as a source

II.3. Food Crops Present or Introduced to Southern Kikuyu Diet,
c. 1890-1990

Date	Common crops in Kikuyu diet
c. 1890	cjahe, njugu, *Phaseolus* (*kaforo*), millet, bananas, sweet potatoes
c. 1905-1930s	English potatoes, maize, *Phaseolus* (rose coco, *gituru, gikara, mwitemania*)
c. 1950s-60s	Maize, chickpeas, rice, green grams (mung), cabbage, *wairimu*
1970s	Maize, *Phaseolus* (*njikariathe, mwezi moja*), *sukuma wiki* (kale)
1990	Maize, *Phaseolus* (especially *nyayo*), English potatoes, cabbage, *sukuma wiki*, cilantro

[87] C. Leakey, "Factors," p. 4; interview 21 Oct. 1992.

[88] Orr and Gilks, *Physique*, pp. 21, 27-28; Lindblom, *Akamba*, p. 235; Fisher, *Anatomy*, p. 75; Hoorweg and Niemeyer, Appendix to *Situation Analysis* IV: 2; Middleton and Kershaw, *Central Tribes*, p. 18; Procter, "Kikuyu Market," p. 19, in 1926 said, "As a rule ... the young women hardly ever get meat; the old women and women who have borne a child get it sometimes; they are only supposed to eat the legs of a bullock. The meat eaten by the women is usually nearly decomposed, as it usually takes a day or two to decide that the men are incapable of consuming it all." Orr and Gilks in 1931 called the Kikuyu diet chiefly vegetarian, with old men getting goats' meat occasionally as part of ceremonial feasts, and women and children a leg and the viscera only.

of protein. In 1945 Humphrey described the women's diet of former times as includ-ing *uji* (maize flour porridge), *muthura* (a mixture of millet, *njahe* and leafy vegeta-bles), cocoyam, sweet potatoes and yams, while men ate lots of meat, milk, bananas, sweet potatoes, yams, and cocoyam.[89] No one ate pork or fish. If men drank beer made from millet or sugar cane, women and children were supposed to drink goats' milk, thus placing women symbolically with children as non-adults. Men and women ate separately, women sending prepared food to the men's huts via the children.[90]

Changes in the Kikuyu diet reflect the socioeconomic differentiation that developed over the twentieth century, as well as gender differences. The rejection of a large number of potential recruits during World War I prompted studies of nutrition that showed calcium deficiencies in particular, caused partly by the decline in the presence of calcium-rich beans in the diet. In 1927-28 a study showed that Kikuyu women were better nourished than the men because they ate green leaves, which had a high calcium and manganese content, and edible earth, as well as red millet rich in iron and calcium, while men were more likely to exist on employers' rations consist-ing mainly of *posho*.[91] In the 1930s squatters added green leaves to their *posho* and ate a lot of bananas, but overcropping was becoming common, reducing consumption of green leaves. Millet was losing popularity rapidly; a 1940s campaign to promote it failed. As class differentiation proceeded among the Kikuyu, along with the decline in the pastoralist economy, meat became a scarce item for everyone. At the outbreak of World War II 90% of Kikuyu recruits were rejected due to malnutrition-related problems.[92] In 1947 the Aaronovitches described the typical Kikuyu diet as including white maize, unripe bananas, English potatoes, and some beans. *Uji*, or *ucuru* (respectively Kiswahili and Kikuyu), was eaten for breakfast, which had mainly supplanted millet gruel. They reported malnutrition to be widespread in Kenya, as did Kuczynski in 1949.[93] Fisher's observations on the agricultural situation in 1950 show the consequences of population pressure on resources. She said that people were looking for less labor-intensive crops (maize rather than millet), with shorter growing seasons (cassava and yams were too long), which brought good

---

[89] Humphrey, "Thoughts," pp. 34-36.

[90] Davison and Women, *Voices*, p. 15; Middleton and Kershaw, *Central Tribes*, p. 18. A polygynous man might have had food sent simultaneously by all of the wives. Fisher, *Anatomy*, p. 81.

[91] Orr and Gilks, *Physique*, p. 21; Worboys, "Discovery," pp. 218-19. Porter, *Food*, p. 71, said that French haricot beans had a lower calcium content than local ones. Van Zwanenberg, *Capitalism*, p. 66. In 1926 Procter, "Market," p. 21, found the diet of everyone but laborers to be reasonable, although salt defi-ciency was common.

[92] Interview Huxley, 12 Oct. 1992; Dept. of Agriculture AR 1930: 39; Agr 4/114 Central Province Agriculture AR 1939: 5; Native Affairs Dept. AR 1939-45: 37; Lonsdale, "Depression," p. 171; Taylor, "Habits," pp. 341-42.

[93] Aaronovitches, *Crisis*, p. 41; Kuczynski, *Survey*, II: 210; In 1943 Philip, "Nutrition," pp. 231-32, described exactly the same diet and said that growing millet and beans "had practically ceased." Calcium and protein deficiencies were common among both urban and rural Kikuyu.

prices, and which were less susceptible to pests than yams, *njugu*, and *njahe*. Cabbage had supplanted green leaves in many areas.

By the 1950s and 1960s beans had become more of a luxury item in the diet purchased occasionally rather than regularly.[94] A 1959 survey showed Nairobi average annual household consumption of staple food crops to be in the following order of importance: maize, beans, English potatoes, sweet potatoes, millet. It noted that wheat bread was increasingly popular among richer Africans in Kiambu, in particular. Middleton and Kershaw found in 1965 that bread, milk, tea, and rice were gaining in popularity. Taylor concluded that the nutritional situation in 1970 was worse than in 1870 due to governmental policies.[95] Thus, consumer preferences were diversifying, at least for those who could afford it, but not necessarily improving in nutritional value. Some women in 1988 claimed that their consumption of green leaves had declined sharply because the bottom land where they had previously gathered them had come under cultivation with no space left for wild plants, another indicator of increasing population density.[96] Therefore, not only the soil, but also the health of Kenyans suffered from the reduction in importance of beans and millet, the triumph of maize, and the reduction in available land. Given the dietary hierarchies described here, the overall effects may have been more profound for women and children.

Conclusion

The history of beans in Kenya gives insight into symbolic and material realms important to Kikuyu women, in particular. Agricultural imperialism is evident in the abrupt change from beans to maize as the primary staple; the trials and introduction of new varieties of beans, some of them unsuited to Kenyan conditions; the unreciprocated exportation of plant genetic materials; the efforts to develop dried bean exports to Europe; and the apotheosis of the green bean export industry. The results were negative for Africans' diet. The situation regarding beans under colonialism fits very well into the pattern described by Wolff:

> The choice of what and where to produce in the East Africa Protectorate resulted from interaction between the needs felt by private interests and government circles in London, on the one hand, and the conditions of soil, climate, transport, protectorate finances, and so forth, under which European settlers functioned, on the other. The colonial administration ... suggested, promoted and financed experiments with specific, carefully selected exportable crops. Rather widespread fears about Britain's economic future determined which crops were selected.[97]

---

[94] Fisher, *Anatomy*, p. 231; interview 14 Oct. 1992; Kershaw, "Changing Roles," p. 187.

[95] Market Research East Africa, *African Income*, pp. 3, 5; Middleton and Kershaw, *Central Tribes*, p. 4; Taylor, "Habits," p. 336.

[96] The best description of the wild or cultivated greens eaten previously is in Procter, "Market," p. 18. Porter, *Food*, p. 72.

The retreat from export-driven research on beans came with Africanization of the Ministry of Agriculture, which pervaded the ranks only in the 1970s; the last big export push for European-preferred white beans came from European holdovers in the Ministry of Agriculture after independence. The switch from *njahe* (black) beans to white beans was interrupted by the preference for red beans. The increasing economic imperatives faced by women farmers only reemphasized the tendency to plant red beans, which had both a local and an export market, a trend that current concerns about food security in Africa are reinforcing. In a sense this trend is a victory for the women farmers, although they have little say within the Ministry of Agriculture. However, there have been some irreversible changes in Kenyan agriculture: reduction in genetic diversity through the diffusion and enforcement of a few varieties only; increasing dependence on foreign seed companies who do not pay royalties for their appropriation of genetic matter; continuing maize mining which not only harms the soil but also raises vulnerability to famine; and the importation of various disastrous crop diseases.[98] The indoctrination of a population with the idea that innovations should come from above in terms of developing new varieties may have been another result of arbitrary agriculture policy, although farmers have a continuing history of appropriating new seeds from others. The attempt to convert beans into an export crop largely failed not only because the colonial administration did not consult African needs and tastes, but also because they took African women's labor in the production of food crops for granted,[99] and ignored their marketing activities. When colonial officers disagreed over bean policy, which they frequently did, it was never over any of these issues.

Njahe were displaced, then, marginalized along with the indigenous Kikuyu religion they symbolized. Beans in general were also displaced, along with millet, by the overwhelming colonial emphasis on maize and women farmers' labor considerations. Meanwhile, new bean varieties were introduced, first with the aim of experimentation, but then increasingly with the aim of producing more export crops. Local mixed beans and non-white varieties were discriminated against in government pricing, marketing, and seed distribution efforts, forcing European food preferences on African growers and traders. After independence, although discriminatory pricing continued, red varieties preferred by Africans assumed importance and eventually became the focus of export efforts with the widening of Euro-American tastes. The autonomy lost under colonial purification and export campaigns reasserted itself somewhat, perhaps because beans were neither a leading export nor thought to

---

[97] Wolff, *Britain*, p. 86.

[98] Some aid agencies, whose efforts have been well meaning, have nonetheless through carelessness imported diseases that have had a destructive impact on key East African crops such as cassava and maize. Jones, *Marketing*, p. 53; interviews C. Leakey 15, 21 Oct. 1992.

[99] References calling the cost of production of beans nothing were routine in the files; when women's labor was accounted for it was minimized. For example, the Central Province Annual Agriculture Report for 1943: 22, stated "in less advanced areas the women always ensure the planting of a sufficiency of food crops."

possess that potential. Most were consumed locally so that local needs and preferences, which had undermined many colonialist attempts to manipulate varieties, prevailed. Moreover, the value of beans as a food crop received Ministry of Agriculture
attention, although few resources. The new beans, although associated with women,
do not have the accretion of symbolic value of the old.

Subsequent chapters that pay specific attention to the history of women's trade
in dried staples demonstrate that indeed the history of *njahe* serves as a symbolic and
material index for the history of these working-class women. Black, indigenous
beans and millet were displaced by maize and imported *Phaseolus* varieties, with
attempts at white dominance. Beans were subordinated in the diet and in their trade,
and went from supporting a staple trade as a staple food to occupying a niche market
and diminishing portion of the diet. Likewise, women were marginalized spiritually
and economically, their trade and their persons discriminated against in access to
critical resources; they were subordinated on the basis of race and ethnicity as well as
gender under colonialism, with attempts at stronger male dominance replacing asymmetrical precolonial complementarity in trade and gender roles (see Chapter III).
Women's labor was relied upon absolutely to market crops and boost agricultural
productivity, but it was undervalued and its cost ignored, just as the cultivation of
beans was both taken for granted and ignored in the pursuit of maize monoculture.

Kenya's independent government continued gender discrimination and segregation, which varied by class, and withheld critical resources from women's trade,
while for international consumption proclaiming the value of women's work for
development. Like beans, women are supposed to be consumed, their labor and their
lives devoted to others. However, some beans and some women have indigestible
qualities. Red imported and indigenized varieties ultimately succeeded by women's
agency, as did maize. Women farmers and traders refused to accede to either the dictates of heightened male demands on their labor or unproductive export campaigns.
They organized themselves, their trade and their crops to maximize the opportunities
presented by the interstitial, often illegal, trade that feeds Nairobi.

III

The Development of Trade in the Nairobi Area, 1890 to 1940[1]

Women's militancy began with labor.[2]

> To disregard internal exchanges, which in some African countries actually dominate the economies, is to distort the reality of African economic processes, aboriginal or post-colonial.[3]

The segregation of maize from beans and different varieties of beans from each other is mimicked in the changes in women's trade occupying this chapter. The motif of increasing segregation of the trade of women from that of men is evident. The first section considers the precolonial and early colonial situation, in which local and long-distance trade was intimately connected. In the late nineteenth century women and men cooperated in trade, but asymmetrically to a certain extent, with women's profits subject to male expropriation, increasingly as conditions became at once more chaotic and hierarchical. The second section looks at trade in the 1920s and 1930s with particular attention to various types of controls and changes in the scale of African trade. Differentiation in both of these then necessitated separate sections on men's and women's trade. Attempts at control of women's trading activities objectified women as one aspect of segregation and were accompanied by self-conscious efforts by some women to achieve autonomy. In the last section male-female trade relations are clearly adversarial, which represented a triumph of colonial divide-and-conquer tactics.

Women, Men and Trade in the Nairobi Area to 1919

This section pays particular attention to the nature and degree of leadership, power and authority women exercised regarding their trade profits and goes on to describe the beginnings of women's trade centering on Nairobi before and during World War I. The vital but little known role of women in precolonial and early colonial trade is stressed, along with the links between local and long-distance trade and the asymmetrical complementarity of women's and men's roles in precolonial trade.

---

[1] Portions of Chapters III, IV and VII are reproduced here with the editors' permission from the author's "Traders and Urban Struggle," *Jl. of Women's History* 4, 3 (Winter 1993): 9-42. An expanded analysis of women's precolonial trade can be found in Robertson, "Gender."

[2] Presley, *Kikuyu Women*, pp. 79-80.

[3] Herskovits, Preface to *Markets*, p. xiv.

Before the foundation of Nairobi in 1899 the area was sparsely populated for the most part, especially at the lower elevations. Both settled and migratory populations of peoples produced goods which were complementary, thus facilitating trade. The heart of this trade was the pervasive daily exchange of ordinary commodities like foodstuffs, utensils and materials for clothing and weapons. All of the local peoples were mobile to a certain extent and trade formed a motivation for new settlements in many cases.[4] Kikuyu and Kamba women, who now predominate among Nairobi traders, were both involved extensively in local trade, and Kikuyu women played a key role also in long distance trade between central Kenyan peoples. These trade networks also included Chagga, Maasai, Embu, Mbeere and Ndorobo women and men. This trade sometimes involved trips of over 200 kilometers and was more extensive and important in providing necessities and widening socioeconomic networks than the occasional caravan trade in the Nairobi area, especially before the 1880s.[5]

In Africa and elsewhere women's trading activities usually began as an extension of their fundamental role as food providers expressed in their performance of a large share of the necessary agricultural labor. With both the Kikuyu and Kamba, women's right to dispose of their own produce was based on a gender division of labor and of property wherein certain crops were cultivated by women and certain fields were designated by their male relatives for women's use. However, women did not own the products of their labor unambiguously, nor did they have an undisputed right to the profits of their trade. There is no incontrovertible evidence that the right of Kikuyu and Kamba women to dispose of their profits independently of men originated in the nineteenth century. This point is crucial to understanding the full impact of women's trading to Nairobi in the twentieth century. Stamp described such trade activities as contributing "substantially to the material resources of their families and to the enrichment of the web of social relations within their society and with neighboring groups."[6]

Women's trading activities and property rights in preindustrial societies fall into four general patterns that range in level of autonomy from a great deal to very little. At the maximum level of autonomy there are such women as the Yoruba and Ga West African traders and London fishwives, whose right to trade and keep their profits was related to a considerable level of independence in property rights and sometimes to an urban situation in which men frequently were absent, especially with those involved in the fish trade. Intermediate in level of autonomy would be an Iroquois-type pattern, where women's control over their crops allowed for considerable autonomy and even parity in political decision-making based on withholding

---

[4] Ambler, *Kenyan Communities*, p. 63.

[5] Kjekshus, *Ecology Control*, p. 114; Wood, "Market Origins"; Muriuki, *History*, p. 106. Lindblom, *Akamba*, p. 440, suggested in the early 1900s that Kamba women did not go alone on long journeys, although Lamphear ("Kamba," pp. 75-86) implies that they traded as Kikuyu women did.

[6] Stamp, "Groups," p. 36.

crops from men when the women's council disapproved of a war initiative taken by the men. Another fairly egalitarian pattern existed in the Trobriand islands, where men and women traded different commodities that circulated separately.[7] At the lowest level of autonomy would be groups in which women had no autonomous property rights and no undisputed rights to their profits, which were considered to derive from selling produce whose ultimate ownership lay with men. By this rubric precolonial Kikuyu and Kamba lay at the lower end of the spectrum of women's trading autonomy, although characterized by a great deal of variability.[8]

The low level of economic autonomy of Kikuyu and Kamba fits the ideal of patrilocality, according to Coontz and Henderson, who pointed out the critical role of residential patterns in determining the level of women's autonomy. Patrilocal residence bore great disadvantages for women's organization of trade, both spatially and in terms of labor. "The source of female subordination lies not in an attack on women by men but in the attempt by both female and male members of specific [patrilocal] kin corporations, under conditions of competition with others, to accumulate and control labour." Women married out, joining their husbands' patrilineages on land whose disposal belonged exclusively to the men of that lineage.[9] A woman's loyalty was henceforth to be to her husband's lineage and her labor devoted to enriching her husband and helping her mother-in-law. Women were often removed from daily contact with the women of their own patrilineages, thus diminishing the possibility for cooperative trade partnerships. Cooperation in trade with in-laws or co-wives took place, but these were necessarily defined by the connecting link through the husband and seem to have consisted more of a division than a pooling of labor. Older women, especially those past menopause, traded and even led trade expeditions to Maasailand which could last for weeks, presumably leaving younger women to perform their share of the household chores. Co-wives might go to a local market together every four days or so, but once there they arranged their goods hierarchically, the senior wife placing hers on the ground in front and the others only being allowed to sell when her goods were gone.[10] Such arrangements did not facilitate the creation of a large-scale business which the pooling of profits and labor might have allowed. Nor did the absence of land rights and the ownership of most livestock by men help in credit arrangements, since goats were a primary form

---

[7] Weiner, "Stability," pp. 270-93.

[8] Ambler, *Kenyan Communities*, p. 7, has aptly described these peoples as belonging to "a social order in the making" in the nineteenth century, rather than a fixed ethnicity. The fluidity of ethnic identity is quite evident throughout this study. I therefore use the conventional terms Kikuyu, Kamba, Maasai, etc., advisedly, especially in the precolonial era. They then become territorial terms once the British assigned boundaries to the African population.

[9] Coontz and Henderson, "Property Forms," p. 129. In some cases, according to Mackenzie and Kershaw, daughters received some land from their mothers' allocation from their fathers, a custom that seems to be largely in abeyance, and which has been challenged by male relatives in the courts; they usually win. Mackenzie, "Marriage," pp. 68-74; interview Kershaw: 4 Aug. 1994.

[10] Interviews A Wangige: 9 June 1988; B Wangige: 13, 24 June 1988.

of wealth. The organization of women's precolonial trade in the Nairobi area, then, while giving ample evidence of a certain level of female autonomy, also indicates a fairly restricted situation in comparison with societies having intermediate and higher levels of female autonomy.

The right of women to control their own profits, their control over disposal of surplus produce, constituted a critical element in precolonial power relations.[11] In what follows I will not assume that uniformity existed in central Kenya in this regard, which is highly improbable, but will critique the available scarce evidence regarding the precolonial situation, paying particular attention to the nature of the sources. Advantages accrued to men not only from the limitations patrilocality imposed on the scale of women's businesses but also in the limits on women's profit accumulation. The oldest women interviewed began trading at the turn of the century and stated unambiguously that their trade profits went to their husbands. One traded with her eight co-wives, each with specialties assigned by their husband, a chief; she sold tobacco that he grew, another bananas and so on, all turning over their profits to him. At his wish she was forced to abandon selling her own things, she said, to do her "husband's work," implying that she had had some (expendable) autonomy.[12] Another, whose husband was not a chief, sold her own produce such as beans and millet, but she and her co-wives turned over their profits to their husband.[13] Senior men therefore organized and profited from both women's agricultural and commercial labor according to this evidence.

The secondary literature presents more conflicting views, one camp claiming that, as women themselves were property, they could not own or control anything, and the other that those who produced the goods could dispose of them at will. Following Radcliffe-Brown, men's rights in women can be divided into different types: *jus in rem* (rights in the wife as an object); *jus in personam* (rights to her services); *jus in uxorem* (rights to her as a wife); and *jus in genetricem* (rights to a wife's procreative power).[14] By these definitions, there is no quarrel in the sources about the latter two sets of rights, the last even extending to a husband claiming any offspring no matter who the genitor was, but the first two are the site of controversy. Were women property themselves, and how much control did they have over the disposal of the products of their own labor? Included among those who believed women were property are a number of Europeans like Cagnolo, a Catholic missionary in Kikuyu country in the 1920s and 1930s, various colonial officers, most notably John Ainsworth, and Gerhard Lindblom, ethnographer of the Kamba in the early twentieth century. Cagnolo is most firm in his statements. "A woman, strictly speaking, does

---

[11] Blumberg, "Income," p. 100, noted that surplus allocation is more important in male/female power relations than the disposal of subsistence production, since withholding food from children is not normally a choice.

[12] Interviews B Wangige: 13, 24 June 1988.

[13] Interview A Wangige: 9 June 1988.

[14] Caplan, "Cognatic Descent," p. 31.

not possess. Having been taken from her parents upon an agreed dowry, she becomes a possession of her husband who exercises his rights on all the fruits originating from her." He stated that many Kikuyu men regarded women as slaves and quoted the proverb, *Mondo moka ndare igweta,* "No one bothers about a woman," or "A woman has no independent identity."[15] Various colonial officers entered into the debate over women's status in the second decade of the twentieth century when concerned about the availability of African labor. Their tendency to want to "free" women from African male control of their labor to serve as cheap labor for Europeans may have clouded their judgment regarding women's status. In 1919 and 1920 Ainsworth, then Chief Native Commissioner, wrote to the Solicitor General, the Attorney General, and the Acting Provincial Commissioner at Mombasa all on the same subject, to wit, "At present no native woman ever attains her majority, she is held to be under guardianship all her life, she is in practice debarred from holding property even when such property is earned by her own labour." Women should be allowed to leave the reserves and work for wages, he said; "if she was made more free to please herself ... in many respects the labour difficulty will be eased."[16] The issue of women as property also came up in the debate over bridewealth, which many missionaries opposed because they felt that it commodified women and, since women could not own property, they could not buy their freedom by repaying the bridewealth. These views were widely shared by colonial officers.[17]

On the other side we have some unequivocal statements saying that women had an unrestricted right to control the disposal of their produce. More contemporary scholars such as Shaw, Stamp, Kershaw, White and Gutto agree on this point.[18] Shaw (Clark) has argued that Kikuyu women had unrestricted power to dispose of their own produce as they wished, giving them power to control men's actions to some extent by withholding food, an argument that has been widely cited. The basis for this claim is a reading of Leakey and Kenyatta, both of whom were anxious to prove to unbelieving colonial officials that Kikuyu women were not oppressed victims.[19]

Jeanne Fisher's study of women in Kiambu and Murang'a in 1950 also leaned toward the unconditional, but with important reservations. "Male and female

---

    [15] Cagnolo, *Akikuyu,* pp. 29, 287. Second translation provided by Njuguna Mwangi, pers. comm. 1 Apr. 1995.

    [16] AG 4/2791. Corres. Chief Native Commissioner to Solicitor General 12 Apr. 1919. Memos. to Acting P.C. Mombasa 22 Mar. 1920, Acting Attorney General 13 Apr. 1920.

    [17] PC/CP 6/4/4. Memo. Acting District Commissioner Nyeri to Senior Commissioner Nyeri 5 July 1922. See also "Women Farmers of Kenya" (1986), p. 6.

    [18] Stamp, "Self-Help Groups," p. 35; White, "Bodily Fluids," pp. 419-22; Gutto, "Legal Constraints," pp. 3-4; Ministry of Finance and Economic Planning, *Situation Analysis of Children and Women in Kenya* III: 15.

    [19] Shaw, *Colonial Inscriptions,* pp. 29ff; Clark, "Land and Food," pp. 365-67. Paradoxically, Shaw has a fine dissection of the agendas pursued by Leakey and Kenyatta but did not fully apply the implications of that agenda to her analysis.

members of the family exercise full control over the management of their plots and the products of their labour, deciding what to plant and the period of fallow, and, with certain reservations in the case of wives, disposing of their crops as they please." She said that a woman's earnings were her own, unless she had an agreement with her husband to give some to him, a fairly important exception. The reservations mentioned concerned a male elder who told her that it was shameful for a husband to interfere in a woman's decisions regarding cultivation, but that a husband could beat her if she did not cultivate well. A woman told her that women could plant whatever they liked in their gardens but if a husband wished a wife to plant certain crops in certain places she had to obey or he would beat her. Kenyatta in the 1930s commented that a woman having a surplus of grain to sell in the market was a good sign of her industry, and that she would consult with her husband regarding the disposition of that surplus and sell it if the family needed the cash for something.[20] The unequivocal position has weaknesses, then.

A historically situated conditional situation constitutes a better explanation for the variation in the sources on the subject of control of women's trade profits. Women's rights to dispose of surplus production were not fixed, but shifting, and a perpetual site of conflict.[21] Perhaps symbolic of the situation regarding women's profits was that in any transaction in which produce was exchanged for livestock it was customary for the produce seller, most likely to be female, to add a tip (Kiswahili=baksheeshi, chai) to the livestock seller, most likely to be male, thus diminishing her profits. Depending on the situation, the amount earned, the location, and even the lineage, women might exercise more or less power over their earnings.[22] Given that this was a contested area, it then behooved women to try to maximize their economic position when faced with insecurity by moving toward an independent situation whenever possible. Only by understanding the locational specificity in time and place of women's control of their profits can we understand essential features of the development of women's trade in Nairobi.

Among the secondary sources Leakey is most elaborate in his description of women's long-distance trade, but almost silent in the area of local trade, by which emphasis he exercised a substantial influence on subsequent writers.[23] Leakey's description of Kikuyu women's roles in trade below has received independent confirmation. By his account Kikuyu women frequently went on expeditions into Ukambani and Maasailand to pursue a lucrative trade selling dried banana flour, njahe,

---

[20] Fisher, Anatomy, pp. 273, 141; Kenyatta, Facing, pp. 61-62.

[21] Here I concur with Kitching, Class, p. 124.

[22] Ngumo, "Trade," p. 24. Wairimu Githaiga-Bowman, interview 21 Jan. 1988, one of the first Kenyan women to attend secondary school, claimed that in her Nyeri lineage, where her father was a wealthy diviner, women could own and manipulate property; many did not marry and were not forced into it because they lacked property rights.

[23] I have analyzed the discrepancies between Leakey's and Muriuki's accounts further elsewhere. Robertson, "Gender."

maize, sorghum, green bananas, sugar cane, chewing tobacco, honey and earthen-
ware cooking pots. In exchange they got from the Maasai women leather cloaks,
hides, brass and copper wire, cowries, goats and sheep. This trade was conducted by
older women who had had at least one child initiated, because young girls were
thought to be vulnerable to Maasai warriors. Up to a hundred women might go on
such an expedition, organizing it themselves.[24] They consulted with a diviner before-
hand, whose blessing was necessary but could be denied, especially if the women's
husbands objected. A *hinga,* a woman captured as a child from the Maasai or a Maasai woman married to a Kikuyu man, would serve as an organizer, guide, and translator. Women would pay one trade bundle to the organizer as a fee for joining the caravan and go in a large group until reaching Maasai country where they split up into
twos and threes and were escorted by warriors to a village, where they became guests
of a Maasai host woman. Each carried a load of fifty to seventy kilograms with a
tumpline slung from her forehead to her shoulders.[25]

Both Jackson and Blackburne-Maze encountered such women, the former calling them "sturdy little women, always cheerful and merry" with loads "so heavy that
the strap [across their foreheads] sank deep into the flesh below the level of the surrounding skin." Blackburne-Maze found women at Nyeri going to Laikipia and others coming from Embu to Nyeri.[26] On the return trip the men of the warrior age-set
would meet them with food and water and help them to carry the loads the rest of the
way, having been notified of their impending arrival by the husband of the leader.
That notification was accomplished by a system of knots tied in ropes to represent
the number of days they intended to travel, one being left with the husband and one
accompanying the woman. Upon arrival a woman handed over the goods and goats
to her husband or eldest son, who had no right to dispose of them without her
consent.[27]

Muriuki and Ngumo, writing in the 1970s and relying on oral sources for the
1880s to 1900, added more detail and disagreed at points with Leakey. They
described women going as far as Lake Naivasha, Narok, Kajiado and Nanyuki on
expeditions, and encountering "untold hardships" such as wild animals, harsh
weather, and robbers. The *hinga* was a male of Maasai descent in Muriuki's description, the implication being that he was a product of trade relations facilitated by a
history of intermarriage between Maasai and Kikuyu. Sometimes there were

[24] Leakey, "Economics," p. 172.

[25] Berman and Lonsdale, *Unhappy Valley,* p. 320, noted that *hinga* in the 1950s meant "hypocrite"
or "dissembler." Leakey, *Southern Kikuyu* I: 480-85. Tumplines are usual in hilly or mountainous terrain,
as in the Andes, and allow the carrying of more weight compared to the usual headload of West African
women traders of about twenty-five kilos.

[26] Jackson, *Early Days,* pp. 171, 174; Blackburne-Maze, *Journals,* pp. 134, 221. Elderly women
now frequently exhibit permanent indentations on their foreheads from carrying heavy loads in such a
manner.

[27] Leakey, *Southern Kikuyu* I: 483-85.

permanent trading relationships between certain locales based on kin and friendship networks. In times of famine permanent markets could be established along the borders of territories. The Kamba exchanged beads, arrow poisons, medicines, chains, brass and iron wire, salt, snuff and snuffboxes, cowries, bows and arrows, and iron ore for foodstuffs, tobacco and ivory from the Kikuyu, while the Maasai wanted red ochre. Poor men might go on these expeditions too, but trade was viewed as a "menial" task, "certainly not the sort of job that appealed to a self-respecting warrior or elder." Trade was facilitated by a widely observed market peace rule, but men accompanying expeditions did not get the "comparative immunity" benefitting the women involved. Muriuki goes on, however, to emphasize the greater importance of the internal trade, which was "more frequent, extensive and affected a larger population than the external trade." It involved well-organized markets with a four-day cycle where foodstuffs were bartered for handicrafts and more pricy commodities like cowries and beads were purchased by the "well-to-do." Warriors enforced order in the markets held on permanent sites and provided a lost-and-found service. Different locales had different specialties--Gakindu for grinding stones and tobacco, Gaturi for poisons, medicines, tobacco and iron goods. Murang'a sold red ochre, pig iron and implements, and tobacco to Kiambu in exchange for soda, skin garments, beads and cowrie shells, which those at Kabete had obtained from passing caravans or the Maasai. Well-maintained roads and bridges served areas with permanent markets (especially Nyeri and Murang'a), cleared or constructed during the handing-over ceremony of one male age-grade to another (the *ituika*). Thus, women and men cooperated to everyone's advantage, each playing a variety of roles in trade. Local trade was well integrated with long-distance caravan trade, and became more so as trade from the coast grew in the late nineteenth century.[28]

In the last two decades of the nineteenth century integration into long-distance caravan trade contributed to the commodification of women. The caravan trade from the coast led by Swahilis had long involved Kamba and increasingly Kikuyu men as porters and traders. The long-distance trade in ivory, slaves and other male-controlled commodities involved women not only as commodities (the majority of the slaves) but also as suppliers of provisions to the caravans through farming and trading. Thus, we are not talking about two unrelated trading systems, but rather concentric circles of trade in which most took place among central Kenyan populations, with the coastal caravan trade entering in to supply certain restricted commodities only in exchange for slaves and ivory at the beginning, and then for foodstuffs to take Europeans to Uganda in the late nineteenth century. In the 1880s Kamba women began supplying the IBEAC outpost at Machakos, as well as passing caravans.[29] The obvious advantages of the Kikuyu granary became evident when the caravan trade

---

[28] Muriuki, *History*, pp. 106-109; Robertson, "Gender."

[29] Kershaw, "Land," p. 139, *Mau Mau*, p. 70; Feierman, *Shambaa*, p. 134; Munro, *Colonial Rule*, p. 35; Collier and Lal, *Labour*, p. 25.

reached southern Kikuyu country in the 1880s. Muriuki stated aptly that "Kabete ... became to caravans what Cape Town had been to the passing ships in the seventeenth century." In the 1880s caravans made regular stops on their way to Uganda at Ngongo Bagas, some fifteen kilometers from present-day Nairobi, and often stayed until they had gathered enough provisions to take them west of Lake Baringo, twenty-one days away and the next source of surplus.[30] Francis Hall, John Ainsworth and others successfully divided and conquered the Kikuyu, Maasai and Kamba in the 1890s, helped greatly by a range of disasters including diseases brought by European caravans (a more virulent form of smallpox, rinderpest), drought, locusts and famine. In 1895 the British government, having already taken over from the IBEAC in 1894 and begun the Uganda railway, declared Kenya and Uganda to be the East African Protectorate. By 1896 there were British forts at Dagoretti and Kikuyu within five kilometers of the boundaries of present-day Nairobi.[31]

All trade in the Nairobi area was affected as both men's and women's commodities entered directly into the Swahili-European caravan trade. The impact on women in particular took several forms:

1. Peaceful intermarriage to cement trade relationships was displaced in this trade by a continuing series of rapes, kidnappings, and sometimes even murder of women.

2. The impact of the slave trade intensified in newly affected areas, while the 1890s famines increased the pawning and sale of girls both into the slave trade to the coast and to the Kikuyu by the Maasai and Kamba.

3. The disasters of the 1890s were to some extent caused by the caravan trade; rinderpest, for instance, spread in the wake of oxen teams imported by the British from India.[32] Epidemics caused a huge loss of both human and animal populations and intensified the burdens of production on the survivors, especially the women.

4. Women's labor also intensified with the increased demand for foodstuffs for the caravans, and became the object of more male competition. Successful male traders became big men and ultimately the vehicles for British rule, which greatly profited them and exaggerated differences in wealth. One of their most outstanding characteristics was their many wives, who generated wealth for them with their labor in agriculture and trade.[33] The complementarity of women's and men's roles in trade was disturbed not only by increased labor demands on women but also by increased hierarchy among men.

---

[30] Muriuki, *History*, p. 33; Miracle, "Change," p. 13.

[31] Dawson, "Change," p. 92; Sorrenson, *Origins*, pp. 15-17; Morgan, "Kikuyu," pp. 61-62.

[32] Rogers, "British," p. 263.

[33] Kinyanjui, a trader appointed paramount chief of the Kikuyu by the British, fits this profile exactly; he is reputed to have had forty-nine wives. Browne, "Kawangware," p. 27.

5. Through trade senior Kikuyu women traders were able to recruit younger women to help them, but probably due to the restrictions imposed by the residential system and lack of control over profits mentioned earlier, could not convert that recruitment into permanent large-scale businesses or the creation of independent women-founded clans except in unusual circumstances.

Looking at these factors more closely, commodification of women is never more evident than in casual violence inflicted upon women, who are viewed as male property to be exploited for profit or revenge, with the more extreme situation being the complete conversion of women into mobile, kinless property as slaves. Most European travellers' accounts mentioned altercations and even occasional attacks on their caravans by local populations provoked by maltreatment or kidnapping of local women by their porters.[34] Lugard described the situation succinctly when stating his opinion that the Fort Smith (Dagoretti) site was unsuitable for a caravan stop due to the dense surrounding population. "Caravans from the coast, halting at the station, would inevitably pilfer from the crops, or cause trouble with the women."[35] One of the more egregious involved one of Hall's men shooting and killing a Kikuyu woman because she refused to submit to rape by himself and another man. Such incidents caused women in the 1890s to raise a warning the minute they saw soldiers approaching.[36] Ciancanelli has suggested that the trade in slaves and ivory effected a heightened gender division of labor in which women specialized in cultivation and men in defense with the increased insecurity of conditions, thus increasing women's subordination to men.[37] Whatever the merits of this argument, which remain untestable due to the paucity of data, it is clear that the caravan trade of the late nineteenth century in the Nairobi area and elsewhere in Kamba and Kikuyu country routinized violence against women in a manner that was previously unknown, pitting those with firearms against local populations whose prior experience of violence was sometimes very little, but certainly always more episodic and limited in scope.

The scale of the caravan trade through central Kenya grew steadily in the late nineteenth century and required ever more provisions in shorter amounts of time. In 1900 Arkell-Hardwick described the scene on his caravan campground as follows, "the camp was fairly buzzing with natives of all ages and both sexes. Most of them had brought food to sell ..." His photograph, reproduced here as Figure III.1, shows several women traders in prominent positions. While Swahili or Kamba caravans averaged only about 300 to 400 persons at the largest, IBEAC caravans were usually over 800. In 1884 Thomson's caravan had over 1500 persons and in 1899 another

---

[34] PC/CP 1/1/2 Hemsted, "Short History," pp. 1-4; Wright, *Strategies*, p. 139, noted the same phenomenon in northeastern Zambia. Kershaw, *Mau Mau*, p. 70, attributed attacks on caravans to Kikuyu warriors escaping the control of the elders, as if engaged in a hobby.

[35] Lugard, *Rise*, p. 325.

[36] Muriuki, *History*, p. 144.

[37] Ciancanelli, "Exchange," pp. 25, 28.

British caravan more than 4000. In the 1890s at Ngong caravans of 1200 to 1500 men were a common sight. In addition, there were military expeditions to feed, punitive expeditions which could be quite large. The principal food-producing area was at Wandegi's, twenty-five kilometers north of Fort Smith in Kiambu. In 1892 Lugard purchased over 10,000 kilos of grain and beans (mostly the latter) in a few days there.[38] The IBEAC outposts depended absolutely for food on the surrounding peoples, which dependence made some officers resentful at the necessary accommodations and gave locals a lever to use against unreasonable extractions. In 1890 the conduct of the incompetent officers at Machakos led to a boycott in which women did not bring food supplies; Lugard and Nzibu Mweu, Masaku's successor in authority, settled it by making a blood brotherhood pact, which was common among traders. In 1893 a dispute with Waiyaki's people led to their refusal to supply provisions, to the great frustration of IBEAC officials, caused the destruction of Fort Smith, and ultimately Waiyaki's deportation and death.[39]

Apparently both chiefs and British officials could organize and control women's labor and trading activities to produce these results. In 1894 over a hundred Kikuyu women were employed grinding maize for the IBEAC at Dagoretti, where in 1896 21,000 kilos of food, mainly dried staples, were supplied in twelve days, and in 1897 55,000 kilos in sixteen days from just the immediate environs. Production intensified with new land being brought under cultivation; large landholders had an advantage in trade. A big man, Mahui, was said to have divided up Kiambu in 1898 into divisions with headmen assigned to collect trade goods and recruit porters, collecting goats to pay them.[40] In the 1898 to 1900 Ulaya (Kiswahili=European) famine insufficient food was forthcoming voluntarily, and caravans regularly extorted it by various stratagems: holding leaders hostage (Mackinder); seizing foodstuffs (Sir Frederick Jackson, Kikuyu entrepreneurs); stealing livestock (most). Those who were most vulnerable in terms of lacking legal and economic rights suffered the most under such conditions: women and children. For instance, Kinyanjui regularly usurped the land use rights of unprotected women.[41]

---

[38] Arkell-Hardwick, *Ivory Trader*, pp. 51-52; Muriuki, *History*, p. 139; Wisner, "Man-Made Famine," p. 4; Miracle, "Economic Change," pp. 14-15; Lugard, *Early Days*, p. 305. Kershaw, /f2Mau Mau, p. 63, described Ng'waro's, halfway between Kiambu and Komothai, as a caravan provisioning stop of less importance, handling a caravan a month by the early 1880s but hampered by size restrictions imposed by the elders due to lawlessness on both sides (no more than forty persons per caravan).

[39] Munro, *Colonial Rule*, p. 35; Lindblom, *Akamba*, pp. 141-42; Kenyatta, *Facing*, p. 46.

[40] Ambler, *Kenyan Communities*, p. 110; Rogers, "British," pp. 261-62; Kershaw, "Land," p. 145, "Roles," p. 178, *Mau Mau*, p. 64.

[41] Mackinder, *Ascent*, p. 160; Rogers, "British," p. 264. Caravans also, besides doing intentional damage, violence to women and others, stripping whole neighborhoods of food even in times of scarcity, and bringing epidemic disease, sometimes caused involuntary disasters like the fire set on Mount Kenya by Mackinder's people that burned for weeks, a high cost indeed to local peoples for Mackinder's desire to attain the dubious glory of being the "first" to climb a mountain (p. 207). Miracle, "Economic Change," p. 17; Browne, "Kawangware," pp. 297-98.

III.1 Buying Food at Murang'a, 1900

The situation was changing rapidly with a strong impact upon social structure. Young men began going away as porters willing to do heavy carrying, despite its designation as women's work, when it allowed them to trade and make marriages (pay bridewealth) independently of male elders.[42] Controlling women's labor was clearly of critical importance in the creation of wealth; polygyny was a much desired goal and necessity for ambitious men. What Ambler has called "the commercialized transfer of women's labor" extended also to pawnship and enslavement. Such a situation meant that, especially as conditions worsened in the 1890s, there was very little of the widespread security needed to carry out long-distance trade, in particular. Violations of the market peace rule were routine, while that rule encouraged higher trade participation by women in chaotic times. Jackson called pawnship "a passage to relief" in times of famine, when "trading parties rarely completed journeys without being ambushed."[43] The escalating violence especially hindered women's large-scale trade. A few women who had emulated male leadership qualities by making many woman-marriages and building large-scale businesses were less likely to be able to establish *mbari* to protect themselves from disruption.[44]

Some tentative conclusions can be extrapolated from this history regarding the status of women's trade and profits around the turn of the century. When men's and women's commodities are mutually exclusive, women's control over them is facilitated. But women's crops, especially dried staples, were fundamental to both local and long-distance trade, and especially important as the caravan trade through central Kenya increased. Big men traders like Karuri wa Gakure with organized age-sets of young men carrying staples for the caravan trade and the Englishman John Boyes with his *njahe* trade were involved extensively in the staples trade.[45] Even if at some earlier point the staples trade might have been the exclusive province of women, by the 1890s it certainly was not. A struggle over controlling this trade might have occurred between big men and the more successful women traders, but we have no evidence to that effect. It is just as likely that women's rights to dispose of their own produce were considered to be contingent on male permission anyway (which most sources agree upon) and were ignored when it suited men to do so. Some men were increasing their involvement in trade in "women's" commodities at the wholesale level to take advantage of new leadership opportunities, extending latent aspects of male dominance to do so. The elderly woman at Wangige who had to stop trading her own commodities in favor of those of her entrepreneur/chief/husband, serves as an emblem for an ongoing process that expropriated most women completely.

---

[42] Wisner, "Man-Made Famine," p. 5; Kershaw, "Land," pp. 165-66.

[43] Ambler, *Kenyan Communities*, pp. 70-71, 82; Glazier, *Land*, pp. 61, 64; Jackson, "Family," pp. 204-206.

[44] A more nuanced discussion of the possibilities for precolonial female leadership buttressed by trade is in Robertson, "Gender." Njau and Mulaki, *Women Heroes*, pp. 6-10.

[45] Mukaru-Ng'ang'a, "History," p. 17; Boyes, *King*.

By 1920 in the Nairobi area there was a well-developed permanent local market system, described elsewhere,[46] which the British had expanded upon, and Kiambu was extensively involved in supplying both dried staples and fresh produce to Nairobi. New pressures on women imposed by increased labor obligations in rural areas, as well as cultural constraints, encouraged some to escape control by entering or expanding trade. Before World War I some went to Nairobi to trade, practice prostitution, or both. At the Indian Bazaar some women rented rooms in the back for prostitution. Such women were valuable assets for the overwhelmingly male town inhabitants because they sold prepared foods and domestic services of all kinds. An observer described the central role of the Nairobi bazaar, "To the native generally speaking Nairobi means the bazaar: the bazaar exists in virtue of the native trade, the volume of which is enormous. There is a daily influx of thousands of natives, of whom the greater number come by road from Kyambu."[47]

The typical Nairobi trade in the first decades of the twentieth century was carried out by women like Wangari, who began as a small girl selling sweet potatoes to Indian and Swahili traders in about 1904 on the rail line in Kabete. Her profits went to help her father purchase livestock. As she got older she took heavy loads of beans to sell at Wangige and Dagoretti markets, and brewed beer for sale to people in Nairobi on weekends. The sale of milk and of English potatoes in Nairobi also began to be important during World War I.[48] Dundas, a district officer at Dagoretti, described milk sales carried out by itinerant traders, who made twenty rupees a day in 1913 by selling five large tins each morning and evening in Nairobi at two rupees apiece.[49] Old trade patterns and market locations continued despite newly imposed illegality in some cases, but new patterns also appeared, especially apparent during and after World War I. Much of the dried staples trade in maize and beans took place at African markets and Indian trade centers in Nairobi and in Kiambu at railway stations, as well as on white settlers' land.[50] Trade, especially urban trade, was becoming ever more important as a livelihood for Africans in the area because land alienation to Europeans exacerbated the calamities of the late 1890s; by 1906 the Kamba had lost half of their grazing areas and been displaced from the fertile Mua Hills, while by 1908 the Kikuyu had lost over 60,000 acres in Kiambu alone.[51] The imposi-

---

[46] Robertson and Fisher, "Terrain."

[47] McVicar, "Twilight," p. 8; White, *Comforts*, pp. 41-42, 45, 71, 75; Governor Philp cited in Dawson, "Change," p. 95.

[48] Interview Chege 4 Nov. 1988; DC/KBU 1/9 Dagoretti AR 1915-16: 45.

[49] DC/KBU 1/4 Dagoretti Handing Over Report 1912-13: 14.

[50] DC/KBU 1/7 Kiambu AR 1914-15: 16; DC/KBU 1/9 Dagoretti AR 1915-16: 22-23; DC/KBU 1/4 Dagoretti AR 1913: 25.

[51] DC/KBU 1/4 Dagoretti Handing Over Report 1912-13: 12; Onstad, "Life," pp. 91-92; Silberfein, *Rural Change*, p. 45; Presley, "Transformation," p. 79.

tion of a hut tax in 1901, to be paid in cash only from 1904, not only forced both men and women to work on settlers' farms, but also sent them to town to trade.[52]

The Organization of Trade in the 1920s and 1930s

After the war, however, the movement of women traders to Nairobi to escape patriarchal controls, landlessness, and/or supplement insufficient rural incomes increased considerably. This movement did not go unopposed, however. That opposition was intimately connected to the issue of women's control over their profits and was premised upon the segregation of women's interests from men's. To understand the ramifications of this development in the interwar period it is necessary to look at changes in the organization of women's trade and at the growing efforts by government in its several guises to stop the women's Nairobi trade. Of particular relevance here is the implementation of maize control laws. The way in which gender entered into these control efforts is emblematic of gender relations among central Kenyan peoples and illustrates how colonialist notions regarding gender, trade and traders intersected with those of Kikuyu male authorities.

The provisioning of Nairobi in the 1920s and 1930s was becoming a large-scale enterprise that required organization suitable to an agglomeration of some 20,000 persons in 1921, 50,000 in 1931.[53] In the 1920s it was primarily the trade in dried staples that increased in scale. The Kikuyu and Kamba response of ever increasing involvement in this trade drew mixed reviews from British administrators. While one remarked in 1927, "The Akikuyu are naturally a methodical and industrious agricultural people, but they are also keen money makers," another was less positive in 1928, saying that the Kikuyu have "a propensity for money making, a thirst for knowledge and a complete inability to be contented."[54] This ambivalence arose from several factors: money sense and involvement in trade contravened common British essentialist assumptions about local peoples, who were supposed to be docile farmers and laborers, unsuited to urban life and unskilled in trade; the economic independence of such traders removed them from the labor market, which made the settlers unhappy; and the urban presence of African traders was sometimes illegal, as were some of their other activities. One reason the stereotype of the East African woman as farmer has persisted is that many administrators assumed that Africans had never traded before, whether they saw Africans as being happy primitives or ignorant savages.[55]

But ambivalence was the milder of administrative reactions involved; some noticed that many Africans did have an aptitude for trade and were inspired to

---

[52] Sorrenson, *Origins*, p. 183; PC/CP 4/2/1 Kikuyu AR 1909-10: 3; Onstad, "Life," pp. 33-34.

[53] Obudho, *Nairobi*, p. 6; Parker, "Aspects," p. 2.

[54] PC/CP 4/1/2 Kikuyu Province AR 1927: 13; DC/KBU 1/21 Kiambu AR 1928: 4.

[55] In PC/CP 4/1/2 Kikuyu AR 1931: 3, E. B. Howe marvelled at how rapidly Kikuyu were learning "trading sense."

invective ranging from racist disdain for moneygrubbers to images of traders as criminals. It is probable that they felt threatened not only because independent African
incomes threatened colonial control, but also because the male traders tended to
come from mission-educated ranks who wore European clothing and aspired to ape
their betters, in this view. In 1924 the Kiambu District Commissioner (DC), C. M.
Dobbs, allowed other ethnocentric stereotypes to show, "The characteristics of the
majority of the Kikuyu in the district are those associated with Jews. They are past
masters in the art of driving a hard bargain and Shylock would find it difficult to hold
his own."[56] Van Zwanenberg and King quoted an anonymous administrator describing male traders in the 1930s as,

> the unemployed and mostly the unemployable ... As they emerge from the mission
> school their main ambition appears to be the achieving of a competency by means
> of petty cheating ... This finds expression in the incredible number of middle-
> men--traders who are found on almost every reserve road trading on a miserable
> capital, but persuading the native producer ... to dispose of his [sic] produce at a
> figure much below the market prices. It further finds expression in the shops ...
> butcheries and 'hotels' which have sprung up like mushrooms and owe their exis-
> tence to that misguided patriotism which is the last refuge of the scoundrel.[57]

Insofar as Kikuyu views can be characterized generally, many initially welcomed new trade opportunities offered by the European presence. But after World
War I when the colonial presence meant the loss of more land and unfavorable terms
of trade (more settlers arrived, took land, and demanded labor bringing about higher
taxes for Africans), their attitudes changed. They were especially contemptuous of
European farming attempts, feeling that the Europeans "were ignorant and poor, they
needed many men to do the work of a few women, they grew the same crops as the
Kikuyu and grew them without regard to type of soil, season or prevention of
weeds."[58] Paradoxically, the very activity that most interested Kikuyu with respect to
the European presence, trade, was also one viewed by the British as highly suspect
among Africans, whether the preferred stereotype was noble savage, Jewish shyster,
corrupt urbanite, or simple primitive. However, in the 1920s such trade went largely
unmolested by the colonial authorities because it was essential to provisioning
Nairobi and provided most exports.

Gavin Kitching suggested that in the 1920s and 1930s,

> a clear bifurcation of produce trading emerges ... with women being restricted to
> short distance, 'subsistence' trading of produce for produce, or produce for handi-
> crafts, and men monopolizing the long-distance trade in the export of each district's
> surplus product. This bifurcation was the equivalent, in the sphere of exchange re-
> lations, of the control exercised by male household heads over the bulk of the

---

[56] DC/KBU 1/17 Kiambu AR 1924: 2.

[57] Van Zwanenberg with King, *History*, p. 213. The term *mushroom* was used by upper-class
British to refer to socially unacceptable parvenus who had made their fortune in trade.

[58] Strayer, *Making*, p. 4; quotation is from Kershaw, "Land," pp. 178-81.

household's surplus product with women being 'relegated' to control over the 'subsistence product.' Since, however, women's labour power appears to have remained predominant in all farm production ... the process of commercialisation would appear to have been appropriated by men at the expense of women.[59]

Although segregation of women's from men's trade was implemented under colonialism, the process of class formation can be seen as beginning as early as the late nineteenth century, depending on how the evidence is read. Shaw, a moderate on this topic, stated that socioeconomic differentiation was not as "structured or conventionalized before the divisive influence of colonialism."[60]

What is clear is that the "big man" complex flourished under new conditions of increased marketing to Nairobi. Cagnolo described rich men as being "surrounded by clients and hangers-on."[61] Many profited from a combination of the perquisites brought by chiefship and trade, especially wholesale trade. Colonialism confirmed the translation of prominence in trade into political eminence. The large-scale bulking of staples was carried out mainly by Asian traders, and increasingly by African male traders in the reserves. The means of transport used were donkeys or oxcarts or, for the most successful, trucks.[62] While trade from Kiambu to other areas continued, its importance diminished in the interwar period with a substantial reorientation to focus more narrowly on Nairobi. Particularly during the late 1920s drought, animals were brought from Ukambani and other dryer areas for sale in Murang'a and Nyeri in order to obtain dried staples. Kiambu's increasing production of fresh vegetables for the Indian and European market in Nairobi by the 1930s helped to make it dependent upon areas like South Nyeri for supplies of maize, while the railroad depended on shipment of African-grown produce for its profits throughout the 1920s.[63] In 1931 a district officer tried to make a precise calculation of the disposition of Kiambu crops and found that, despite a plague of locusts, Kiambu Native Reserve was consuming only 46% of its production, selling or bartering 4% to other African areas, 41% to settler areas and Nairobi, and exporting 9% abroad.[64]

One of the big men in Kiambu extensively involved in this trade was Chief Josiah Njonjo in the 1930s. He was part of a system in which chiefs confiscated produce, or were bribed with it by people wishing to avoid forced labor. His people

---

[59] Kitching, *Class*, p. 178. Unfortunately, the situation of women disappears from his subsequent analysis.

[60] Shaw, *Colonial Inscriptions*, pp. 119ff.

[61] Cagnolo, *Akikuyu*, p. 212.

[62] Marris and Somerset, *African Businessmen*, pp. 46, 49, and Leo, *Land and Class*, p. 50, suggested that by the 1920s African men had forsaken caravan trade for shops in the Masai Reserve at Narok, and that by the 1930s their donkey trade selling to Europeans in Nyeri had been displaced by Asians with trucks.

[63] PC/CP 4/1/2 Kikuyu Province AR 1927: 16; 1929: 15-16,18,39; DC/KBU 1/21 Kiambu AR 1928: 4; 1/22 Kiambu AR 1929: 60-61; 1/26 Kiambu AR 1933: 27; Native Affairs Dept. AR 1927: 30,49.

[64] DC/KBU 1/24 Kiambu AR 1931: 28.

transported maize, beans, and English potatoes to Nairobi in oxcarts. From the mid-1920s Kikuyu men began opening a number of wayside shops and *posho* mills, even forming partnerships to do so.[65] Murang'a led the field in number of such African-owned shops in 1928 with 208. One of these shopkeepers had a contract to supply Nairobi with fresh produce, in one week providing 5000 pounds (2275 kgs.) of sweet potatoes, 8000 (3640 kgs.) of bananas, and forty (18 kgs.) of African-grown tobacco. In the mid-1920s and increasingly in the 1930s Kikuyu men formed cooperatives or companies for the purpose of conducting large-scale trade. In the 1920s the focus of such companies in Kiambu was more likely to be dried staples; by the 1930s the export of vegetables to Mombasa to supply ships was a lucrative trade.[66]

Further down the wholesale pyramid than the large shopkeepers were the wholesaler-collectors, who were in the habit of "visiting individual holdings or way-laying women on their way to market," purchasing produce at "well below fair market value." In 1933 a Kiambu district officer estimated that "a large proportion of the Kikuyu" indulged in this form of trade, bringing wattle as well as green vegetables to sell.[67] In 1926 the growing involvement of Africans in business provoked a repressive measure intended to limit the scale of African-owned businesses, while its stated purpose was the paternalistic goal of protecting them from excessive debt. The Credit to Natives Ordinance imposed a limit of Sh.200 on the amount of credit that could be advanced by non-Africans to Africans. It was in force until 1960, but after 1945 it became easier for well-connected Africans to get the DC to grant an exemption.[68]

In addition to legally licensed shops, there were also less prepossessing illegal ones, as described by the Kiambu DC in 1933. At the Ngong Road-Dagoretti junction (now called Dagoretti Corner) there was "a collection of disreputable huts and shops built of old corrugated iron and flattened petrol cans." This "embryo Pangani" (the oldest Nairobi African residential area considered to be a slum by officials) was demolished with the approval of the Kiambu Local Native Council (LNC). Kiambu had had LNCs since 1908, when the governor announced that the councils of Kikuyu male elders (*kiama*) were henceforth to be so designated, but their composition

[65] Interview Chege 4 Nov. 1988; PC/CP 4/1/2 Kikuyu Province AR 1924: 5; 1926: 20.

[66] Native Affairs Dept. AR 1928: 23, 46; PC/CP 4/1/2 Kikuyu Province AR 1927: 32; DC/KBU 1/23 Kiambu AR 1930: 7; Agr 4/440 Safari Diaries, entry at Makemei, Kiambu, 22 Oct. 1935. All diaries in this file are by agriculture officers working in Kiambu. This development was ignored by Himbara, *Capitalists*, who uncritically accepted the negative evaluations of African entrepreneurs by colonial officials, especially in the post-World War II crisis.

[67] Native Affairs Dept. AR 1936: 45; DC/KBU 1/26 Kiambu AR 1933: 26-27. Kitching, *Class*, pp. 64-66, said that wattle production in Kiambu was encouraged by the government to supply a British-owned multinational, Forestal, but that many Kikuyu preferred making charcoal out of it rather than selling the bark.

[68] Swainson, *Development*, p. 176. Such exemptions helped Harry Thuku, an exile in northern Kenya to 1933, to amass a prosperous fortune with the help of a cooperative DC with whom he was in business. Thuku, *Autobiography*.

changed in 1925-26 to consist of government-appointed officials and chiefs, whose goals included profiting from trade opportunities and assuring monopolistic advantages for their members.[69]

Perhaps the best indicators of the growing popularity of trade among mission-educated Kikuyu men are various pronouncements by Kenyatta and others extolling the virtues of trade in the 1920s in *Muigwithania*. Although couched in terms of the virtues of promoting agriculture, what was really meant was the promotion of growing and selling cash crops. In November 1928 Petro N. Kigendu wrote that mission schoolchildren needed to learn about agriculture and cooperative buying and selling of maize, beans, livestock, milk and eggs, as well as artisanal skills, so as to buy motorcars ("if this were possible") as part of a patriotic effort. This sentiment was echoed in several other letters and summed up most elegantly by Kenyatta himself. After stressing the importance of cultivating large fields, he said that Kikuyu should,

> send our produce in quantities to distant countries and get good prices for it; ... this is the way to enrich our country, for ... a country is made rich by selling the produce of its soil so that the gold which is dug in other countries can come to our country ... [F]or without these objects called 'shillings' we can do nothing; ... it is they which remove mountains.

However, men like Kenyatta found competition from women in production and trade quite threatening; Kenyatta even advised that fields be divided into trade (male) and food (female) crops.[70]

If men eagerly seized various opportunities to expand their trade, their efforts rested ultimately upon women's continuing agricultural and trade activities. The women's increasing disadvantages, however, confined them to more small-scale efforts also characterized by different levels of involvement. Few women were like Wangeci wa Kang'ethe, who, when she was widowed in 1930, took over complete responsibility for farming ten acres at Kabete and raising twelve children belonging to herself and her deceased co-wife. She hired farm labor and incorporated her sisters, daughters, and grandchildren into a business selling maize, beans, sweet and English potatoes, sugar cane, bananas and arrowroot to Nairobi. From her profits she sent children to Alliance Secondary School, the first for Africans in Kenya, and founded the prosperity of her descendants. She described herself as a "rich woman" before she died in 1981 at over ninety years of age.[71] More typical was Njoki, who began trading as a child with her mother in Murang'a. Like Wangeci, her mother was a widow forced to supplement her income through trade.

> I was taught to trade by my mother. We would go to the *shamba* [Kiswahili=farm]

---

[69] DC/KBU 1/26 Kiambu AR 1933: 5; Kitching, *Class*, p. 188.

[70] Barnett and Njama, *Mau Mau*, p. 37; DC/MKS 10B/13/1 *Muig.* I, 7(Nov. 1928): 1-4, 7-8, 13; Berman and Lonsdale, *Unhappy Valley* II: 387. The 1929 famine, however, provoked second thoughts about exporting staples, especially *njahe*. DC/MKS 10B/13/1 *Muig.* I, 10 (Feb.-Mar. 1929): 8.

[71] Interview Chege 4 Nov. 1988.

in the morning; in the afternoon we were off selling things. She would cook beans--I would go and sell them along the road. She would make porridge and I would sell that too. The following day, back to the shamba.[72]

Wangeci and Njoki represent respectively the largest and the smallest scale of women's trade, but there were also intermediate levels involving retailers, described in a 1935 memorandum. "There are in the Kikuyu reserve a great many natives who live alongside the European boundary and border on coffee farms to which they are accustomed to sell their maize by private treaty."[73]

But most women traders went to markets, which were well described by contemporary British observers. In the 1920s Procter commented that markets were the chief social centers for the Kikuyu. He paid particular attention to the prepared foods and produce sold by the women, which he said dominated the market. He walked up and down the rows of sellers noting women selling *uruu*, ladling it out in small half-calabashes, maize porridge (*ugali*), curdled milk (*iria imata*), many legumes including *njahe* and *njugu*, sweet and English potatoes, cocoyam (*nduma*), lots of bananas, shallots, wild figs, many different kinds of consumable green leaves including those of *njahe*, pumpkins, and boiled or roasted corn on the cob. Commodities sold by men included salt earth dug from marshes or imported salt, natron (soda), castor beans and red ochre. Around the edges of the market were *dukas* (anglicized Kiswahili=shops) carrying imported finery like beads, necklaces, dancing bells and various pigments. There also were teashops, largely patronized by men, "where the exhausted male may recover from the arduous toil of watching the women do the work, and may discuss the news of the day."[74] Norman Leys in 1924 added more commodities to the list of those available in markets, especially imported goods: tobacco, firewood, sheep and fowls, dressed and undressed skins, baskets, pots, wire, calico, thread, needles, combs, mirrors, crockery, enamelware, umbrellas, women's pottery and men's ironware.[75] Because the organization of markets incorporated sex segregation by commodities and women had little capital to open shops, men and women were somewhat separated both in the open air portions of the markets and in the shops.

There was also another form of trade in the 1930s involving more adventurous types described by Louis Leakey. Women went to Nairobi, sometimes traveling eighty kilometers daily. "Every day vast numbers of Kikuyu women and girls walk into Nairobi from outlying districts and sell potatoes and sugar cane and bananas, etc. Most of these commodities are sold to the house-boys of Nairobi, many of

---

[72] Interview 185 Gikomba: 26 Feb. 1988.

[73] CNC 10/9 Memorandum No.1, "Marketing of Maize Enquiry Order in Council," p. 12.

[74] Procter, "Kikuyu Market," pp. 15-18.

[75] Leys, *Kenya*, p. 58; see also Cagnolo, *Akikuyu*, pp. 41ff.

whom make the arrangements for a regular weekly supply of such food."[76] Nyikamba, a woman trader in her nineties, described her early career in the 1920s trade. At 3 A.M. she and her cohorts started from Gitaru each carrying a *debe* of English potatoes and nine trays of eggs. At about 8 A.M. they would arrive at Kileleshwa market in a newly settled Nairobi suburb, where she sold to regular European customers. At 3 P.M. they would leave for home. In the 1930s the first truck transport became available at Gitaru, a truck owned by Musa Gatonyi (many early Kikuyu male traders and Nairobi residents adopted Islam and Muslim names through Swahili influence). This allowed Nyikamba to sell at Wangige and Dagoretti Markets.[77] Nyikamba's activities are yet another example of the pervasiveness and continuity of the involvement of women in daily trade transactions at the local level, also evident when squatters in the forest traded potatoes for maize from squatters on farms; when women, still the chief porters, trudged with heavy loads to local bulking centers, which were continually growing in number; and when maize and beans were still the chief commodities traded and barter still the chief method.[78]

Women, however, clearly were at a disadvantage in trying to increase the scale of their trade. Domestic and agricultural responsibilities kept them home; it is not accidental that Leakey described unmarried girls as dominating the Nairobi hawking of produce. Women generally made the lowest level of profits in a system in which the profit margin increased in proportion to the amount handled. Areas far distant from the railroad, unlike Kiambu, suffered from lower produce prices, a factor capitalized upon by male traders, who bought maize cheaply from women in the 1930s and transported it by donkey in caravans to places where better prices prevailed.[79] Women lost out at mills where more was charged when they paid in kind instead of cash (in Kiambu cash transactions appear to have become dominant from the mid-1920s on). Wholesalers sometimes cheated women sellers; in 1936 an agricultural officer investigating an Indian-owned duka at Gitaru market found four different-sized measures, all called a bushel measure.[80]

Cooking and water pots, the production of which was a women's specialty surrounded by taboos on male participation, continued to be sold, despite the incursion of imported goods. Potting, a women's skill handed down in certain clans located in areas with suitable clay soil, continued unabated in the 1920s and 1930s. Other commodities sold by women were sheep and goat skins, which they rubbed with castor oil and red clay to make soft and smooth, and used as clothing. With the exception

[76] Leakey, *Contrasts*, p. 137; interview Mwaura: 4 Mar. 1988.

[77] Interview D Gitaru: 6 July 1988. This name derived from Kamba-Kikuyu intermarriage brought by trade contacts.

[78] Furedi, "Squatter," p. 4; Agr 4/440 Safari Diaries, entry 20 July 1936; PC/CP 4/1/2 Kikuyu Province AR 1924: 9; DC/KBU 1/22 Kiambu AR 1929: 9; Native Affairs Dept. AR 1924: 4; Kenyatta, *Facing*, pp. 59-60.

[79] DAO/KBU 1/1/92 Liversedge, "Report on Marketing of Potatoes," 7 May 1931, pp. 1-5; PC/CP 4/1/2 Kikuyu Province AR 1932: 27. Marris and Somerset, *Businessmen*, p. 48.

[80] Kitching, *Class*, pp. 118,175; Agr 4/440 Safari Diaries, entry 25 Mar. 1936.

of those at missions, women at this time continued to process, wear and sell skins. Kenyatta attributed this to their "conservatism" compared to the men, who had taken to wearing European clothes or European-manufactured blankets.[81] But women could less afford the new types of clothing and few attended mission schools.

The early 1920s and 1930s depressions seem to have affected Kiambu trade less than areas further north, which were experiencing more difficulties in finding buyers for maize, beans and potatoes. In the 1930s Kikuyu male traders began forming buying cooperatives in large numbers, as well as producer cooperatives for wattle and maize in Kiambu, a trend that took hold later in Ukambani. Trade diminished across the borders of settler areas and the reserves.[82] Since no new land was available by the early 1930s, intensification of agricultural production became more common, meaning more work for women and less for men, whose task of clearing the land eased. By 1928 40% of adult males were absent from some Central Province districts. Kiambu's relative prosperity reflected the continuing necessity of feeding Nairobi, an "unfailing market for charcoal, firewood, poultry, eggs, vegetables, fruit and flowers in addition to wattle bark and the usual native crops." The market for dried staples, in particular, increased with the advent of a number of African restaurants in Nairobi catering to the growing number of single male workers.[83]

It is clear, then, that in the 1920s and 1930s areas that could profit from trade to rural settler areas and Nairobi did so. The organization of trade became less hierarchical as the relatively few "big men" of the late nineteenth century who were in the best position to capitalize on the opportunities provided by the caravan trade yielded to an influx of more men into trade in the interwar period. This evidence sharply contradicts the 1924 account of Norman Leys, who in his estimable desire to promote African agriculture and get rid of forced labor on plantations, said that European settlers had killed the African export trade because they were afraid of competition and that settler cotton and maize growers had "brought the trade in native produce nearly to extinction."[84] To the contrary, it was flourishing, pervasive, and still produced a large proportion of Kenyan exports. It was, however, more hierarchical as regarded women's participation. Women increasingly were confined to local trade only and gender segregation was more pervasive in markets. Because male traders were often better capitalized, they opened shops or tea stands, or traveled around collecting produce as wholesalers; they did not sit on the ground selling green leaves or half-calabashes of beans at open air markets. Their sense of status

---

[81] Kenyatta, *Facing*, pp. 84-90; Blakeslee, *Curtain*, p. 33; Leakey, *Southern Kikuyu* II: 344-48, has an excellent description of women's garments. Roscoe, *Years*, p. 271; van Zwanenberg, *Capitalism*, p. 223.

[82] Dept. of Agriculture AR 1932: 73-74,79; DC/KBU 1/27 1934: 11; PC/CP 4/2/2 Ukambani AR 1920-21: 48; PC/CP 4/1/2 Kikuyu Province AR 1931: 19-20; DC/KBU 1/24 Kiambu AR 1931: 12.

[83] Mosley, *Economies*, p. 80; Heyer, "Policy," p. 95; DC/KBU 1/25 Kiambu AR 1934: 21; DC/KBU 1/28 Kiambu AR 1937: 30.

[84] Leys, *Kenya*, pp. 221, 295-96, 374n.

and decorum forbade it. Nor did they carry loads unless paid for it. Two Kikuyu proverbs regarding trade both charge women with disrupting it, not men: *haro ni ya mika uri thiri* ("quarreling characterizes a woman who has debts"), and *giathi githaragio ni gaka kamwe* ("a market can be spoilt by one woman").[85] In ideology and in reality small-scale trade belonged to women. It therefore fell upon women not only to do the carrying, but also the subsistence trade that enabled their families to survive on increasingly smaller plots of land. Their former role in long-distance trade vanished with confinement to Reserves and increasing labor obligations.

In pursuing this trade women took an active role in the spread of an increasingly efficient and ubiquitous market system in Kiambu and Nairobi.[86] One Kiambu market, Wangige, housed three types of trade: export in wattle, maize, beans, potatoes and hides; retail in clothing, soap, and small luxuries; and "market day" trade in which "local consumable produce" was bought and sold. It was one of the most developed in 1935.[87] In the development of markets wealthier Kikuyu men used forced or voluntary women's labor to prepare market infrastructure (for clearing, for instance, formerly assigned to men in the gender division of labor). Their alliance with colonial officers at the local level presaged postwar efforts to reduce the access to resources of younger men and women. As will be shown in the next two sections, such efforts were not successful at this time either in keeping out many younger men, who sometimes chose illegality to force an entrance into trade, or in stopping women traders going to Nairobi.

Attempts to Control Men: the Wholesale Staples Trade in Kiambu

The development of markets was one aspect of government efforts to impose controls over, and tax, small-scale trade. The 1920s and 1930s saw the beginnings of government efforts to control the staples trade in general, and especially wholesalers in Kiambu. As time went on local African authorities joined in these attempts--to secure control over the wholesale trade for their members and to eliminate Asian dominance of the trade. While the measures focused on large-scale traders, they also affected small-scale traders. Moreover, the invention of such controls in this period when enforcement lacked vigor established precedents for more stringent efforts during and after World War II.

The usual focus of attention regarding Kenyan government control over trade in staple grains and pulses is on the Maize Control Act of 1942 and subsequent legislation, but well before that date there was substantial interference in that trade which disrupted precolonial trade routes and afflicted African trade with rules aimed at profiting white settler agriculture regardless of the consequences for African traders

---

[85] Interview Huxley: 12 Oct. 1992. Men carried only weapons. Barra, *Proverbs*, pp. 20, 8.

[86] Robertson and Fisher, "Terrain."

[87] DAO/KBU 1/1/92 corres. Agriculture Officer Kiambu to Secretary, Kiambu LNC Wangige Market Committee, 22 Feb., 5 Apr. 1935.

and producers. From the viewpoint of the mass of traders the colonial government created far more hindrances than help.

The nascent attempts at maize control are of primary concern here, along with the evasions they fostered by disrupting the old system. Ironically, given the ultimate effects of produce trade legislation, some of the first measures affecting the trade in foodstuffs were taken to even out food supplies during famines. Before and during World War I, when two-thirds of Kenya's export earnings came from African-grown produce, the British colonial administration was satisfied that the staples trade had been sufficiently facilitated by the building of the railroad, other roads, and the imposition of (local) "peace," which allowed free movement of produce.[88] It was only after World War I with the increasing importance of white settler produce that measures were taken to privilege that produce in the guise of bettering exports by improved quality control. The proposed Grading of Maize Ordinance of 1919, modeled after a South African act of 1917, established four grades of maize: choice and fair average for European-grown maize, and native white and native colored for African-grown maize. White growers were associated with white maize, Africans with colored, but even African white was assumed to be inferior. "Native" grades were allowed to have more imperfect grain but none could have a high moisture content or weevils. A penalty was imposed for misrepresentation of "native" maize as European-grown maize. An elaborated form of this ordinance promulgated in 1923 included seven grades of maize with "native mixed" at the bottom. Higher grades were supposed to bring better prices.[89]

More pesky for local traders were the movement controls applied by district officers to *prevent* local staples from being exported outside of the district. By the 1920s Nairobi's dependence on Kiambu African produce was such that in 1923 attempts were made to stop local movement of maize in other directions and to stop all hawking. The first British agriculture officers to go into the African reserves arrived in 1923; their duties included carrying out these rules. The Kikuyu, however, continued their older trading route by selling maize to the Kamba, which then was defined by the authorities as a blackmarket. The 1928-29 drought and famine brought the first systematic movement control attempts, which drew in the LNCs. From January to October of 1928 the Dagoretti area had an embargo placed on the export of grain and beans.[90] The 1929 Food Control Ordinance promulgated in February provided for the establishment of a Food Control Board with the power to prohibit exportation of staples (maize, wheat, potatoes and pulses) colony-wide or locally, to impose price controls, to requisition and transport staples, to prohibit

---

[88] PC/CP 4/2/1 Ukambani AR 1914-15: 2; Lonsdale, "Depression," p. 99.

[89] ARC(MAWR)3 Agri 3/257 Grading of Export Maize Ordinance (1919): 1-2; Director of Agriculture to Chief Secretary of Agriculture and Attorney General 18 Sept. 1920; same to Secretary of London Corn Trade Association 1 May 1923.

[90] Native Affairs Dept. AR 1923: 50-51; Smith, "Overview," p. 117; DC/KBU 1/21 Kiambu AR 1928: 10; PC/CP 4/1/2 Kikuyu Province AR 1928: 23; Kitching, *Class*, p. 195.

forward buying of stocks, to distribute famine relief, to license dealers in foodstuffs, and to effect forcible entry to inspect food stocks without compensation to the owners.[91] Thus, even before the 1930s the Kenya government had assumed wide-ranging powers affecting how traders could conduct their businesses.

Set in this context, the 1935 Marketing of Native Produce Ordinance repre-sents a widening of the earlier legislation that centralized markets, licensed traders, and extended and made compulsory the produce inspection and grading system (dis-cussed with respect to beans in Chapter II) to cover more staples.[92] The Kiambu LNC appointed a buying agent who worked on commission with the LNC getting a share in the form of a tax, or cess, which was used to fund schools, finance busi-nesses belonging to its members, and pay clerks at marketing centers. Despite cor-ruption, these betterment funds ultimately contributed substantially to improvements in African locations. The centralization of marketing, however, led to efforts by the Kenya Farmers' Association (KFA) to corner the maize market. In 1937 the Legisla-tive Council passed a motion that any African squatter with a marketable surplus was to notify the master first.[93] Both African advisory councils and white settlers there-fore gained from these laws.

The advent of produce inspection in 1934-35 generated far more opportunities for producers and traders to break the law. It was always difficult to enforce, espe-cially since there was no requirement that locally sold produce be inspected. Kiambu, with its relatively well-developed road network, provided ample opportuni-ties for evasion of inspectors. At first in 1935 fourteen inspection stations were envisaged for "native produce," most of which was destined for Nairobi, but very quickly more were needed and thirty-nine were established. Even so, inspectors could only hope to cover the largest centers. By May 1936, defeat was acknowl-edged and the number of inspection centers reduced to five.[94] Evasion was widespread by wholesalers taking produce to Nairobi by truck and even taxi.[95] Although the KFA attempted to monopolize maize supplies, they failed to dominate the dispersed trade filtering through the Kiambu patchwork of settled areas and reserves. The exemption from inspection of produce being purchased for home con-sumption or sold in private markets in settled areas was necessary not only to benefit

---

[91] AG 4/3233 Kenya Colony, *Official Gazette* XXXI, 9 (5 Feb. 1929): 319-23. See also corres. from 1929 in AG 4/3231, AG 4/3233, AG 4/3235.

[92] MCI 5/1 Marketing of Native Produce Ordinance.

[93] Kitching, *Class*, pp. 188-193; Dept. of Agriculture AR 1933: 99; Cone and Lipscomb, *History*, p. 70; Kanogo, *Squatters*, p. 60; Lonsdale, "Depression," pp. 111,126; Tignor, *Transformation*, p. 308; Agr 4/114 Kiambu Agriculture AR 1936: 7.

[94] Agr 4/334 corres. Agriculture Officer Central Province to Deputy Director of Agriculture Pro-duce Inspection Nairobi 12 Jan. 1935; same to Agriculture Officers Kiambu and Machakos 4 May 1936; Agriculture Officer Kiambu to Divisional Chiefs 14 Apr. 1936; MCI 5/1.

[95] Agr 4/334 Marketing Officer Dept. of Agriculture Nairobi to Deputy Director Produce Inspection 12 May 1936; latter to Provincial Agriculture Officer Central Province 25 Sept. 1936; Assistant Agricul-ture Officer Embu to Provincial Agriculture Officer Central Province 1 Oct. 1936.

employers but also because any further efforts at inspection were not feasible due to lack of finances. It was the small wholesalers, both African and Asian, who bore the brunt of the inspection effort. In Ukambani the advantage given to the KFA by the regulations caused the DC to question allowing it to operate in the African reserve, saying that it was driving Kamba traders out of business. Mobile African whole-saler-collectors were, according to the 1936 Agriculture Report, completely stopped from visiting farms or dealing with women on their way to market. Women not only had to sort beans, but they also had to clean the maize in order to sell it. It is not sur-prising that some traders and farmers objected. A Kiambu agriculture officer found it necessary to stop his work laying out market sites because "the district [was] in such an unsettled state" due to objections to the discriminatory prices. In July 1936 a group of Asian wholesalers assaulted an African produce inspector.[96]

The regulation of trade was increasingly used by British and LNC authorities to drive Asians out of their well-established niche in the Reserves. In 1923 almost two-thirds of the 117 traders' licenses issued in Kiambu went to Asians. The devel-opment of better roads improved the Asians' mobility as buyers; they were more likely to use motorized transport than African wholesalers. Some were even involved in market gardening for the Nairobi market. Asians were especially domi-nant in wholesaling produce and in selling imported goods to Africans such as soap, razors, tinned milk, tea, coffee, sugar, wheat bread, and bicycles.[97] As imported goods drove out some local products and Kiambu people developed a taste for them, taxation was raised on them to increase colonial revenues. African consumers then focused their ire on Asian traders who passed this cost on to them.[98] In the 1920s a concerted campaign against them waged by the LNCs and DCs largely succeeded, resulting in a decline in numbers of Asian wholesalers that began in the late 1920s. By the end of the 1930s Asian traders were more or less confined to central markets, while African male traders had secured control over local marketing centers.[99]

The nature of the 1935 regulations made their widespread evasion inevitable.[100] In addition to limiting inspection to only a few centers, the regulations

---

[96] Agr 4/493 Marketing of Native Produce Ordinance, p. 8, Amendment 28 Aug. 1937; Munro, *Colonial Rule*, p. 182; Dept. of Agriculture AR 1936, I: 96; Agr 4/440 Safari Diaries, entries 14, 20 July, 23 Mar. 1936.

[97] DC/KBU 1/16 Kiambu AR 1923: 1-2. The rest went mostly to Africans engaged in the livestock trade to Ukambani (30), while twelve went to Europeans. Dept. of Agriculture AR 1928: 24; DC/KBU 1/20 Kiambu AR 1927: 9; 1/23 Kiambu AR 1930: 7; PC/CP 1/1/2 "Short History," p. 45.

[98] Brett, *Colonialism*, p. 194, described the public outcry by reformers in Britain over the raise in the African poll tax implemented after the Harry Thuku demonstration in 1922. Subsequently, the poll tax was lowered but customs duties on cheap consumer goods were raised, and became a larger proportion of overall revenue.

[99] DC/KBU 1/22 Kiambu AR 1929: 9; 1/27 Kiambu AR 1934: 37; DAO/KBU 1/1/92 Agriculture Officer Kiambu to DC Kiambu 31 Jan. 1935; Lonsdale, "Depression," p. 109.

[100] DAO/KBU 1/1/92 Assistant Agriculture Officer Kiambu to Agriculture Officer Central Province 28 May 1936; same to J.A. Shukla Co. 14, 16 June 1936. DC/KBU 1/28 Kiambu AR 1937: 31. Agr 4/574 Agriculture Officer Embu to Senior Agriculture Officer Central Province 3 Feb. 1939.

forbade purchase and sale of produce at places within three miles of the inspection centers, the purchase of produce between 6 P.M. and 6 A.M., and trading in produce outside of the buying centers in the reserves. All produce consigned to places outside the district (and therefore subject to inspection) was to be marked. Buyers were to have licenses, which were often granted on an exclusive basis, so that certain companies or individuals had concessionary privileges. Any competition at the wholesale level was therefore discouraged. For instance, in 1938 when Kikuyu sawyers began selling timber to Nairobi at half the price charged by the mills, mill owners protested and sawyers were forbidden to sell to Nairobi traders. The many African-owned shops on settler farms also evaded further restrictions established by the Crop Production and Livestock Ordinance in buying produce.[101] The 1937 Native Produce Marketing Weights and Measures Rules required the use of standardized English units, but calabashes were the most common measures for beans even in areas close to Nairobi until the 1970s. LNCs resisted enforcement efforts by district officers directed at restricting trade to designated centers and reducing the number of traders, and requested more buying centers. Kitching argued that it was the very impossibility of implementing produce inspection rules that shifted enforcement efforts to the burgeoning African-owned shops in the reserves and license infractions.[102]

The impact on Central Province of the inspection legislation was immediate; later it was extended to other areas, to Rift Valley Province in 1938, for instance. Because of the proximate necessity of feeding Nairobi, Kiambu was closely scrutinized regarding supply conditions and subjected to more bans on the export of maize and beans. Conversely, its centrality mitigated the impact of the weights and measures standardization, since at the wholesale level they had already been using British measures for some time. In 1934 while under a voluntary inspection system 100 produce traders in Kiambu had already registered, each having installed "an approved produce cleaner on his premises." The new licensing system was more restrictive, leaving the granting of licenses up to an administration with discriminatory policies in mind.[103]

The first effort at price controls was contained in the proposed Maize Control Bill of 1936, which enshrined maize as the chief staple, extended coverage to all British East African territories, and established the principle of a central marketing board to purchase all supplies. The chief losers under this act would have been the Asian traders, whose mobile and shop trades in the reserves would have been sub-

---

[101] Dept. of Agriculture AR 1936 I: 5; Native Affairs Dept. AR 1935: 153; DC/KBU 1/29 Kiambu AR 1938: 37; ARC(MAA) 2/3/1 VIA Thika AR 1938: 26.

[102] MCI 5/1; Kitching, *Class*, pp. 195, 169-70; DC/KBU 1/28 Kiambu AR 1937: 33.

[103] MCI 5/1 Director of Agriculture to Attorney General, to Acting Provincial Commissioner Nyanza 7 Jan., 9 Mar. 1938; Native Produce Marketing Weights and Measures Rules, 1937; DC/KBU 1/29 Kiambu AR 1938: 9, 31; 1/27 Kiambu AR 1934: 8.

stantially damaged,[104] and the small African traders, who could not afford the produce cleaner. The Federation of Indian Chambers of Commerce lodged a number of criticisms of the Maize Control and Produce Marketing bills, most of which proved to be justified when maize control was later implemented. They said that the bill provided a subsidy for "European maize grown at an uneconomically high cost of production," and harmed small traders. The new marketing mechanisms would interfere with free trade, "rendering activities of the trading community cumbersome, hampering, not facilitating trade ..." They mentioned the problems involved with requiring petty traders to keep accounts, given the prevailing illiteracy, and deplored putting small traders "at the mercy of exporting agencies" and "unscrupulous harassing." Their objections were dismissed summarily but those of large plantation owners who did not want to pay more to feed their labor were accepted and the effort abandoned for the moment. However, other regulations indicate that the government's intentions to eliminate "unsatisfactory and uneconomic traders by the gradual induction of produce into suitable channels of trade" seen as desirable in 1934 were being implemented.[105] African wholesalers, in particular, as well as Asians, had to worry about all facets of their businesses, while becoming increasingly proficient at evasive measures.

"MODESTY LIKE FIREWOOD": Attempts to Control Women's Retail Trade to Nairobi

In the 1920s and 1930s the authorities' attempts to control women traders, as with men, were also mostly unsuccessful; they are particularly interesting insofar as they illuminate aspects of the prevailing gender ideology related to women's control of their bodies and their profits. Gracia Clark noted that in Africa "loss of economic control over traders is equated with loss of sexual control over women."[106] Nowhere is this more clear than in the reactions of local Kikuyu authorities when faced with numbers of women going off daily or permanently to Nairobi. The ineffectiveness of the LNC's actions indicates the limits of the power of the LNCs when unsupported by the colonial administration, a situation that was to change later. Both in the urban and the rural contexts escalating efforts to control women illustrate the objectification of their status, while women's actions, especially in the early period, often seem imbued with a desire to seek autonomy and adventure, rather than simply economic desperation. The history of attempts to control urban women began before World War I with arrests of prostitutes. Prostitution and drunkenness of women were not acceptable behavior in Kikuyu culture but also were becoming uncontrollable before

---

[104] CNC 10/9 "The Selling of Kenya Maize," p. 1; MAA 8/53 corres. Acting Chief Native Commissioner to Chief Native Commissioner 7 Aug. 1934: 1, 4. See also 22, 27 Apr., 21 May 1936. The LNCs were consulted about the bills before their promulgation. Native Affairs Dept. AR 1933: 47.

[105] CNC 10/9 Summary of Criticisms Received and Replies [regarding Maize Control Bill]; van Zwanenberg with King, *History*, pp. 211-12; DC/KBU 1/27 Kiambu AR 1934: 11.

[106] Clark, "Introduction," p. 8.

World War I.[107] Despite women's hopes of escaping control by going to Nairobi, coercion by men did not necessarily disappear in town. Violence against women early on became an established fact of life.[108] Thus, some women may have found it more appealing to seek protection with missionaries. In 1913 the Dagoretti Handing Over Report stated that

> Mission influence and interference in native affairs are constant sources of trouble. In particular, the practice of native girls and women abandoning their homes to go and live at mission stations is a cause of keen resentment among the natives. Most of the missionaries have now agreed to submit these disputes to the District Commissioner for settlement.[109]

This quotation is important in illustrating the tone of official British-Kikuyu interactions regarding control of women. For British administrators the important "natives" were men whose resentment needed to be palliated; the source of women's discontent provoking them to such drastic action was not worth exploring; the DC would henceforth attempt to deal with this petty distraction to the satisfaction of the Kikuyu men; and others were not to interfere. The Acting DC at Dagoretti, M. W. H. Beech, had insights into women's grievances that did not, however, make it into the dominant discourse. In an article entitled, "Suicide Amongst the A-Kikuyu of East Africa," he claimed that suicide was far more common for women than for men. Why? Anger, physical pain, quarrels with their husbands.[110] Both elder and younger Kikuyu men took advantage of British authority to assert control over women. Forest guards robbed women gathering firewood of axes and cords and, if the women were beautiful, insisted upon submission to sexual intercourse.[111] This, then, was the setting for the first public attempts to stop women traders going to Nairobi. It can be surmised that many private ones preceded them of which we have no record.

Although both local and long-distance trade were well established as women's activities in Kikuyu culture by the 1920s, when women wanted to pursue it in Nairobi men found it objectionable. Older men felt they were losing control over young men and women; young men did not want women claiming the same freedom that they themselves obtained from wage work allowing them to pay their own

---

[107] Stichter, "Women," p. 10; PC/CP 4/2/1 Ukambani AR 1908-1909 Prison Report; DC/KBU 1/5 Dagoretti AR 1913-14: 15.

[108] DC/KBU/1/3 Kiambu AR 1911-12; PC/CP 4/2/1 Nairobi AR 1909-10: 2b. White, *Comforts*, pp. 45, 71, 75.

[109] DC/KBU 1/4: 14. The Kiambu AR of 1909-10 (DC/KBU/1/1) also noted that men were having trouble controlling women because of "women being able to leave them and go to Nairobi or other places."

[110] Men's reasons for killing themselves were listed as impotence, physical pain, theft, and conviction of a crime. PC/CP 1/4/2 Kikuyu District Political Record Book II, 1912-14: 4.

[111] Two warrior age-sets, Kianjeku and Kamande, initiated respectively in 1898 and 1902, became the Kikuyu Reserve police force. PC/CP 1/4/2 Kikuyu District Political Record Book II, 1912-14, Beech, "Kikuyu Point of View"; DC/KBU/1/7 Kiambu AR 1914-15: 8.

bridewealth and choose their own brides.[112] Leaving home temporarily or permanently was the one sure way that women could achieve control over their profits and their bodies. Urban trade involved moving into a situation where men had great difficulty in controlling women's sexual activities, and those activities were likely to be with strangers. Moreover, for some women who stayed permanently in town wealth accumulation might result, thus freeing them completely from male economic control.

For their part, British officials were not overly concerned about women hawkers coming to Nairobi at this time--they supplied the town; they usually went home at night to Kiambu; and they were not troublesome. British officials did not make the connection between trade and prostitution and required the services of the traders, while deploring prostitution. Prostitutes were routinely cleared by the police. Traders were not specifically enumerated as undesirable in the pass law of 1921, although hawking without a license was forbidden by the 1903 ordinance.[113] There is evidence of illegal hawking of foodstuffs by Africans in the World War I era but none of systematic arrests. While those selling their own produce did not need licenses in the 1920s, those who could afford licenses, market stalls, and legality were more likely to be men.[114]

Meanwhile, Kikuyu men had ample reason to worry about keeping their authority intact. In 1923 a census of Nairobi prostitutes showed that over half were Kikuyu. Some rural women were using trade as an excuse to go to Nairobi for prostitution, while others saw prostitution as a supplementary source of income. Amina Hali, a long-time Nairobi resident, described picking beans by the river in Nairobi as a routine excuse used by women who derived income from prostitution.

> She would take a [gunny sack] which ... she would use ... as a blanket... When they saw a woman lying on [it] they would take out their money, and she would motion for him to lie down with her. They paid us and sometimes they gave us babies, so we were rich, we had money and babies that way.[115]

Huxley described 1930s headmen, who sent their wives to sell produce in Nairobi and return with imported goods for sale in a shop. But such women sometimes went to Nairobi and never returned, or came back in bad shape from hard living and sexual abuse.[116]

Leakey's 1937 description of women trading to Nairobi was included in a chapter about prostitution, and went on to explain how prostitution might arise out of trading arrangements in Nairobi. As an anthropologist raised in Kenya, who self-

---

[112] PC/CP 1/4/2 Kikuyu District Political Record Book II, 1912-14, Beech, "Kikuyu Point of View."

[113] PC/CP 4/1/2 Kikuyu Province AR 1924: 9; Nairobi Administrative District AR 1926: 55; Wood, "Origins," p. 39.

[114] Onstad, "Age Mates"; East African Protectorate *Official Gazette* 1 June 1904; 5 Oct. 1921.

[115] White, *Comforts*, pp. 71, 45, 75.

[116] Huxley, *Lizard*, p. 161; interview A Wangige, 22 July 1988.

identified as Kikuyu, he found it necessary to explain to his predominantly European audience just how prostitution was linked to trade.

> When the same girl brings the supply of potatoes week after week a flirtation often ensues, and not infrequently the girl becomes a kind of a concubine, spending an occasional night in the boy's quarters and telling her parents that she had been delayed and slept with friends on the way home. In these cases the man very seldom has any intention of taking the girl as a second wife, and he probably tires of her before long. Nor in most cases does she take the matter very seriously, sometimes she is actually betrothed to someone in the Reserves and in due course marries and settles down, but on the other hand it is from this class of girl that many of the prostitutes are derived and although by no means all the girls who become temporary concubines to servants in Nairobi turn to prostitution, a fairly large percentage of them undoubtedly do so.

He also disapproved of Kikuyu women being employed by Europeans as childminders (Hindi=*ayah*), since that also sometimes led to prostitution.[117] Crowded housing conditions, a highly uneven sex ratio, the lack of wage earning opportunities for women, and the vagrancy laws which subjected women alone on the street to arrest, extortion, and sexual harassment, all were factors promoting prostitution.[118]

As a consequence young politically conscious men involved in the Kikuyu Central Association (founded in 1924) took up the cause of stopping the women's Nairobi trade with nationalistic fervor, securing the backing of the LNC and the chief, Kinyanjui wa Gathirimu. The subsequent struggle is documented in *Muigwithania* (Kikuyu=The Unifier). Grievances expressed in 1928 were consistently vehement on the subject of loss of control over both married and unmarried women. Xenophobia was evident in some protests; control over women was seen as determinant of a nation's greatness. When women are considered to be male property, control over them may become a matter of national or ethnic pride. One correspondent from Kahuhia stated that the chiefs should

> look after the matter of those Kikuyu women who live amongst the Foreigners, in the towns of the Foreigners. Because this custom is one which causes the Kikuyu nation to decrease, for these women bear children among the foreigners and are taken to other nations and, further, these women have given for them not even a bean ... to be eaten by the Kikuyu ... [no bridewealth]. If we allow our nation to become scattered in this way, how shall the seed of the Kikuyu be made to increase? Will it not just become stunted?[119]

---

[117] Shaw, *Colonial Inscriptions*, p. 98; Leakey, *Contrasts*, pp. 137, 146, could find no better English word than concubine, which implies a kept woman, to describe a situation in which women clearly were no such thing.

[118] White, *Comforts*, pp. 71, 41, 75.

[119] DC/MKS 10B/13/1 *Muig.* I, 7(Nov. 1928): i. The correspondent was Gideon M. Kagika, the translator the missionary Bible translator, A. R. Barlow.

In response Kenyatta asserted that the strength of nations is symbolized by their maintenance of control over women:

> Raise your eyes and see how the powerful nations and those who are most fa-mous--how they have exalted their women and girls and made prohibitions con-cerning them ... Guard against dropping your child (or daughter or wife) like a millet stalk by the wayside, lest you make yourself despicable, while all the time you look upon it as a joke.[120]

He was clearly not fooled by the gilt on British middle- and upper-class women's cages. He and the KCA embarked upon a nationalist campaign which made control over women's bodies, reproductive and economic activities, an essential part of the construction of Kikuyu male identity.[121] The women's puberty rite, arguably a site for autonomous authority for senior women (see Chapter VII), and other customs were being newly constructed as sites of social control by African men. Another cor-respondent said that people in Nairobi were impugning Kikuyu manhood because of Kikuyu women's immodesty, while Kenyatta went on to say that it was women's trading that was leading them to corruption.[122]

The most purple prose was in an article by George Ndegwa and Dishon Wai-henya entitled "The Trading of Girls and Women in Potatoes and Other Things in Nairobi--This is the Cause of the Beginning of Insubordination."

> The trading ... is a danger to the girls and newly married women, being produce not from their own gardens ... frequently it is the road to the beginning of PROS-TITUTION, although the woman did not desire it ... When they are selling they ... are spoken to by people of many nations and shameless things are said to them ... We are being exterminated at a blow ... Oh you Bride of Kabete, you have done wrong without knowing it: would you deceive your husband by saying that you are going to sell potatoes [but] when noon arrives you are sitting at a table [drinking is implied]? ... These days, on account of trade and other things pertaining to profit-making they have all burned their MODESTY LIKE FIREWOOD, for even any stranger whatsoever can stop a Kikuyu girl or woman on the road to talk to her. If it were the old days the childless thousands who are now prostitutes ... would be in Kikuyuland with their fathers and husbands, and would have children as numerous as they ... ARE WE TO DIE THUS WITHOUT PROTEST?"[123]

"Insubordination" more than immorality was disturbing to the authors; controlling

---

[120] DC/MKS 10B/13/1 *Muig.* I, 7 (Nov. 1928): 2. In 1942 Kenyatta was equally unequivocal in his view of women as property, "There can be no ground for friendship with one who seeks to deprive you of your land, your women and your cattle." Kenyatta, *People*, p. 22.

[121] This phenomenon fits exactly into Ortner's connection of control of women's sexuality to nation-making. Ortner, "Virgin."

[122] DC/MKS 10B/13/1 *Muig.* I, 7(Nov. 1928): 10-11.

[123] DC/MKS 10B/13/1 *Muig.* I, 8 (Dec. 1928-Jan. 1929).

women's procreative power rather than sexuality was the chief issue.[124] Clearly, the men were also worried about perpetuating their own lineages, while women like Amina Hali liked having their own money and children. According to one anonymous contributor, even girls in rural areas used trade as an excuse to profit from prostitution. He signified his outrage at overhearing two girls at Maragua Market in southern Murang'a plotting to deceive their parents. They had come to sell around 6 P.M.; the next morning one said, "I shall deceive my mother by telling her that when one goes to sell maize she should spend the night at Maragua so as to get a good price for it! ... Should I want to come often there is no one to stop me!"[125]

But most of the protest centered about women going to Nairobi and becoming what one contributor called *"njara-ruhi"* (Kikuyu=stretchers out of the palm, or beggars), wicked city women who rejected the authority of their fathers and husbands and exploited men by taking their bodies and their possessions. K. Kirobi, a work-seeker in Nairobi, was outraged that a Kikuyu man in Pangani had been *murdered* by a woman. He went on to say that such women made bad wives (!) since they would not settle down; after all, they had left their homes for reasons such as disobedience to their menfolk, or not wanting to repay bridewealth.[126]

Women's Nairobi trade became a dominant issue in the late 1920s' protest over uncontrolled women, usually termed the female circumcision controversy by scholars. It might equally be called the women's trade tumult. Women who controlled their own profits not only threatened individual men's control but also the survival of the clan by detracting from its corporate wealth, while prostitution threatened its posterity. In 1930 one KCA member wrote to another, "A woman's wealth makes no sense, ... like stinging nettles which have not been mashed."[127] Ire also focused upon girls going to European-run schools. School attendance was associated with a wide range of evil consequences. Girls ran away to missions and were put in schools to become Christians. Not only were they out of the control of Kikuyu men, but they were also likely to marry foreigners (here the nationalist construction of ethnicity is evident) and lose their own culture. One result of these feelings was an increased impetus given to the independent schools movement of the 1920s.

The missionaries had raised objections to bridewealth and clitoridectomy, both of which Kikuyu felt were central to the fabric of their society. In 1938 Kenyatta stated that "No proper Gikuyu would dream of marrying a girl who has not been circumcised and vice-versa," and claimed that a man who did so would be disinherited.[128] Female genital mutilation at initiation was not only an important part of Kikuyu culture, but also symbolic of the subordination of junior women to senior

---

[124] Berman and Lonsdale, *Unhappy Valley* II: 386, have an excellent analysis of this material.

[125] DC/MKS 10B/13/1 *Muig.* I, 7(Nov. 1928). Regarding rural prostitution see also PC/CP 4/1/2 Kikuyu Province AR 1924: 4; PC/CENT 2/1/4 minutes Kiambu LNC 19-20 Mar. 1934.

[126] DC/MKS 10B/13/1 *Muig.* I, 8 (Dec. 1928-Jan. 1929): 14.

[127] Berman and Lonsdale, *Unhappy Valley* II: 387.

[128] Presley, *Kikuyu Women*, pp. 87, 91ff; Kenyatta, *Facing*, pp. 132-33.

women and to men; it will be dealt with at length in Chapter VII, where its implications for women's gerontocratic authority are explored. Some of the more violent incidents in the controversy took place in Kiambu, including the murder of a female missionary, Hulda Stumpf.[129]

There were also moves by colonial authorities regarded as highly suspect by many Kikuyu that had negative implications for women's fertility. In 1927 an unannounced tour by a food committee concerned about diet and wishing to experiment with food additives, involved weighing children, which caused the Kahuhia Mission converts to run away "en bloc." Rumor had it that stepping on the scales would cause girls to become barren and boys impotent. There was, then, a whole complex of issues regarding women pressured by the intensifying impact of the colonial presence which came to a head in the late 1920s, with one of the foci being control of women's trading activities. The fact that some prostitutes in Nairobi were becoming independently wealthy must have only added fuel to the fire. Many men felt that whites were highly hypocritical in trying to stop practices like clitoridectomy and bridewealth, which were essential to proper morality of women (chastity and marriage), while not doing anything fundamental to clean up Nairobi, a cesspool of immorality exercising a deadly fascination upon young women.[130]

One reaction by both elders and young politicos was to try to stop women going to Nairobi to trade. This effort was most possible in Kiambu, especially Kinyanjui's area, whose proximity to Nairobi permitted men to pursue wage work and farm, while exercising more control over women and the young. In his youth Chief Kinyanjui was thought to be promiscuous by his contemporaries and made many girls pregnant without marrying them, causing his family to disown him. In his later years he was consistent in his negative view of women, refused to let his daughters to go to school and, under pressure from the LNC, forbade women to trade to Nairobi.[131] This prohibition was preceded by a host of Kiambu LNC resolutions aimed at controlling women's chastity that prohibited young men and women bathing together at the river lest it lead to "indecent assault," and certain dances held at midnight "for the purpose of violating virgins," while asking that women workers' lodgings on settler farms be isolated from men's camps and men forbidden entry (a request attributable to the frequently reported sexual abuse of young girls). On 22-23

---

[129] PC/CP 8/1/1; Murray, "Controversy," pp. 176-77. Three orphan girls from Canon Leakey's Kabete school ran away to be initiated with Leakey in hot pursuit. He recaptured them but there was then a mass exodus from his school. Stumpf was forcibly excised according to the Medical Examiner, but the most immediate witness who examined the body was a medical doctor and missionary, Virginia Blakeslee; she left a written account that calls the excision into question. Blakeslee, *Curtain*, p. 191. Pedersen, "National Bodies," pp. 647-680, has an excellent analysis of how the "ritual unmaking and reworking of women's bodies became so central to the construction of national identity" (p. 648). Other accounts of these events can be found in Sandgren, "Kikuyu"; Strayer, *Making*, pp. 128ff; Welbourn, *Rebels*.

[130] PC/CP 1/1/2 Hemsted, "Short History," p. 42; White, *Comforts*, pp. 124-125; Stichter, "Women," p. 11; Berman and Lonsdale, *Unhappy Valley* II: 391.

[131] Browne, "Kawangware," p. 54; Kinyanjui, "Biography," pp. 22, 42.

November 1928 they discussed prohibiting women from going to Nairobi to sell produce, "as it leads to prostitution and disease." But M. R. Vidal, the DC, said it was a "domestic affair" and that legislation was "incapable of controlling women's morals." While in 1927 the Kiambu LNC had acknowledged that one of the contributing factors to prostitution was men taking and discarding mistresses, their attitude in 1928 was generally condemnatory of women.[132] Both British and Kikuyu authorities considered the main problem to be controlling women's sexuality, not men's, sharing a common assumption about women's bodies as men's property.

Although without the DC's support, the Kiambu and Dagoretti LNCs passed resolutions forbidding women to trade to Nairobi, securing Kinyanjui's help in setting his police to patrol their routes and turn them back. Kinyanjui's effort was his last act as chief. Before setting off on a trip to Maasailand he confirmed the prohibition despite opposition from the DC When he returned with a fatal tetanus infection, he was told that the DC had arrested and fined his men set to stop the women and had said, "Anyone again picketing the woman or preventing a woman from passing and going to trade, I will imprison him for six months without a trial [hearing]." Nevertheless, Kinyanjui insisted that the prohibition should remain. He was then taken to Dr. Arthur's Mission Hospital where he died, Canon Leakey presiding at his funeral (since both Arthur and Leakey were strong opponents of clitoridectomy, this was surely an irony of fate).[133]

Nonetheless, the patrols stopped and this incident marked the failure of Kikuyu men's efforts at that time to stop women trading to Nairobi, efforts that were predominantly based in rural areas. The DC's actions were surely not concerned with protecting women's rights, given that he shared Kikuyu men's negative opinions of women's morals. In the 1928 Kiambu *Annual Report* Vidal wrote, "There is a strong movement in the Reserve to forbid women and young girls going to Nairobi to sell produce owing to the laxity in morals of such women and the well founded risk of their becoming prostitutes; the establishment of markets on the borders of the Reserves and the Nairobi district is being considered." He was more concerned about the necessary services and produce supplied by women to the predominantly male Nairobi population. Alternative supplies of fresh food were difficult to come by, and a cheap urban food supply was a cornerstone of British administrative policy to promote a cheap labor supply. If Kikuyu elders and intelligentsia objected to women

---

[132] PC/CENT 2/1/4 minutes Kiambu LNC 4 Apr. 1927, 22-23 Nov. 1928; Ross, *Kenya from Within*, pp. 111-13. The telegram that earned Harry Thuku so much opprobrium from the authorities among other demands asked the Prime Minister to repeal, "compulsory taking of girls married women for plantation work culminating into immoral practice." Thuku, *Autobiography*, p. 87.

[133] DC/MKS 10B/13/1 *Muig.* I, 7 (Nov. 1928): 11; Obituary for Kinyanjui wa Gathirimu, *Muig.* I, 10 (Feb.-Mar. 1929): 3-4.

trading, there were surely other men involved in market gardening who needed the women's help in realizing cash for their produce.[134]

In Nairobi those viewed as undesirables by the administration continued to be deported to the reserves, but neither prostitutes nor traders were greatly harassed in the 1930s. A ninety-four-year-old Kamba woman who began hawking at that time said that she was not bothered by European officials; most regarded her as a beggar, gave her bits of cash, and told her, 'here, go eat something.'[135] In 1934 the municipal trade licenses inspector claimed that hawking was uncontrollable by himself and two African assistants. Produce hawkers paid only one shilling per month for a license, a sum that the KCA appealed on behalf of vegetable hawkers in 1931. In 1939 only one person was arrested for hawking without a license compared to hundreds for remaining in the Municipality without work for over thirty-six hours and for breaking the 10 P.M. curfew.[136] But African authorities continued the effort to stop women's trade to Nairobi in the 1930s, the Nairobi Native Advisory Council going so far as to ask that the rigorous 1921 pass law be extended to women for this purpose. The fact that African men but not women at this time were restricted by pass laws must have caused considerable resentment and heightened concern over women escaping men's control. Like local courts in Ghana and Zimbabwe, the Nairobi Native Tribunal, established in 1930, spent much of its time on adultery cases, which "in deference to native law and custom" the British authorities allowed to be criminalized so long as a fine was the punishment.[137] The Kiambu and Dagoretti Local Native Tribunals dealt with a steady stream of cases in which men sued each other for enticing away their wives or daughters. In August 1932 the Kiambu DC commented, "this enticing away of women causes great resentment and in many cases the men who do it are without property, and the girl is returned with great trouble and difficulty and is by this time 'soiled goods.'" Chief Muhoho complained that young men were coming out from Nairobi on Sundays and inducing girls to return with them "where they become prostitutes."[138] Clearly, diminishing control by propertied men was used by those who were landless to secure women, a phenomenon also evident in some marriages in the 1987-88 sample of fifty-six women.

The DC left the adultery cases to the Native Tribunal, but rape and indecent assault were tried as criminal offenses under British law, not subject to customary law that treated women as property and compensated men for property damage or

---

[134] DC/KBU 1/21 Kiambu AR 1928: 12; Onstad, "Life," Ch. 2; Kitching, *Class*, p. 67.

[135] Onstad, "Life," p. 128; interview 77 Ngara: 11 Nov. 1987.

[136] In Kiambu the number of trade licenses granted went down due to staff shortages and enforcement was nil. Onstad, "Life," pp. 12, 67-68, 129. DC/KBU 1/30 Kiambu AR 1939: 27; White, *Comforts*, p. 98; LG 3/3207 Nairobi Municipal Native Affairs Dept. AR 1939: 47.

[137] CNC 10/29 corres. Nairobi Municipal Native Affairs Officer with Attorney General 18 Mar., 5 Oct. 1935; 4 Sept. 1939; Schmidt, *Peasant Traders*; Allman, "Adultery."

[138] PC/CENT 2/1/4 minutes Kiambu LNC 19-20 Mar., 2-4 May 1933.

loss.[139] The Nairobi Municipal Native Affairs Officer, Eric Davies, was not willing to back control efforts. He stated that *malaya* prostitution (involving domestic services in addition to sex) was a necessary part of African urban life and saved the cost of housing families, while making it unnecessary for employers to pay men enough to support a family. Nonetheless, there were occasional campaigns to deport "undesirable females" from Nairobi.[140] Desmond O'Hagan, a Nairobi DC in the 1940s, commented that most cases brought to district officers in the 1930s concerned property rights in women and cattle. Women left their husbands because they had been maltreated or the bridewealth had not been paid, meaning that by Kikuyu custom they were not really married. In 1939 Davies noted that the 8:1 male:female sex ratio in Nairobi created a huge demand for prostitutes and encouraged young women to leave home.[141] The combination of unpleasantness, constraint, and want at home and the prospect of mobility and independence in Nairobi, whether as traders or prostitutes, must have been irresistible to some women. Women, then, were no more controllable than young men and sometimes had far stronger motivations for leaving home.

Conclusion

Women's trade, especially in dried staples, has a long history in central Kenya and considerable socioeconomic importance. Essential foodstuffs like beans supplied by women's agricultural labor and trade were the key link between local and long-distance trade, which involved complementary efforts by men and women. Women's labor, profits from trade, and bodies were increasingly subject to male manipulation with the impact of the late nineteenth century caravan trade. But the growing intrusive colonialist challenge to African trade and to customs newly constructed as means of social control of women in the 1920s provoked resistance and innovation. The many manifestations of control and insubordination regarding trade in the interwar period represented a testing on both sides of the limitations on both. Women found their horizons narrowing in terms of rural long-distance trade but widening in terms of urban opportunities and markets, while the forces arrayed against their efforts looked for effective means to keep them subordinate, and control their bodies, their labor, and their profits. Kikuyu men, divided by age, education, and socioeconomic status, nonetheless allied themselves against women's efforts to escape by going to Nairobi. In so doing African men contributed to the objectification and segregation of women and women's interests fostered by colonialism. The colonial government pioneered ways of using taxation to profit from African trade and set up a market system in alliance with, and following in the footsteps of, African authorities. When trade was involved they tended not to support the LNC attempts to control women, but when order in urban areas was at issue, vagrancy and

---

[139] CNC 10/45 corres. Attorney General with DC Kiambu 18 July 1931; Solicitor General to DC Kiambu 10 Aug. 1931.

[140] White, *Comforts*, p. 94; ARC (MAA) 2/3/1VIA Nairobi AR 1938: 15.

[141] Interview O'Hagan: 8 Nov. 1988; Nairobi Municipal Native Affairs Dept. AR 1939: 34.

anti-prostitution measures were implemented. The nascent licensing and produce inspection systems were inconsistently enforced due to lack of personnel, but monopolistic efforts which hurt small traders were encouraged. Paternalistic "protections" for African traders were instigated to limit the scale of their businesses and to reduce Asian competition. All of this happened in the context of major increases in the scale of the business of supplying Nairobi with dried staples and, increasingly, fresh vegetables, and a progressive segregation of women's and men's trade most evident in the differing scale of their businesses.

The groundwork was laid in this period for an increasingly segregated women's and men's trade, for the enforcement of very strict controls on traders and for evasions of those controls. Chapter IV will document the next phase of interactions between traders and various branches of government, when the exploratory and somewhat tentative efforts of the 1920s and 1930s were overtaken by unabashed autocracy. In the 1940s and 1950s not only was experimentation with beans largely abandoned in favor of export attempts that treated African farmers and traders arbitrarily, but also government efforts to control Africans acquired a more authoritarian nature. Regarding trade, persuasion was abandoned in favor of coercion which, inevitably, fell most heavily upon those with the fewest resources available to combat it, women farmers and traders. Both the arbitrariness of the controls and the ingenuity of the evasions then played a strong role in the creation of the Emergency situation of the 1950s.

III.2 A Kikuyu Market, 1930s

IV

"Various Nefarious Happenings": Trade, Wars, and Traders' War, 1940 to 1963

If in the 1920s and 1930s various manifestations of the Kenyan colonial government experimented with beans and explored forms of control over traders and trade, from the 1940s more rigorous efforts were implemented until the failure of that policy was manifest in the early 1960s. African trade lost autonomy under war conditions but developed adaptability and further capacity to evade controls. The struggle to maintain that autonomy became a fundamental part of the conflicts that evolved into the Kenyan independence movement. Women traders pursuing their usual rounds found that much of what they were accustomed to doing was becoming criminalized as regulations proliferated in the face of several wars--World War II, the 1950s Emergency, and what I have termed the first hawker war from about 1940 to 1963. Indeed, as trade and trade networks were becoming more elaborate, with women expanding their local trade into Nairobi on a more permanent basis, their commodities became subject to produce movement controls while their bodies were subjected to population movement controls enforced under the pressure of several political crises. From about 1940 to 1958 a more or less continuous state of emergency existed with regard to controlling the movement of Africans into and out of Nairobi. The declaration of Emergency in force from 1952 to 1960 was aimed as much at controlling a burgeoning contumacious Nairobi trading population as it was at putting down guerrilla warfare in the forest.[1] From about 1959 to 1963, although the formal Emergency was mostly over, an informal one continued with respect to controlling hawkers. The difficulty and expense of controlling the Nairobi African population, in fact, formed one motivation for some British officials to give up on the effort and pass it on to African successors.

The changes in women's trade entailed the further establishment of trade as a full-time occupation, lack of access to critical resources provided to certain male traders by government agencies, and controls aimed more at their economic than their sexual lives. Paradoxically, the general conflagration of World War II seems to have presented more opportunities for women traders than otherwise, while the Emergency presented more problems. The Emergency, along with the implementation of the Swynnerton Plan's privatization of land ownership, made many irrevocable changes. The Kikuyu population was scrambled in many areas by villagization

---

[1] Lonsdale, "Explanations," p. 168, unfortunately omitted Nairobi traders from his listing of groups who were particularly active in support of Mau Mau. Kershaw, *Mau Mau*, p. 221, noted that after World War II women were becoming more subject to urban problems like low wages, lack of housing, and crime.

and internments.[2] Many lost their land rights and never returned home, seeking land to buy or rent elsewhere. Before colonialism the Kikuyu were mobile and expansive, especially in the Kiambu frontier area. Colonial policies first fixed their boundaries with the establishment of the ethnically segregated African Reserves and then attempted to keep members of one African "tribe" from entering other "tribal" areas, a restriction which traders constantly contravened by maintaining old trade routes and connections, and eventually opening new ones. Despite the restrictions, many Kikuyu migrated as squatters to the Rift Valley and elsewhere; in the 1940s there were campaigns to repatriate squatters that placed more population pressure on Kiambu. Then, under the Emergency Nairobi became a haven for the landless, who made a living by their wits. Some traders continued their activities making the necessary adaptations for illegality, bore risks, rescued interned husbands' businesses, and proved themselves to be indomitable in the face of increasing government threats. Others stopped trading, were attacked, killed, or intimidated by the complications of alliance with either side. Whatever the actions of individual women traders, they and their men were caught up in a process of gendered class formation that irrevocably changed the division of labor in trade and the nature of patriarchal controls, while separating the interests of women from those of men.

The first section of this chapter analyzes elaborations in the organization of trade in and around Nairobi. The second continues the story of the evolution of the dried staples trade in Kiambu and its control. The third looks at an expanding market system in Kiambu and Nairobi, and at efforts at class formation by administrators expressed in granting privileged access to trade infrastructure for loyalists. The fourth documents the increasing repression of small-scale trade and traders in the 1940s and 1950s that played a strong role in fomenting both the urban rebellion of Mau Mau (the term applied by the British to the Land and Freedom independence movement), and a more intense hawker war. But the gendered nature of the growing class conflict changed, as will be evident in looking at the role of women in, and the impact on women traders of, the critical changes that took place in the 1940s and 1950s. These changes are clarified by the increased use of oral sources that show women's own perceptions of change.

Changes in the Organization of Trade

In the 1940s and 1950s a growing number of women traded as a full-time occupation in and around Nairobi, in a few cases influenced by a mother or mother-in-law's substantial involvement in trade. The pioneers were the relatively few women of the 1920s and 1930s and earlier who developed trade as a full-time occupation; those of the 1940s and 1950s who followed this pattern were also not numerous. Their numbers were reduced by government persecution but they persevered,

---

[2] ARC/MAA 2/3/36VII Central Province AR 1955: 35, estimated that over 80,000 huts were built by local authorities to house the "villagized" population.

some joining the Land and Freedom Army (LFA) or various trade and/or nationalist organizations. They were part of a mass of thousands of women whose daily activities fed Nairobi.

Men's and women's wholesale and retail trade continued their trajectories of specialization and differentiation in the 1940s and 1950s, with governmental efforts bent increasingly toward privileging some male traders. The intensity of these efforts heightened in the mid-1950s as part of the divide-and-conquer tactics undertaken to defeat the LFA, carrying out intentions already clear in the 1930s and 1940s. African male traders continued their efforts to form cooperatives or partnerships, the most successful operating small restaurants or chicken and egg businesses during World War II. In 1944 the Nairobi DC described the sensation caused by a group of African restaurateurs who purchased a downtown property for £15,000 at auction, especially when it was discovered that they only had £8500 in cash with which to do so (they were forbidden by law from borrowing the rest).[3]

Women's trade was also experiencing differentiation with the development of a relatively small group of those who could be called professional traders. A woman at Kawangware described the differences developing in women's trade in talking about her mother's activities in the 1940s. "It's not that she bought [sweet potatoes] then sold, no, she grew them. There's a difference because one can buy and resell or grow and sell. When I was a child, of course, we did grow and sell maize in debes at twenty-five shillings per debe." Her mother lived at Thogoto and sold at Wangige and Dagoretti Markets.[4] She differentiated between three levels of women's trade: the usual wholesale selling of maize, the selling of one's own produce at a market, and traveling around buying and selling at various markets. Officialdom did not usually pay much attention to the first two types in terms of regulations, but the third type, which involved more profits and mobility, incurred displeasure.

Humphrey exhibited a distinctly negative attitude when describing an increase in petty trading in South Nyeri in the early 1940s:

> An ugly development recently has been the petty trading done by women who, buying produce at one market, take it to a different part of the district and dispose of it at a handsome profit... The spread of petty trading ... has clearly gone too far, perhaps because of natural inclinations but largely because the cleverer Kikuyu see in it one way of adding to incomes that would otherwise be quite inadequate for their needs.

He was unusual among administrators in seeing both sides of the situation. If he condemned Kikuyu for moneygrubbing, he also saw their need to supplement their incomes. He spoke of them experiencing a rising sense of economic insecurity, cash crops squeezing out food crops, and the inability of many households to meet basic

---

[3] PC/CP 4/4/2 Nairobi AR 1944: 13. In 1941 a Municipal Native Affairs Officer estimated that while unskilled wage workers in Nairobi earned 12c per hour, hawkers could earn 40c. Onstad, "Life," pp. 47-48.

[4] Interview 581 Kawangware: 14 June 1988.

needs from subsistence agriculture. He therefore devised a strategy to be employed by Kikuyu households in which trade (presumably by men since he disapproved of women doing it) would add to their incomes. He estimated how much could be sold off as surplus from agricultural production by Kikuyu households; he assumed that 23% of the maize crop would be sold, 83% of the bean crop [!], and most of the English potato crop. Consistency was not his forte, since he also complained of Kikuyu selling too much of their production and therefore suffering malnutrition. His production figures were based on the assumption that each family would have about twelve acres of land, meaning that almost half would need to leave the land. No suggestion was made as to where they should go.[5]

There were, therefore, conditions that increasingly made trade an absolute imperative for most households. Women flocked to Nairobi, with the heightened demand of the military presence offering opportunities. If unwanted marriages, abusive husbands, forced labor, and landlessness through widowhood or divorce still exerted pressure on women to trade, so did the increased burden of rural labor obligations with the exodus of men from agriculture and the low level of plantation wages. The 1942 Nairobi Municipal Native Affairs Department Annual Report said that it was more due to difficulties at home than to the attractions of town that women ran away, adding, "Kikuyu girls require less excuse and now predominate amongst the young girls who have run away to town for its attractions... [I]t is not easy to make a girl stay home who has once enjoyed the idle life of town."[6] In the late 1940s and early 1950s the proportion of women among the Nairobi Kikuyu population rose sharply. Kamba women also began coming to Nairobi but not to stay, following "peregrinating habits." The situation in the Reserves was not good economically and the position of women in the household division of labor had been undermined. Kiambu, in particular, was becoming a bedroom community for Nairobi, with men leaving their wives to do more of the agricultural labor than previously, while socioeconomic differentiation proceeded apace.[7] The vegetable and fruit trade from Kiambu boomed during World War II and pineapples became a cash crop. At Wangige trade was enlivened by the presence of Italian prisoners-of-war, who traded clothes for tobacco and grew tomatoes as a cash crop. But the war also coincided with several droughts and trade restrictions occasioned by the necessity of feeding the military in Nairobi. Produce movement controls fell most heavily on traders going to Nairobi and were causal in the formation of a large underground economy. Commodities traded included fresh vegetables, maize, English potatoes,

---

[5] Even after land consolidation in Kiambu in the 1950s, the average landholding was 5.3 acres. Trench, *Men*, p. 270; Humphrey, "Thoughts," pp. 37-38, and "Relationship," pp. 9-10. See also PC/CP 4/4/2 Nairobi AR 1944: 13, for a negative view of Nairobi small traders that recommended furthering "fewer and more substantial traders with ... some training in commercial practice."

[6] ARC(MAA) 2/3/8III: 27.

[7] AA 13/1/8/9 Nairobi AR 1954: 3-4; Throup, *Origins*, pp. 77, 89.

pineapples, onions, and bananas, in particular.[8] For instance, in the early 1940s a number of women from Banana Hill near Karuri sold fresh vegetables, potatoes, and bananas door-to-door in Nairobi. They carried their babies in front and produce in *ciondo* (Kikuyu=baskets)[9] on their backs and traveled at night to avoid arrest. They often would stay several nights to do so. It was more profitable than local trade, partly because it was more risky.[10]

At the same time there was also the legal trade being carried out mostly by male traders, and we start to see the equation of legal with male, relatively capital intensive, licensed, infrastructure-based trade and illegal with female, poorly capitalized, unlicensed, little infrastructure trade. In 1940 the Kiambu DC described a typical transaction in produce as follows (I have added the probable gender of the participants). A (male or female) producer sold to a (male or female depending on the commodity) small itinerant trader at a village or from the farm, who sold to an African (male) plotholder in a local market, who sold to a small African (male) trader outside Nairobi wholesale market, who sold to an Indian (male) retailer inside the wholesale market, who sold at Nairobi retail market to consumers, the usual number of middlepersons being three to five.[11] The nature of the controls forced illegality on women's trade and affected its organization.

Households differed in their involvement in trade. Even though women were concentrated in small-scale retail trade, more were moving into mobile trade as retailers and wholesalers. If they were landless they had no choice. But even with land trade was often essential. Over a steaming mug of sweetened tea and milk around a hearthfire in 1988 three old friends in their seventies living at Githega (between Kiambu town and Gatundu) explained why they got involved in trade in the 1940s. They said that women older than themselves had seldom traded. One of them spoke for herself and her long-time companions in summing up reasons why even women with access to land traded at that time.

> Hey, hey! Why wouldn't anybody want to trade and earn a little money?! And buy a good dress. If you waited for your husband, a herdsman, where would you get that money? And with trading we'd be able to buy good clothes and be left with some profit. And we enjoyed it, of course. And what about keeping the children fed? We'd buy the beans, sell some, and take some home to cook for the children. We didn't want anything else. And besides, we didn't spend the whole day at home like the other women. *Their* children would come wailing about they were hungry, while *our* children were healthy.

---

[8] DC/KBU 1/41 Kiambu AR 1950: 8; LG 3/733 DC Nakuru to Commissioner for Local Government 16 Feb. 1942; Fisher, *Anatomy*, pp. 134-36.

[9] The type of sisal woven basket still used for hauling produce is a larger version of the Kenyan ones imported into the U.S. in large numbers in the 1980s and used as purses or bookbags.

[10] Interview Mwaura 4 Mar. 1988.

[11] DC/KBU 1/31 Kiambu AR 1940: 6.

These women traveled on foot to Limuru, some twenty kilometers away, carrying debes of beans. Paying school fees was not yet an issue for them, but extra income was certainly needed in the late 1940s.[12]

In this generation a few women learned about business from their parents, whereas previous generations were taught only agricultural skills (this was still true for a majority of traders in the small sample of fifty-six individuals with no significant difference by age group). An elderly woman living at Ndeiya described aptly the typical upbringing of most women. When asked what skills her parents taught her that were useful for trade, she replied, "What did they know? They only knew farming--a girl would work on the farm, fetch water and firewood, and work for the parents until married."[13] But some slightly younger women had different stories. A woman at Gikomba built an image of a prosperous cooperative family enterprise when she was growing up in Murang'a in the 1940s.

> My parents even as I was growing up were doing business. My father kept animals, cows and goats, and the farm. He even used to cut wattle bark and we'd take it for collection to factories where it was purchased. We also built houses on my father's plots; he has six plots in our shopping center. At the same time we were working on the farm to get food--bananas were plentiful, maize, beans and we had cows for milk and even sheep. Hence there's no problem at my father's even today because of the example he set for us.

A Kamba woman was taught the livestock trade by her father because he had no sons and therefore treated his seven daughters as if they were sons.[14]

Such training could also come from relatives by marriage. Sarah, a relatively prosperous stallholder selling fresh vegetables at Ngara, said that her mother-in-law taught her to trade in the 1940s. They pooled their crops of potatoes, green beans and peas, and fresh corn and traded to Limuru. This partnership lasted until her mother-in-law died during the Emergency, when Sarah continued alone. In 1987 Sarah was traveling around to various markets and farms in Kiambu to secure her supplies, helped by her twenty-five-year-old daughter with both farming and selling. This trading dynasty was one of the few of its kind among all of the samples.[15]

The power of example was extremely important for these women and sometimes gave them an advantage in trade. Sarah used her networks to maintain her supplies and knew every facet of the trade from growing to wholesaling. Njeri, raised in Nyeri, spoke proudly of her mother's activities in the early 1950s. She used to help her mother take bananas to sell at Karatina Market. "I realized doing business is good because I could see Mother with money. So even at the time I was picking

---

[12] Interview E Githega: 12 July 1988. Kershaw, *Mau Mau*, pp. 162-63, stressed that educating sons had become a high priority by this time, but not daughters.

[13] Interview C Ndeiya: 28 June 1988.

[14] Interviews 175, 253 Gikomba: 1 Mar., 8 Apr. 1988.

[15] Interview 51 Ngara: 22 Oct. 1987.

coffee on the plantations I used to say, if I had money I would start a business because my mother was doing it." On the plantation she had a consensual union with a landless coffeepicker. When he died, she continued picking coffee at Ruiru near Nairobi until she had saved Sh.250 to start trading. When she was sick for more than three days and could not work, she and her five children were evicted from the company housing they shared on the plantation. She then began traveling daily to Nairobi to sell beans at Nyamakima, but was having a hard time supporting her four children still at home, two older sons at school, and her oldest daughter's child. Moreover, Njeri herself was pregnant with her ninth child.[16] Clearly, Sarah's experience in Kiambu was more useful to her in establishing herself in business than was that of Njeri, who in any case lacked resources to do the successful juggling of farming and trade that Sarah managed. The differences between them well illustrate stratification among women traders.

The statistics regarding sources of starting capital from the large sample (N=995 persons in 1,492 trade occupations), when segregated by age cohort, confirm the increasing importance of family help in starting trade in the 1940s and 1950s. For instance, women over age fifty in 1987-88 got very little help with starting capital from relatives, while there was a steady increase in self-financed capital as a proportion of all sources as women got older (most starting capital, in 54% of the businesses, was derived from traders' own savings). While less than 1% of the businesses of women seventy and over ever received starting capital from parents, 23.2% of the businesses of women aged twenty to twenty-nine in 1987-88 did, with steadily increasing percentages for intermediate cohorts. A parallel change occurred regarding help with starting capital from spouses; no woman seventy or over ever got starting capital from her husband, compared to husbands being the source of starting capital in 29.9% of the businesses operated by women aged twenty to twenty-nine. The critical changes in family-supplied capital took place among women aged forty to fifty-nine, who relied on a number of relatives, affinal and agnatic, for starting capital. Male traders showed similar patterns, with 59.7% of businesses based on starting capital supplied by their own savings but less dramatic chronological differences. This change suggests that family attitudes toward women's involvement in trade were shifting toward approval, perhaps as an adaptation to necessity in the 1940s and 1950s.

In 1950-51 Fisher found that some women in Murang'a and Kiambu were traveling around from market to market bulking produce for sale. The older women were more likely to trade and leave younger women to do more of the farming. Profits were about 25 to 50% of the value of the produce, and traders varied the profit margin not by bargaining over the price but by varying the quantity per measure, a practice that is still prevalent. Most households' cash income came from trade. Men

---

[16] Interviews 142 Nyamakima: 7, 15 Jan. 1988. She had three more children by lovers after her husband's death.

who owned water mills for grinding maize skimmed off a profit of 30 to 60c per debe. Most traders had markets available to them within a twenty-minute walk,[17] although that did not mean that their trade was confined to that area.

By 1951 there were a number of changes in women's trade evident in markets, which surfaced in Fisher's survey of twenty-one markets in Murang'a and two in Kiambu.[18] This glimpse of older patterns and changes in process showed a gender division of commodities in markets related to the old gender identification of crops. Women were selling dried staples (*njahe* were most important among pulses), root crops except yams and Irish potatoes (usually called in Kenyan sources English potatoes), fresh vegetables except peas and cabbage, fruit, sugar cane, cooked foods and beverages except *chapatis*[19] and milk, firewood, pottery, baskets and sleeping mats, seeds, salt and ochre. Commodities sold by men included tobacco products, sponge tree yeast for making sugar cane beer, calabashes, ropes and leatherwork, wood and metal utensils and tools, furniture, livestock and related equipment, farm implements, imported goods, secondhand clothes, tire sandals, wooden combs, beads, *ciondo*, and beeswax. Commodities shared were green peas, yams, cabbages and potatoes, milk, cooking oil and fat, tea, basketry, vines for feeding livestock, pumice and talc, castor oil seeds, and dyes. While men were not nearly as numerous in the market as women, they were there in significant numbers selling both old commodities like livestock, tobacco and metalwork, and new imported goods like tin products and rubber sandals, both products of male industries generated under colonialism. Men also ran shops around the perimeter of the market selling an array of imported goods, some of which were becoming household necessities like soap and sugar. In addition to old commodities like dried staples, women were selling newly introduced produce like tomatoes, carrots, oranges, pineapples and passion fruit, as well as baked goods like scones and bread, and fritters. Boys were selling *chapatis*. By the 1950s, Fisher said, men had overcome some of their old reluctance to sell in the market; Kamba men were continuing their calabash trade, in any case. Some commodities had disappeared--skins, for instance. Most women were wearing European-type clothing. Women had created new industries from some imports, as men had. They brewed new dyes from teapackets and pencils, for instance.

The Dried Staples Trade: Exploding Controls in the 1940s and 1950s

Nowhere are the effects of increasingly draconian measures aimed at controlling trade more evident than with dried staples; they threatened women's attempts to increase the scale of their trade in the 1940s and 1950s. Kiambu's dried staples trade was deeply affected by World War II's emergency conditions. The swift growth of Nairobi provoked further desire by large maize producers to improve their profits. Kenya was also being asked to feed other British colonies, so export production was

---

[17] Interview Fisher 14 Oct. 1992. Fisher, *Anatomy*, pp. 130-41.

[18] The full results of her survey are presented in Robertson and Fisher, " Terrain."

[19] Originally an Indian food, a flat wheat bread similar to Lebanese pita bread.

encouraged.[20] African producers were forced to grow maize and women's compulsory labor was also employed in terracing, with British administrators judging chiefs' efficiency according to how much terracing had been accomplished. Military recruiting and wage labor removed most ablebodied men.[21] These conditions increased not only the scale of the regulation and the trade, but also of illicit trade. Price controls were imposed on staples in Nairobi at the beginning of the war; maize control was promulgated in 1942 and remained relatively unchanged through 1990. The establishment of marketing boards proliferated; by 1945 coffee, sisal, pyrethrum, passion fruit, flax, dairy and pork products, as well as maize and pulses were covered, by 1961 cotton, beef, wheat and canning vegetables.[22] The desire for protected prices for plantation/ranch products is evident from this list, as well as widening efforts to eliminate Asian and African large-scale traders.

The pricing function of what is now called the National Cereals and Produce Board differed according to the race and gender of the producers and the crop. The grading process evolved into a policy of imposing hidden costs on African producers, who were in effect paid less for their produce, which was presumed to be lower in quality. White producers were paid more because they were said to have covered their own processing and transport.[23] But kinds as well as quality of crops received different treatment. The profits from beans went mostly to their small-scale female producers; they were systematically underpriced in relation to maize. The production of beans was more expensive than of maize, requiring more labor and yielding less per acre. Since the control price of maize was usually artificially high, we can expect that the ratio of bean to maize prices for controlled produce would be lower than for retail uncontrolled prices, and so it proved. From 1912 to 1939 (before price controls) the ratio of bean to maize retail prices was 1.74:1 compared to 1.58:1 for control prices between 1942 and 1962.[24] Agricultural officers frequently complained about the artificially low bean control prices.[25] Price controls for beans furthered illicit trade and removed incentives to produce them for export.

---

[20] Agr 4/527 Director of Agriculture to Senior Agriculture Officer Central Province, 11 Feb. 1942.

[21] Trench, *Men*, p. 206. Kershaw, *Mau Mau*, p. 162, noted that women did far more government-required communal labor than men did in the late 1940s, and especially resented the terracing work that took away from planting time.

[22] Jones, *Marketing*, p. 198. PC/CP 4/4/1 Nairobi AR 1939: 12.

[23] The history of maize control in Kenya after World War II has received extensive treatment elsewhere. See van Zwanenberg and King, *History*; Jones, *Marketing*; Miracle, "Appraisal"; Keyter, *Maize Control*. One topic needing further examination is the diversity of control agents, in particular the role of the LNCs. See, for example, PC/CENTRAL 2/1/13 minutes Kiambu LNC: 29 Aug.-2 Sept. 1948.

[24] These figures do not reflect the full discrepancy before independence since they are based on control prices to African producers rather than European. The ratios were calculated from over a hundred sources ranging from area annual and marketing board reports to informants in 1987-88 markets. Prices in the same currency for the same amounts of the same type of maize or beans were used.

[25] Agr 4/239 Assistant Agriculture Officer Kiambu to Senior Agriculture Officer Central Province 21 Oct. 1946.

IV.1 A Snack Bar at Geitwa Market, 1951: Women and Men Share *Ucuru*

IV.2 Geitwa Market, 1951: Men, Women and Calabashes

Price controls were difficult to enforce, especially when there was also a prohibition on selling commodities until the market for them was officially declared open.[26] In 1941 thousands of bags of maize were traded along the boundaries of white settler and African areas in Kiambu according to L. A. Elmer, a seasoned agriculture officer, which caused him to doubt the wisdom of even trying enforcement. The beginning of maize control in 1942 "caused a great deal of dislocation of normal trade channels."[27] Various agriculture officers fretted about how to get the situation under control. They felt that they had the roads fairly well covered, but illegal produce was headloaded and carried on donkeys. G. J. Gollop, an assistant agriculture officer, said that the biggest "leakage" was by hawkers to Europeans' houses in Nairobi. As it would have been difficult and too costly to hire enough staff to do the necessary night work to enforce the prohibitions, he suggested that the police should simply round up Nairobi hawkers. This consideration undoubtedly combined with the security concerns to promote the change in hawker policy described in the last section of this chapter. But the inequity of arresting hawkers and not customers disturbed him.

> I deplore the idea of prosecuting natives selling produce illicitly to Europeans who offer prices so high as to tempt the natives to sell. When the person who creates the black market is to be prosecuted together with the supplier then we shall have a fair chance of clearing up the matter in an equitable way.[28]

Since it was out of the question politically to arrest European customers, the hawkers bore the brunt of official displeasure.

Persistent food shortages caused bans on the export of maize and beans from Kiambu in 1942, 1943 and 1945, and routine evasion of export controls.[29] All produce suffered "meteoric" price rises with a drought and famine in 1943-44, causing stringent control efforts. Officials worried constantly about insufficient food supplies in Kiambu. But by 1943 Kiambu was wholly committed to growing vegetables for export to Nairobik, which were not eaten locally to any significant extent; the Kiambu DC warned the LNC that local growers needed to replace growing export vegetables with food crops. The value of export vegetables exceeded that of all other exports put together in both 1943 and 1944. War conditions also prevented the importation of cheap consumer goods, which usually did not make it to areas outside of Nairobi and so were in high demand by traders. Aside from futile efforts to stop produce movement, there were other policies implemented to boost food supplies.

---

[26] Agr 4/527 corres. Agriculture Officers May-June 1942.

[27] DAO/KBU 1/1/92 Assistant Agriculture Officer Kiambu to Senior Agriculture Officer Central Province 17 Feb. 1941; ARC(MAA) 2/3/8 IV Central Province AR 1942: 1.

[28] Agr 4/574 Assistant Agriculture Officers Meru and Fort Hall to Senior Agriculture Officer Central Province 29 Dec. 1942, 4 Jan. 1943; Assistant Agriculture Officer Kiambu to Senior Agriculture Officer Central Province 29 Dec. 1942.

[29] DAO/KBU 1/1/92 Assistant Agriculture Officer Kiambu to V.K. Jani and Co. 22 June 1943. DC/KBU 1/36 Kiambu AR 1945: 12.

The Kiambu LNC was given large sums of money to purchase and distribute food but could not find enough. Nonetheless, according to the DC, no one starved to death.[30]

Things were worse in Nairobi, where colonialist values regarding African persons were evident in the rationing of foodstuffs established in 1942. The DC boasted that only the "native community" had suffered food shortages and listed categories of persons to whom food coupons had been refused: "some women, numbers of independent workers like superfluous hawkers and also employed Africans whom we thought unnecessary, e.g. large staffs of golf courses." In such matters women's and children's identities were recognized separately from men's in order to deny them coupons; that is, there was no family coupon just as there was no family wage for Nairobi Africans. Africans were allowed less meat than Europeans and Asians. African women were given one-way tickets to leave Nairobi to ameliorate the shortages. A municipal soup canteen was opened to feed the African population, the first of several war-induced city-owned businesses which competed with women's trade.[31]

Feeding Nairobi was not helped by the complications imposed by the controls, which some officials realized. The Kiambu DC refused to impose further price controls, saying that they would just create a blackmarket. The amount of disappearing produce rose considerably; maize was always of chief concern but beans also drew attention. Estimates came in that between July and December of 1942 over 3500 90 kilo bags of maize had been sold illegally at Nyeri, and 4000 bags of beans at Fort Hall (Murang'a) in 1944. The Central Province Agriculture Officer made an interesting distinction between "women's" and "trade" markets in describing the illicit trade in staples at Fort Hall and Embu. "Big sales are taking place in the womens' [sic] markets of Fort Hall and Embu to Machakos, Kitui and Nyeri natives, who come on foot or by taxi to buy small loads at very big prices. While this price temptation holds it is thought unlikely that the surplus produce will reach trade markets." Only unpopular Boston beans were being sold to Control; Canadian Wonder were selling to Machakos at astronomical prices.[32] This widespread evasion of the price and movement controls took place in the face of stringent laws punishing infractions; the 1943 Defence (Controlled Produce) and 1944 Defence (Control of Maize) Regulations imposed a fine of up to £500 or two years of imprisonment (these were still in force during the Emergency).[33]

---

[30] KNA Reel 85 of microfilm: minutes Kiambu LNC 16-17 Sept. 1943: 7; DC/KBU 1/34-35 Kiambu AR 1943: 5; 1944: 8-9.

[31] PC/CP 4/4/2 Nairobi AR 1943: 1-2, 6-7.

[32] PC/CENTRAL 2/1/13 minutes Kiambu LNC 7-9 Feb.; 3-5 July 1944; Agr 4/574 Assistant Agriculture Officer Nyeri to Maize Controller 15 Feb. 1943; Director of Agriculture to Senior Agriculture Officer Central Province 1 Mar. 1944; Agr 4/527 Senior Agriculture Officer Central Province with Produce Controller Nairobi 1, 4 Oct. 1943. He noted that most beans were being headloaded out of Central Province (to Director of Agriculture 7 Oct. 1943).

[33] Agr 4/527 Director of Agriculture to all agriculture officers 17 Mar. 1944; Assistant Agriculture Officer Northern Frontier to Senior Agriculture Officer 5-6 Apr. 1944; DAO/KBU 1/1/93 Kiambu Monthly Marketing Reports Mar. 1957: 8; Apr. 1957: 3.

The magnitude of the evasions of controls, with produce and livestock moving freely in many directions, accompanied by genuine concern about feeding Nairobi, prompted exasperation, ethnic slurs, and a shifting of blame among authorities. The Director of Agriculture was highly offended when the Fort Hall Agriculture Officer in March 1944, upon being asked for figures regarding surplus beans available for marketing, sent back a terse telegram saying, "No beans expected come on market whilst black market flourishes," and demanded to know what he was doing to stop it. The Kikuyu were said to have an individualistic "me-first-and-damn-everyone-else" profit-seeking mentality reckless of the consequences of selling off all surpluses. When they persisted in continuing the illicit produce trade to Machakos and Kitui, one official eventually gave up on enforcement efforts, saying, "the Kikuyu would undoubtedly have evaded the Regulations and managed to make all the maize to disappear from the markets and subsequently sold it [*sic*] at an even blacker price."[34] The Kiambu LNC passed the buck (after requesting that the price of livestock be controlled because of inflation in bridewealth payments) saying, "It was difficult to control as there was very little authority Chiefs could exercise over the women as it was possible for them to buy or sell wherever they pleased throughout the district and particularly at villages or in the bush." Agriculture officers spent much of their time trying to stop illegal movement of produce at the expense of more productive activities.[35]

When the war ended the controls did not, nor did Kiambu's export of produce to Nairobi diminish. In 1946 the street price of beans was frequently twice the control price.[36] Price controls on pulses were therefore removed with the encouragement of agriculture officers concerned about soil conservation. As a consequence acreage under beans increased at the expense of maize to the dissatisfaction of the Supply Council in charge of ensuring maize supplies and promoting exports to Britain. Bean exports were going mainly to France and India, and it looked as if maize would need to be imported. Therefore, in 1948 control prices to African producers were reimposed on beans that reflected deductions for traders' commission, transport, a marketing charge, storage and shrinkage, an inspection fee, and a cess for the African [formerly Local Native] District Council (ADC). Discriminatory price structures that effectively halved the price of maize and beans to African producers, as well as poor crops in the late 1940s, kept official supplies low and promoted covert market-

---

[34] Agr 4/574 Director of Agriculture to Senior Agriculture Officer Central Province 1 Mar. 1944; DC/KBU 1/33, 1/36 Kiambu AR 1942: 2; 1945: 12.

[35] PC/CENTRAL 2/1/13 minutes Kiambu LNC 7-9 Feb. 1944. In 1945-46 attempts to control livestock movement impinged upon a lively Kikuyu-Maasai border illegal trade and became embroiled in a series of raids and counter-raids (MAA 7/736). Dept. of Agriculture AR 1945: 115, 24, 9-10.

[36] Dept. of Agriculture AR 1946: 52; Agr 4/239 Ass't Agriculture Officer Kiambu to Sr Agriculture Officer Central Province 21 Oct. 1946; Acting Director of Agriculture to R.P. Armitage, Agriculture Production Board 5 Nov. 1946.

ing. Evasion of maize inspection and movement prohibitions continued on a large scale, especially in the Ukambani trade.[37]

Meanwhile, African traders wishing to buy produce legally faced daunting obstacles. Petrol rationing made motorized transport more difficult. Musa Nderi wrote to the Kiambu Senior Marketing Officer in May 1949 concerning his wish to buy dried beans at Limuru, only to receive a curt reply from Gollop, then Senior Assistant Agriculture Officer, saying that in order to do so he had to rent a plot in a government-gazetted (see below) market class A or B, but that the export of these crops from Kiambu was in any case forbidden. The beans purchased had to be inspected to ascertain that they were without weevil damage, clean, dry, had no more than three discolored (presumably colored differently from the rest) beans per 100, and were properly sewn and packed in new bags. If the bags were reused or faulty the price of new ones was deducted from the purchase price. Buyers paid five to ten cents per bag inspected, and re-inspections took place at central markets.[38]

Leading up to the declaration of the Emergency in 1952 things were clearly completely out of hand from the point of view of enforcing controls on trade. Despite prohibitions on produce movement in 1950-51 a September 1950 crop inspection report stated,

> The headload traffic of Maize, Beans, etc., from Embu, Meru and Kikuyu into Ukambani has achieved vast proportions. It is estimated in Fort Hall that practically the whole bean surplus has gone out through Thika to Machakos. In lower Embu literally hundreds of bags are leaving daily by several routes... [T]raffic of this magnitude is not entirely by foot safari and must be assisted by lorry transport at both ends.

A produce inspector at Meru who refused to yield to bribes or mild physical intimidation finally was held up with a shotgun; thousands of bags escaped control. At the other end it was estimated that only 25% of the produce reaching the Nairobi market had been inspected.[39]

In this context the Emergency regulations on African trade represent a last ditch effort by British and African authorities to control and profit from it. The conduct of legal trade in produce from African areas to Nairobi was restricted to "known loyalists." In 1958 there were no more than 4000 certificate-holding loyalists, who

---

[37] Agr 4/71 memos Director of Agriculture 6 Apr. 1948; Acting Director of Agriculture to Produce Controller Nairobi 18 Oct. 1948; DAO/KBU 1/1/92 Senior Assistant Agriculture Officer Fort Hall to Marketing Officer Kiambu 2 Dec. 1947. DC/KBU 1/39 Kiambu AR 1948: 9. Dept. of Agriculture AR 1948: 66.

[38] Agr 4/527 Asst Agriculture Officer Embu to DC Embu 17 Oct. 1941; DAO/KBU 1/1/218 corres. 10 May 1949; Agr 4/68 Marketing Officer Nyeri, Instructions to Produce Inspectors 10 Sept. 1951. PC/CENT 2/1/13 minutes Kiambu LNC Trades and Markets Sub-Committee 25-27 July 1950.

[39] Dept. of Agriculture AR 1950: I, 30, 37; DC/KBU 1/42 Kiambu AR 1951: 16, 30; Agr 4/510 Central Province Crop Inspection Report Sept. 1950.

were mostly chiefs, headmen, teachers and government employees,[40] categories which either excluded women completely or included very few indeed. Registration of private land ownership carried out in Kiambu under the Swynnerton Plan also privileged male loyalists. The interests of small traders were regarded as inimical to the government, partly because of the growing evasion of controls. Many male owners of small shops in urban and rural areas led the resistance movement, their resentment fuelled by the many restrictions on trade and their skills in evading the laws honed by participation in illegal trade. Especially important were squatter traders and artisans on European farms.[41]

Women traders, however, faced so many obstacles that many abandoned their efforts. Movement restrictions were not only increased but also enforced. Emergency measures included impediments to illicit trade such as curfews, confinement to strategic villages, confiscation of trucks, barbed wire, ditches around villages, and clearance of vegetation around settlements, while very few women could afford or obtain licenses. Beating and robbing traders was a sport practiced by both sides. Those who supplied the forest fighters or urban guerrillas ran great risks. Some helped voluntarily and were usually interned for it. Others had no choice.[42] The congestion of Nairobi offered more opportunities than the villages. "What one had to do in the village was to make sure she did not meet with either the Mau Mau or the government police for fear of being killed," one woman commented, while another said, "Both were our enemies." In Kiambu over 12,000 Africans were detained by 1956 and many more confined to strategic villages. By 1955 over a million Kikuyu and Embu had been forced into 854 villages with quarter-acre plots to cultivate, on which loyalists were allowed to build square houses and suspected Mau Mau round huts.[43] Among the casualties were 12,590 considered to be Mau Mau and 1880 persons killed by the LFA (including fifty-eight whites and approximately 600 loyalist Homeguards). If the killings were unequally distributed in favor of the Europeans, the propaganda was also and generated much fear of Mau Mau. Many people fled to Nairobi because of increasing landlessness, compulsory labor levies in rural areas, starvation due to restrictions on cultivation associated with villagization, and persecution when chiefs used the Emergency to settle old scores.[44] Despite these measures and perhaps partly because of the commotion, the illicit marketing of produce into Nairobi continued, but was restricted to supplying Africans. The considerable trade

---

[40] AA 13/1/8/9 Nairobi AR 1954: 20; Manley, *Marketing*, p. 49.

[41] Furedi, "Composition," pp. 499, 503.

[42] Two traders of the fifty-six in the small sample were interned for helping. Mugo, "Role," pp. 215-16.

[43] Davison and Women, *Voices*, pp. 161, 52; Bates, "Origins," pp. 13-14; Etherton, "Mathare Valley," p. 6.

[44] Lonsdale, "Mau Maus," pp. 398-99; Dickerman, "Africans," pp. 12, 18-20, 37-41. Thuku, *Autobiography*, pp. 69-72, by then a prominent prosperous loyalist, claimed that he hated Mau Mau because they killed women and children, and that some women took refuge in his compound for protection. He sometimes listened to confessions along with British officials.

of livestock with Ukambani, however, diminished substantially because of compulsory destocking and the Emergency movement restrictions.[45]

In Kiambu it was clear that unlicensed trade in produce was dangerous; the number of purchasers of licenses went from sixty-seven to more than 850 in 1954, accompanied by bribery of corrupt ADC officials and the imposition of a new cess in 1956 on fruit and vegetable transport. Annoyance at the corruption caused the marketing officer to entertain no new license applications for two years.[46] Administrators' concern about controlling the rural produce trade related more to leakage of food to the guerrilla fighters than to eliminating illegal trade per se. Movement and marketing controls on staples like maize and beans hit Kiambu hard because of its greater dependence on imported staples and the necessity to feed Nairobi. By this time feeding Kiambu alone required importing approximately 100,000 bags of maize annually. Thus, a 1957 African Foodstuffs Ordinance specifically prohibited export of maize, maize meal, sorghum, millet, and dried peas and beans from the Kikuyu Native Land Unit in Kiambu.[47] The rural focus of controls on Kiambu, Fort Hall, Nyeri, Embu and Meru left the illegal Nairobi trade relatively unimpeded, but better suited to tough individuals who could protect themselves either physically or by corruption. Dried staples from Ukambani continued to move by illicit routes into Nairobi.[48]

Paradoxically, the Emergency population movement restrictions aimed particularly at Kikuyu, Embu and Meru privileged those closest to Nairobi by granting them superior access to Nairobi markets. This aspect especially applied to the relatively uncontrolled fresh vegetable and fruit trade. In 1953 the Kiambu Agriculture Officer complained of the large illicit banana trade to Nairobi; by 1958 when some of the Emergency controls were being lifted, a surplus of bananas flooded the Mincing Lane (now called Wakulima, Kiswahili=farmers) wholesale market in Nairobi through legitimate channels. The Kiambu Marketing Officer seconded the request by some "loyal individuals" to be allowed to ship some of the surplus bananas to the Rift Valley, but noted that, "Most of the Banana traders would fall in the category of 'small fry' but between them they regularly export 100 tons of bananas per month to Mincing Lane." He conveyed to his superior complaints from women traders regarding the drop in (uncontrolled) prices, and noted the privileged position of Kiambu traders.

> Vegetable traders are complaining of difficuly [sic] in disposing of produce at reasonable prices in Mincing Lane. Having had the complete monopoly during the

---

[45] CS 1/14/33 minutes Kiambu African District Council (ADC) Trade and Markets Sub-Committee 21 Jan. 1954; DC/KBU 1/45 Kiambu AR 1954: 13.

[46] CS 1/14/33 minutes Kiambu ADC 6 Apr. 1954; 13-14 Feb. 1956 App.C.

[47] DAO/KBU 1/1/93 Legal Notice 107. Such action normally took the form of temporary bans by proclamation.

[48] Nairobi African Affairs Dept. AR 1955: 165; DAO/KBU 1/1/93 Report of Marketing Survey in Central and Southern Provinces 31 July 1956: 18-19, 2-3.

Emergency, I feel Kiambu traders must now accept a spirit of competion [*sic*] from other districts and capture this market, as they should be able to do instead of sitting back and complaining bitterly.[49]

On the eve of independence, despite continuing and widespread evasion of controls[50] and investigative reports encouraging the Kenyan government to lift trade restrictions such as price controls, the regulations continued. The most bizarre evidence of this persistence in the face of criticism comes from a Ministry of Agriculture Working Party's response to the 1956 Royal Commission Report. One recommendation of the Report was that "Government policy should aim at bringing about a situation where it will not be necessary to rely on a system of local self-sufficiency in food production; this entails improving communications and removing unnecessary obstacles to trade." The working party accepted this recommendation but blamed recalcitrant African farmers who wanted to feed themselves for the problems with marketing. "This is in fact the aim of controlled marketing in Kenya and the objective of Government policy. The reluctance of the African to give up growing his own food, and the need to develop the right balance in his production, must make the change gradual." This stunning and, one suspects, willful ignorance of the impact of the severe regulations in force in 1956 upon Kiambu, not self-sufficient in staples by any means, shows the distance of upper British administrators from the local African population, as does the subsequent denial of the importance of cash crops and the underground economy. The Commission recommended that, "Efforts should not be wasted in trying to regulate the market where it is impossible to do so owing to extensive black-marketing." The response was, "The investigations of the Price Controller may show that the wiser course is to overhaul the system rather than to abandon it. It is agreed that administrative officers should not waste their time on these matters, where such time really is wasted." Indeed. In both responses recommendations were accepted and then undermined.[51]

There are several aspects of the controls affecting trade in the late colonial period worth analyzing beyond the usual critique of price controls that focuses on impediments to free market mechanisms. The Central Province chief agriculture officer raised one of them in 1954 when he described the functions of his four marketing officers. "This title is a complete misnomer and will remain so until Assistant Agriculture Officers with an active interest in marketing are seconded for Marketing duties." He went on to complain that they were paid and appointed by Maize Control and, "consider their duties begin and end with diverting controlled produce into the Controllers' Godowns [warehouses]. Their interest in finding markets and

---

[49] Agr 4/365 Kiambu Agriculture AR 1953: B1. DAO/KBU 1/1/148 Safari Reports Marketing Officer Kiambu to Agriculture Officer Kiambu 21 June, 27 Sept., 15 Nov. 1958, 24 Jan. 1959.

[50] For the early 1960s see DAO/KBU 1/1/218 Marketing Officer Kiambu to Agriculture Officer Kiambu 17 Feb. 1960. Central Province Marketing Board Second Annual Report 1960-61: 4.

[51] MAA 9/993 "Report of the Ministerial Working Party Set Up to Consider Chapter 7 of the Marketing and Distributive System" [of the Royal Commission Report, 1956], pp. 8-9.

improving the quality of non-scheduled crops is conspicuous by its absence." It is doubtful that this result was envisaged when the first Kiambu marketing officer was appointed for African produce in 1936 through a Carnegie Trust grant.[52] The original rationale for imposing controls was to improve African cash income and therefore their ability to pay taxes. But, when many traders proved recalcitrant, this policy was eventually corrupted by the colonial mission into a desire to control trade as an extension of controlling traders. It prevented all but a few elite African collaborators from profiting lest they threaten the survival of the colonial state. Dried staple movement controls, originally imposed in order to even out supplies during famines, ultimately fought the attempts by a lively underground economy to do exactly that. Marketing cesses, originally aimed at providing funds for local development, were used for operating expenses and as slush funds by ADCs, whose powers were greatly increased by the Emergency regulations.[53] All along the line monopolistic tendencies grew, especially at the wholesale level. If African farmers were subject to a discriminatory official price structure, African small traders faced equally oppressive oligopolistic trade conditions, as well as physical and political barriers. Resources devoted to controlling trade absorbed most of the Kiambu local budget, while cesses collected by ADCs furthered monopolies. The model presented to Kenya's future rulers was not a felicitous one: a government that demanded that most of its citizens do for it what it would not do for them.

The Market System in the 1940s and 1950s: Privileging Access to Infrastructure in Kiambu

In the 1940s and 1950s further trade controls were promulgated that focused on an expanding legal market system, developed by the administration to increase both profits from the taxation of trade and to confine trade to certain areas. Hence a new category of regulations developed, market-based controls aimed at more prosperous traders selling from fixed locations. The distinction of market-based controls from hawker policy aimed at small-scale often mobile traders is emblematic of class formation among traders, the segregation of the insiders from the outsiders. Market policy became one element of a broad-based attempt by the colonialists to promote loyalist interests by giving them privileged access to infrastructure. The sections below on market-based policies in Kiambu and Nairobi not only demonstrate how the colonial administration privileged certain male traders in order to create a "propertied" entrepreneurial class, but also how Emergency policy purposefully strategized gender roles for those traders by providing unequal access to practical education. Hawker policy will be looked at more specifically in the last section.

---

[52] Agr 4/116 Central Province Agriculture AR 1954: 12-13; Dept. of Agriculture AR 1936: I, 91.

[53] DAO/KBU 1/1/93 Report of a Marketing Survey in Central and Southern Provinces 1956: 24; Kitching, *Class*, p. 197.

Before the 1930s most Kiambu markets were local creations, sometimes ratified by administrative approval. In the 1930s, however, the administration for the
first time began taking the lead in platting new markets for the purposes of controlling the staples trade. By 1945 there were sixteen gazetted markets and 108 trading
sites in Kiambu. The administration of markets was the responsibility of the fourteen
chiefs of the LNC that allocated market plots, always a matter of great moment for
its Trade Committee.[54] Most African applicants received one, but war veterans got
preference. Asians or their agents did not prosper in this process, however. Competition with Asians over selling space surfaced in a conflict over hawkers' licenses
issued to traders from Nairobi. The World War II consumer good shortages persisted
to some extent in the late 1940s and 1950s. Some Asians used African agents in the
reserves to sell profitable imported goods, which were given out to sellers on a quota
system based on past performance, putting many traders at a disadvantage.[55] Some
tried to get around the problem by group buying, but many had to buy at retail prices
from Asian traders, meaning that the final sale price was inflated. Less desirable
goods were often sold to shopkeepers in rural areas by Nairobi wholesalers, disad-
vantaging the shops in the competition with the hawkers who were serving as agents
for Asian merchants. Hence the attack by the LNC on Nairobi male hawkers was
understandable. The LNC managed to persuade some British officials to try to even
up the situation regarding supplies of imported goods, but not to prohibit hawking in
Kiambu in 1945.[56] By 1948 hawkers were defined as a "menace" in Kiambu markets,
were banned, and remained so throughout the Emergency.[57]

The Kiambu LNC and British officials agreed upon the desirability of keeping
women from going to Nairobi during and after World War II, as did male traders.
The Kenya African Traders and Farmers Association requested the government to get
chiefs to stop "native women from selling things in towns," except in markets.[58] The
attempt to stop women hawking to Nairobi entered into deliberations over the siting
of markets. Consistent with British efforts to promote large-scale trading by making
the supply process more efficient in their view, the Provincial Commissioner told the
Kiambu LNC in 1944 that women wasted a lot of time carrying loads from one market to another and that, if they created a good central market in Kiambu, people could
bring large quantities and "save sale by head loads," a solution that would have cut
most women's profits. After the war the LNC took up Vidal's earlier suggestion that

---

[54] PC/CENT 2/1/13 minutes Kiambu LNC 4 Feb. 1946: 1-3; 15 Oct. 1946.

[55] DC/KBU 1/32 Kiambu AR 1941: 11; (Reel 85) minutes Kiambu LNC: 12-13 Aug. 1941; Native
Affairs Dept. AR 1946-47: 69-70; 1939-45: 22; ARC(MAA) 2/3/36VI Central Province AR 1947: 23.

[56] DC/KBU 1/38 Kiambu AR 1947: 13; 1/36 Kiambu AR 1945: 18; PC/CENT 2/1/13 minutes Kiambu LNC: 8 Feb. 1950: 3; 13-15 Mar. 1945: 2; ARC/MAA 2/3/36VI Central Province AR 1945: 27.

[57] DC/KBU 1/39 Kiambu AR 1948: 19. The hawker "menace" was also a subject of much discussion among white settlers over a long period. MCI 6/881 District Council Office Clerk Supervisor
Naivasha to Commissioner for Local Government 17 May 1941; DC/KBU 1/46 Kiambu AR 1957: 35.

[58] Agr 4/68 minutes Kenya African Traders and Farmers Association 29 May 1942.

IV.3 No Time to Waste: Basketweaving while Selling Pots, 1951

IV.4 Geitwa Market, 1951:
Women Sellers in Mixed Dress

peripheral markets be established around Nairobi by recommending that a market be established in the Muthaiga area "with a view to stopping women hawkers from entering the town." They asked the Nairobi Municipal Council (NMC) to stop issuing hawkers' licenses to women and to enforce the law against hawking without a license. Later, when problems were encountered in finding a market site at Muthaiga, the Kiambu LNC President said that barring women hawkers from going to Nairobi was only a stopgap; "the real answer to the whole question was cooperative [male] marketing of produce."[59] In other words, men and women were seen as being in direct competition and women's niche as small retailers or wholesalers was to be eliminated by more organized male selling. Mobile selling by women was particularly frowned upon.

Kiambu was involved in the 1950s freedom struggle early on (oathtaking there first came to the attention of the authorities in 1950, when it was declared illegal).[60] But rural markets did not serve the purposes of freedom fighters well in the 1950s. They were easier to control than the dispersed homesteads. Far from being places where Africans organized, prosperous Africans and Asians there were viewed as likely collaborators with the regime. Markets were raided by the LFA and a few shopkeepers killed.[61] Shopowners also had to worry about the other side. Homeguards hung around the markets, sometimes vandalizing the shops of those viewed as Mau Mau sympathizers. The existence of smaller markets and isolated shops worried the authorities lest their shopowners be helping Mau Mau; they were routinely closed down. In the late 1950s when markets were allowed to reopen, loyalists got preference in license allocations; ex-detainees were denied them.[62]

Nairobi Markets and the Emergency

If rural markets lost their function as a political gathering place for men under the Emergency, with shopkeepers suffering persecution from both sides, urban markets became focal points for African political action, their volatile crowded spaces providing solidary anonymity. A number of factors helped make the Land and Freedom movement an urban phenomenon as well as a rural one. Among them was discontent with the Nairobi trade infrastructure. Nairobi had a critical shortage of

---

[59] PC/CENT 2/1/13 minutes Kiambu LNC 11-14 Dec. 1944; 23-25 Nov. 1948; 26-28 Apr. 1949: 2.

[60] DC/KBU 1/41 Kiambu AR 1950: 1; MAA 9/835. Governor's Order in Council 12 Aug. 1950.

[61] LG 3/2434 Secretary of African Affairs to Secretary for Local Government, Health and Housing 11 Sept. 1957; Itote, *Mau Mau,* p. 140. Kershaw, *Mau Mau,* p. 250, mentioned both the notoriety some Homeguards earned for their violence and extortion and that some "gang" members who carried out the Marige massacre were "boys" who hung out at Marige Market in Kiambu.

[62] CS 1/14/33 minutes Kiambu ADC: 30 Oct. 1956; ARC/MAA 2/3/36VII Central Province AR 1953: 37; 1954: 24; LG 3/2700 minutes Kiambu ADC 29-30 July 1957: 7. LG 3/2434 Draft Minute Council of Ministers Nov. 1957; Permanent Secretary for Commerce and Industry with Secretary for Local Government, Health and Housing 19 Nov., 16 Dec. 1958; Commissioner for Local Government to Clerk Nakuru Town Council 29 Nov. 1958; LG 3/2701 minutes Kiambu ADC 3 Feb. 1956: 2; DC/KBU 1/45 Kiambu AR 1956: 30.

market space; yet, rather than improving it, further constriction was caused by the application of regulations. For instance, in 1951 the structures at Shauri Moyo Market were quite dilapidated, but they were required to accommodate traders evicted from verandahs along River Road. In July 1952 there was an attack on the Master of Municipal Market, which was then raided twice by the police to arrest illegal African traders. A successful two-day boycott of vegetable supplies organized by the vegetable traders ensued. The mayor of Nairobi was then forced to negotiate a settlement to stop it.[63] The traders were clearly fed up with such harassment and organizing to resist.

Then there was the issue of the competition offered to traders by municipally owned shops. From the beginning of the policy in the 1940s there were protests over it. By 1950 the number of municipally owned shops had grown to forty-eight. In the 1950s the managers of such shops were African men selected for their loyalist sentiments; they complained of competition from milk hawkers. In 1951, while trying to eliminate milk hawkers, officials raised the price of milk by 20%, causing resentment.[64] That the aim of the authorities was to control trade as well as traders is shown by the enforcement of Emergency regulations and the tinkering with market and shop trade. By 1957 there were sixty-four municipally owned shops. While privately owned shops in African locations always outnumbered those of the municipality, the Emergency caused their numbers to drop from 174 in 1950 to 146 in 1957. Meanwhile, African retail market fee collection rose steadily and dramatically during the Emergency because of the restrictions that were being enforced on people trading outside of the markets, the raising of fees, and the reconstruction of markets. In 1951 only Sh.107,286 was collected; by 1955 the sum was Sh.345,925, a jump of over 300%. The number of market stalls available to traders dropped from over a thousand in 1951 to just over 500 in 1956, and the number of legal African markets went from four to two, meaning that fewer people were paying more taxes. In 1953-54 the legal portions of both Shauri Moyo and Kariakor Markets were extended, which was one reason for the large jump in market tax income in 1953, as was the increase in market fees.[65] Clearly, the government used the Emergency to get the markets under control, and to make a profit in doing so. All along it was also clear that only draconian measures could accomplish that goal.

---

[63] LG 3/3141 minutes NMC African Affairs Committee 25 Jan., 3 Oct. 1951; NMC AR 1952: 17, 23, 30.

[64] LG 3/2825 minutes Nairobi African Advisory Council Trade Committee 11 June 1957; AA 13/1/8/9 Nairobi AR 1958: 17; LG 3/3204 NMC AR 1951: 16; Nairobi African Affairs Dept. AR 1950: 23.

[65] NMC AR 1951: Appendix C; 1957: 63; NCC ARs 1951-55, Market Appendices; LG 3/2958 NCC AR 1956: 74; NCC AR 1954: 44. The daily rates for selling at the new Shauri Moyo Market were Sh.1 compared to 15c. at Burma Market. In Oct. 1953 rates were raised again and stallholders at Shauri Moyo and Kariakor Markets had to pay Sh.2 instead of Sh.1 daily, effective three weeks retroactively.

If the immediate cause for the imposition of the Emergency was the assassination in Kiambu of Chief Waruhiu, an LNC member, on 7 October 1952 the urban variation on the same theme was the assassination of Tom Mbotela on 27 November 1952 near Burma Market. Mbotela was a Nairobi African Advisory Council member popularly considered to be an arch-collaborator. Burma Market accommodated displaced traders from Shauri Moyo Market, which was undergoing renovations involving permanent construction in stone. As a result of the assassination, the police raided Burma, finding it "ramshakle," arrested all of the traders and took them to Kingsway Camp for interrogation. Two hours later a fire broke out at the market, widely supposed to have been set by Homeguards, and it was completely razed. The opening of the renovated Shauri Moyo was then moved up from the eighth to the first of December.[66]

Kariakor Market was also thought by authorities to be "a black spot and a gathering place for spivs and thugs." *Spiv* was an acronym for "Suspected Persons and Itinerant Vagrants," and was applied constantly to traders, as was "drones."[67] In May 1953 the police raided it, destroyed some 600 temporary market stalls at its rear, and arrested the occupants. Later that month they tore down illegal stalls at Shauri Moyo. Traders at Shauri Moyo and Duke Street experienced frequent police raids, arrests, and detentions. In 1954 both Kariakor and Shauri Moyo were closed down completely at various points.[68] The demolitions, closures and arrests were a response to the various violent incidents centering on markets and municipally owned shops. Officials said that Mau Mau activists were carrying out a campaign of intimidation and had instituted a type of protection racket aimed at Asian and other non-Kikuyu shopowners. The Duke Street Market also burned down on 13 August 1954.[69] Two Homeguards were killed at Kariakor on 21 January 1955. Despite a demonstration organized by loyalist Kikuyu traders against the murderers, all Kikuyu-, Embu- and Meru- (acronym KEM used by authorities) owned shops were closed down for three months by the authorities as a result. Armed raids on municipally owned dairies and butcheries resulted in their closure.[70]

A comparison of stall allocations in the Nairobi Annual Reports for 1949, 1952 and 1956 makes the overall impact of the Emergency regulations on access to marketing infrastructure very clear. Between 1949 and 1952 the number of stalls increased by 44%, but between 1952 and 1956 it dropped by 70%. Changes in stall

---

[66] NCC AR 1952: 18; *East African News Review* 5 Feb. 1948; Onstad, "Life," p. 104.

[67] African Affairs Dept. AR 1952: 59; Mbilinyi, "'City,'" p.WS-89, has an excellent analysis of the language applied to African urbanites in colonial Tanganyika.

[68] LG 3/3143 minutes NCC African Affairs Committee 6 May 1953; Finance Committee 18 May, 19 Oct. 1953; NCC AR 1953: 27, 38, 53; 1954: 44.

[69] Nairobi African Affairs Dept. AR 1953: 157; LG 3/3144 minutes NCC African Affairs Committee 1 Sept. 1954. The origins of this legal market remain a mystery; it seems to have existed only in the early 1950s and was not rebuilt.

[70] NCC AR 1955: 2, 48; ARC(MAA) 2/3/16IV Intelligence Report Dec. 1944; NCC AR 1953: 53.

allocations by commodity at legal African markets in Nairobi (Kariakor and Shauri Moyo in 1949 and 1956, plus Burma and Duke Street in 1952)[71] had definite gender and class implications. From 1949 to 1952 there was a rise in the number of artisanal skills and services such as shoemakers and barbers from occupying 7.6% of the stalls to 13.8%, and then to 22.4% in 1956, despite the disappearance of potters (the only ones likely to be women), tinsmiths and bicycle repairers. There was also a rise in general stallholders, purveyors of mostly imported goods who usually required more starting capital and were male. The number of cooked food stallholders, likely to be women, declined sharply during the Emergency; *uji* (maize gruel) and beansellers disappeared. Male-dominated meat and chicken businesses increased in number, but offal sellers disappeared; they were more likely to be female. The number of fishsellers, never large, increased; they were most likely to be Luo serving a population relatively unaffected by the Emergency arrests. The number of calabash sellers declined, probably because of competition from imports. The number of fresh vegetable sellers went down because they were mostly Kikuyu cleared out by Operation Anvil. Overall, in 1952 12.3% of the commodities/occupations of stallholders were most likely to be female, and 17.6% likely to be highly capitalized. By 1956 only 3.2% were likely to be female and 36.9% highly capitalized. The relatively highly capitalized male general store proprietors seem to have taken over the gaps left by women and poorer male traders removed by the Emergency arrests, detentions and repatriations. Poor people were overrepresented among detainees. When municipally owned butcheries and dairies came under attack during the Emergency, the risks and the proprietorships were shifted to African private ownership. Market fees went up, as we have seen, and the new stallholders were more likely to be relatively prosperous wage earners; 60% of the applicants for stalls in 1955 fell into this category.[72]

Although before Operation Anvil about 1000 Kikuyu per month were being expelled from Nairobi, the Operation itself in April 1954 was undoubtedly the worst single event for the traders during the Emergency. More than 37,000 of those identified as KEM were removed from Nairobi, a deportation that fought a counterwave of immigrants fleeing villagization and starvation in the Reserves.[73] The majority of traders were arrested and either interned or repatriated. The authorities were particularly concerned about traders not only supporting Mau Mau by complicity in acts of violence, but also about their funding it and banking for it. As a result, Kikuyu dominance in access to trading facilities and housing was lost. Most stalls at Shauri Moyo, Kariakor and Duke Street Markets were vacated and reallocated to non-KEM. Male detainees abandoned their businesses perforce, left their wives to look after

---

[71] Nairobi Municipal/City Council *Annual Reports* 1949: Appendices C-D; 1952: App. F: 28; 1956: App. H: 77-78.

[72] Bates, "Origins," p. 24; NCC AR 1953: 53; 1955: 72.

[73] Hake, *Metropolis*, p. 61; Dickerman, "Africans," pp. 12-14, 20.

them, which was not always successful as wives were routinely repatriated or detained, or searched for others to help them retain possession. Most small businesses at Kawangware, which was predominantly Kikuyu, went under.[74]

Even Kikuyu loyalists had problems, and were not exempt from shop closures. Those who formerly did business at Ziwani in central Nairobi were forbidden both to enter or live there. But they also got benefits in terms of stall allocations and exemptions from prohibitions on occasion. Some traders in new housing estates were permitted to operate temporary shops out of their homes. Perhaps as an incentive to loyalty, the vegetable stalls at Mincing Lane were all allocated to Africans. However, some traders in the African housing locations were said to be making "fortunes," perhaps due to the decline in competition.[75]

Creating a Male-Dominated Middle Class: Differentiation among Traders

Once the clashes of 1953-55 died down the class issue came to the fore regarding expansion of Nairobi market facilities that were even more woefully inadequate than before. Foreign capital got involved in the mid-1950s not only in financing market construction in middle-class housing estates, but also in promoting the creation of a prosperous Kenyan male-dominated middle class including businessmen. A U.S. government African trader loan program was implemented under conditions that excluded women.[76] It went beyond loans to train traders and liberalize credit restrictions. The 1954 U.S. International Cooperation Administration (ICA) development project proposed a revolving loan fund for "Africans who are already engaged in enterprises or show particular aptitudes." The loans were to maximize opportunities for businessmen who had trained at the Jeanes School at Kabete in commercial subjects. A pilot program was established at Nyanza, avoiding troubled Central Province. Eligible industrialist, artisan and businessmen participants were literate and drawn from male-dominated occupations (smiths, mechanics, construction, shoemakers, carpenters, hotelkeepers). ADCs were to provide matching contributions for the project.[77]

If African women were implicitly excluded by the design of the project, they also were explicitly excluded from the implementation of its financial training. The Jeanes School had only men enrolled in the business courses, but also offered an attractive array of other courses aimed at improving male skills in a variety of fields, some with obvious implications for control operations: agriculture, citizenship, hygiene, cooperatives, community development, languages, probation officership,

---

[74] Nairobi African Affairs Dept. AR 1954: 178, 184; 1953: 154; NCC AR 1954: 4, 19; 1955: 72. CS 1/14/85 minutes Nairobi African Advisory Council 15-16 Mar. 22-23 Nov. 1954; Brown, "Kawangware," pp. 64-65.

[75] NCC AR 1955: 30; AA 13/1/8/9 Nairobi AR 1954: 16.

[76] Gordon, *Decolonization*, pp. 230-33.

[77] MCI 6/1272 "Expansion of a Project for Assistance to African Industrialists, Artisans, and Businessmen" (FOA-10-1Bx.8/54), pp. 2, 4-5, 7-8.

trade unionism, baking, librarianship, physical education, music and drama. There was a separate school to rehabilitate Mau Mau. Both of these were boarding facilities. Women also had Jeanes courses available to them in needlework, cookery, laundry, and child welfare on a non-residential basis. A nursery school was provided for the children of women students.[78] If a few African men were to be taught trading skills in order to raise their status to that of petty bourgeois, then it was considered suitable that they marry Western-style housewives. Changed thinking regarding women's education was a logical accompaniment to the labor stabilization policy forced by the Emergency. British East African officials met at the 1958 Ndola Urban Conference (whose African attendance consisted of one stenographer), deplored the expanding "septic fringe" around East African towns, and said that urban residence should be encouraged for African families, whose women should have home economics education and whose men should be paid a family wage. Whereas missions had previously assumed the function of educating girls for domesticity, the government was now making small-scale efforts to do so involving adult education for women, who could have benefitted more from literacy and accounting skills.[79] Home economics was also taught through local cookery demonstrations sponsored by the African Women's Training Center at Wangige. The only "economics" taught to Wangige women, however, was rabbitkeeping; a local agriculture officer was skeptical of the value of this exercise since, as he wryly noted, that location already had more rabbitkeepers than anywhere else.[80]

To the annoyance of officials, the beneficiaries of the loan scheme had a poor repayment rate; the funds were used to purchase cattle, cars, or for bridewealth (in this context good investments). Corruption in the ADCs had led to unwise granting of loans, some felt. Defaults were so common that a U.S. consultant was brought in to advise on remedying matters in 1959.[81] In any case, due to restrictions on the use of funds imposed by the ICA (they were not to be used for building shops, for instance, which eliminated much of their value for smaller aspiring traders), the Nairobi African Affairs Department refused to participate; sometimes ADCs could not come up with the requisite matching funds, even in Kiambu.[82]

---

[78] MCI 6/1272 Jeanes School attendance rolls Jan., May 1955; Report of Jeanes School Principal 26 July 1955.

[79] "Report on Ndola Conference," pp. 201-205; JA/LG 5/1 officers, Kariakor African Traders Association to Town Clerk Nairobi 28 Apr. 1960; LG/2702 minutes Kiambu ADC Trade and Markets Sub-Committee 2 Feb. 1960: 3.

[80] Agr 4/154 Kiambu Marketing AR 1957: 4.

[81] MCI 6/1385 M. S. Klein produced a report entitled "African Trade in Kenya" as part of his consultancy project. In general, women traders and farmers have had better repayment rates in recent loan programs than men in Africa.

[82] MCI 6/1385 Deputy Secretary Commerce and Industry to Principal Secretary Commerce and Industry 30 Jan. 1962; LG 3/2958 NCC African Affairs AR 1956: 63; 1958: 27; LG 3/2704 minutes Kiambu ADC Finance and General Purposes Committee 16 May 1962: 5.

International capital also entered in to pressure the Kenyan government to improve road networks in the Reserves so that multinationals could improve their distribution systems. Consideration was being given to Africanizing tobacco and beer distributorships. A 1957 report described a tobacco distribution system in which a European supervised "Recognised Wholesalers," who were mainly Asians with shops and trucks, or in a few areas Africans with handcarts, and "Stockists," who were African men on bicycles with smaller turnovers. Only Asian distributors had stores and were allowed credit and to sell retail over the counter. Those who were distributors in the 1940s and 1950s then often became manufacturers in the 1960s.[83]

The issue of credit to approved African traders (male) also exercised policy-makers in the 1950s. African wholesalers had an especially difficult time securing imported goods to sell with the legal credit limit at Sh.200. The law was therefore often flouted in this regard; many Africans were indebted to Asian suppliers.[84] In the 1940s administrators mainly held to the Sh.200 rule; the 1948 Credit to Natives (Control) Ordinance merely established that businesses registered under the Business Names Ordinance were exempted. All others still had to have exceptions approved by the DC. Few were made. But in the mid-1950s the issue was reopened with various officials pushing for higher limits. At a Council of Ministers meeting on 12 January 1956 the Credit to Africans Bill was approved establishing a credit limit of Sh.2000. Even then a number of male traders were granted exceptions by June 1956. By 1959 sentiment was moving toward repeal, which came in 1960.[85]

Between 1946 and 1963 only 3% of registered companies were owned by Africans. Expansion in the number of African-owned companies was steady from 1946 to 1952, but the preeminence of Kikuyu among the owners and the repressive measures taken even against relatively prosperous traders during the Emergency caused a drastic reduction until after independence.[86] The Emergency, then, also affected relatively prosperous traders. Nonetheless, in 1987-88 several men traders recounted their experiences, which showed how their wives' labor and profits were crucial resources they used to re-establish themselves. Following a usual 1950s pattern identified by Kershaw, in which men were shopkeepers and their wives assistants,[87] a male trader revived his business after emerging from internment by borrowing money from his two wives, who had continued in business during the Emergency. A shopkeeper at Nyamakima was interned for three years from 1954 to 1956. Before the Emergency he had managed to buy land at Kiambaa, on which he

---

[83] MCI 6/1272 "Report on Interview with the East African Tobacco Company's Representative Regarding Their Distribution System in Kenya," 22 July 1955; Swainson, *Development*, pp. 180-82.

[84] MCI 6/1272 J. W. Kent to Director of Trade and Supplies 6 June 1955.

[85] MAA 9/959 corres. and ordinances from 1941 to 1959; Swainson, *Development*, p. 172.

[86] Werlin, *Governing*, p. 106; Swainson, *Development*, p. 194.

[87] Sluter, "Confidential Report," p. 55.

had established his wife. She supported their three children by farming. When he was freed he was able to use profits from cash crops to get a shop and buy a truck for hauling potatoes; he then built up a produce haulage business first from Nyandarua to Nairobi and then Nairobi to Mombasa. In 1987 he had sold that and settled into selling dried staples from a shop.[88] These accounts show that the control of women's labor was still essential for male traders to be successful and suggest the class-dependent nature of that control. The mass of poor women traders who were struggling at the bottom were effectively segregated from those who cooperated with their husbands in trade and turned profits over to them.

By 1960, then, there was very defined differentiation among traders. This was recognized by the Kariakor African Traders Association in their demands concerning selling space. A long letter sent to the Nairobi Town Clerk by the all male, multi-ethnic officers in April 1960 is interesting not only for its evidence that the organization existed, but also for its advocacy of differential market fees by commodity. Restaurant owners were to be charged most, followed by general stores, secondhand clothes and tailors, mattress makers, butchers, and fish and chicken sellers. Lowest were barbers, vegetable, tobacco, snuff, and calabash sellers and sandalmakers. All but the fish and vegetable sellers were likely to be exclusively male. These fees indicate the hierarchy of profits by commodity among traders. They complained of competition from hawkers and included a list of requests regarding better market amenities.[89]

The 1950s are widely recognized as being a watershed in terms of class formation in Kenya. The British policy of creating a business bourgeoisie of African male traders and businessmen succeeded to some extent largely due to African efforts in that direction (the credit restrictions, in fact, hindered this development). Women whose husbands had shops were becoming subordinated to their husbands' business needs as unpaid employees, a trade version of the common gender division of labor in agriculture. In the best executive tradition, such assistants did much of the actual work, sometimes all of it, but their contributions were neither conceptualized as crucial nor recognized by ownership or monetary rewards. Women preserved the lives and businesses of their families during the Emergency by feeding them through farming and trading. Many women did small-scale, often illegal, undercapitalized trade, while some men, despite Emergency setbacks, continued to evolve larger scale companies, to serve as agents for multinationals, or to establish shops. Access to permanent selling space in legal markets became a sign of privilege, especially awarded to loyalists. The hierarchization of trade was mirrored in the growing split between the less numerous, skilled, relatively well-paid Nairobi workers and the more numerous,

---

[88] Interviews 265 Gikomba: 25 Mar. 1988; 138 Nyamakima: 16 Dec. 1987.

[89] JA/LG 5/1 Kariakor African Traders Association to Town Clerk Nairobi 28 Apr. 1960.

unskilled, poorly paid workers.[90] The poorer traders formed the nucleus of an under-class which suddenly exploded in size with the lifting of Emergency population movement restrictions in 1960. The result was a victory for hawkers in the first hawker war.

Gender and the Attack on Hawkers: Nairobi's First Hawker War, 1940-1963

If the staples trade in Kiambu suffered from the concentrated attention of colonial authorities, a policy which at least originally had some economic justification, urban hawkers were the subject of widespread fears in which growing class formation among the Kikuyu during the Emergency played a role. The focus of men's efforts to control women traders shifted from controlling women's bodies, their sexual and childbearing functions, to stopping their movement and business activities. The first serious attempts to enforce pass and vagrancy laws and hawker regulations efficiently were provoked by the three wars of the period,[91] while the resentment caused by that enforcement also helped to cause the Land and Freedom movement. In the 1940s and 1950s the British and the loyalists constructed gender so as to consolidate their control. Thus, if in the 1920s and 1930s colonial officials often did not abet elders' attempts to control women, in the 1940s and 1950s the emphasis on controlling population movement in general, and on helping local collaborators with the regime in particular, changed the picture considerably. The alliance of young and old Kikuyu men against women broke down when young militants joined the Land and Freedom movement and treated some women better in order to secure their necessary help. As independence approached in the early 1960s efforts to maintain male dominance were becoming embedded in class struggles and therefore translated onto a more general plane.

Class divisions were apparent early on in the 1940s when a new element joined in the effort to control hawkers: African shopkeepers, who objected to competition from hawkers and were organizing to protest. In April 1942 the East Africa Traders Association wrote to the Nairobi Acting Town Clerk urging tighter restrictions on the granting of hawkers' licenses saying, "the majority of hawkers obtain licences to cloak various nefarious happenings."[92] Such class differentiation among traders was regarded as desirable by policymakers, who intended not only that some African shopkeepers be male and better capitalized, but also that some male hawkers become shopkeepers. Gendered class formation was a conscious aim of British administration. Colchester, the Nairobi Municipal Native Affairs Officer, stated in the 1941 Annual Report,

---

[90] Dickerman, "Africans," p. 74; Bates, "Origins," p. 27.

[91] Furedi, "African Crowd," p. 226, said that overcrowding in the 1930s prevented enforcement of laws aimed at African population movement control.

[92] LG 2/125 Document 2, 22 Apr. 1942. In 1948 the first African businessman was appointed to an important trade advisory committee. MAA 8/22 Chief Native Commissioner to Municipal African Affairs Officer 6 Jan. 1948.

The aim is to evolve a class which will, with a little capital, be able to supply more people at lower prices... [T]he native hawker is usually a Kikuyu from 60 to 70 miles away taking advantage of temporary booms to earn Shs. 25/- to Shs. 30/- a month by 3 or 4 hours work a day. He usually lives in the most overcrowded parts of Pumwani and rarely has his wife or family with him. What is desirable is a more stable figure living at a higher level of subsistence and more knowledgeable in his trade.

Why did such people come to Nairobi? The pay from hawking was better, he said, than either rural or urban laborers' pay, and the war had caused a jump in the prosperity of the town.[93] Labor stabilization policy included concern for male traders, most without wives in town. But since colonial policy discouraged the presence of African women in town, this became another reason to limit the number of African male traders in Nairobi. Nairobi's African population went from 41,000 in 1939 to 70,000 in 1941.[94] Thus, Colchester was willing to encourage those men who could afford fixed selling places/licenses, but came down hard on itinerant unlicensed male traders, in particular. Women were invisible in his thinking.[95]

If rural officials were worried about hawking as an alternative to farm labor for Africans, urban administrators were increasingly concerned about simply keeping control over a bumptious population. The most important shift in government policy in the early 1940s was that it was agreed that trading licenses, "which were at present only a revenue producing measure should be a *control* measure" [emphasis mine].[96] This decision was evident in the 1941 Nairobi Annual Report, which stated, "With a view to limiting the native population and particularly the prostitutes, passes are now being issued for permanent residents in the town and the number of hawkers' licences is to be reduced from 500 to a maximum of 300."[97] The lower number of licenses did not accommodate most of the hawkers; Parker estimated that in 1942 there were 470 itinerant hawkers, 225 traders, 145 shopkeepers, 150 proprietors of eating houses, 280 skilled artisanal workers, and 235 service workers among the self-employed African population of Nairobi. Women seem to have been mainly omitted from these figures, as were the hundreds of Kiambu hawkers who traveled into Nairobi daily.[98] Nairobi women now had to carry passes, whether hawking or not. While the NMC was not willing to forbid hawking altogether, it adopted the policy

[93] ARC(MAA) 2/3/8III: NMC AR 1941: 22; interview Colchester 19 Oct. 1992.

[94] Onstad, "Life," p. 64.

[95] Himbara, *Capitalists*, p. 80, in praising British efforts to promote African entrepreneurship, ignored the gender aspect, the counter-insurgency motive behind British efforts to promote African class formation, and the progress of inequality.

[96] LG 3/733 DC Nakuru to Commissioner for Local Government 16 Feb. 1942; MCI 6/881, Sixth Annual Conference of District Council Representatives 11-12 Sept. 1945.

[97] PC/CP 4/4/1: 4.

[98] Parker, "Aspects," p. 20; DC/KBU 1/34 Kiambu AR 1943: 7. This source also states that there were 550 known traders in Kiambu, or about one for every sixty families, in addition to the hawkers.

of gradually widening the number of commodities that required licenses to sell. Under a 1942 Nairobi spiv law, 200 persons a month were picked up and deported to the reserves as vagrants in 1949.[99]

How did this situation of increased regulation affect the women traders in particular? Prostitution, venereal disease, and women escaping husbands were of increased concern to the Kiambu LNC and the Nairobi Native Advisory Council, the Kikuyu Houseboys Association, and the Kikuyu Progressive Association. The military presence provided not only a booming market for prepared foods, but also for prostitution. Some traders had a profitable sideline practiced in the bushes near the small markets established at the gates of military compounds.[100] The colonial administration cooperated to an extent unknown in the 1920s and 1930s. The Kiambu District Officer fined men for taking young girls to Nairobi for European-type dances; compulsory medical examinations for prostitutes were introduced. Women could not obtain urban employment as maids or childminders without "it first being established that she was not a runaway girl or wife." Wives living in overcrowded conditions did not get their passes renewed, probably as much from the fear of prostitution as from desire to reduce population density. Prostitution itself was changing into mere sexual encounters without other services, which made it less useful to British administrators concerned about labor stability. Women were forbidden to enter African eating houses.[101] Neither the Kiambu nor the Nairobi African councils had a woman member.

In 1945 Askwith came up with a plan to reformulate the government of African Affairs along the lines of indirect rule through "native associations," a move designed to prevent the "drift to the towns of women and girls," and to improve taxation and control of the Nairobi African population. Once the war was over, a top priority among Africans was to regain control over women. In 1945 a Joint Tribal Committee was formed to advise the Nairobi Native Advisory Council about the control of women; they requested that the DC refuse trade licenses to women. Askwith noted that the administration of African Nairobi consisted of a Swahili headman plus a Kikuyu assistant headman, who had two Kikuyu retainers "whose only work is the control of women."[102] Another reason British authorities were willing to reverse their policy and cooperate with African men wishing to control women

---

[99] LG 2/125 Doc.27, 1942 Amendment to Hawkers By-laws; MCI 6/881 Crown Counsel to Chief Secretary, Ministry of Commerce 2 Mar. 1945; African Affairs Dept. AR 1949: 57; Onstad, "Life," pp. 110-11.

[100] PC/CENT 2/1/13 minutes Kiambu LNC 3-5 July: 3, 11-14 Dec. 1944; minutes Nairobi Native Advisory Council 3-4 Sept. 1945. Stichter, *Migrant Labour*, p. 171; interview Colchester, 19 Oct. 1992; DC/KBU 1/31 Kiambu AR 1940: 5; White, *Comforts*, p. 173.

[101] White, *Comforts*; CNC 10/45 D.O. Kiambu to Crown Counsel 26 Jan. 1946; PC/CP 4/4/2 NMC AR 1944: 12; CS 1/14/11 minutes Nairobi Native Advisory Council 9 May, 11 July: 3, 19 Aug.: 1, 1944.

[102] MAA 7/491 memo Askwith to Chief Native Commissioner 14 Sept. 1945: 1; Hake, *African Metropolis*, p. 54; MAA 7/491 Askwith, report 22 Aug. 1945: 3.

was that the commercial infrastructure of Nairobi was better developed in the 1940s than the 1920s. Europeans, in particular, were therefore not so dependent on hawkers.

Neither the underground economy nor the militancy of hawkers disappeared when World War II ended. Without the diversion of the war the internal socioeconomic crisis became more evident--and acute, resulting in part in an escalated hawker war. The authorities responded with ever more stringent efforts. A February 1946 ordinance allowed any authority to remove any African from the Municipality for any reason without warrant or appeal. In 1947 disorder was rampant in Pumwani and Shauri Moyo, and the trade licensing officer said that without more help he could not control increased trading activities involving more than 2000 unlicensed traders.[103] Armed Kikuyu gangs were said to be roaming the African locations kidnapping Kikuyu women to use for prostitution, while the Kikuyu General Union (KGU) rounded up wayward girls for trial and repatriation to rural homes, contradictory goals for different groups of men. A widow who went to Nairobi in 1943 to seek work and sold *uji*, was first queried by the KGU about being on her own in Nairobi and then recruited to spy on "would-be prostitutes." Again younger activists supported controlling women; the KGU carried out campaigns to force uninitiated girls to be excised, causing one initiation group to be called *Haraka* (Kiswahili=Hurry).[104] Askwith acceded to the Native Advisory Council's request and forbade granting trade licenses to women. This 1945 ruling was cancelled, however, due to a protest from "porige sellers" and the hardship imposed on urban women. The Nairobi Native Advisory Council agreed that the restriction was only to apply to women coming from the Reserves, and made so many exceptions for *uji* sellers, who were supplying most African workers with their meals, that the prohibition became meaningless. The result of these conditions was another rash of laws in 1949 attempting to control both hawkers and "voluntarily unemployed persons."[105] By the late 1940s the legal restrictions on both marketing of foodstuffs and movement of traders were such that most urban Africans were dependent on the underground economy, chiefly produce hawked by women from Kiambu and Thika.[106] One observer of the scene in 1950 commented,

If one of the happier pictures of colonial Africa is that of the District Officer and lo-

---

[103] Aaronovitches, *Crisis*, p. 121; Throup, *Origins*, p. 172; LG 3/3139 minutes NMC General Purposes Committee 17 Feb. 1947; MAA 8/22 Askwith to Superintendant C.I.D. 29 Oct. 1947.

[104] NCC 2/281 Document 1, Verandah Trading By-laws; ARC (MAA) 2/3/36VII Central Province AR 1950: 54; interview 728 Gitaru: 17 Aug. 1988.

[105] MAA 8/22 Superintendant of African Locations to Superintendant C.I.D., 28 Oct. 1947; White, *Comforts*, p. 191; Mungai and Awori, *Kenya Women*, p. 166.

[106] PC/CP 2/1/13 minutes Kiambu LNC 13-15 Mar. 1945: 9; NCC 27/10 DC Nairobi to Town Clerk 4 Oct. 1945; LG 3/3140 minutes NMC Native Affairs Committee 6 Jan. 1949; CS 1/14/11 minutes Nairobi Native Affairs Committee 15 Oct. 1945: 4; 13 Nov. 1945: 1; White, *Comforts*, p. 153; Throup, *Origins*, p. 188.

cal chief proudly surveying a cotton crop or a new village well, the most gloomy is
that of the police of East Africa harrying the vegetable sellers, usually women, on a
periodic roundup of unauthorized markets in an urban estate.

In concert with the British authorities, the African councils renewed their push
to ban women trading,[107] associating it as always with prostitution. The views of
many Kikuyu men regarding women hawkers in Nairobi were expressed by Dedan
Githegi, Assistant African Affairs Officer, in a memorandum entitled "Immorality of
Kikuyu Women." He said that the immorality of Kikuyu women had gotten worse in
recent years because they were allowed to come to town without chiefly permission
to hawk foodstuffs, because there was no chief in town, and because many fathers
were not interested in the welfare of their children (implying that the women were
single mothers). Most of the women had children to support but house-to-house
hawking was fatiguing, he said. In his view, more judicious than some, only a small
proportion became prostitutes because of housing problems, which pressured
women to share with men, who became their lovers, or with old prostitutes. But
because of the necessity to keep down the cost of living food supplies needed to be
assured. He thus agreed with others before him in suggesting that markets be set up
on the periphery of Nairobi to keep women out of the center of town. When the
Nairobi African Advisory Council concluded that no more hawking licenses should
be given for Pumwani, the African Affairs Officer responded, "it is gratifying that
responsible African opinion has appreciated this danger."[108]

Conflicts between hawkers and authorities were at the heart of the urban incar-
nation of the Land and Freedom Army movement in the 1950s. The struggle for land
and freedom was explicitly gendered; women entered into it as freedom fighters,
messengers, secret agents, oathgivers, and as traders and farmers supplying food.[109]
The issue of social and economic control of women was prominent among freedom
fighters, as well as loyalists. White has pointed out that the LFA issued far more
statements regarding "the nature and proper organization of marriage than it did
about land or freedom." The difference was that among freedom fighters in the forest traditional gender roles were eventually challenged and overthrown in some
cases,[110] while among the loyalists the pressure remained on women to conform.
Thus, a part of the conflict in Nairobi also concerned controlling women.

---

[107] Werlin, *Governing*, pp. 56-57; Furedi, "African Crowd," p. 230, noted that at that time many
Nairobi Native Administrative Council members were close relatives of chiefs and headmen in the Reserves, Kiambu in particular.

[108] MAA 8/22 memo. 28 Jan. 1948; LG 2/39 Nairobi African Affairs Dept. AR 1949: 48.

[109] Furedi, "African Crowd," p. 237, said that by 1952 more than 90% of Nairobi's African population had taken at least one Mau Mau oath. Kanogo, "Kikuyu Women"; *Squatters*, pp. 143ff. A Kiambu
DC described women as "the eyes and ears of Mau Mau" in 1953. DC/KBU 1/44 Kiambu AR 1953: 3.

[110] White, "Separating," p. 15. Women freedom fighters had to take oaths, which indicated that they
were no longer the jural minors of precolonial times.

In Nairobi "petty traders were natural recruits for [the LFA]: most of them had a strong impetus to fight the colonial government while their livelihood gave them a perfect cover for subversive activities." By 1952 when the Emergency was declared, both rural and urban traders had organized themselves to dispute various ordinances aimed at controlling their activities. Early 1940s attempts at organization were small scale; in 1942 there were cobblers' and banana sellers' guilds with about eighty members each, for instance.[111] But by the late 1940s large-scale organizations were forming to protect traders' interests. The United African Traders Association protested the proposed 1949 Verandah Trading By-laws, which prohibited conducting business on the porches of houses except in Asian areas, and the anti-spiv measures. The chairman, Kigondu wa Machira, met with the Town Clerk and Labour Officer and informed them that his organization had 4000 members in twenty branches, including mostly male-dominated occupations such as tailors, shoemakers, painters, charcoal sellers, tinsmiths, blacksmiths and vegetable dealers. Despite widespread administrative support, the Verandah Trading By-laws were dropped when the Solicitor General advised against the feasibility of outlawing this method of trade. Women traders may also have been organizing themselves into Kamba dancing troupes at this time.[112]

This organizing was facilitated by the changing nature of the Nairobi population. If in the early 1940s Colchester found most of the Nairobi traders to be rural residents who came in daily and left again, by 1950 more were established permanently in Nairobi and staking their claims to existence there. In 1953 about 40% of Nairobi's African population had been there for at least five years; some members of the United African Traders claimed to have been in business for over fifteen years at the same location in Nairobi. Many had their families with them.[113] Landless squatters forced back to Kiambu in the 1940s often turned to trade, putting more pressure on local resources and heightening competition. According to Furedi, squatter traders, as well as Nairobi petty traders, were particularly active as leaders of the LFA.[114]

---

[111] Onstad, "Life," p. 110; ARC(MAA) 2/3/8IV Nairobi AR 1942: 4; 2/3/8III NMC Native Affairs AR 1941: 22.

[112] LG 2/281 Nairobi Municipal Verandah Trading By-laws, 1949; Kigondu wa Machira to Town Clerk 24 Aug. 1949; Labor Commissioner to Acting Commissioner for Local Government 21 Dec. 1949; Solicitor-General to Commissioner for Local Government 29 Dec. 1949. Rural traders were more represented in the Central Province African Merchants and Growers Association, which had political links to the Kenya African Union (later KANU, the present ruling party). DC/KBU 1/42 Kiambu AR 1951: 4; African Affairs Dept. AR 1950: 5.

[113] Dickerman, "Africans," pp. 5, 55; LG 2/281 Kigondu wa Machira to Town Clerk 24 Aug. 1949; DC/KBU 1/41 Kiambu AR 1950: 8.

[114] This movement was called *Kifagio* (Kiswahili=broom) and referred more specifically to destocking of squatters' animals from the 1920s on. Interview E Githega: 12 July 1988; Kanogo, *Squatters*, pp. 46-50, 99-100. See also Manley, *Marketing*, pp. 44-45. Squatters were particularly enraged at the maize pricing system by which in 1950 European landowners paid Africans Sh.14-15 per bag, and then turned around and sold it to the Control at Sh.32 per bag, misrepresenting it as European-grown maize. Furedi, "Social Composition," pp. 493, 499, 503.

But in the 1950s struggle male traders seem to have been more likely to support the LFA than females. The problem was that LFA activists carried out considerable sexual harassment against women. In some cases force was used by the LFA to
secure not only sex but also help. Veronica Wanjiru, a trader who came to Nairobi in
the early 1950s to peddle vegetables and fruit, said, "I could see that the Mau Mau
harassed the beautiful girls, the ones who were older than myself. The Mau Mau,
they would like to 'marry' the girls by force." Women were sometimes kidnapped by
forest fighters. But loyalists also harassed women. Two women in the small sample
were interned as young teenagers in the 1950s and forced to "marry" loyalists in
Kiambu, no bridewealth being paid and no consent asked from their parents. Both
commented on the need for security involved in making these forced liaisons. Rape
by Homeguards was common.[115] Possibly many women had more interest in avoiding any political involvement as too risky. Likimani has described one common
Kikuyu reaction to the Emergency political situation as *komerera* (Kikuyu=lie low,
keep out of trouble), which was also the term for the buses which secretly transported traders back and forth to Nairobi during the Emergency.[116]

The situation in Nairobi contrasted with that in Kiambu, which the authorities
thought had less involvement in Mau Mau than both areas further north and Nairobi.
In Nairobi the increase in petty theft around markets and illegal hawking prior to the
Emergency made getting illegal trade under control a prime objective once the law
allowed a crackdown.[117] Court records tell the story. In Kiambu in 1952 there was
only one trade-related case against a woman (.8% of the 123 cases) and 2.6% of the
1463 cases brought against men fell into this category. Wide participation in illicit
trade seems to have been unmolested. By 1960 in Kiambu the situation had only
changed a bit; 1.8% of the cases brought against women related to trade, 3.4% of
those against men. In Nairobi in 1951 very few cases were trade-related, none
against women, but in 1960 7% of the cases brought against women and 5.8% of
those against men involved hawking without a license.[118]

During the Emergency the colonial administration turned its attention to controlling hawking in Nairobi by drastically reducing the number of licensees. From
1952 to 1957 the number of *uji* (sold by women) licenses stood at 105, but the total
number of hawkers' licenses fell from 667 to 185. From 1953 to 1954 alone the

---

[115] Onstad, "Life," p. 115; Browne, "Kawangware," p. 256.

[116] Likimani, *Passbook,* pp. 76, 92. Lonsdale, "Mau Maus," p. 419, discusses the concept of *komerera* for LFA, which paired idleness with concealment, an analogue for the British term "spiv."

[117] DC/KBU 1/44 Kiambu AR 1953: 1; 1/45 Kiambu AR 1954: 3; ARC(MAA) 2/3/36VII Central
Province AR 1951: 3; LG 2/40 NCC African Affairs AR 1952: 2, 13-14. Similarly, the Emergency allowed strong rural measures by the Department of Agriculture, like the use of Parathion to kill 4,500,000
quelea birds at Mwea to save the wheat crop. Dept. of Agriculture AR 1958 I: 56.

[118] MAA 2/24, 2/26, 2/16 Kiambu and Nairobi African Tribunal Records.

number dropped by 400.[119] The cheap provisioning of workers was the chief argument used to preserve this number, which was not affected by Operation Anvil's removals. This argument did not save the KEM tea hawkers, however, who were usually among the more prosperous male traders. They were forbidden to sell completely in 1953 because they were thought to be witnesses or accomplices to Mau Mau crimes who refused to inform the police.[120] Forging a hawker's armband was made a criminal offence when several people tried it. Hundreds of people were arrested for hawking without a license or hawking outside of permitted areas. People were even arrested for picking flowers, sorting over garbage, and spitting. Fences were built around African locations and curfews enforced. There were shortages of commodities like charcoal and sugar due to the movement restrictions on traders. Spot raids were conducted to catch violators of the many restrictions and squatter villages like Kariobangi were destroyed. Plans were made to limit Kikuyu to no more than 25% of Nairobi's population.[121]

After the most violent part of the Emergency died down the authorities decided to crack down further on hawking; in 1958 only eighty *uji* licenses were given and in 1959 only sixty.[122] When a group of widows appealed the reduction, the Chief Municipal Inspector of markets gave them short shrift, saying, "all unlicensed hawking must stop and the offenders will be relentlessly prosecuted until that end is achieved. It is therefore necessary for the widows ... to take up some form of livelihood that is lawful." Former licensees got nowhere upon appeal. At the same time the General Secretary of the Nairobi People's Convention Party complained to the Town Clerk about the arrests of women hawkers, who were fined Sh.50 or got two months in prison. Other protests concerned the initiation of the policy that itinerant hawkers could only sell in their own "racial area."[123] For most women traders licenses and infrastructure and the bribes necessary to get them were in any case too expensive, nor were they granted licenses in rural areas when the few who could afford it applied to the ADC.[124]

The articulated goals of government policy aimed at obliterating the hawker population concerned the security risk (with particular attention to the fact that most

---

[119] Onstad, "Life," pp. 81-82; Dickerman, "Africans," pp. 37-39.

[120] Ross, *Grass Roots*, p. 20.

[121] NCC AR 1952: 12; 1953: 12; 1954: 12-15, 60; 1955: 12-16; Dickerman, "Africans," pp. 20, 38, 41, 18-19, 12; AA 13/1/8/9 Kiambu AR 1957: 1.

[122] LG 3/3147 minutes NCC African Affairs Committee 12 Oct. 1957; LG 3/3149 minutes NCC General Purposes Committee 4 Sept. 1959.

[123] NCC 27/10 Chief Municipal Inspector to Githuka s/o Kikuyu Feb. 1959; LG 3/3149 minutes NCC General Purposes Committee 6 Feb. 1959; LG 3/734 Salim Faraj to Town Clerk 17 Dec. 1959.

[124] If we assume that the proportion of loyalists was the same among women as among men, then gender appears to have triumphed over political loyalty as a criterion for awarding licenses at Fort Hall, where women were refused them. CS 1/14/63 minutes Fort Hall ADC 9 Feb. 1954; 8 Nov., 16 May 1955; 8 Nov. 1956; minutes Fort Hall ADC Trades and Transport Committee 9 Feb. 1954; Government of Kenya, *Commission of Inquiry Report* 1955-56: 44-5; CS 1/14/33 minutes Kiambu ADC Trade and Markets Sub-Committee 28-29 Jan. 1954: 1.

traders were Kikuyu), the presumed unsanitary methods of operation for cooked foods, general dirtiness, traffic congestion, the nuisance of traders' importunities to European housewives, and their assumed involvement in crimes more serious than the elementary one of illegal hawking. Another argument, joined into by prosperous African traders, involved hawkers posing unfair competition for shopkeepers. According to Likimani, Europeans perceived women traders during the Emergency as being, "dirty Mau Mau savages." There was also anxiety about the possibly dangerous political consequences of poverty. The 1954 Kenya government *Report on Destitution* said,

> The tendency to reduce the numbers of open-air traders may make a contribution to the number of indigents. Questions of hygiene, traffic problems and no doubt many other factors induce the desire in those responsible to impose severe limitations on the numbers of African petty traders, but we would nevertheless urge that the opportunity of a modest livelihood that these activities afford should be provided whenever possible.[125]

As we have seen, this recommendation was ignored whenever possible.

Emergency policies probably harmed women more than men because they were legally more vulnerable. Even the more prosperous suffered. Because a married woman's right to live in Nairobi was contingent upon her husband's status, she was automatically removed along with her husband. An example of what could happen is provided by a letter from a woman shopkeeper of 28 April 1956 to the Nairobi DC. Wangui w/o (wife of) Chege was left to watch her husband's shop for him after he was repatriated. She complained that the Ngara chief Owiso was harassing her in saying that she had no right to sell. But, she asserted, she was respectable, always paid the rent, had a legal pass, and four children to support.

> Whilst I maintain my loyalty to her Majesty's Government I feel extremely injustified [*sic*] by Chief Owiso's action against me. Had I been a woman without proper standings and left to roam in the town then his actions would be justified and fair, however he is on the contrary and has no mercey [*sic*] upon my future being together with my children. It is not the intention of the Government to make the women poor and I believe the Government is doing the best it could to see that the African women are advanced, but with [this] action it is to reverse our progress and stir hatred or bad feelings by misusing the Government Policy to the loyal citizens. I lay my trust on nobody but the British Government and I pray that Chief Owiso be stopped from his merciless actions on me.

The Nairobi DC told the Municipal African Affairs Officer that he was not going to reply to her as she had already been repatriated and was supposed to have gone with her husband in the first place.[126]

---

[125] Werlin, "Hawkers," pp. 199-200; Likimani, *Passbook*, p. 65; *Report on Destitution*, p. 5.
[126] MAA 9/904 corres. 28 Apr. 1956.

Several women in the small sample stopped going to Nairobi to trade at that time because they could not get passes from the loyalist chief, whether they were LFA supporters or not, and/or because "they were beaten so hard." Since getting a pass to trade required political involvement in the shape of declaring one's loyalist sentiment, some traders quit. In 1954 over 10,000 persons were refused daily passes to enter Nairobi from Kiambu.[127] A woman at Kangemi said that she stopped going to Nairobi to sell beer and potatoes and traded locally only. Why? "Mainly because I supported our people and not the colonialists," and so could not get a pass from the chief.[128] Among the 1018 men and women traders included in the large sample only about forty were trading during the 1940s and 1950s. Of these only six were trading to or in Nairobi: three who quit, two men who were detained for long periods, and the woman mentioned above. Two women used the situation to improve their businesses by selling foodstuffs and tobacco to prisoners and guards at prisons outside of Nairobi. A woman not included in the random sample was already in her sixties during the Emergency and was arrested while trading at Wangige and interned; because of her age she was set to supervising others doing farmwork. A curfew was imposed, meaning that traders at Wangige Market could not stay later than about 3 P.M. Under conditions where by the end of 1954 over 77,000 Africans had been detained, most Kikuyu women had no defense and no recourse.[129] Young girls were sometimes snatched off the street at the pleasure of the Homeguards. One of the saddest stories from the lives of the fifty-six women in the small sample concerned a woman who at age twelve was captured and detained for three years. Her parents had no idea what had happened to her and she suffered the full brunt of doing meaningless hard labor like moving piles of stones from one place to another and back again, or grinding stones into powder,[130] a form of torture also used in Nazi concentration camps.

One of the major changes that came about as a result of the Emergency and changing socioeconomic and political conditions was the abandonment not only of attempts by ethnic associations to govern Nairobi, but also of their efforts to control women's sexual and childbearing functions. Anti-hawker measures became separate from those aimed at controlling women's bodies. In the early 1950s it is clear that ethnic associations still expected to be able to control women. In 1950 the KGU said that four groups of women should be allowed to stay in town: those who were legally married and living with their husbands, registered domestic servants,

[127] Interviews 667 Kangemi: 25 July 1988; 561 Kawangware: 23 June 1988; LG 2/40 NCC African Affairs AR 1954: 173, 176-77, 183. The same source described Mau Mau as a "virtual seizure of [Nairobi] by an unruly tribe," and stated that strong measures were needed to "break the Kikuyu clutches on the city." The mayor's response, however, was to distribute Christmas presents to children of all races and allocate money to groups to form town bands.

[128] Interview 667 Kangemi: 25 July 1988.

[129] Interviews B Wangige: 13 June 1988; A Wangige: 9 June 1988; Leo, *Land*, p. 60.

[130] Interview 728 Gitaru: 17 Aug. 1988. More detail on the treatment of women prisoners is in Presley, *Kikuyu Women*, pp. 141-45.

householders, and "old prostitutes who have lived this way for a long time and cannot find alternative means of employment." Also, taxi drivers carrying prostitutes and prostitutes' customers were to be punished. In practice, however, they harassed prostitutes more by using salaried female informers to interrogate runaways, who had to show proof of marriage and explain why they had left their husbands or parents. Both the KGU and the Kalenjin Union asked that unsatisfactory maids be reported to them.[131]

However, by the end of the 1950s the chief loci of efforts to control African women were British laws and authorities. The decline in the efforts by loyalist African authorities to control women's bodies, and in the expectations of African men that this was possible, are indicated clearly in cases heard by the African tribunals. Between January and October of 1952 5.8% of the 1,463 cases with male defendants brought before the Kiambu Native Tribunal involved accusations of adultery or seducing away a woman from her husband or father.[132] In Nairobi between January and July of 1951 and August and October of 1952, such cases composed 7.7% of the 947 with male defendants brought to the Native Tribunal, a clear indication of the severity of the perceived problem there.[133] Many of the defendants were Luo and most plaintiffs Kikuyu, thus lending credence to Kikuyu men's complaints about strangers seducing away women. Or it may be that Kikuyu men objected most when the offender was a stranger; the issue of uncircumcised males was a sensitive one.

By the end of the 1950s adultery and related cases were becoming insignificant in both Kiambu and Nairobi. From January to May of 1959, 2,818 cases in Kiambu had male defendants but only .4% concerned such offenses, from February to June of 1960 only 1.5% of the 1,850 cases. In Nairobi from July to December of 1960 there were 3,029 cases with male defendants brought before the Extra-Provincial Civil Court (which replaced the African Tribunal), of which only .8% concerned adultery or related offenses.[134] These were disappearing among the overwhelming number of liquor- and pass-related offenses. This change was clearly *not* because women were being more obedient, especially in Nairobi. In 1949 Parker mentioned both the increasing frequency of interethnic marriages and the growing possibilities for women's economic independence. The court cases with women defendants rose from 7.7% of the total in Kiambu in 1952 (123 cases) to 12.9% in 1960 (275 cases), while in 1951 in Nairobi 6.5% of the cases had women defendants (59 cases)

---

[131] White, *Comforts*, pp. 192-93.

[132] CNC 10/46. Note the persistence of the status of women as property of men, as in the European tradition.

[133] CNC 10/30; CNC 10/29 Acting Native Courts Officer to DC Nairobi 12 July 1950. Although the records were not available, the Provincial Commissioner for Central Province on 26 Feb. 1948, in a letter to the Attorney General said that "There are scores of adultery cases every year in Nairobi." Unfortunately, the outcome of the cases in the records are often unclear; many seem to have been dismissed.

[134] MAA 2/24; 2/26; 2/16.

compared to 12.3% in 1960 (425 cases). The Nairobi records leave a growing impression of rowdiness by women--assault cases in 1960 were 5.6% of those brought against women, liquor offenses 55.8%, compared to 1.8% and 12% respectively in Kiambu in 1960.[135] Clearly, the growth of Nairobi made controlling women ever more difficult and priority was given to other goals considered to be more important with the approach of independence.

Women traders were involved strongly in the heightened intensity of the hawker war in the early 1960s, which was directly precipitated by the late Emergency measures to get rid of hawking and by the subsequent lifting of the Emergency restrictions on movement that allowed thousands of traders to go to Nairobi. By late 1956 the authorities had trebled the number of passes for individuals and vehicles to trade to Nairobi, while allowing many shops to reopen. Beginning in 1957 the government was returning many Africans to Nairobi, and by the end of 1958 entry during daylight hours was unrestricted for passholders.[136] Housing, underfunded by a government which frowned upon private African attempts, in 1960 had again achieved the high level of overcrowding of 1952, while there were an estimated 18,000 unemployed African men in Nairobi, a situation exacerbated further by the influx of 50,000 more people between January and March of 1960.[137] This influx only grew because of the increasing landlessness provoked by the 1954 Swynnerton Plan, which furthered the considerable privatization of ownership already present in 1941 in Kiambu. Women's landlessness was confirmed by registering land only in men's names. By November 1960 there were an estimated 130,000 landless families in Kenya, many of them in Central Province.[138]

The impact of these conditions on governmental attempts to control hawking was immediate. The lifting of population movement restrictions "nullified" attempts to control the overflow of hawkers at Mincing Lane, according to the Provincial Marketing Officer, who got the NCC Marketing Advisory Committee to pass a resolution forbidding retail trade at Mincing Lane altogether, to no effect.[139] Congestion there was extreme, with many hawkers selling uninspected produce less than 100 yards

---

[135] Parker, "Aspects," pp. 45-46; MAA 2/24, 2/26, 2/16 Kiambu and Nairobi African Tribunal Records. Months as listed above.

[136] DC/KBU 1/45 Kiambu AR 1956: 5; 1958: 1; Leo, *Land and Class*, p. 62; Hake, *African Metropolis*, p. 58, estimated that by 1957 there was a shortfall in Nairobi housing of space for some 22,000 Africans, despite daily repatriations.

[137] Dickerman, "Africans," pp. 37, 59. One of the Emergency measures aimed at reducing Nairobi's African population involved removing subsidies for African housing, meaning that only European government officials living in Nairobi had help with meeting housing costs. NCC AR 1954: 49.

[138] Throup, *Origins*, p. 78; Davison and Women, *Voices*, p. 165, described the impact of the Swynnerton reforms on women as including marginalization of women's usufruct land rights, making it impossible for women to use land as collateral; further encouragement of export production which absorbed women's labor to the exclusion of food crops. The land consolidation and privatization eventually included 7.6 million hectares (18,316,000 acres) registered to men by 1978. Leo, *Land and Class*, p. 62.

[139] LG 3/3148 minutes NCC Marketing Advisory Committee 14 Nov. 1958.

away. Much of this produce came from Kikuyu and Kiambaa Divisions. The chief staging area for the illicit trade in produce was the Ngong area. Underground economy prices of maize and beans were very high. In 1959 the General Manager of the Central Province Marketing Board described the futility of regulations under conditions of a "free-for-all with every Tom, Dick and Harry pouring into Nairobi with his produce and the bedlam in Mincing Lane is hopeless." Produce inspectors launched a "blitz" on Mincing Lane to catch offenders.[140] Some traders took matters into their own hands to try to keep down competition and regulate the situation. They formed the Mincing Lane Market Traders, Wholesalers and Farmers Union in 1960, which collected money for produce inspection and cesses, and hired watchmen for the market. Wholesalers had to pay Sh.10 for membership and 30c per bag marketed, which drove down Kiambu ADC revenues. But the Union was not a legally registered organization and was dissolved in several months.[141] The Kiambu District Marketing Officer described the situation in 1960:

> The easing of movement restrictions and curfew has caused an absolute flood of uninspected produce into Nairobi in the form of baskets, headloads and even small hand carts. Hawking is rife within the City and this burden is being carried by legitimate wholesalers who continue to support Mincing Lane and have quantities of produce left over at the end of a morning. For this very reason some buyers are now not bothering to use the Market when produce can be delivered to the doorstep... [If the produce inspectors do not do something] in a month or two months, the market will be run by the African and Asian Traders not the City Council which to my mind is almost the position now.

Whether traders were coming or going, control mechanisms were ineffective. Trucks were racing each other to the market and arriving earlier and earlier. Mincing Lane revenue dropped in the face of a boycott by traders and hawkers.[142] Less than half of the vegetables were now going to Mincing Lane; most were being hawked around Nairobi or were sold directly to Asian wholesalers. Hawkers seeking selling space formed illegal markets at Doonholm Road, Bengal Road and Dagoretti Corner. Adding to the chaotic marketing conditions and violation of urban land use rules were a number of urban farmers who were selling some of their produce.[143]

The escalating situation pressured an immediate increase in the number of licenses given (with the restriction that no hawkers were to be in the Central, a.k.a.

---

[140] Agr 4/69 Kiambu Monthly Marketing Report: 10 Apr. 1960; Fortnightly Reports 20 Apr., 5 May, 15 Sept., 2 Nov. 1960; 21 Jan., 6 July 1961; General Manager Central Province Marketing Board to Assistant Director of Agriculture Nyeri 10 Nov. 1959.

[141] LG 3/3148 minutes NCC General Purposes Committee 10 Oct. 1958; Agr 4/69 Kiambu Fortnightly Marketing Report 21 Jan. 1961; Monthly Marketing Reports 5 May, 4 June 1960: 2.

[142] DAO/KBU 1/1/93 Kiambu District Marketing Monthly Report Feb. 1960; Fortnightly Report 18 Mar. 1959.

[143] LG 3/2702 minutes Kiambu ADC, Marketing Report Aug. 1960; LG 3/3150 Resolutions NCC General Purposes Committee 16 June 1961; DC/KBU 1/46 Kiambu AR 1959: 3; *Nairobi Food and Fuel Survey* 1957, p. 59.

European, city). Mincing Lane and City (formerly Municipal) Market traders asked
for a reduction in stall rents, citing the hardships imposed by the granting of 800
hawkers' licenses, a protest which illustrates the conflicting goals of traders' and
hawkers' organizations. For not only the traders but also the hawkers were organizing. A key political factor influencing the liberalization of license policy was the rise
of a number of hawkers' organizations, formed by men in order to defend their interests. They organized both by market and generally.[144] Another was the colonial government's reluctant recognition of the inevitability of independence, fostered by their
problems with keeping control. Both led to the Africanization and politicization of
the hawker struggle in Nairobi, as African politicians sought to secure hawker support. In July 1960 it was decided to issue over 400 trading licenses (100 for *uji*), and
in November of that year over 800 (200 for *uji*). The first African mayor of Nairobi,
Charles Rubia, made the granting of more hawkers' licenses a priority in 1962,
despite the fact that 1500 had already been issued in August. Nevertheless, illegal
hawkers still predominated--by 1963 over 2000 of them. Most of the unlicensed
traders were selling prepared foods; many were women.[145]

By mid-1961 administrators felt that the situation was completely out of control. The 1961 Nairobi District *Annual Report* noted the dramatic increase in hawking and in the number of illegal markets (called *Uhuru*, Kiswahili=freedom, markets)
but said that the authorities had decided to tolerate them because the government was
unwilling to use the "last tier" of Emergency legal powers to do so.[146] Three major
hawker organizations were formed between 1960 and 1962 and fought to obtain legal
permanent or itinerant selling space. Onstad described the situation cogently in
mid-1961; it was "as if defeated Mau Mau had risen from the ashes, phoenix-like, in
the form of militant hordes of petty traders." Their agenda included not only the
right to secure selling space of their choice, but also an increased number of licenses,
relaxed regulations to allow permanence and expansion of businesses and capital
accumulation, and the cessation of police harassment.[147]

As effective as the written petitions and protests were the boycotts of designated trading locations, protest marches, and the constant street fights in which
bystanders came to the aid of hawkers resisting arrest. A typical case from the Crime
and Incident Reports occurred on 8 July 1960 when police constables from Shauri

---

[144] LG 3/3150 minutes NCC Finance Committee 21 June 1961; see Onstad, "Life," for an elaboration of this subject. JA/LG 5/1 officers, Kariakor African Traders Association to Town Clerk Nairobi 28
Apr. 1960; AA 13/1/8/9 Nairobi District AR 1959: 20.

[145] Minutes NMC General Purposes Committee 22 July, 4 Nov. 1960; Onstad, "Life," p. 160; Werlin, "Hawkers," pp. 200-201; AA 13/1/8/9 Nairobi AR 1960: 17.

[146] AA 13/1/8/9 Nairobi AR 1961: 3.

[147] Onstad, "Life," pp. 151-52, 166-71, 188-89. LG 3/3048 Kenya Auctioneers, Hawkers, Marke-
teers and Traders Union to Town Clerk 25 Oct. 1962; Nairobi Hawkers Traders Association to Prime Minister Kenyatta 4 May 1964; KAHMTU and Nairobi Vegetable, Fruits, Hawkers Traders Association to
Governor of Kenya 5 Jan. 1963.

Moyo were attempting to arrest illegal hawkers at Machakos Country Bus Stop, still a center for illegal trading. The police were stoned by the crowd, only succeeded in arresting one juvenile, and had to send for reinforcements to extract themselves from the imbroglio. Three incidents on 16 November 1960 at Shauri Moyo Market included one in which a large crowd prevented two plainclothes officers from making an arrest by pushing them out of the market, one being bitten on the finger, and two incidents in which police were stoned by the crowd. Machakos Bus Stop became notorious for its rowdiness.[148] By the end of 1962 the Nairobi City Council had given up on trying to stop hawking altogether and instead hoped to control it somewhat. In the scramble in 1963 for new bylaws aimed at controlling hawkers (the old ones were invalidated by the court in 1962 as not applicable to itinerant hawkers and too general), the old ones were inadvertently repealed with no new ones yet passed, and governmental disarray was complete.[149] The Nairobi Assistant Commissioner of Police wrote to the Permanent Secretary for Local Government, "To be perfectly honest, the Council have got themselves into such a mess in connection with hawking that it is really immaterial what amendments are made to the By-Laws," while the latter informed his Minister, "Unfortunately, like many problems, [hawking] has been allowed to grow because it could only have been solved by colonial/imperialist methods and these were becoming less and less appropriate as Uhuru drew near."[150] The remaining British officials felt a bit disconnected from what they were observing and perhaps somewhat maliciously satisfied that Africans were having as difficult a time establishing control as they had had. Although the bylaws were reinstated, this situation serves as a symbol of the inadequacy of colonial hawker policy under the onslaught of postcolonial conditions.

Conclusion

Nairobi African markets became a locus of political and economic protest in the period from 1940 to 1963, protest that was not segregated by gender. Both women and men took part in the escalating level of street violence in and around markets--fighting the police, hiding miscreants, and generally refusing to accept the dictates of authority where their livelihoods were concerned. Both the nature and the role of gender concerns in the struggle over hawking had changed irrevocably by 1963. More particularistic concerns about controlling women's sexuality, which were so prominent in earlier attempts to stop their hawking, had by 1963 been supplanted by class-based efforts to promote wealthier male traders and to maintain law and order, which further criminalized many traders' activities. While prostitutes were still being persecuted on moral grounds, traders were being attacked primarily

---

[148] LG 3/3048 Inspector General of Police to Minister of Internal Security and Defence 16 Mar. 1964; Crime and Incident Reports, 1960-64.

[149] AA 13/1/8/9 Nairobi AR 1962: 4. Onstad, "Life," pp. 158-59.

[150] LG 3/3048 Assistant Commissioner of Police Nairobi to Permanent Secretary for Local Government 17 Nov. 1962; latter to Minister for Local Government 2 Sept. 1963.

on economic grounds. For women the change by about 1960 was from controlling traders to controlling trade, where women's disabilities derived more from discrimination in access to training, capital, loans and trade sites than from their sexual and childbearing functions. This shift was a logical result of the increased tendency for trade to become a full-time occupation for some women and of the rapid class formation consciously furthered by the British administration as part of counterinsurgency efforts.

This transformation symbolized the increasing dominance among the upper classes of concerns over controlling the lower classes rather than over ethnic or gender conflicts. It is clear that before independence, the colonial government both in the heat of Mau Mau and in the cooler venues of trader and hawker policy succeeded in promulgating gender and class distinctions. After independence they were promoted with enthusiasm by Kenyan merchants and rulers, whose accession to power and influence was rooted securely in the events of the 1950s, in particular. The history of small-scale traders in Nairobi--their burgeoning numbers and militance along with the failed attempts to control them--lends urban illustration to Leo's image of a government powerless to control an expanding peasant sector.[151] More women joined the urban trading population to seek increased incomes, but they were not organized to the same extent as the male traders were in this period. That was to change, as we shall see in Chapter VII, when after independence women traders' organizations grew along with their level of urbanization and their increased needs. If the first hawker war was led by men, the second saw increased female participation and leadership, a consequence of the progressive segregation of women and men traders detailed in Chapter V, which continues the history of women's trade by illuminating startling differences between contemporary male and female traders.

---

[151] Leo, *Land and Class*, pp. 186-87.

V

"Here We Come Only to Struggle":[1]
Changes in Trade, 1964 to 1990

In the 1960s Nairobi began to take on the aspect of a big city; the population's annual growth rate was 7.9% from 1948 to 1962, 5.8% from 1962 to 1969 and 5% from 1969 to 1979. In 1990 the population was pushing two million, with a projection that by the year 2000 25% of Kenya's population would be urbanized. Despite punitive population density, the supply of legal housing grew, if anything, at a slower rate than in the latter years of colonialism. From 1964 to 1971 urban land values inflated by 300% in Nairobi. In 1972 there was a shortfall of about 60,000 housing units, while by one estimate over 70% of families could not afford even the cheapest two room conventional housing. In 1977 there were 30,000 names on a waiting list for 1000 NCC public housing units. The city government came under stricter central government control, and very little money was allotted for the maintenance of infrastructure and services. But immigration continued, with an increasing proportion of women joining the stream, many of whom took up trade as an occupation.[2] In 1973-74 the female migration rate to Nairobi was twice that of men. From 1973 to 1982 the Central Bureau of Statistics estimated that the informal sector in Nairobi grew from employing 41,415 persons to 172,214, more than a 400% increase, and by 1987 it was thought to be generating employment at a rate three times faster than the formal sector. In 1984 the NCC estimate of 30,000 hawkers in Nairobi was regarded as too low by the press, who added another 15,000 to it.[3] There were also the perpetual migrants; the insecurity of life in Nairobi, heightened by ongoing squatter settlement clearances carried out by authorities, confirmed for many women the wisdom of living elsewhere and trading to Nairobi, a commute facilitated by better transportation.

---

[1] Interview 241 Gikomba: 31 Mar. 1988. Portions of Chapters V and VI appeared in Robertson, "Trade."

[2] Ominde, "Population Distribution," pp. 55, 60; Muwonge, "Urban Policy," pp. 599-601; Ames, "Migration," pp. 249-62; Stren, "Urban Policy," pp. 179-208; McCormick, *Manufacturing*, p. 91; Werlin, *Governing*, pp. 222, 231. Women formed the majority of applicants for site and service housing schemes in eastern Nairobi; they were usually heads of households with informal sector jobs. Nimpuno-Parente, "Struggle," pp. 70-72. A contributory factor to the housing shortage was government adherence to a fairly expensive standard of construction in legal housing (ILO, *Employment*, pp. 231-32; Kimani, "Structure," pp. 398-99).

[3] Opinya, "Pressure," p. 73; Onstad, "Street Life," p. 6; Mitullah, "Hawking," pp. 10, 15.

General changes in Kenya's economy only reiterated the necessity for women to trade. Economic growth between 1963 and 1973 was at 6.5% per annum, and economists touted the benefits of the Swynnerton Plan in boosting agricultural productivity, especially in the area of cash crops. But in the 1970s the overall terms of trade declined for primary products like coffee and tea; there were oil crises in 1973-74 and 1979-80, and droughts in 1979-80 and 1984. Ukambani had serious famines in 1961-62, 1965, and 1970-74, in addition.[4] Pressure toward structural adjustment was exerted on the Kenyan government by the International Monetary Fund and the World Bank to reduce government spending, which contributed to Nairobi's housing crisis. The real wages of government workers, so critical to Nairobi's prosperity, dropped by a third between 1974 and 1988. Serious thought was given to establishing an export processing zone in Kenya (in which women would probably be at least 75% of the labor force) as in Mexico or Sri Lanka, but by 1990 this had not been done.[5] Fragmentation of landholdings once again drove down agricultural productivity while cashcropping continued to drive out food crops. In order to feed Nairobi dried staples were becoming cash crops in ever widening areas.

The cumulative impact of these conditions contributed largely to the transformation of women's involvement with trade in the period after independence. If dried beans for local use became the focus of limited government interest, green beans developed into an important export crop to Europe, but were not consumed locally to any significant extent. Likewise, women's trade expanded but remained marginalized in many ways, not least by government persecution of traders and continued privileging of maize, but also by the dominance of neocolonial interests including foreign capital in setting Kenya's economic priorities. The changes in trade involved: 1) an increased intensity and scope of involvement of women in trade; 2) an elaboration in functions that differentiated women traders considerably, as with men's trade, and built upon the specialization that had developed in the 1940s and 1950s, with some women establishing businesses of scale; and 3) the organization of women traders, as well as many other Kenyan women, to achieve wider goals. The first two changes in women's trade occupy most of this chapter, which will also include sections on the construction of gender in attitudes toward trade, how trade worked as a coping strategy, and an analysis of women's lack of access to critical resources that drove them into trade. Even the success that some achieved demonstrates the relatively narrow parameters of accumulation for indigenous capital in most cases.

---

[4] Wisner, "Man-Made Famine," p. 18.

[5] Nzomo and Staudt, "Impact," pp. 36-37.

Attitudes toward Trade: The Work Ethic and Women's Businesses

The construction of gender for central Kenyans has long included a strong work ethic. Kikuyu culture is rich in proverbs promoting hard work, a key virtue for a wife, while the role of a man as provider is also highly valued. Some of the proverbs are: "fear of toil keeps your house poor"; "if you help yourself you will be helped"; "buying and selling has neither mother nor son."[6] In 1987-88 these sayings were mirrored by ubiquitous slogans posted on the walls of shops lifted from various sources or invented, which not only praised hard work but also sharp business practices. "Do not mix business with friendship." "Mind your own business." Some were jokes. "We only give credit to those over eighty-five years of age, who must be accompanied by both parents." An ambivalent attitude regarding mixing personal relationships with business is evident. My favorite was, "Struggling is the real meaning of life. Victory and defeat are in the hands of God, so one must enjoy struggling."[7]

The exuberance in this last saying came out in the attitudes of some women. Women's reasons for liking work often went beyond meeting economic needs. One woman wanted work which would "widen her horizons."[8] A Mutira woman said,

> The way I learn is by comparing myself with other people and trying to work better than they do. The Agikuyu say that 'a woman never challenged does not give birth.' We also say, 'Going wide is seeing and learning much.' The one who just stays in one place is a fool. When I move outside I learn something new and when I come back I try to use new methods I have learned.[9]

If women felt trade was educational, they also saw advantages such as self-reliance, solidarity with friends, freedom from supervision, and suitability to women's skills. Some used professional metaphors in referring to their work, calling the market jokingly their "office," and their profits their "wages." They sometimes took pride in their abilities to trade. One woman boasted, "I am the best calculator in Kiambu." These attitudes conflicted sharply with those of some struggling male traders, who were ashamed of having to yell *Mali kwa mali* (Kiswahili=Goods for goods, signaling barter) to sell used clothing, or of having to pound maize, seen as women's work.[10]

But most traders, female and male, were most interested in the economic aspects of trade. Economic reasons for liking trade were cited by 86.3% of the women and 83.9% of the men traders in the large sample; unprofitability was the most frequent reason for disliking it. Women especially liked the dried staples trade

---

[6] Barra, *Proverbs*, pp. 12, 104; Ngumo, "Trade," p. 17. See also Ngugi, *Devil*, p. 101.

[7] Interviews 132 Ngara Bean: 11 Dec. 1987; 16 Ngara: 14 Oct. 1987.

[8] Interview 184 Gikomba: 25 Feb. 1988.

[9] Davison and Women, *Voices*, p. 167.

[10] Interviews 61 Ngara Bean: 27 Oct. 1987; 581 Kawangware: 3 June 1988; 808 Kiambu: 12 Oct. 1988; 385 Gikomba: 19 Apr. 1988.

because they could feed their families with unsold inventory and because staples took longer to spoil than other produce. More women than men cited supporting their families as most important for liking trade (27.8 versus 8.2%). Perhaps the most revealing statements about the nature of women's relationship to trade, however, came out in their overall assessments of the importance of business to them. Few could maintain the philosophical view of the forty-seven-year-old woman at Nyamakima who said, "What I can say is, business is like gambling. You can buy something, sell and get money. Other times you lose. It is not the same throughout." But her equanimity dissolved into determination despite pessimism, an attitude typical of most traders. "I think along the lines of doing the little things that will sustain me, because I have realized that I can't buy land, and I can't make it into big business. So I have settled for small things, very little things that keep me alive."[11] Traders grappled constantly with the realities of survival on few resources. A Gikomba woman insisted on impressing upon us a last point,

> About business, it is good but for me it really isn't. I can't do it very well because of lack of capital because I have to buy food. And like now, we are buying beans at Ksh.14 back home. On Monday I took food home--as you have heard there's another wife--so it can't really be good if you see your children suffering.[12]

A forty-three-year-old woman from Kirinyaga told us,

> Even if I try digging [farming], I can't. I try for two days, having to buy milk, sugar, what all, and I realize, 'hey, I'm going broke!' Because if I were here I can buy three debes of potatoes and sugar. Next time I buy soap, so at home I don't feel peaceful in my mind. It's retrogressive.[13]

This determination, edging on desperation in some cases, feeds into the struggle for space, autonomy, and profits waged by Nairobi traders.

Nairobi Trade outside the Markets in the Postcolonial Period
       In the 1960s and 1970s the present conformation of trade in and around Nairobi was emerging. A 1966 government survey of 8,313 self-employed traders in Kenya found that 69.5% of them were retail, 26.2% wholesale and 4.3% both.[14] The world of trade outside the Nairobi markets attracted some researchers who explored the range of possibilities from hawking or shopkeeping to the macro-level of international corporations. In the mid-1960s McVicar in his Pumwani research encountered hawkers including four young male Kikuyu partners in a scrap metal and bottle collection business who also shared a room. Each day they collected whatever they could find and sold it to Asian merchants or to local people. They existed on *ugali*

---

[11] Interview 133 Nyamakima: 15 Dec. 1987.

[12] Interview 244 Gikomba: 25 Mar. 1988.

[13] Interview 72 Ngara Bean: 20 Nov. 1987.

[14] Republic of Kenya, *Statistical Abstract 1969*, Table 110.

(maize meal porridge), and worked for ten or twelve hours a day to earn Ksh. 4 or 5 profit. When asked why they did not return home, one said,

> If I say that to work on the land is better than selling bottles, I'm wrong, because my land is too small. A man has to have enough land to have a good life at home. I know I can't stay here all my life; I won't get any pension here so I'll have to go home sometime, but I don't know when it will be. We are always looking for better jobs. We go to the labor department; we get employment cards but the cards wear out before we find any work.[15]

Nairobi was a difficult place in which to find a comfortable living in trade, more difficult than Kiambu for aspiring traders wishing to set up shops. In rural areas by 1967 there were thirty-three District Trade Development Boards and in urban areas four Municipal Loans Committees which gave loans to over 1000 small businessmen, meaning that in the whole of Kenya such loan recipients numbered perhaps less than a sixth of the number of illegal hawkers in Nairobi. Kikuyu men had successfully reasserted their preeminence in markets, dominating the trade in most commodities.[16] Profitable businesses run by men or men and women that grew out of small-scale trade included operating *matatus* [Kiswahili=small bus or van],[17] restaurants, and wholesale dried staples, fruit and vegetable businesses. By 1990 one of the largest of the latter was a family business operated by a middle-aged Kikuyu couple, whose four sons all worked in the business at some point, the eldest permanently. They had a contract to supply Kenyan army bases with fruit from Mombasa and cabbages from Kiambu and the Rift Valley. They attempted to expand their cramped premises in east central Nairobi in 1990 by paying half a million Kenya shillings in bribes to take over the store next door, which, however, was then immediately vacated to another businessperson upon payment of Ksh.1,000,000.[18]

One of the most successful enterprises for women was running kiosk restaurants. Mukui observed Cecilia, a woman supporting herself, her husband and her children in the 1970s by running a small restaurant selling tea, bread, and cooked food like *uji*. She employed three men and a girl as helpers (none related to her), kept no books, and served low income workers like messengers, sweepers, and shop assistants. Her husband had two-and-a-half acres at Ndeiya of poor quality land, on which his first wife farmed to meet subsistence needs. After subtracting her costs of doing business including renting a room at Kariobangi, Cecilia turned over the profits to him, which formed the sole cash income for the family. Their livelihood was severely imperiled by the 1975 closing down of all such kiosks due to a cholera

---

[15] McVicar, "Twilight," pp. 206, 209.

[16] Author's estimate. Werlin, *Governing*, p. 107; McVicar, "Twilight," p. 92.

[17] The *Standard* for 12 Sept. 1988 headlined an article, "Behind Matatu Business ... are rich locals and foreigners" (p. 3). See Lee-Smith, "Management" for an examination of the matatu industry.

[18] Interview J 22 Sept. 1991.

epidemic.[19] Wanjiku, nicknamed "Mama Githeri," a restaurant owner in Nairobi, demonstrates similarities to Cecilia but also significant differences. She began as a hawker in 1982 selling eggs, boiled maize and sweet potatoes on the street, but stopped because of police harassment. She then started a small-scale prepared food business from a fixed location, whose clientele rapidly increased tenfold. She diversified her menu but still charged only Ksh.2 or 4 per plate of *githeri* or beans. The cheapness, friendly efficiency, tasty food, and central location of her restaurant made it one of the most popular in 1988. Wanjiku's son, a university student, had come into the business with her. The *Daily Nation* report on her business ended by saying, "You may not take Wanjiku seriously, but for the hordes of men and women who rush to the Maskan every lunch break, she is somebody." In her case there was no husband evident and certainly no handing over of profits since she was saving to open a "big hotel."[20] Despite their success, these women still had problems meeting family needs, especially Cecilia. They do provide a sense of the possibilities that must spur on some traders, however.[21]

At the level of big businesses and multinational corporations, Swainson described the 1970s "struggle" between the bourgeoisie and the petty bourgeoisie to obtain distributorships for foreign-owned firms. The former was represented by the Kenya Association of Manufacturers and the latter by the Chamber of Commerce. The battle for Kenyans to gain entrance into multinationals and to control smaller business was cloaked in nationalist terms and facilitated by hostility toward Asian merchants. Marris found four years after independence that "there is still hardly an African shop to be found in the main streets of Nairobi." Not until the early 1970s did Asians begin to lose their dominance of urban shops to any significant extent; in 1987-88 parts of the central Nairobi business district (the old European areas) were still overwhelmingly Asian in ownership, although in the northeastern area African-owned shops dominated.[22] Many Europeans and Asians took up Kenyan citizenship to avoid the provisions of the 1967 Trade Licensing Act which excluded them from trade in rural and suburban areas; it did not apply to Nairobi, however. Himbara argued that capital formation in Kenya mainly occurred through Asian-owned businesses.[23] Foreign-owned manufacturing firms were usually given protected status to avoid competition from locals; when in 1977 Nanyuki Textile Mills failed and reopened in 1979 under new management, one of the government guarantees

---

[19] Mukui, "Anatomy," pp. 129-30.

[20] Reported by Alfred Omondi, 4 Nov. 1988.

[21] Gerry and Birkbeck, "Petty Commodity Producer," p. 148, emphasized the functionality for maintaining exploitative class relations of the "hard work brings success" ideology for both the upper classes ("if you are poor you must be lazy"), and for the poor, disguising the difficulty of social mobility.

[22] Marris, "Barriers," pp. 1-2; MA 12/54 Kiambu AR 1972: 4. By the late 1960s in Kiambu most Asian traders had fled. MA 12/42 Kiambu AR 1968: 2.

[23] Himbara, *Capitalists*, p. 75.

involved banning the importation and sale of secondhand clothing.[24] This ban made illegal one of the most profitable (and useful for poor consumers) male-dominated trades. Its contravention became routine, the secondhand clothes trade occupying large areas of illegal markets and even space in open air legal markets. In 1987-88 the newspapers were full of pictures of bales of secondhand clothing confiscated by police being burnt, either at the Tanzanian border or in Nairobi.[25] If government policy privileged big business at the expense of small ones and poor consumers, secondhand clothing nonetheless remained a quite profitable trade for those who could avoid prosecution. Its profitability has, however, no doubt been reduced by its legalization in 1996.

In the 1970s the government intervened further on behalf of the Kenyan bourgeoisie by requiring all goods manufactured by foreign firms in Kenya to be distributed through the Kenya National Trade Company, a parastatal employing only citizens as agents. The Kenya Commercial Bank, under local control from 1976 on, gave loans on a preferential basis to Kenyan-owned businesses from 1974 on. Benefits for large Kenyan-owned businesses accrued greatly from such policies as ICDC loans, preferential licensing forcing Asians to sell out between 1972 and 1975, and especially implementation of the Ndegwa Commission's recommendation of 1971 allowing civil servants to own businesses. Throughout the 1970s, however, there were few Kenyans in directorships of foreign-owned corporations,[26] a situation that government pressure was used to change in the mid-1980s. Multinational corporations were reluctant to lay themselves open to political manipulation by appointing government ministers as directors. Swainson agreed with Leys in concluding that during this period the Kenyan government "constructed the machinery through which to control foreign capital in the interests of indigenous accumulation." In 1993 the Goldenberg Limited scam was exposed in which millions of shillings were looted from the government treasury in the form of payments to a company without assets owned by the Vice-President and his associates; the evening before a magazine was going to print the story its premises were raided and all copies destroyed.[27] As Swainson noted, however, "it matters little to the Kenyan worker or peasant whether his [sic] exploiters are based in Nairobi or London."[28] A bottom-up view is more cogent for exploring the consequences of monopoly capitalism for most Kenyans.

---

[24] Swainson, *Development*, p. 187; Bates, *Markets,* pp. 63, 70.

[25] *Daily Nation* 30 Oct. 1987: 1; 14 June 1988: 3; 3 Nov. 1988: 26; 10 Aug. 1988: 3. Most of the Kenyan garment manufacturing trade uses cheap nylon fabric, so that cotton clothing is available only in used clothes or at expensive tourist boutiques. Most of the used clothing comes from the U.S. or Germany. A stimulating analysis of this trade in Zambia is in Hansen, "Salaula."

[26] Swainson, *Development*, pp. 189-204. MA 12/57 Kiambu AR 1973: 3, reported drily that "of course" Africanization had not extended to big industries.

[27] Reported on National Public Radio, "All Things Considered," 26 May 1993. The name Goldenberg refers to a mythical mountain of embezzled gold.

[28] Swainson, *Development*, pp. 235, 290; Leys, "Accumulation," pp. 241-66.

If upward mobility was becoming very difficult for Nairobi retail traders, rooted at the base of a pyramid whose top they could view daily, it was becoming impossible for those in rural areas. The Nairobi hawker problem remained with rural areas dependent on Nairobi for supplies not only of manufactured goods, but also for services like mechanical repairs (parts were frequently imported), dressmaking and tailoring, and metalworking.[29] Moreover, feeding Nairobi required drawing on ever more distant agricultural production, especially for dried staples, but also for vegetables. Heinrich looked at supply sources for Wakulima Market in the early 1970s and found that Kiambu was supplying less than a third of the vegetables, Naivasha 27%, Machakos 17% and suburban areas of Kabete and Nairobi itself 8%. Kiambu was losing its monopoly, with most of the produce acquired directly from farmers by wholesalers, rather than going to markets. Wholesalers from Kiambu hired small vans to carry the produce into Nairobi, while groups of traders from further away hired large trucks.[30] Supply sources for beans also diversified. The dispersal of Kikuyu settlement across Kenya, helped along by Kenyatta's Million Acre scheme in the 1970s, diversified local diet and production and increased Kikuyu involvement in the fresh fruit trade from Mombasa. Improvements in transportation made trade at once easier for some in well-served areas and also more competitive with a more elaborate structure of middlepersons.[31] Mechanized transport has now become key to the trade in staples. To the north and northeast of Nairobi women go to Limuru to buy supplies that come off trucks and trains from the Rift Valley. They used to buy at Dagoretti, but it is no longer a train stop; its market suffered accordingly.[32] Women wholesalers from Loitokitok on the Tanzanian border, another area of Kikuyu settlement, bring bags of beans to Nyamakima for sale. The chief supply sources are more distant from the Nairobi area, which is now losing land rapidly to urbanization. Kiambu people now concentrate more on trade and less on production.

Changes in Trade: the Intensity of Women's Trade, Landlessness and Education

This is the setting, then, for a more detailed look at the elaboration of petty trade in Nairobi, with particular attention to dried staples. The best place to begin looking at changes in the patterns of women's involvement in trade is by considering the retrospective occupational patterns of women and men in the large sample. Table V.1, drawn from women's work histories, has occupational patterns by year going back to 1940 in the form of time slices which show a pattern of overall change for this sample in their labor force involvement. The numbers represented in each year

---

[29] Kongstad and Monsted, *Family*, pp. 139-41; MA 12/66 Kiambu AR 1976: 60.

[30] Heinrich, *Marketing*, p. 8; Freeman, *City*, p. 60.

[31] MA 12/48 Kiambu AR 1970: 27; Jones, *Marketing*, p. 70; interview C Ndeiya: 28 June 1988.

[32] Interviews 595 Kawangware: 29 June 1988; 843 Karuri: 17 Oct. 1988; fieldnotes Githunguri: 29 Aug. 1988.

diminish as we move back in time and more traders drop out due to their youth or noninvolvement in the labor force.

The earlier histories of most women involved farming. The usual pattern was for women to farm, perhaps trading in a local rural market, until some kind of family crisis forced larger involvement in trade. Therefore, as one moves later in time more crises occurred to more women and they began trading. The rural origins and continuing rural connections of many of these women are evident in the sample; in 1987-88 31% were selling in rural markets, a majority of whom were living nearby. But even the more than two-thirds who were selling in urban and suburban markets mostly had strong rural roots. Although 73.2% of women selling in urban markets lived in Nairobi full-time, 12.8% lived there part-time only and farmed in rural areas the rest of the time, while 14% traveled daily to Nairobi from their rural homes.

Table V.1's results regarding women's participation in other occupations revealed that the next most common occupation for women was casual labor in agriculture, such as picking coffee. Women sometimes derived their starting capital from those wages. Next in importance was skilled labor of some sort, usually

V.1. Historical Occupation Patterns of Women Traders by % of Occupations, 1940-1987

Occupation: Year:	Trader	Farmer	Agri-cult-ure/Fishery	Service/Skilled	Com-merce	White Collar	Manu-fact-ure	Domes-tic	Unskilled Ser-vice
1987 N=983	64.3	26.1	.4	7.2	1.6	.2	0	.1	0
1985 N=921	50.1	32.6	1.6	7.6	1.5	2.2	0	1.4	1.5
1980 N=649	39.1	45.1	3.4	4.5	1.2	2.0	.8	2.2	1.7
1975 N=485	27.4	58.6	4.7	2.1	1.4	1.6	.4	2.5	1.2
1970 N=348	20.1	67.2	6.3	1.4	1.7	.6	0	1.7	.9
1965 N=255	18.0	72.2	5.5	.8	.8	.8	0	1.2	.8
1960 N=191	17.8	75.9	4.2	0	0	0	0	1.0	.5
1955 N=132	16.7	76.5	5.3	0	0	0	0	.8	.8
1950 N=86	15.1	79.1	4.7	0	0	0	0	0	1.2
1945 N=52	9.6	82.7	3.8	0	0	0	0	0	1.9
1940 N=31	9.7	87.1	3.2	0	0	0	0	0	0

dressmaking or basketweaving. The sample included the legal part of Gikomba (called Quarry Road Market), three buildings inhabited mainly by a substantial portion of Kenya's garment industry employing many women, a number of sisal basketweavers belonging to a marketing cooperative at Kariakor Market, and a few hairdressers at Ngara Market. Domestic service occupied a few women at various times, but most found it too confining and quit; only one woman had done it for a number of years. The few white-collar and commerce jobs listed involved teaching, nursing, sales or clerical work, and were not available to many women before independence. Women's white-collar jobs in Kenya tend to be gendertyped as in Western economies.[33] The range of skills was therefore fairly narrow for women.

Women's historical work patterns contrast sharply with those of men, as shown in Table V.2. The chief differences between men's and women's occupation patterns involve more diversity and consistency in men's occupations, as well as much less unwaged farmwork for men. The figures indicate a higher frequency of involvement in skilled work by men than women both historically and in the present. No woman

V.2. Historical Occupations of Men Traders by % of Occupations, 1960-1987*

Occupation: Year:	Trader	Farmer	Agriculture	Service/ Skilled	Commerce	White Collar	Manufacturing	Domestic/Service	Military	Unskilled
1987 N=369	72.1	6.2	0	14.1	6.8	0	0	0	.3	.5
1985 N=365	42.2	15.1	1.6	18.4	6.8	2.7	4.7	1.4	1.4	5.8
1980 N=191	34.0	16.2	1.6	24.1	5.8	4.2	5.8	2.6	2.6	4.2
1975 N=114	24.6	10.5	2.6	28.9	6.1	5.3	5.3	7.0	7.0	7.9
1970 N=62	24.2	11.3	3.2	27.4	3.2	6.5	9.7	4.8	4.8	6.5
1965 N=44	22.7	13.6	9.1	20.5	4.5	2.3	11.4	4.5	4.5	11.4
1960 N=28	21.4	21.4	10.7	17.9	3.6	0	10.7	3.6	3.6	7.1

*Before 1960 the numbers drop too low to be of statistical significance.

---

[33] Women historically and in the present are poorly represented in administrative and executive positions in both the public and the private sectors in Kenya. In 1979 only 4.5% of the total female labor force was in formal wage employment compared to 23% of the male labor force, while less than .05% were in top executive or managerial positions, 2% in middle management or professionals. For excellent analyses of the position of Kenyan women in the wage labor force see Zeleza, "Women," pp. 69-107, and *Situation Analysis* III: 82. In Adagala and Bifani's sample of women traders in eastern peri-urban markets of Nairobi, trade was a less important occupation, a stopgap undertaken as a survival strategy along with domestic service and prostitution; *Self-Employed Women*, p. 98.

mentioned skilled work as an occupation before independence. The list of men's skilled jobs is varied: shoemaking, metalwork, tailoring, leatherwork, repairwork of various kinds, carpentry, masonry, woodcarving, and numerous others. Among the most poorly paid were the maizepounders at Gikomba, who worked for women sellers on a piecework basis. The consistency of men's work patterns is shown by less exponential growth in trading activities than women had and steady employment not only in skilled jobs but also in commerce and manufacturing, where very few women had any employment. Men had/have more occupations available to them and did more shifting around in and out of trading.

Mwangi's career, a success story that could be entitled "From parking boy to prosperity," is a good illustration of both the variety characteristic of men's careers and the struggle for existence of landless men.

Mwangi, a fifty-three year old proprietor of a kiosk restaurant that occupied two rooms in a shack next to the river at Gikomba, was a member of the governing committee of the market and very proud of his accomplishments. He moved to Nairobi when he was a young boy and lived hand to mouth as a "parking boy," the ubiquitous boys who haunt the streets of central Nairobi picking up tips for helping motorists to find a parking space. Eventually he got scutwork washing dishes in a kiosk restaurant but quit that when he had saved a little in order to begin selling housewares, peddling them house to house at Kariakor. He went bankrupt at that and so began collecting and selling scrap metal in the Nairobi Industrial Area. Again he saved a little and began selling tea to railway workers, which was more profitable and yielded Ksh.240 to begin peddling food from a handcart. When competition in that trade grew too fierce in the late 1960s he began a kiosk restaurant using Ksh.1,000 in savings. There were problems with getting supplies in the late 1970s, however, so he began selling fresh vegetables at Gikomba, which evolved into a wholesaling business. In 1988 he had quit traveling to Embu and Kiambu to buy, and restricted himself to buying fresh vegetables from wholesalers at Gikomba, which he both sold from a stall in the market and used in his restaurant business, which was three years old and employed six males. His income from one-shot Ksh.1500 fees allowing usage of market stalls was substantial. He spent virtually all of his waking hours at the market, an average of 94.5 hours per week. From his income he was able to pay school fees for his nine children, who had all either completed middle school or were still in school. His wife provided for their subsistence needs by growing food on a small farm at Nyeri.[34]

---

[34] Interview 173 Gikomba: 19 Feb. 1988.

V.1 Gikomba Market, 1988: A Sturdy Shelter in a Prime Position

V.2 Growing Up at Gikomba, 1988

Male traders were more likely to have had a wage job which allowed them to save up some starting capital, whereas women often began by selling their own produce. Men were also more likely to be permanent Nairobi residents, which is reflected in their lower participation in farming. Men were 40.5% of the traders in urban markets compared to only 18.7% in rural markets, and 28.4% in suburban markets.

Mwangi's lack of active participation in farming was typical of men traders, while such a situation was also becoming more common for women traders, evident in the rising intensity of their participation in trade and landlessness. Changes in the intensity of women's involvement in trade are evident in the number of hours worked weekly. Women in the large sample averaged over fifty hours weekly trading, despite their simultaneous labor in farming in many cases. Over a fourth of the small sample of fifty-six women reported that they had had to raise their hours spent trading in order to increase earnings. Nevertheless, women put in fewer hours in the markets than men did. Men averaged 66.9 hours a week compared to 50.6 for women, and more days selling per week, 6.3 versus 5.1 for women. Women were more likely to sell at rural two-day markets like Gitaru and Karuri, although many circulated among three of these in order to sell daily. More of women's time was spent farming and meeting domestic obligations. Commonly, a woman would cook breakfast for her family, see the children off to school, and then go to the market in the morning. Some men were employees of bigger men traders and therefore had little discretion about their hours. They showed up early each morning at the market looking for employment. Not included in the sample were porters who worked on a per load basis hauling large bags of produce or unloading trucks. Men were more often young wage jobseekers with few or no dependents, and younger than women. The lesser number of days spent selling cut substantially into women's profits.

Aside from family obligations pressing women to put more hours into trading, landlessness is an increasing problem. There was a steady diminution in the amount of land available to women who had access to land; those aged seventy and over averaged 7.5 acres each, compared to 1.8 acres for those aged twenty to twenty-nine, with steadily diminishing amounts in intermediate age groups (N=272 with information given). Men had an opposite pattern with more landlessness in older age groups and steadily increasing amounts as men got younger for those who had access to land (N=42). These figures for men are unusual; one would expect that older men would have been able to purchase or inherit more land. They reflect both inheritance patterns and the scramble for land in areas surrounding Nairobi. A large wave of landless men came to Nairobi in the 1960s; they are now in their 50s and 60s or over. Many became traders; those who could not purchase land remained in Nairobi. Some may have lost their land due to their absence from home, just as several women were victims of husbands' rapacious relatives. The next wave arrived later and found it more possible to straddle, as Cowen put it,[35] leaving their wives to farm their land while trading themselves, and even to purchase land, especially in the 1970s. They were not numerous, however. Land access figures for the large sample (N=1016) amply illustrate the severity of landlessness pushing people into trade. Only 1.9% of women and 3.6% of men traders owned land. Among all women traders 24.8% had access to land through their husbands, 3.5% through their fathers, and 3.8% rented it. Altogether 43.5% of women traders had access to land in some fashion. Among men 3% had access to their father's land and .6% rented it. A total of 15.7% of men traders had access to land in some way. For both men and women land ownership was minuscule and 65.6% of all traders had no access to land.[36] The number of women claiming land use rights through their husbands was equivalent to less than half of the women married at the time of the survey, indicating substantial landlessness among their husbands. The dominance of young landless men in urban markets was evident in the land access statistics. Women's strategies for survival often included growing their own food, sometimes on small plots of rented land on which they housed their families.

The best way to secure land for women was to purchase it. On average women who had land owned 4.6 acres they had purchased, but had access to only two acres through marriage, 2.4 acres through inheritance, and 1.1 acres through rental. All of the women who had inherited land got it through their fathers indicating that, even if a few senior women managed to acquire land, none was passed on to daughters. In contrast, men with land had an average of 3.6 acres through purchase, 5.2 acres through inheritance, and 1.7 through rental. If for women marriage was the most common method of access to land, purchase secured them more land. Men with access to land had more land on the average, but women had purchased more. Women selling or living in Nairobi had acquired more land than either rural or suburban women; none of the women traders in rural markets had bought land, although five women in the large sample who lived in a rural area but did not sell there had purchased it. Men's best access to land was through inheritance. Stamp and Mackenzie have documented the conflict over land in which male reinterpretation of customary law is being used to deprive women of access to land by inheritance. Mackenzie has argued, borne out here, that women's land use rights have now become dependent on individual male action rather than corporate kin, a more fragile position. These women had numerous stories of landlessness caused by husbands or sons selling land or husbands' relatives seizing it sublegally.[37]

---

[35] Cowen and Kinyanjui, "Problems."

[36] For purposes of comparison, Mitullah's sample of 425 Nairobi street hawkers in 1988-89 had a landless rate of 73.4% with an average of 1.8 acres for those with land. Mitullah, "Hawking," p. 41. Rutten, *Wealth*, p. 35, described Kenya as belonging to the group of countries in Africa in 1988 with the highest inequality in land distribution, with female farmers as particular victims.

[37] Stamp, "Burying," pp. 808-45; MacKenzie, "Gender," pp. 68-74. Mackenzie further asserts that the construct which says that women had no property rights and were property themselves is a relatively recent one, but aside from some women being granted use rights by their fathers until they married, there seems to be no basis for this assertion. Women's ownership of their houses was acknowledged, but this

The sum total of this landholding evidence indicates both the vulnerability of women traders, most of whom would farm if they could, to landlessness, and the differentiation among traders themselves. The few who did own land had substantially more than the average landholding in Kiambu and Murang'a, less than one acre per household. However, this is partly because of the proportion of Kamba in this sample. Land scarcity is not as prevalent in Ukambani, although the land is less fertile; among those with access to land the thirty-three Kamba women had an average of 6.5 acres each compared to 2 acres each for Kikuyu women. Even when ethnicity is taken into account, then, traders with access to land had more than did average households. But when the amount of land is divided among all traders including the landless, each individual had only .78 acres, below the average household holdings for Murang'a, Kiambu and Ukambani.[38]

The rural/urban statistics concerning land access confirm the increasing class differentiation going on between rural and urban areas and suggest that trading income can, in fact, improve family economic status or at least help to avert landlessness. Conversely, those with more land may have more surplus to sell or more money to hire farm labor freeing them to trade. Those who lived in Nairobi or traded in urban markets had access to more land than those in either rural or suburban areas at a significance level of .00. Nairobi-resident women traders had 6.4 acres, while women who traded in urban markets had six acres, compared to 8.4 and 7.5 acres respectively for men. Women traders who lived part-time in Nairobi had 3.2 acres (there were no men in this category). Women traders who lived in rural areas had 2.5 acres and men had access to two acres. Women who traded in suburban markets had 3.3 acres compared to 5.8 for men, while women sellers in rural markets had 1.5 acres and men 1.4. The magnitude of rural/urban differences was reduced somewhat when ethnicity was factored in (the Kamba were concentrated in central Nairobi markets), but still held strongly within ethnic groups. For instance, urban resident Kikuyu women had access to far more land on the average (5.8 acres for those with access) than rural Kikuyu women (1.75 acres), while part-time Nairobi Kikuyu women residents had four acres. This trading population, then, illustrates not only widespread landlessness, for men in particular, but also differentiation among traders in which a few traders have a fair amount of land, but most have none.

In general, men traders who had any involvement in farming were able to secure more land. They had three acres on the average compared to 2.6 for women who farmed.[39] A comparison of several of the more prosperous groups of traders confirms this impression. A group of eight Nyamakima male storeowners aged

---

was a weak position since husbands regularly now sell land regardless of the houses on it. What seems to have lapsed is the courtesy of asking the woman's permission to do so. See also Davison and Women, *Voices*, p. 172.

[38] *Situation Analysis* I: 30.

[39] Freeman, *City*, pp. 83-85, also found that men involved in Nairobi urban farming had more land, but that women did more of the farm labor.

V.3 Gikomba Market, 1988:
A Chickenseller and Her Wares

V.4 Gikomba Market, 1988: Selling in the Hot Sun

forty-eight and over had an average of 9.9 acres of land, all of it worked by their wives and most of it purchased. A comparable group of seven Shauri Moyo women stallholders aged forty-five and over were also not farming themselves and owned no land, except for one woman who had access to thirty-five acres owned by her deceased husband and worked by her wife acquired by woman-marriage. So, even women who were relatively prosperous with a long trading history had not usually been able to buy land. Moreover, most of their spouses were not farming (five out of seven), so they could not supplement their earnings with rural food. They were more likely to be sending food to rural areas. The Nyamakima men, in contrast, were often getting income from cash crops sold by their wives.

The diminishing amount of land available to women is probably the single most crucial factor that heightened their involvement in trade, but another contributory factor was their lesser access to Western-type education, which has become a critical resource for Kenyans. Far more women traders had had no formal education than men: 29.3% versus 3%. About the same proportion had completed some primary school, 43.4% of women versus 44.9% of men, but only 24.9% of women had gone to middle school compared to 50.5% of the men. Very few of both (.1% of women and .3% of men) had gone to secondary school. The most significant difference lies in the number of traders with no formal education, who are mostly older women. Fewer men in the sample fell into the age groups not likely to have gone to school. The largest expansion in provision of primary education for Kenyan girls came in the 1970s.[40] This differential access to education carries over into the level of education attained by those in the sample who did go to school; only 24.4% of all of the women traders mostly completed primary school, reaching Standard 6 or 7, compared to 32.9% of the men. To set these statistics in the context of the whole Nairobi population, 27.2% of the women traders in the sample reached middle school, completing Form 1 or more, compared to 38.3% of the women fifteen and over in Nairobi in 1979. For men 51.1% of the traders had completed Form 1 or more compared to 43.9% of men fifteen and over in Nairobi. The case is apparently quite different for men and women traders, then. Women simply lacked education as a result of a number of factors like age, fewer available school places and poorer schools, pregnancy terminating school attendance, parental reluctance to send them to school because of their labor value, among other things, and poverty forcing that parental choice.[41] In contrast, the chief difficulty facing men was not access to schooling--male traders had above-average access, in fact--but finding a job commensurate with that schooling. There are good reasons for the increasing intensity and scope of women's involvement in trade, then: they have fewer choices than men do in terms of occupations and training; they are more vulnerable to landlessness in

---

[40] Robertson, "Education," pp. 95-97.

[41] Kenya, Central Bureau of Statistics, *Population Census 1979* 3: Urban Population: 24-25; *Situation Analysis* III: 51-77.

V.5 Market Men: Used Clothing

V.6 Mud and Dirty Work

that they rarely *own* land; and they have less land when they are farming than men do. In Chapter VI the social factors contributing to this increased vulnerability are considered, especially changing marriage patterns.

The Scope of Women's Involvement in Trade: Mobility and Differentiation among Traders

In 1987-88 it was very clear that there was a sharp differentiation among traders in their involvement in trade, which was reflected in profits and amount of starting capital. Table V.3 shows the mean average number of hours worked according to whether the selling location was a periodic or a daily market,[42] and the mean average amount of starting capital and gross profits (on a good day) in the two types of markets. The relatively long trading hours spent by those in periodic markets have to do with circulation among three markets or extended hours at two markets. Many rural women have become full-time traders, while some of those selling in rural markets came from urban areas. About equal proportions of men and women traders lived in Nairobi and traded in rural markets (8.9% of the men and 9% of the women). However, the numbers show more mobility among women than men traders; 36.1% of women traders (N=670) were trading outside of their home areas compared to 19.7% of the men traders (N=314). These men mostly came under the rubric of the "Nairobi hawker problem" mentioned previously, often selling imported goods like hardware and used clothing, while the women were more likely to be produce wholesalers. The mobility and hours worked by these women contradicts the stereotype of women trading close to home only as a minor sideline to farming and represents a change in the scope of women traders' operations.

V.3. Mean Average Hours Worked, Starting Capital, and Daily Profits by Gender and Market Type (Daily or Periodic), 1987-1988

Market type	Gender	Hours worked weekly N=979	Starting capital (Ksh.) N=835	Profits (Ksh.) N=1012
Daily	F	58.3	1004.13	135.9
	M	69.4	2542.16	301.5
Periodic	F	38.2	523.8	126.8
	M	54.5	1931.2	386.8

---

[42] Periodic markets included Wangige, Limuru, Gitaru, Karuri, the open air sections of Kiambu, Kawangware and Kangemi markets, and the open air section of Gikomba. Daily markets included Gikomba, Shauri Moyo, Kariakor, Westlands, Toi, Gachui, Ngara and Ngara Bean, Nyamakima, and the stalls at Kiambu, Kawangware and Kangemi.

In 1980 Kongstad and Monsted noted what they felt to be a new development in women's trade, the movement into long-distance efforts to the west--to the Rift Valley, Nyanza and Western Province. They considered it to be a longer distance and more intensive profit-making enterprise than the precolonial barter trade involving Kikuyu women.[43] Of the 403 Rift Valley traders in their sample, 40% were trading full-time. Among rural women householders 70% were involved in trade and half sold their own crops. Planting time was the least profitable for traders due both to shortages of supplies and the absorption of women's labor in agricultural tasks, which was confirmed by women in my samples. They also noted the separate venues for sales of women's and men's crops, marketing boards for male-owned cash crops, and local open air markets for women's food crops. They calculated that about 20% of produce sales in 1974-75 went through women traders in rural markets, 50% through rural male-owned shops, and 30% directly to marketing boards.[44] The establishment of Kikuyu women's trade across Kenya was evident in 1988 at Mbale on the Ugandan border, where there were four Kikuyu women shopkeepers, reportedly doing a "good business."[45]

In the Nairobi area, however, the mobility and scale of women's trade did not make a significant difference for their gross profits. Gender differentiation was always far more significant than either of these characteristics. As shown in Table V.3, profit levels did not differ much for women trading in daily versus periodic markets, although starting capital did. If gender differences were highly significant in Table V.3, they were even more evident in the short- and long-distance trade profits. Men who lived and sold in the same areas made significantly lower profits on good days than those who sold in different areas from where they lived: Ksh.262.95 daily versus Ksh.341.98. But for women there was no significant difference; those who lived and sold in the same area made Ksh.138.88 on an average good day versus Ksh.134.47 for those leaving their residential areas to sell. The gender differences here mark men who sell imported goods in rural areas off from poor rural women who turn to Nairobi trade due to landlessness and lack of capital; many are hawkers but some are wholesalers. Greater mobility did not bring a significant upward shift in profits for most women, nor did involvement in wholesaling.

Selling in a legal location also failed to make a big difference for women. Women selling in enclosed premises with a roof constructed in permanent materials made Ksh.138.88 on an average good day, compared to Ksh.131.38 for those selling legally outdoors, and Ksh.131.05 for those selling from illegal premises with no permanent infrastructure. Men paid more for selling space because they could afford more; they built illegal premises more frequently, for instance, or rented legal ones.

---

[43] Muriuki, *History*, p. 107, reported that precolonial women traders went as far afield as Nanyuki, Narok, Naivasha and Kajiado, perhaps half of the distances traveled now, an impressive feat considering that they traveled on foot heavily loaded.

[44] Kongstad and Monsted, *Family*, pp. 100, 119, 113-14, 107, 104.

[45] Pers. comm. Abwunza 10 Jan. 1988.

While more than half of the women were selling with no infrastructure compared to less than a quarter of the men, the number of men selling in enclosed legal market space was about equal to the number with no infrastructure. Unlike women, men showed significant differences according to the legal status and infrastructure of their selling space. Those selling in legal permanent enclosed premises made Ksh.221.96 on an average good day. Those selling legally in outdoor markets made Ksh.328.65, while those selling from illegal premises made Ksh.380.27. The latter results were strongly affected by the high profits of the used clothing trade. For men there was a strong disincentive to sell in legal premises, which applied to both genders when the costs of selling space are considered. The cheapest method of obtaining selling space was to sell in rural outdoor periodic markets for a fee calculated according to the quantity of goods brought there to sell. Next in cost was illegal space, subject in some areas to rents or initial fees charged by market committees. Highest in cost by far, at two or three times that of illegal space, were the rents charged for permanent selling premises in legal markets. But those in illegal space often needed to construct premises themselves, so their building costs were usually higher than for those with legal space. Adding building and acquisition costs of selling space together, women in the large sample paid an average of Ksh.227 for legal enclosed premises compared to Ksh.410 for men. Legal outdoor space cost women traders Ksh.35.5 on average compared to Ksh.85 for men, while illegal selling space cost women Ksh.211 compared to Ksh.265 for men.

The stunning results regarding starting capital and profits illustrate the relative success of women and men traders. In accordance with women's lack of access to critical resources like land, education and wage jobs, the mean average starting capital for those traders who used cash (many women began by using their own produce; cash starting capital is already a sign of greater resources) was Ksh.836.39 (approximately $50 in 1988) for women traders compared to Ksh.2353.91 (approximately $139) for men (N=1064 businesses). The ratio of average male starting capital to female starting capital was 281.4, which was exceeded by the ratio of average male profits to female, 292. Table V.4 shows the mean average differences by age and gender for profits made on good and bad days of selling (N=835 for good day, 828 for bad day).

On both good and bad days men's profits averaged more than twice those of women.[46] The reasons for men's greater profits included higher starting capital that allowed them to deal in commodities like imported goods, which had greater unit value than dried staples, for instance, or on a larger scale; lesser domestic work obligations; and longer work hours. Family obligations weighed heavily on women, not only in reducing their selling hours, but also in withdrawing capital from the business. Table V.4 shows that women's earnings dropped off sharply when women were

---

[46] These differences would have been even greater had the older male storeowners at Nyamakima been included, but the sample here is restricted to market and street traders.

V.4. Gross Profits of Traders, Good and Bad Days, by Age and Gender
in Kenya Shillings, 1987-1988

Age: Sex:	15-19	20-29	30-39	40-49	50-59	60-69	70+	Overall average
Female								
Good	153.6	140.4	151.8	120	114.8	97.8	105.1	132.9
Bad	90.0	45.4	46.6	40.4	28.0	24.7	35.0	41.5
Male								
Good	274.0	363.8	254.8	346.5	57.8	116.3	128.0	318.1
Bad	74.5	106.9	64.8	113.4	11.9	50.8	55.6	93.3

in their 40s, mainly because they withdrew capital to pay school fees, which increased as children got older.[47] Women's profits diminished at age sixty and over. For men the numbers are unreliable in the older, usually more successful, age groups because of the high incidence of missing data.

The relationship of land use rights to profit levels among traders ties together this section and the preceding one and makes a fitting ending to both. We have already seen that men with access to land had more than women did on the average, although more men were completely landless than women (87.6% versus 61.2%). Table V.5 shows that for men, in particular, a strong positive relationship existed between land access and trading profits. The association is uneven, but those with access to more land did tend to make more profits trading, especially men. They were also likely to have more starting capital. For women, however, profits fell somewhat when access to land rose above eight acres, probably because they put in more work farming. This evidence indicates strong differentiation among men

V.5. Distribution of Land Access and Trading Profits by Acreage
and Gender, 1987-1988

Gender:	% of those of same gender with land access:		Mean average profits (good day)	
	F	M	F	M
Acreage:				
Less than 1	33.1	19.1	109.80	150.00
1 to 3.9	46.6	56.1	107.42	342.64
4 to 7.9	11.7	14.6	208.58	286.17
8 and over	8.6	9.8	142.09	395.00

---

[47] This data answers the question posed by Parker and Dondo, "Kibera," pp. 30, i, regarding why women's businesses at Kibera showed lower survival rates than men's; had their survey research lasted longer than twenty-two days they might have confirmed this finding.

traders but only weak differences among women traders; virtually all the statistical differences between women and men were significant at the .00 level.[48]

"That's What You Eat": Change in the Dried Staples Trade in the Nairobi Area

Some of the increased mobility of women traders in and around Nairobi had to do with changes in the dried staples trade, an enduring and fundamental part of women's trade and the locus of success for a few of the wealthiest traders. Here I will situate this trade first in terms of its relationship to other trades after World War II, and second with regard to its profitability. Third, I will describe present conditions in this essential trade that feeds Nairobi.

The best way to understand the importance of the dried staples trade for women traders is to look at women's work histories regarding their involvement in selling different commodities. These results are presented in Table V.6 going back to 1965. Table V.6 shows that for women traders the dried staples trade formed the base from which most began.[49] Second in importance in 1987 were fresh vegetables at 35.5%, which showed a steady diminution back to 1960, when 17.6% of the commodities women sold fell into this category. Fresh vegetables, when combined with fresh fruit as they often were, were the most important commodity occupying women traders in 1987-88 at 43.9%, but in 1960 they comprised only 20.5% of the commodities sold by women compared to 58.8% for dried staples. Moreover, women have been taking over from men in this category. For men the largest growth was in the sale of used clothing, which had spread to rural markets and was overwhelmingly male dominated; women in the garment industry were more likely to be selling dresses, lingerie, or cloth, or operating dressmaking businesses.[50] It is clear, then, that for women traders there was more diversification over time, with increased involvement in selling clothing, fresh fruit and vegetables.

The selling of prepared foods, however, did not prosper, which differentiates these women traders from those in many other areas of the world, where they are a popular commodity for women traders. Until 1960 there was more involvement of women in selling prepared foods, but this tapered off in the late 1960s and early 1970s, only to begin again later. The earlier involvement occupied about 15% of the

---

[48] A USAID study of Kutus Market, one of the fastest growing markets in Central Province, found similar gender differences in 1988: women had a fourth to a third of the starting capital and half the sales that men did, less access to capital, and greater time constraints due to domestic chores. Women traders spent more on locally produced products and had a higher rate of return on their capital, indicating their willingness to put in long hours for little profit. USAID Kenya, *Newsletter* Oct. 1989.

[49] It should be remembered that this sample is overwhelmingly a market sample. In Mitullah's 1988-89 sample of hawkers there were only 2.9% dealing in dried staples; most (63.5%) sold vegetables or fruit, 18.8% sold prepared food, and 3.8% sold fish. Mitullah, "Hawking," p. 47. Although in my sample dried staples sellers were intentionally overrepresented, the historical data presented in Table V.1 justifies this procedure when the earlier years are considered.

[50] See McCormick, *Manufacturing*, for an extensive description and analysis of the Kenyan garment industry.

V.6. % of Commodities Handled by Traders by Gender, 1965-1987

Commodity:		Dried Staples	Fresh Vege- tables	Fresh Fruit	Pre- pared/ Canned Foods	Cloth- ing	Meat/ Fish/ Milk	House- wares/ School	Agri- cult- ural Supply	Other Supply	Total
Year	Gender										
1987	F N=631	36.6	35.5	8.4	1.6	10.6	3.3	3.6	.3	0	99.9
	M N=264	6.8	19.7	4.9	2.3	49.6	1.9	12.9	1.1	.8	100.0
1985	F N=461	38.4	33.2	9.3	2.0	7.6	5.2	3.9	.4	0	100.0
	M N=152	9.9	19.7	5.9	4.6	41.4	2.6	15.1	0	.6	99.8
1980	F N=251	38.2	34.7	10.7	2.0	6.0	4.4	4.0	0	0	100.0
	M N=64	14.1	10.9	6.2	7.8	37.5	4.7	17.2	0	1.6	100.0
1975	F N=131	42.7	32.8	7.6	2.3	2.3	6.9	4.6	.8	0	100.0
	M N=27	22.2	7.4	0	14.8	25.9	14.8	14.8	0	0	99.9
1970	F N=70	50.0	25.7	11.4	0	1.4	5.7	4.3	1.4	0	99.9
	M N=15	33.3	13.3	0	6.7	13.3	26.7	6.7	0	0	100.0
1965	F N=46	60.9	23.9	6.5	0	0	4.3	4.3	0	0	99.9
	M N=10	10.0	20.0	10.0	20.0	20.0	10.0	10.0	0	0	100.0

women traders from 1950 to 1960, and usually consisted of selling *uji* or *ugali*. The later less numerous involvement was more likely to include women who had managed to get enough capital to start a kiosk restaurant or a duka selling canned items. *Uji* is not usually sold separately in markets now and tends to be sold by itinerant hawkers. The profits from such small-scale efforts are not sufficient to pay for permanent selling space. Most small-scale prepared foodsellers are on the streets, among hawkers like the ones surveyed by Mitullah in 1988-89.[51]

From looking at changes in traders' commodities over time and the relative profitability of those commodities it is possible to make some educated guesses about changes in profit levels, although it is not safe to assume that commodities retained the same profit relationship as we move back in time. Table V.7 ranks commodities by groups and profitability while also giving the distribution of their sale by gender. Profits are average gross profits for a good day. Some commodities have

---

[51] Mitullah, "Hawking," pp. 34-35, 46.

V.7. Profitability of Trade in Various Commodities and
Distribution by Gender, 1987-1988

	Mean average gross daily profits (Ksh.) N=823			% of traders selling N=1000		
Gender:	F	M	All	F	M	All
Commodity:						
Clothing - used	285.04	546.92	462.63	4.7	25.5	11.6
Agricult- ural supply	140.00	550.00	345.00	.3	.6	.4
Clothing - new	262.94	286.51	276.30	9.9	20.2	13.3
Housewares/ School sup.	250.60	278.00	195.79	3.7	14.4	7.2
Prepared/ canned food	94.43	229.50	166.45	3.3	7.4	4.6
Clothing - accessories	n.a.	162.66	162.66	.3	4.3	1.6
Fresh vege- tables	109.17	277.85	140.84	32.4	15.6	27.0
Meat/fish/ milk	147.27	32.85	136.87	3.0	.9	2.3
Fresh fruit	130.15	148.21	133.49	8.4	4.3	7.1
Dried staples	105.70	167.90	110.14	33.9	6.1	24.9

undoubtedly fallen in level of profitability, the sale of fresh vegetables, for instance, under the impact of better transport and more competition. Nelson's 1979 study included some vegetable sellers whom she considered to be quite poor.[52] Thus, women's entrance into it in large numbers may have coincided with a loss in profitability. Conversely, the used clothing trade may have been more profitable due to its illegality. It existed as far back as World War I but has now grown considerably. It was extremely profitable for the business owners, but not for the many young sellers paid low daily wages by the owners.

The most significant results in Table V.7, however, are the lower profits of women than men in all trades except meat, fish or milk sales (where only two men gave profit information), and the lesser involvement of women in trades where profits

---

[52] Nelson, "Women," p. 293. Livingstone, *Rural Development*, pp. 6, 18-19, gave the following order of profitability for the informal sector from highest to lowest, omitting many women's trades: 1) auto repair, metalwork, food kiosks (average weekly income Ksh.500-600); 2) retailing, making furniture (Ksh.300); 3) charcoalmaking, tailoring, shoemaking, hairdressing (Ksh.110-190); 4) shoeshining and repair, clothes repair (Ksh.60-100).

are higher. The dried staples trade was lowest by far in terms of profitability. For most traders it is the equivalent of subsistence farming, subsistence trade. The attitudes of many women dried staples sellers about profits fit this profile. They calculated their profits insofar as they met the basic needs of themselves and their families. Some examples of responses to the question, "How do you calculate your profit?" were "By buying the children clothes"; "I don't calculate the profits. What I count on is the daily bread that I get... If I can afford a packet of maize meal, this is my profit"; "That's what I spend ... I first count to insure that the money used in buying is back, then the rest I can spend."[53] A woman at Karuri told us about her bean trade in the 1960s and 1970s: "the best thing was to find a sympathetic wholesaler who would sell to you using a bigger calabash." When asked about the problem of eating her capital, she replied, "What do you do if you care? I used to go there for my consumption needs and nothing else."[54]

Moreover, the profit margin in the dried staples trade has diminished substantially. As late as the 1970s and early 1980s (depending on the location) half calabashes (Kikuyu=*ciihuri*) were used as measures. Most traders owned more than one set of calabashes and preserved them carefully, sewing up any cracks. They were amazingly consistent in size. There were four sizes used by retailers, two for maize and two smaller ones for beans. The custom was to buy maize in the largest one, which held about half a kilogram, and sell a little less than half the amount in the second to the smallest calabash for the same price. Beans were bought in the second largest calabash and sold in the smallest one in the same manner, meaning that gross profits for both maize and beans were at least 50%. But in 1987-88 the usual measures were metal margarine tins (Kimbo or Blue Band) and maize and beans were sold in the same size tins for the same amount of profit regardless of price. For instance, beans sold for Ksh.12 to 18 per two kilo tin, including one shilling profit.[55] Maize sold at Ksh.7 or 8 per two-kilo tin with one shilling profit, meaning that gross profits for beans were 5 to 8% per kilo and for maize were 12 to 14%. The differences between calabash measures and margarine tins was well understood by some traders; one said, "The problem with the Kimbo tin is that you get very little [profit] because the Kimbo tins are equal in size." She meant that one buys *and* sells mostly in two-kilo tins. She thought people began using the tins because the calabash measures were too small, although we have seen that the government pressured wholesalers, at least, to standardize the measures.[56]

---

[53] Interviews D Gitaru: 6 July 1988; 118 Nyamakima: 7 Jan. 1988; 123 Nyamakima: 18 Dec. 1987.

[54] Interview H Karuri: 26 Oct. 1988.

[55] Kilogram equivalents for the old calabash measures are as follows in descending order of size: .5kg. (used to buy maize), .25kg. (used to buy beans), .22kg. (used to sell maize), .11kg. (used to sell beans). The metal tins come in four sizes: 2kg., 1kg., .5kg., .25kg. and may be used for either maize or beans.

[56] Interview 804 Kiambu: 12 Oct. 1988. Another woman claimed that the profit margin with calabashes was even greater--400%. Interview 731 Gitaru: 24 Aug. 1988.

V.7 Cartoon Commentary on Male Consequences of Female Action, 1988

V.8 Limuru Market, 1988:
Market Day at a Bulking Center

The diminution in the profits from the sale of dried staples is also evident in the historical information given by sellers in the small sample of fifty-six dried staples sellers. Traders were asked to give the buying and selling prices that prevailed when they began in business and those prevailing in the present by commodity. The results, a set of prices stretching back to 1952, allowed the calculation of sell:buy price ratios in a time series. Those who began selling beans before 1979, when calabashes were still in use in many locations, had an average ratio of 172(sell):100(buy). Those who began in the 1980s had 142, and the ratio at the time of the study was 124. Maize showed a similar pattern but the data were too sparse for a chronologically reliable breakdown; the average starting trade sell:buy price ratio was 160 for beginning trade compared to 126 for 1987-88. The ratios show less of a discrepancy between beans and maize than the information derived from measures would suggest. In 1987-88 beans were somewhat less profitable to sell than maize, despite their higher price. They were becoming a luxury food compared to maize, and were often sold in conjunction with maize or other foods like green vegetables. Many women carried an eighth of a bag of *nyayo* alongside other items, and *irio* was often made with very few beans. For poor people they were becoming a condiment rather than a staple.

In the markets about 15% of all traders were selling beans in 1987-88; in the census beans were 9.6% of commodities sold and maize 7.3%, indicating the widespread selling of small quantities of beans mentioned. Maize tended to be sold alone in larger quantities. Those who specialized in dried staples were likely to carry several bags of maize plus two or three varieties of beans; a few who specialized in beans had large inventories including more than a dozen varieties in colors ranging from bright pink and purple to chartreuse. Many sellers polished the beans to make them more appetizing and remove dust and pesticide residues. Dried staples had a significant presence in some markets but were absent from others for the most part. Legal market buildings at places like Ngara and Westlands tended to have very few dried staples sellers--one or two at most, whereas outdoor legal and illegal markets had more. At Gikomba about a fourth of the sellers dealt in dried staples and the rural outdoor markets all had their row or two of dried staples sellers.

The scale of traders' businesses can be differentiated on the basis of the amount they bought per buying trip. This was more constant than daily turnover, which varied extremely for individual traders according to season, supplies, and other responsibilities. If they could, traders tried to buy about the same amount daily or weekly, or whenever they had sold what they had. Thus, the amounts given here are also not calibrated to reflect buying within the same amount of time, which also varied. Rather, they reflected the amount of credit or capital available to traders. Most (41.9%) were concentrated at the level of purchasing one bag (90kg.) or less per buying session (these amounts are totals of all dried staples purchased). About a quarter (25.6%) of the forty-three women who gave information purchased two to four bags at a time, while 20.9% purchased four-and-a-half to six bags. Only 11.6% purchased seven to ten bags. When divided between wholesalers and retailers, the range of amount purchased for wholesalers was from thirty kilos to ten bags, and for retailers from five kilos to ten bags.

Qualitative data reinforce the impression of differentiation among traders illustrated statistically above. Among traders the poorest were normally the hawkers, lightly represented in the sample.[57] Hawkers who sold fresh vegetables or dried staples often went door to door selling to Asians or Europeans. Ngara Bean market served as a congregating point for such hawkers, who purchased from wholesalers on credit before trudging out with their heavy loads to sell. They were mostly Kamba, tightly organized into a women's group with an elected market head and secretary who zealously watched out for their welfare. Hawking territory was carefully apportioned; trespassers aroused hostility. A common story among them involved starvation during the drought of 1984, sitting at home in despair over feeding their children.[58] Sometimes the woman and her husband then devised the strategy of her going to Nairobi to trade, or more commonly, a woman friend already involved in the Nairobi trade helped her get started with credit, beans and contacts. These and some women at Gikomba formed the majority of those who lived part-time in Nairobi and the rest of the time in Ukambani, where they tried to keep up their farming activities. They and many of the Kamba basketweavers at Kariakor slept wherever they could, not being able to afford permanent accommodation in Nairobi. Sleeping accommodations included the benches of several kiosk restaurants, charcoal depots, and various shops at Gikomba, whose proprietors charged a nightly rate, usually Ksh.1/50 (approximately a dime). The Kariakor cooperative members had purchased a bus, in which they slept until it broke down.

The Nairobi *Standard* of 13 July 1988 carried an article by Joy Mutero about "Mama Mboga" [Kiswahili=Mama of the vegetables], Nyina wa Muiruri, a Kikuyu vegetable hawker. It was illustrated by a picture of a heavily-laden woman with a large burlap bag of fresh vegetables on her back held with a tumpline and a *kiondo* on her arm, dodging trucks in a Nairobi street. Nyina wa Muiruri lived at Banana Hill near Karuri and traveled before dawn by bus to Nairobi with other women friends/sellers to Wakulima Market to buy supplies and then to her selling route in Parklands. At Wakulima she bargained with wholesalers before going to sell to her Asian customers. She normally carried her toddler with her, when he was younger nursing him at stops where customers asked her to shell peas (at no extra cost). Nyina wa Muiruri and her cohorts were not selling at the roadside because of the

---

[57] This is particularly true for dried staples sellers. Mitullah's results ("Hawking," p. 52) showed that street hawkers' profits were generally somewhat higher than those of the dried staples hawkers. Commodity differences in profits in the markets are mirrored by those on the streets.

[58] Interview 94 Ngara Bean: 4 Nov. 1987; Mitullah, "Hawking," p. 45. An older Kikuyu woman who was one of the founders of this market said that before 1984 she would bring the dried staples to Ngara and then tell the Asian customers to fetch them. But with the famine the Kamba women started coming and bought them from her to go hawking for smaller profits. Interview 59 Ngara Bean: 26 Oct. 1987.

problems of illegality and police persecution, nor could they afford to sell in markets with their high costs and competition. Sometimes the women carried cold *irio* with them in plastic bags to feed themselves as they went along, since customers objected to them doing so on their property. Unsold vegetables were taken home to feed their children. When interviewed Nyina wa Muiruri was later than usual because she had had to cook for her son. She was twenty-eight years old in 1988 with one son to support, no husband visible.[59] Her profile fits that of many dried staples sellers, who bought supplies on credit or for cash to sell in Nairobi. Mitullah's sample of 1988 included 425 roadside hawkers, 67.6% of whom were female, with an average age of 33.9 years, 59.8% Kikuyu, 54.3% of whom were married, 88.7% unlicensed, and 36% of whom had been selling for over five years.[60]

Such hawkers are a long way from the farmers who sell small quantities of homegrown produce in rural markets, even though they may live in the same village. But not all rural traders are farmers. In the 1987-88 census 31% of the women were selling in rural markets but only 26.1% were farming. In a 1979 study Schmidt described typical rural dried maize traders. He said that most moved between two markets or more, usually within a fifty-kilometer radius, that most had working capital of less than Ksh.500 and handled less than 340 bags of maize per year.[61] The impression given is not one of generalized prosperity.

The middle of the spectrum is well represented by the 400 or so dried staples sellers occupying a hillside at Gikomba, an illegal location containing the largest dried staples market in Nairobi. These women plied their trade daily, sitting in the sun with open bags of staples spread out in front of them on wooden platforms. Their infrastructure varied with the whims of the police; in 1984 they had elaborate flimsy structures of plastic sheeting which made the hillside into a veritable rabbit warren. In 1987 they had been reduced to no covered shelter, for the most part, and their stock was being adversely affected by weather conditions, especially rain, while they themselves suffered both from the high-altitude intense sun and heavy rain that turned the black cotton soil into muck several feet deep.

At Gikomba the dried staples sold differed from those at Ngara; Ngara served the Asian market selling rice, chickpeas, green and black grams, coriander, and even millet grown in Ukambani or Kirinyaga. They also sold *phaseolus* beans, but these were found in much greater profusion at Gikomba, where *nyayo* and pinto beans outsold competitors. Even *njahe* could be found there. Most women carried more than one kind of bean and many sold maize also. They usually purchased supplies from wholesalers, women who arrived with truckloads early in the morning, the delivery involving frantic offloading in five minutes for fear of police interference. Occasional small wholesalers with a few bags arrived later.

---

[59] *Standard* 13 July 1988: 11.

[60] Mitullah, "Hawking," pp. 29-43, 46, 55.

[61] Schmidt, "Effectiveness," p. 161.

The Gikomba sellers participated in group buying to try to secure the best price from the wholesalers (a widespread practice at many markets) and also decided the selling price among themselves. Anyone trying to undersell the others was ostracized and prohibited from selling there.[62] At other less tightly organized markets[63] individual women calculated their own selling prices, as described by the proprietor of a well-stocked stall at Kiambu Town Market:

> When I buy a bag of beans or *njahe* I sell it in tins. So I calculate how many [2kg.] tins are in a bag. They could be about forty. I then decide for how much I am going to sell each tin so as to have a profit. You have to learn these things for this is like education. Many people do not even know how many tins are in a bag. Business is like a school where some excel while others fail. Depending on how the prices are, I fix my prices and decide I cannot sell lower than that. Customers have faith in me because I always have everything.[64]

Damaris, handsome and vigorous at age fifty-two, was a reasonably successful staples trader at Gikomba who stood out not so much because of her business, which was prosperous but not spectacular, but due to the lively personality and energy that led her to be elected to the market governing committee by the staples traders. The day we first interviewed her was hot; the car parked near the beansellers was sweltering despite open windows. She sat composedly with her five-year-old granddaughter on her lap, who idly swung a foot against the dashboard.

> Damaris was born at Masi in Machakos. She grew up farming with her parents, and married a man from Makueni when she was only fifteen. She continued farming but he went to Nairobi, quit providing any support, and ran around with other women. They had ten children, three of whom died as infants. Her childbearing ended when she effectively left him in 1975 to go to Nairobi to trade (she still considered herself to be married, however). She left the children at Makueni; by 1988 all but one had left home and the youngest daughter, a fourteen year old, was staying with Damaris' husband on the farm.

Damaris' work history encapsulated the transition from rural-based suppliers to urban-based businesses, and from beans to maize.

> Damaris began trading when her husband's support disappeared by selling cowpeas she had grown. With those profits she progressed to collecting cowpeas and mung beans, and bringing them to Nairobi to sell at Gikomba. But this was not profitable enough so she established herself in Nairobi and began selling full-time at Gikomba in 1975, dealing in cowpeas, *njugu,*

---

[62] Interviews 214 and 241 Gikomba: 16 Mar., 22 Aug. 1988.

[63] There is no free selling space at Gikomba except in the small periodic market for fresh produce attended by sellers who came from as far away as Kisumu.

[64] Interview 808 Kiambu: 19 Oct. 1988.

nyayo, pinto beans and maize. Maize was her principal commodity; on a good day she would sell up to six bags of it. Beans had become more of a sideline; she would sell only about one bag total divided among several varieties on a good day. Normally she was buying supplies at Gikomba; only if there was a scarcity would she go collecting herself. She was still spending about three months a year at home farming, but most of the time she stayed at a rented room in Kitui Village in eastern Nairobi, a squatter settlement upgraded by a development project. Nonetheless, she invested her profits at home; by 1987-88 she had built a market stall in her local market and a five room brick house with a metal roof for her family on her husband's land, which they had obtained by squatting and then official allocation when ownership was privatized. Her ambition was to purchase land at Yatta for her eldest son, but she feared that the cost, Ksh.22,000, would be too much. She said, "I'm searching! I'm trying!"[65]

Similar processes that supply Nairobi with dried staples go on at many locations. The chief supply points for dried staples to Nairobi were Gikomba for Rift Valley staples, Ngara for Ukambani products, and Nyamakima for Loitokitok beans sold to storekeepers and street traders there. A visit to Loitokitok yielded a picture of a dusty frontier town with one main street lined with small shops and trucks bearing the owners' names stenciled on the sides. The owners of the pickups are the most successful women dried staples wholesalers.

Dried staples wholesalers were not numerous; they made up about 6% of all dried staples traders and only 4.8% of the women staples traders. More sold both wholesale and retail (7.6%), while an overwhelming proportion (87.6%) sold retail only. The dried staples wholesalers in the large sample made significantly higher profits than other dried staple sellers at an average of Ksh.185.23 on a good day for women versus Ksh.580 for men. The women who sold both ways (there were no men in this category) made an average of Ksh.118.23 on a good day, while retailers averaged Ksh.33.48 for women and Ksh.42.21 for men. Retail maize traders tended to make more on the average than retail bean traders (Ksh.100.77 versus Ksh.83.94 daily on a good day), while bean wholesalers made somewhat more (Ksh.324 versus Ksh.300 per good day for maize). Only the dried staples wholesalers did better than the Ksh.130 average for all women traders.

There is therefore no strong incentive to go into dried staples wholesaling, especially since the costs are significantly higher for transport and accommodations away from home.[66] Moreover, wholesaling staples is not for the elderly or infirm. It is a strenuous life in which traders go as far afield as Taveta, Nakuru, Loitokitok,

---

[65] Interviews 241 Gikomba: 17, 31 Mar. 1988.

[66] Bryceson, *Liberalizing,* p. 199, also found little differentiation between the profits of women wholesalers and retailers.

V.9 Kawangware Market, 1988:
Crowded Conditions in a
Suburban Dried Staples Section

V.10 Ngara Market, 1988: Mixed Crowds, Prosperous Customers in a Legal
Urban Market

Eldoret and even Malaba Market on the Ugandan border.[67] Although in theory wholesalers should make significantly better profits than retailers, in this sample they showed a virtually identical profit margin to retailers and lower differences in quantities bought than one would expect (wholesalers averaged 413.35 kilos per buying trip versus 220.08 kilos for retailers). In effect, the wholesale dried staples trade was often a transition point for farmers and traders; they began by selling their own produce wholesale and worked up to having enough capital to set themselves up in retail trade. From this beginning a few of the very successful then went into large-scale wholesaling, but many wholesalers operated on a small scale with only about five bags turnover per week.

Rahab is a good example of a staples wholesaler.

In 1987 Rahab was forty-seven years old, selling chickpeas and black grams at Ngara Bean market. She was not sent to school; her parents thought it would corrupt her into prostitution. Nor was she taught to trade. "Problems taught me to trade," she said. She started trading in the late 1950s by selling her own produce for twelve shillings. With that money she purchased maize and beans at Kagio Market to sell at Kandongu Prison in Kirinyaga. When the prison moved she sold at Kandongu Market, accumulating capital of Ksh.600 with which to start trading to Nairobi. Rahab's seven children were getting older and she needed to pay school fees. The transition into the Nairobi trade was enabled by a woman friend who showed her how to do it. For four years they traveled together. They also began growing coriander, black grams and chickpeas, popular commodities at Ngara Bean market, where they sold both wholesale in large quantities to hawkers and retail. When her mentor died Rahab continued on her own. By 1987-88 she had been coming to Nairobi for some fifteen years, spending half the week at home in Kirinyaga farming her son's five acres, and half the nights in Nairobi sleeping at a charcoal seller's.

Despite the years put in selling, Rahab's weekly turnover was only five bags of beans. She could not always meet family expenses and sometimes had to borrow from friends (five of the children were in school, one at boarding school). Her husband's sporadic earnings as a casual farm laborer were not sufficient to provide for the family's cash needs. Her oldest daughters both had completed Form 4 and were helping their younger siblings when they could. Sometimes she rented land to supplement their subsistence needs. Her mother-in-law helped with farming and by cooking for the children, who stayed at Mwea while Rahab came to Nairobi. The children still at home, aged twelve to twenty-two, also helped with farming

---

[67] Interview 153 Gikomba: 4 Mar. 1988.

in off-school hours. Rahab had built a three-room, mud-and-thatch house for her family.[68]

Rahab demonstrates well the lack of differentiation between the profits of wholesalers and retailers; indeed, her profits were substantially lower than those of Damaris and her struggle to keep both farm and business going considerably more, despite the help of her relatives.

There were and are, however, successful businesswomen in Nairobi, although few of them are involved in the dried staples trade (including one shopowner at Nyamakima). Some started in it, as did so many traders, but moved on to bigger profits in other commodities. One of the most successful Nairobi businesswomen in the 1960s was probably Wanjiru wa Rara, a Muslim Kikuyu woman. Her career started long before that, however. Under colonial rule Wanjiru occupied land on the present site of the Norfolk Hotel until dispossessed by Colonel Grogan. She farmed along the Nairobi River, growing and selling vegetables, and grazing a large herd of cattle and sheep. She was then removed and resettled on twelve acres at Ndeiya. Despite the poor quality of the land, she developed it and built a large European-style house there, and also moved into the business of renting houses at Pumwani. She lent support and encouragement to politicians like Kenyatta and Koinange from their earliest days and was among the first to visit Kenyatta upon his release from prison in 1960.[69]

Another prominent Nairobi businesswoman, Lisa Syokau Munyao, began selling maize and beans in Nairobi in 1959, returning to her home at Kaungundo to sell foodstuffs. She then moved into selling beadwork, mats and *ciondo* from Ukambani to tourists in Nairobi. She organized a women's cooperative, but she continued to do small-scale farming of staples at her home. Her ambition in 1983 was to open a shop in Nairobi to sell the cooperative's products. She complained of not being able to use the family land as collateral for loans, saying, "Don't treat women as men's property but as individuals in their own capacity."[70] Clearly, some women are building up enough capital to set up businesses of some scale. Barriers are also falling for those

---

[68] Interviews 61 Ngara Bean: 27 Oct., 10 Dec. 1987.

[69] Urban real estate is successful urban women's most popular investment; it is most achievable in squatter settlements like Mathare Valley and Kibera. Parker and Dondo found that 49.2% of the rental property in Kibera was female-owned in 1990. Parker and Dondo, "Kibera," p. 23. In contrast, the ambitions of women in my surveys focused overwhelmingly on rural land ownership. In the small survey only three women (5.4%) got income from rental properties, two of which were in villages. Mungai and Awori, *Reflections*, pp.x-xi.

[70] Mungai and Awori, *Reflections*, pp. 51-52. There are a few very successful corporate businesswomen, including the CEO of a large Kenyan branch of an American multinational and the owner of several cinemas and *matatus*.

with enough capital to establish shops in rural markets; 14.3% of the shops at Gitaru Market in 1987 were allocated to women.[71]

Most dried staples sellers, however, were poor women selling in space that cost little, in accordance with their means, and that in Nairobi was illegal. Their very concentration in those areas increased competition, to which some reacted by group buying and setting prices. The poorest of the poor were the hawkers described above, but even the average staples traders were poor. As a consequence they and many other traders generally had a low commitment to selling their commodity; most said they would rather sell anything more profitable but lacked capital to do so. This is a fragile foundation for the trade that does the most to feed Nairobi, made even more precarious by the government persecution that will be considered in Chapter VII.

The chief dilemma facing most traders is poverty. Their profits illustrate clear gender differences and can be situated in relation to standard of living requirements in Nairobi in 1987-88. After subtracting the costs of doing business, net profits were approximately 12% of gross profits according to information given by traders. On this basis mean average daily earnings of women traders were Ksh.10.45 (approximately $.61) compared to Ksh.24.7 (approximately $1.45) for men, both of these well below minimum daily wages in Nairobi of Ksh.30.8 (approximately $1.81) in June 1987. The 1987 *Statistical Abstract* for Kenya defined households with poor incomes as earning less than Ksh.700 ($41.18) per month (middle was Ksh.700 to 2499, up to $147, and upper was Ksh.2500 and up, over $147).[72] Male traders were earning an average of Ksh.669.12 (approximately $39.40) per month compared to Ksh.229.12 (approximately $13.50) for women, who less often had household income supplemented by other earnings.[73] In the small sample a quarter of the women had supplemental income beyond that from trading, which averaged Ksh.193.65 per month, or Ksh.6.45 daily not counting costs (of rental maintenance or farming inputs, for instance).[74] Most of that income came from selling crops or milk separately from the market trade. It was clearly not enough to make a significant difference to the standard of living for most women.[75]

---

[71] *Standard* 14 Sept. 1988: 4; interview Muigai: 12 Aug. 1988.

[72] Kenya, Central Bureau of Statistics, *Statistical Abstract 1987*: 257, 260ff.

[73] This calculation factors in the lower average number of days worked per month for women than men cited above. It also assumes the lower profit margin associated with the dried staples traders, who were most numerous in the sample and almost universally female. It therefore understates the earnings of men and women dealing in more profitable commodities.

[74] Mitullah, "Women," p. 19, found that the vast majority of Nairobi hawkers had no supplemental source of income outside hawking.

[75] Except for the three who got more than Ksh.700 per month. Only one woman did wage work in addition to trading, casual agricultural labor that yielded Ksh.700 per month on the average.

V.11 Kiambu Market, 1988: A Talented Businesswoman and Her Well-Stocked
Dried Staples Shop

V.12 Gitaru Market, 1988:
Spacious Shaded Grounds,
Stores Surrounding Square

Traders' Coping Strategies

Trade as a survival strategy for women is intimately affected by their great family obligations. Women began trading at an older age than men, 30.6 versus 25.1 years, not just due to family crises. The usual pattern was for older women to trade and leave younger women (their daughters and daughters-in-law) to farm and care for young children. The average age of women traders was 39.6 years compared to 33.6 for men (N=1017). When traders were asked why they began selling, over a fourth of the women cited family needs as primary compared to less than 7% of the men. Moreover, 13% of the women, but no men, mentioned landlessness, widowhood, divorce or insufficient earnings by a spouse.[76] In general, women pointed to economic necessity in their reasons more than men did (58.3% versus 50.1%), and men's reasons in this category were more often to support themselves rather than their families (16.1% versus 8% for women) or the failure to find wage employment (23% versus 6.8% for women). Among positive factors attracting people to trade, profitability was most important for both men and women (25.3% for men and 20.1% for women), and men were more likely to be seeking economic independence (13.7% versus 6.7% for women).

It is in the patterns of women's and men's involvement with trade, however, that the most crucial differences are evident. Although women averaged more years in their businesses due to their older age (6.1 years per trading business versus 4.1 for men), for most age groups men's businesses had endured longer, signalizing both women's greater potential for bankruptcy and women's tendency to begin later (N=897 trading businesses). However, 43.1% of the businesses of the women trading in 1987-88 had lasted five or more years, compared to 28.9% of those of the men, and fewer women had businesses with durations of a year or less (15% of women compared to 20.6% of men). The biggest difference favoring men was in the one to 4.9 years duration range, where 50.6% of men and 41% of women had businesses. These results reflect both women's lack of other opportunities and their greater age, and men's tendency to move in and out of trading with wage work providing other options. A few men had even taken up trading as a retirement occupation. Women averaged fewer occupations over their lifetime than men did; among those aged fifty to sixty-nine women averaged 2.9 occupations compared to 3.9 for men (N=132). Women aged seventy and over averaged only two occupations--farming and trading. Most importantly, women staples sellers (N=56) had erratic patterns of growth and shrinkage in quantities bought--over time half of their businesses grew and half shrank, with length of time in business making *no* difference to that pattern. In 1989 Parker and Dondo's study of small enterprises in Kibera found the same pattern for women's businesses but steady growth as a characteristic of men's businesses. Moreover, when businesses failed women were more likely to become unemployed,

---

[76] Women also cited generalized poverty among their reasons about twice as often as men did (6% versus 3.2%).

whereas men were more likely to start up again. McCormick in 1988 also found that women owners of garment businesses had more family expenses than men and shorter-lived businesses.[77]

The same patterns prevailed when traders listed reasons for quitting occupations. Both women and men named unprofitability as their chief reason in identical proportions (38.7% for women and 38.6% for men), but for women family reasons were next at 19.1% compared to 1.8% for men (2.6% of the women cited the husband's disapproval as a reason among these). For men reasons related to wage jobs were most important--being fired or having a wage work opportunity open up, for instance--which applied to 28.5% of the men, but only 11.7% of the women. Among other reasons for quitting women named problems with the following more often than men did: harassment or licensing from authorities (3% versus 2% for men), supply or spoilage (7.6% versus 6.1% for men), high competition or a poor selling location (3.8% versus 1.8% for men), and health (7.6% versus 5.9% for men). Men seemed more willing to quit a job for personal reasons such as disliking the boss or wanting self-employment (14.4% versus 8.5% for women). Overall, it is clear that family reasons loomed most important for women, while wage-related opportunities were more likely to affect men's choice of occupation.

Individual women's coping strategies show creative management of extremely limited resources. Four abbreviated life histories encapsulate the experiences of two very poor women, one rural and one urban, and two middling-to-prosperous traders in urban markets.

> Wairimu, a wiry woman full of nervous energy at age forty-seven in 1988, had three teenage children and was selling beans at Gitaru Market. She never married and therefore had no land, but made do by farming a quarter of an acre of poor quality government land, which was too small to grow maize. To help support her children she had also joined two women's associations. For one she made sisal bags much in demand on the international market. A woman wholesaler from Meru bought them at a low price for resale. The other one was a cooperative farmwork group composed of church members. These efforts plus selling her produce two days a week in the market were insufficient to earn a living, however. Her nineteen-year-old daughter helped her farm, but the two sons were respectively unemployed and underemployed. Wairimu was also doing casual farm labor five or six days a week for Ksh.20 per day wages (approximately $1.18). Her employer wanted to reduce these further by giving her a monthly wage, but Wairimu refused because she could neither afford a pay cut nor a wait for her wages. At one point she was employed digging ditches for the Nairobi City Council, but that paid even less.

---

[77] Parker and Dondo, *Kibera*, pp. 22, 27; McCormick, "Enterprise," p. 223.

Wairimu worried a lot about their survival. She did not blame the father of her children for his non-support, as her reputation was impaired by having been interned at age thirteen during the Emergency in the 1950s for several years. Girls in such a situation were routinely molested by Homeguards, although Wairimu said that this did not happen to her because her breasts had not developed yet. A male friend was instrumental in putting her in touch with her parents after she was summarily removed to the detention camp, and remained her faithful friend until they later became lovers. But he was poor and her parents disapproved of the liaison; she had to devise various pretexts to meet him and never did spend a whole night with him. Eventually they had a disagreement over her joining the Anglican Church and he married another woman. He never paid bridewealth for his "wife" either, so both of his unions remained in common-law status. He had four children with his wife and never gave Wairimu or her children any support. Her younger brothers had too many children themselves to help her, so she soldiered on, perforce on her own. She said, "I will do anything to get money."[78]

The next woman was an urban vendor selling beans on the street at Nya-makima.

Wambui was thirty-seven years old in 1987. Her careers undertaken to feed herself and her five children spanned the legal to the illegal. She moved to Nairobi from Murang'a when her husband, who was selling sec-ondhand clothes, sold his farm with her house on it. She and the three chil-dren were starving and left. She considered herself to be divorced. In any case, she felt that her husband had betrayed her in some sense by not telling her before they married that he had had another wife before her, who ran away because of ill treatment. Upon coming to Nairobi she lived for some time from liaisons with men, especially a long-term one which produced two children, so that in 1987 she was supporting five children aged nineteen down to five years. She took up residence at Mathare Valley and began selling vegetables at Wakulima Market. When that business failed she turned to beerbrewing, a risky but sometimes profitable occupation.[79] In this case it worked for three years but then she was arrested and jailed, effectively ending her business and putting her chil-dren's welfare in jeopardy. After six months she emerged from prison in 1985 and began selling beans at Nyamakima. In November 1987 the police were raiding that location at least once a week, confiscating the

---

[78] Interviews 728 Gitaru: 3, 17 Aug. 1988.

[79] For a description and analysis of this industry mostly conducted by poor women in the 1970s see Nelson, "Buzaa Brewers," pp. 77-98.

traders' commodities and/or fining them, with the encouragement of local dried staples shopowners.

Wambui formed part of a youngish tough group of traders in a tough neighborhood, for whom illegal activities were a way of life and necessary to survive. Her battle for survival made her a strong believer in birth control, at least for other women. She felt that women should have only one or two children because of the difficulty of supporting them. Her oldest daughter at age nineteen was unemployed; her fifteen-year-old son sold vegetables at Wakulima. Her twelve-year-old daughter also stayed home, but the eight-year-old was in school. None had gone to school past Standard 4. She stressed the importance of educating the children and the extremities brought on by her fourth pregnancy, which also bore the stigma of illegitimacy. "I almost committed suicide because of the pain I was feeling. But I said I won't abort and persevered ... and again with the fifth child. I actually cried ... I knelt down and prayed to God not to give me another child... I have never conceived again. Maybe it is God who helped after hearing my prayers."[80]

Despite their divergent experiences, these two women shared not only their poverty but also some characteristics contributing to that poverty. Both had little or no formal education; Wairimu was taking adult education classes to learn to read and Wambui had had no schooling. The men involved did not take any major responsibility for their children. Wambui's husband occasionally gave money for food and clothes. He also paid bridewealth and the union was sanctioned by her parents, but the marriage ended after eight years and his irresponsibility endured for much of that time in Wambui's view. Both women adopted various strategies to earn a living, Wairimu more than Wambui. Both grew up in rural areas and had worked farming and in Nairobi (Wambui farmed until the land was sold). These women worked very hard at their occupations, more than sixty hours a week not counting domestic work. But despite their labor, they and their children were at risk. None of their children had progressed past Standard 6 in school, and both had unemployed grown children to support, posing the risk of also supporting grandchildren. Their move to the Nairobi area also signalized the beginning of the formation of multigenerational female-headed households. Contrasting the experiences of Wairimu and Wambui, it is clear that Wairimu had a slight edge over Wambui. Although most of Kenya's worst poverty is rural, Wambui was worse off because of her complete landlessness, her higher dependency burden (she was also helping to support her mother back in Murang'a), and her sole dependence on a marginal trade perpetually vulnerable to police harassment. Her income was, in fact, substantially below that of Wairimu, who herself was one of the poorest in the sample.

---

[80] Interviews 114 Nyamakima: 27 Nov. 1987, 7 Jan. 1988.

There are, however, somewhat better off traders whose earnings are in the middle to higher range among traders. One had the great advantage of having an official market stall, and represents a female rags to riches story.

Florence, an attractive, slim and vigorous extrovert, left her husband when he lost out in a land dispute with his younger brother. She was forty-five years old in 1987 and the mother of nine children, running a restaurant at Ngara, a legal Nairobi market, with several employees. She had been in Nairobi for seventeen years, working her way up from selling green maize at Wakulima and peddling fresh vegetables from home to home. This activity was interrupted by a bout with tuberculosis in 1984, at which point the Nairobi Senior Medical Officer intervened and requested city officials to provide better housing for her and her family. A large loan was given for the purpose of building a house at Dandora, a self-help housing scheme, to replace the paper shack at Mathare. In 1987 Florence was living there with six of her children, and three grandchildren by an unmarried daughter. Some of the money saved by not putting a door on the two room house went to set up the business.

Three of Florence's children had reached Standard 7, and her eldest daughter was pursuing adult education and sewing classes. Florence herself had been to Standard 4. Three of the children had acquired skills enabling them to get jobs (two sons and a daughter), while one daughter was also trading. The youngest four children, aged fourteen down to eight, were in school at levels appropriate for their ages. Florence said that none of her grown daughters, aged twenty-seven, twenty-four, and nineteen, had married because her own experience was so bad. Her in-laws had harassed her and her husband had abused her, none of them providing any support. She left partly because she sought "the freedom to rear her children." She preferred not having her daughters help her in the business because she saw a conflict between their roles as mother and as employee. Since the older daughters all had children (an average of three apiece), she felt that it made more sense for them to stay with their children to avoid childcare problems.

Florence's TB was cured, but she said that she could not work as hard as previously. Nevertheless, she had great plans for the business, which required capital to carry out. She wished to divide the stall and make part of it into a canned goods shop. She wanted her daughters to have their own businesses. "I can make my own way," she said. "A husband is good for what??"[81]

---

[81] Interview 26 Ngara: 16 Oct. 1987.

The last history returns us to dried staples sellers.

Caterina was a fifty year old Kamba woman selling chickpeas and millet at Ngara Bean market. She had six living children in 1987, four others having died as children of measles. She and her husband were farming at Embu, which met their needs until the 1984 drought. At that point their cattle died and her husband asked her if she could do something to earn cash to help with the children's school fees. They then adopted the strategy that he would look after the children in Embu while she traveled to Nairobi to sell dried staples. She began trading with the help of her coworkers, who taught her how to do sums so she would not lose money. First she hawked from door to door and then she worked up to selling larger quantities on credit to hawkers. She was buying staples in rural areas and taking them to Nairobi for sale in a small wholesale and retail business. Caterina's earnings were going for food, clothing and school fees for the children and for occasional support for her husband's sister and her five daughters.

The strategy seemed to be paying off with regard to paying school fees, helped along by Caterina's membership in two women's groups. Caterina boasted, "My daughter has never been sent home from middle school because fees are not paid." The oldest daughter reached Form 2, the next son Form 1 and was still continuing, as were the younger children. But the life was strenuous and exhausting. She would spend six weeks in Nairobi, sleeping at a carpentry shop in a large market, and then two weeks at home. Her husband did not cook for the children, so she relied on her eldest daughter to do so. Caterina was adamant, however. Once when she was sick her daughter was helping her trade and complaining about how tiring the work was. Caterina said, "That's what you eat."[82]

Conclusion

In this chapter the increasing intensity and scope of women's involvement in trade,[83] its expansion, and changes in the commodities sold, as well as the large socioeconomic differentiation between women and men traders were shown. Indeed, these differences may have been minimized to some extent by the concentration on a female-dominated commodity like dried staples; Thomas-Slayter and Rocheleau chronicled increasing competition between men and women in the Murang'a banana trade, for instance.[84] The fragile economic position of many traders makes the construction of a trade system that feeds most of Kenya a miraculous achievement. If a

---

[82] Interviews 71 Ngara Bean: 29 Oct., 1 Dec. 1987.

[83] Monsted, "Division," pp. 293-94, has demonstrated a similar phenomenon in South Nyanza among the Luo.

[84] Thomas-Slayter and Rocheleau, *Gender,* pp.94-95.

few women were able to accumulate capital, more had substantial impediments to doing so imposed by women's lack of access to critical resources and disproportionate burden of domestic responsibilities. This aspect provides a cautionary note to those who would blithely ignore gender differences in assigning small traders to a class. There are far fewer nascent bourgeois among women than men traders. However, those who do exist are in town, as the land access statistics showed. Paradoxically, rural women traders had less access to land and more poverty than urban women traders, showing that urban trade contributed to bettering the economic well-being of some of its women participants. Also demonstrated here was the strategic necessity for women to trade and the possibilities that trade could offer for success. Although most women traders suffered multiple handicaps to achieving success in business, trade still offered some enticing possibilities. Not the least of these was economic independence from men (even the customers were mainly women). Women who achieved economic independence did not have to tolerate abuse from men, a possibility that will be expanded upon in Chapter VI, where long-term changes in marriage are explored to refine our understanding of the reasons for women's trade suggested in this chapter. Another possibility offered by trade is the forming of solidary links with other sellers which alleviate women's burdens, increase their business options, and reduce their vulnerability to persecution. Chapter VII analyzes these facets of trade.

But the best possibility offered by trade for most women traders is assuring their survival in an uncertain world. A woman at Kawangware conveyed to us an urgent message for other women,

> As you move around, when you find somebody that is suffering, advise them to try and sell whatever little that they have. They could help themselves and their children, because husbands these days, even if they work, will enter that bar and meet Kamau's father and Njoroge's father. By the time he gets home you have eaten saltless food. Women must wake up and learn not to depend on people.[85]

---

[85] Interview 561 Kawangware: 23 June 1988.

VI

"Seeking the Freedom to Raise my Children": Changes in Marriage[1]

One does not always know when changes are occurring but realizes later on that the things she is seeing are different from what they were before.[2]

The significant role of family obligations in motivating and setting limits to women's trade was evident in Chapter V. Changes in marriage patterns have affected women's trade and vice-versa; they renew the gender segregation motif of this study. Marriage[3] is a key factor in determining women's status and wellbeing in such patrilineal societies. To get at the complexities of marriage I have integrated material concerning ideals and attitudes toward gender and marriage, the arrangement of marriage and husband-wife relationships, wife abuse, and the use of fertility control methods into a consideration of intrahousehold economics in the widest sense. Broad changes in central Kenyan marital patterns from 1890 to 1990 will be delineated here, with particular attention to the period from the 1920s on. The 1920s and 1930s will form a baseline from which to establish change, albeit not a pristine or reified "traditional" one in any sense. The picture that emerges here is fragmented in many ways, with inherent contradictions that resist easy assignment to stereotypical categories making women either subjugated or free. Marital relationships are historicized, rather than essentialized. In the 1940s and later the contradictions become, if anything, more extreme, with marital crises accompanying erosion of the economic basis of marriage. Socioeconomic change is more easily observed over a long period of time, so that its analysis is compressed here into one chapter. The changes entailed women's growing efforts to control their own marriages and their bodies. It is not accidental that women traders demonstrate higher rates of change than among the general population, for they are, through circumstances or self-selection, more likely to be women faced with all of the challenges of independence.

I will concentrate here mainly on Kikuyu social structure, for which the early documentation is vast compared to the Kamba, and which meshed at many points with that of the Kamba due to their proximity and trade connections fostering

---

[1] Interview 26 Ngara: 16 Oct. 1987.

[2] Davison and Women, *Voices*, p. 102.

[3] The definition of marriage used here corresponds to that of my informants, meaning that it changed over time and referred to a number of different kinds of arrangements in which women called a partner husband; similarly, divorce here means an acknowledged permanent separation of the spouses, which might or might not have been formalized.

intermarriage. They seem to have had many similarities in older times and differences exaggerated as Nairobi grew and urbanization became an important facet of life for Kikuyu from Kiambu and Murang'a, in particular. Only recently have Kamba women been coming to Nairobi to trade in large numbers so that similarities are growing once more. The small sample upon which many of the conclusions here are based was 80% Kikuyu and 20% Kamba in composition. There were few observable differences rooted in ethnicity pertinent to this discussion of marriage.

MARRIAGE IN THE 1920S AND 1930S

The oldest group in my samples first married in the 1920s and 1930s when central Kenya was experiencing the late 1920s crisis discussed in Chapter III regarding female genital mutilation, independent schools, and women's mobility as traders. At various points leviratic marriage, the use of bridewealth to cement marriage alliances, customary dance celebrations, polygyny, clitoridectomy, puberty rites, and arranged marriages all came under attack from missionaries. But missionaries and administrators set up counterdiscourses regarding African women to some extent and had differing goals. The legal status of African women as minors was put at issue early on because of the desire by some administrators to make them responsible parties under the Masters and Servants Act, so they could not renege on labor contracts without punishment. Little compunction was felt about subjecting local cultures to arbitrary attacks under the law or from missionaries. In 1919 the Crown Counsel said, "there is nothing to prevent the Legislature from repealing or modifying existing Native law and custom," and in 1933 this position was reiterated with particular reference to African women by the Attorney General.[4] The missionaries staked their claims to African women, especially in the arena of marriage, and the ensuing conflicts challenged African male control of women. The standard of leaving intact customs "not repugnant to humanity" fell where Christian women converts were concerned. Such women, many missionaries and administrators felt, were not to be forced into leviratic marriages or marriages with "pagans," or under pagan guardianship. Christian girls chose their own husbands. One option for girls wishing to avoid forced marriages was to flee to mission stations, which were relatively thick on the ground in Kiambu.[5] For African men another chief issue concerned retaining polygyny while becoming Christian, an untenable position so far as the missionaries were concerned. A few who tried it were imprisoned for bigamy in 1928.[6]

---

[4] AG 4/2791 Crown Counsel to Chief Native Commissioner 16 Apr. 1919; Attorney General to Secretary, Kenya Missionary Council 16 Feb. 1933.

[5] PC/CP 6/4/4 has a lively correspondence among missionaries and administrators on the status of African women. See especially Appendix B of "Memorandum on the Status of African Women" to the Senior Commissioners' meeting of 22 July 1921. DC/KBU 1/14 Kikuyu District AR 1920-21: 39; Blakeslee, *Curtain*.

[6] Kenyatta, *Facing*, pp. 261-62; DC/KBU 1/18 Kiambu AR 1925: 3; PC/CENT 2/1/4 minutes Kiambu LNC 24 Nov. 1925; 22-23 Nov. 1928; PC/CP 4/2/1 Roman Catholic Mission Report 1914-15.

However, before World War II there seems to have been very little actual impact of Christianity on most marriages in the area. Many schoolgoers still made polygynous marriages. In Nairobi in 1918-19 there were only twenty African marriages under the 1902 Marriage Ordinance establishing a European-style contract entailing monogamy and spousal inheritance rights. The missionaries were frustrated by their lack of converts; very few men, in particular, had become Christians even in the early 1940s.[7] The oldest women in the small sample did not come from early Christian convert families, many of whom have now become quite elevated in socioeconomic status due to early access to Western-style education. Only one fits the pattern so deplored by male elders in the 1920s and 1930s; she went to school for five years after her initiation, got pregnant by a boy met there, ran away to Nairobi and married him. Nonetheless, bridewealth was given and the parents consulted after the fact.[8]

What was the situation regarding marriage among the oldest women in the small sample of fifty-six women interviewed in 1987-88? An examination of marriage can be resolved into three topics: the arrangement of marriage, the formalities accompanying it, and spousal relations, which include polygyny and divorce. In looking at the arrangement of marriage it is necessary to keep in mind that arranged marriage is not synonymous with forced marriage; the data here show a continuum regarding choice of spouse by women. Among the dozen women aged sixty and over, 40% arranged their marriages themselves together with their future husbands, 26.7% had the marriage arranged for them by their parents, and 33.3% by the husband and their parents. In only 11.1% of marriages were the parents not consulted at all before the marriage. In 30.8% of marriages the women and their future husbands were already lovers when she went to join him, often when the woman was pregnant. This evidence of independent decisionmaking in the matter of choice of spouse was somewhat overbalanced in this group by that regarding parental choice.

In 1919 an assistant DC said that the High Court's ruling that no marriage was valid without the mutual consent of the partners was nonsense given the customary arrangement of the marriage by the fathers of the bride and the groom.[9] Only a third of the women in arranged marriages had met the husband before the marriage was arranged, and only a fourth felt that they could have refused to marry the proposed spouse. In almost half of the marriages women felt that they had had no choice in the matter, even when no overt coercion was used by the parents. Marriage without the bride's consent was a feature of three-quarters of the arranged marriages, and in half of them the women were not consulted by their parents at all. The usual method for making a marriage involved the parents arranging the marriage, more often than

---

[7] DC/KBU 1/12 Ukambani Province AR 1918-19: 14; Sluter, "Confidential Report on Migrant Labour and Connected Matters in Four Villages in the Kiambu Reserve of Kenya," [1958] p. 102.

[8] Interview 667 Kangemi: 25 July 1988.

[9] AG 4/2791 Assistant DC Nyiaki to Provincial Commissioner Mombasa Feb. 1919.

not with the future husband's participation, although Lindblom claimed that a rich man might arrange his son's marriage without consultation.[10] Several women gave good descriptions of usual Kikuyu or Kamba methods of arranging a marriage. A Kikuyu woman in her sixties said,

> The man decides, 'I would like to wed so and so's daughter,' then he would go to her home and pause at the gate, then the girl would go, they would talk. If the girl refused, no wedding; if the father refused, said he didn't want that relationship, no marriage ... You might meet at dances where he would ask, 'whose daughter is that?' He is told. 'Is she good? Is she humble? Is she good for a wife?' He is told. It was not that you would meet and talk.[11]

Porridge figured largely in the symbolism of another woman's account.

> This is what used to happen. If you wanted a girl, you sent a friend and he told the girl, then the girl went home and said, 'Mother, I've been told to make porridge for so and so's son, can we get married?' If you were told yes, then you did.[12]

A Kamba woman mentioned a less direct version.

> During our time the parents would look for a girl for their son because they feared that the son would look for a girl who was not admirable, who was lazy and so on. The son would report to his parents that he needed a wife. The parents would mention to their son a certain girl whom they thought was good enough for a daughter-in-law, and then it would be their son's duty to watch the character and the movements of that girl. For example, the young man would follow me to the forest when I went to collect firewood or to the river when I fetched water. I would run away from him because it was not allowed to talk freely. After some time he realized that I needed him for a partner... We courted then, but in a very secretive way.[13]

It was considered to be a sign of virtue if the girl had never met the man before; this was more likely if the man was older and arranging his own marriage than if both potential spouses were in a first marriage negotiation. First marriage partners were more likely to have grown up together or to have met at one of numerous dance celebrations which served as the chief method of socializing for young people. Boys and girls usually danced separately, and girls were not supposed to talk to men (a common cautionary tale is the story of a girl who goes off with a handsome man met at a dance, who turns out to be an ogre). After the initial vetting by the husband-to-be his parents went to see those of the girl carrying beer as a gift; if it was accepted by the girl then the negotiation of bridewealth was on.

---

[10] Lindblom, *Akamba*, p. 78.

[11] Interview 59 Ngara Bean: 26 Oct. 1987.

[12] Interview 185 Gikomba: 26 Feb. 1988.

[13] Interview 65 Ngara Bean: 5 Jan. 1988. No one mentioned the permitted petting (Kikuyu=*ng'weko*) which was also the object of missionary disapproval.

There were, however, ways that couples could shortcircuit this system, which might have been more necessary if the prospective groom was poor. The ritual kidnapping that formed a part of the procedure for escorting a girl to her husband's home after all negotiations and ceremonies were concluded was sometimes arranged between the partners without consulting the parents. Alternatively, a woman might simply go to her future husband's home and stay there overnight, or stay with him elsewhere overnight, forcing a marriage, as would a pregnancy. A poor man was more likely to elope or marry a widow.[14] Occasionally a man would kidnap a woman to force her to marry him. If a rich man did it then the bride's father was entitled to take as many goats as he wanted from him; if a poor man there was no remedy and the bride's parents might not recognize the union as a marriage due to the absence of bridewealth. One woman never was allowed to join the man she regarded as her husband, although they had three children, because he was poor.[15] Class relations played a role in marriage; forced marriages may have been more common for girls whose parents were ambitious to marry them to wealthy, politically influential older men, as suggested by incidents described by Blakeslee at Kijabe in the 1920s.[16]

Leviratic marriage was viewed by many Europeans as a form of forced marriage.[17] There were aspects of women's position that made it difficult to avoid; the only way a widow could absolutely be assured of having access to land was to marry her deceased husband's brother, even if she had sons. Leakey assumed that the universal practice of the levirate meant that there were no destitute widows.[18] This practice and that of all children born during a marriage belonging to a husband, whoever their genitor, meant that the only way a woman could "own" her children was to remain unwed when she had them, which not only bore a stigma but also meant landlessness unless her father was willing to give her land to cultivate. No one in the small sample got land from a father, nor did anyone have an infant betrothal, another form of imposed spousal choice (Middleton and Kershaw and Lindblom reported it was common).[19]

This variegated pattern concerning arrangement of marriage conforms neither to Kenyatta's glowing 1930s' description of marriage as a "free choice of one another by the boy and girl" based on "the freedom of association and physical intercourse which has been allowed to them before marriage [which] ought to have made

---

[14] Lindblom, *Akamba*, pp. 75, 81, 35, in 1920 denied that ritual kidnapping took place with the Kamba, but described a faked kidnapping as a means for a couple to arrange their own marriage.

[15] Interview Mwaura 4 Mar. 1988. *Kugurana na gitanda* refers to marriage without bridewealth. In order for the husband to claim bridewealth for a daughter he was supposed to pay it for his wife. Pers. comm. Mwangi Apr. 1995. Interviews 82 Ngara Bean: 9-10 Nov. 1987.

[16] Blakeslee, *Curtain*.

[17] Blackburne-Maze, *Journals*, p. 231; Cagnolo, *Akikuyu*, pp. 289-93; PC/CP 6/4/4 E. K. Figgis, Memorandum on the Status of African Women, Appendix A June 1913.

[18] L. Leakey, *Southern Kikuyu* I: 12.

[19] *Central Tribes*, p. 59; interview Kershaw: 4 Aug. 1994; Lindblom, *Akamba*, p. 78.

each of them competent to select a mate with good judgment,"[20] nor to colonialist suppositions of forced marriage as the norm. Nor was the desire among administrators to "free" African women such that they were willing to abrogate the rights of the parents of Christian women to control their daughters' marriages. In 1931 the Native Christian Marriage and Divorce Ordinance abolished the necessity for Christian widows to practice the levirate and gave them the right to be guardians for minor children, but also said that their marriages had to be registered with their parents' consent. An investigation of the situation in the late 1930s by several administrators and missionaries disproved the common assumption expressed by a DC in 1921, who said that a girl was only consulted regarding choice of spouse if her "accepted lover has as many goats [used for bridewealth] as the other man."[21] The investigation concluded that the ritual protests of girls at marriage were just that and that most men "found that a really unwilling wife was usually more trouble than she was worth." Alfred Mutheri, a Kikuyu clerk in the Kiambu DC's office, wrote a memo stressing the ritual obligation of girls to protest against being taken away from their parents and dismissed the missionaries' claims that many girls were running away from forced marriages. Those who ran away, he said, were "trouble givers." The issue of religion was raised on both sides, with Kikuyu men complaining that missionaries encouraged such runaways, while the Municipal Native Affairs Officer in Nairobi in 1936 said forced marriage did not arise there since "pagans" married elsewhere "or else bloom out after a month or two in Nairobi as fully fledged Mohammedans." In Nairobi there were many marriages between Muslim porters and Kikuyu women, forming a cohesive Islamic community.[22]

Having established that neither the degree of freedom nor of coercion regarding choice of spouse conformed to the descriptions of authorities on the subject, how does one explain that the most reliable ethnographers of the 1930s agreed that there was no forced marriage among the Kikuyu? After all, in 47% of their marriages the oldest women claimed that they could not have refused parental choice of a partner. There is, of course, the male dominant ideology that says that women only marry men out of preference and the tendency to ignore women's views. Also, ethnographers could have been harkening back to an idealized precolonial situation when women were less commodified and bridewealth was lower, before the crises of the late nineteenth century. Ethnographers could also have been, as Leakey was, looking

---

[20] Kenyatta, *Facing*, p. 302-03; L. Leakey, *Southern Kikuyu* I: 10;II: 750, also said that marriage was made by consent of the woman only.

[21] AG 4/2791; LG/1/57 minutes Nairobi County Council Kiambu Road Board 6 Dec. 1921: 49. The frequent discussions of such matters by this body was probably due to lack of other venues for such topics, but may also have alleviated boredom.

[22] PC/CP 19/1 Memo. Alfred Mutheri to Provincial Commissioner Central Province 9 Oct. 1936: 1-2; DC S. Nyeri to Provincial Commissioner Central Province 26 Oct. 1936; DC Nairobi to PC Central Province 27 Oct. 1936; Bujra, "Ethnicity," pp. 5-7, 18. In the 1950s some Kikuyu took Muslim identities to avoid repatriation to the Reserves.

VI.1 "Forced" Marriage in the 1930s: "The Bride Dragged to Her
Mother-in-Law's"

at daughters' first marriages among wealthier families, where the bride was most likely to be consulted,[23] whereas women traders were more likely to come from families undergoing economic stress who might have been trying to mend their fortunes by making an advantageous marriage. Whatever the reason, marriage was a lineage affair and women not usually left to choose their spouses alone; those who wished to do so did so covertly and ratified their choices either by consultation with the parents or elopement. Mwangi claimed that in the old situation a girl could not have refused to marry her parents' choice because of "a beating or worse force."[24] One woman said, "I couldn't have refused, since it was the approved and routine method for making a marriage. If I had refused, I would have been taken there by force."[25]

The administration's reasons for minimizing the importance of forced marriage are clearer. H. E. Lambert, ethnographer and colonial administrator, said that it was not a "serious evil" and the administration should not deal with it. "On the one hand we must avoid any step which will weaken parental authority over girls, and the indirect encouragement of immorality, and on the other stimulate and encourage any modification of marriage custom which will render forced marriage in that district [Meru] impossible."[26] Getting rid of "forced" marriage, as with the abolition of domestic slavery, would have been difficult to impossible, expensive to enforce and caused rebelliousness among groups the British wished to keep subordinate. Therefore, leaving patriarchal controls intact was found to be the best policy except when British economic interests were directly affected, as with the labor issue.

The Formalities of Marriage: Bridewealth and Ceremonies

By the 1920s and 1930s there had been substantial inflation in bridewealth and a partial conversion to cash in some cases. In 1920 Lindblom described Kamba wives fleeing their husbands to elope to Kikuyuland, while Kikuyu men working in Ukambani were sometimes given poor widows as wives, thus allowing poor Kikuyu men to avoid paying bridewealth.[27] There was an influx of livestock into Kiambu in the 1930s that enabled men to attract brides from Murang'a.[28] Wage work allowed some young men to arrange their own marriages and reduced their dependence on senior male relatives for bridewealth. A rearguard action was fought by the elders to stop the monetization of bridewealth, which helped to delay its spread until the

---

[23] L. Leakey, *Southern Kikuyu* II: 750-52. I am indebted to John Lonsdale for an enlightening exchange on this topic. Pers. comm. 26 Jan. 1994.

[24] Mwangi, *Folktales*, p. 124.

[25] Interview 167 Gikomba: 23 Feb. 1988.

[26] PC/CP 19/1 PC Central Province to Colonial Secretary Nairobi 9 Nov. 1936.

[27] Lindblom, *Akamba*, pp. 82ff.

[28] Kitching, *Class*, p. 223; DC/KBU 1/14 Kiambu AR 1920-21: 3; White, *Comforts*, p. 35; PC/CENT 2/1/4 minutes Kiambu LNC 12-14 Jan. 1932; Kanogo, *Squatters*, p. 23; Leakey, *Southern Kikuyu* I: 172.

1940s.[29] Some missionaries and colonial officials complained that inflation was making it impossible for some men to obtain wives and privileging wealthy elders, and supported rather than attacked bridewealth. Missionaries, scholars, colonial officials, and Kikuyu elders deplored the consensual unions and prostitution they felt were caused by inflation.[30] In the small sample the husband's parents paid the bridewealth in 75% of the marriages of the oldest women, so control seemed to be fairly firm, especially since those who paid their own were usually older men. The one divorce was insisted upon by the woman's parents over her objections because of nonpayment of bridewealth.

For most people the marriage ceremony appears to have been far more elaborate than anything surrounding birth or death, an aspect which differentiates central Kenyans sharply from coastal West Africans, and resembles strongly patrilineal European systems in some ways. Kenyatta described the importance of marriage, which

> means the linking of two families in bonds which are social and economic as well as biological, and which are, in fact, the connecting links of tribal life. The code which regulates the behaviour of relations by marriage is, therefore, a most important matter in its bearings on the whole of social life and has to be carefully learnt and punctiliously followed. Marriage, and especially parenthood, gives a man his full share in the common happiness and qualifies him to think for the common good.[31]

Women also assumed maturity with motherhood, the payment of bridewealth establishing the husband's and his lineage members' exclusive rights to her labor, body and children.

The negotiations surrounding marriage were complex, therefore, and not extensively described by my informants, who often said that since they themselves had not participated in them they did not know details like the amount of bridewealth (a notable exception was the ninety-four year old who boasted, "Hey! I cost a lot!"

---

[29] PC/CP 6/4/5 DC South Nyeri to Senior Commissioner Kikuyu Province 10 Apr. 1926. Sometimes there was what L. Leakey called (*Southern Kikuyu* I: 10-11) matrilineal marriage with strong influence by the mother's brother. See also PC/CP 4/2/1 Ukambani AR 1912-13: 1-2; PC/CP 4/2/2 Ukambani AR 1920-21: 17; DC/KBU 1/13 Handing Over Report Ukambani Province 1919-20: 2; LG 1/57 minutes Nairobi County Council Kiambu District Commission and Road Board 18 Mar. 1919; Mathu, "Gikuyu Marriage", p. 25; DC/KBU 1/18 Kiambu AR 1925: 3; DC/KBU 1/19 Kiambu AR 1926: 8-9; ARC (MAA) 2/3/1 VIA Nairobi Municipal Native Affairs Dept. AR 1938: 8.

[30] PC/CP 6/4/5 DC S. Nyeri to Sr. Commissioner Kikuyu Province 11 Jan. 1927; LG 1/57 minutes Nairobi County Council Kiambu Commission and Road Board 6 Dec. 1921; DC/KBU 1/13 Handing Over Report Ukambani Province 1919-20: 2; PC/CENT 2/1/4 minutes Kiambu LNC 6-7 Aug. 1931; LG 1/57 minutes Nairobi County Council Kiambu Commission and Road Board 6 Dec. 1921. Leakey, "Problem," p. 281n., blamed the inflation on missionaries who insisted that the whole bridewealth be paid before the marriage so that it became a brideprice instead of a guarantee.

[31] Kenyatta, *Facing*, pp. 302-303.

and proceeded to enumerate items and livestock).[32] In the negotiations, as described by Mathu,

> each stage and set of rules [were] meant to fulfill specific purposes and obligations in consolidating the entire marriage relationship ... and publicly commit[ted] the people of two different families to increasingly binding obligations such that they must be full participants rather than mere spectators.

In this process "female children [were] ... looked upon as the connecting link between one generation and another and one clan and another, through marriage, which [bound] the interests of clans close together and [made] them share in common the responsibilities of family life."[33]

The actual ceremonies showed individual, class, regional and temporal variations, the following description pertaining to the 1920s and 1930s. Generally, after the initial exploratory period and the acceptance and drinking of beer, which sometimes occurred twice and was supposed to symbolize each time the bride's giving consent, the groom's parents began collecting bridewealth of thirty or forty sheep and goats. The groom's family also provided a fat sheep for slaughtering at an engagement ceremony where arrangements were made to finalize the marriage. Kenyatta mentioned that a written contract would be signed at that time. The final ceremony involved a big dance and a feast at which six fat sheep provided by the groom were consumed. After that the bride could join her husband at any time; his young female relatives would escort her, while she lamented loudly with her age-mates, to her husband's home.[34]

The ceremonies described by my informants usually involved only one feast, in contrast with the more elaborate precolonial forms entailing five beerdrinkings described by Leakey.[35] The ceremonial aspects described by this woman were typical of Kikuyu marriage among the oldest group in the sample.

> It would begin with the man sending other young men who would tell the girl's father [about the man's interest]. The father would refer the issue to her mother, 'Ask your daughter what I heard.' If confirmed and they had no objection, the man's household would brew *njohi* [beer]. The two clans would drink and the announcement be made. The parents were now friends and they began *matega* [exchanging gifts]. As the friendship grew, the negotiations began and the man would start bringing bridewealth. My husband first brought Sh.800 ... then six cows in calf. He was told to pay ninety goats ... he could only afford seventy so he pleaded with my father. Then he brought the ceremonial two he-goats for the feast. I was already pregnant so that is where it rested.[36]

---

[32] Interview 77 Ngara Bean: 11 Nov. 1987.

[33] Mathu, "Gikuyu Marriage," p. 3.

[34] Kenyatta, *Facing*, pp. 157ff.; Mathu, "Gikuyu Marriage."

[35] Interviews 185 Gikomba: 2 Mar. 1988; 144 Gikomba: 23 Feb. 1988; L. Leakey, *Southern Kikuyu* II: 761ff.

[36] Interview 175 Gikomba: 1 Mar. 1988.

Kenyatta called marriage "an adoption ceremony," in which women became members of their husbands' lineages. Mathu stressed the negative in describing the giving of *kiande* meat by the bride to the groom, a part of the ceremony which "sever[ed the bride's] right and her future children's right to inherit any property of her father or her children's maternal grandfather."[37] An essential purpose of marriage was the perpetuation of the clan by bearing children. Middleton and Kershaw called birth "the means by which the present recreates the past and the future," referring to the belief that continued communication with the ancestors by young members was necessary to secure the clan's well-being.[38] Marriage and control of women in order to assure reproduction of legitimate children were therefore a duty to assure the welfare of the clan, transposed by Kenyatta into the welfare of the Kikuyu nation. For lineages, the issue of control over women's bodies focused primarily on women's biological reproductive function rather than on their sexuality, since any children born during a marriage (or after it, for that matter, given the proper ceremonies) were attributed to the husband.

Spousal Relations among the Oldest Women

A successful marital relationship for a woman depended upon how far she was effectively incorporated into her husband's lineage; the construction of wifehood stressed docility and humility as appropriate behavior for women. Among the expectations of wives listed by informants in the small sample, which were fairly consistent over all age groups, 14.2% concerned obedience to the husband and/or his relatives, 22% involved fidelity and loyalty to the husband, while 4.3% of the obligations specifically concerned wives tolerating husbands' infidelity. Twelve percent concerned wives providing care for their husbands, yielding a total of 52.5% of obligations entailing caring for or pleasing the husband and exercising restraint in one's behavior. The major obligations of husbands as seen by the women, however, were more restricted to their role as provider; 28.8% of the obligations concerned supporting children with an additional 4.6% involving school fees, in particular, while 32% concerned supporting wives, and another 5.9% involved the desirability of a hardworking provider.

Among the oldest group of sixty and seventy year olds most women said that they did not socialize with the husband after marriage; before marriage their socializing mainly involved going to dances. This pattern, also stressed by Lindblom for that period,[39] conforms to the usual separate socializing of the genders noted for much of Africa. A strong majority reported liking (90%) and trusting (85.7%) their husbands, while a minority reported verbal (28.6%) or physical (33.3%) abuse from

---

[37] Kenyatta, *Facing*, pp. 166-67; Mathu, "Gikuyu Marriage," p. 12. The aspect of marriage involving abandonment of rights by women has often been ignored by ethnographers. Kershaw, for instance, concentrated upon its establishment of land rights. Kershaw [Sluter], "Land," pp. 197-98.

[38] Middleton and Kershaw, *Central Tribes*, p. 38.

[39] Lindblom, *Akamba*, pp. 408, 436.

VI.2 Waithera, A Retired Beanseller, and Her Husband of Seventy Years, Peter, at Their Home Near Wangige Market, 1988

the husband. Husbands and wives were fairly similar in age, the husbands averaging 3.3 years older than the wives. The average number of husbands per woman over her lifetime was 1.2 due to several leviratic marriages. Forty-three percent of the marriages were polygynous, the largest number of wives a husband had at once being three, and 30% of the oldest women approved of polygyny. The average duration of marriages was 27.4 years.

Using the women's priorities expressed in their narratives about their relationships with their husbands I devised a rating system for marriage relationships with a scale from 1 to 5, 5 being the best.

5.   Very good marriage: good understanding between spouses, good level of communication and contentment, good financial support by husband, little or no abuse.
4.   Fair marriage: usually got along, some support by husband, abuse uncommon.
3.   Mediocre: business-like relationship, sporadic support, some quarrels and abuse.
2.   Poor: frequent quarrels, little support from husband, regular abuse, may have separated though still married.
1.   Bad: divorce, lots of abuse, nonsupport by husband.

In the oldest age group the average marriage rating was 3.6, higher than for any other group, and the incidence of reported abuse was the lowest, a finding supported by the Routledges' observation in 1910.[40]

Most of the women said that they were happiest during the courtship period and early in the marriage, especially before any children died. The death of a child, experienced by most, was their most grievous experience, and they were happier before there were many children to feed. In a few cases the love lasted throughout the marriage. A Kikuyu woman in her seventies described an idyllic marriage for her,

> I love him because we have been together since our youth and now we are old. We have always been happy. He never struck me and there were no quarrels. He is my husband, my darling. We used to say that we were married when he was a *kihii* [lad] and I was a *kirigu* [lass] and we are still together.[41]

Infatuation played a lesser role for a Kamba woman in her sixties, but she appreciated her husband's good qualities.

> I loved him and he also loved me a lot. He was a good man; he never stole anything or fought anybody. He was also hardworking. I never saw a fault in him, not one. He never struck me or yelled at me and he was always ready to help me

---

[40] Routledges, *Prehistoric People*, p. 135.
[41] Interview 185 Gikomba: 2 Mar. 1988.

whenever I asked. He trusted me and never asked me where the children came from [infidelity is implied].[42]

The oldest women generally believed either that their husbands had fewer opportunities for infidelity and were faithful, or more commonly, said that they did not know if they were or not, and that it did not matter in any case. They agreed that male fidelity to wives is a contemporary expectation by women.

The views of a proper marital relationship reported by 1920s' and 1930s' written sources are, logically enough, more male dominant than those of my informants. Lindblom said that in marriage, "woman's artfulness is more than a match for man's wisdom," in describing women's use of manipulatory mechanisms such as spirit possession to extract benefits from husbands like meat and clothing. Although he felt that most Kamba marriages were based on "mutual attachment," he also stressed economic factors. "Every native [sic] desires to have many wives since the number of wives he has is to a material degree a criterion of his importance and wealth."[43] Cagnolo cited several proverbs illustrating patriarchal values: "starting a home is the beginning of troubles"; "a man should be master in his own house." Kenyatta, whose project included restoring the reputation of Kikuyu women for a British audience, stressed the submissive behavior incumbent upon wives: women were to be bashful and respectful toward their in-laws, not eat in their presence or expose the body improperly, not to utter unpleasant words and to speak sweetly. They were not to look directly at men while speaking to them.[44] Men were to avoid their mothers-in-law and be respectful toward their elders. Women's sexuality was to be controlled by the husband to the extent of entertaining a member of her husband's age-set with sex if the husband so directed. But any choice of sexual partner by the wife without the husband's knowledge was regarded as adultery and could bring a beating or divorce, and a fine for the lover. Prohibitions on sexual intercourse outside the homestead or when the husband or children were away also contributed to enforcing women's marital fidelity.[45]

The generally positive view of marriage by the oldest women included accounts of peaceful ways of solving disputes, as well as some abuse. A woman in her sixties at Gikomba said, "Yes, we had quarrels here and there, but then we sat down and I told him if I was offended and he told me too. So we cleared the air." One woman complained of repeated beatings but said that it was never done in public and no one knew about it, which seemed to excuse it in her view since she was not publicly humiliated (the assumption that the beating was provoked by her shortcom-

---

[42] Interview 82 Ngara Bean: 9 Nov. 1987.

[43] Lindblom, *Akamba*, pp. 229ff., 72, 79.

[44] Cagnolo, "Akikuyu," pp. 211-18; Kenyatta, *Facing*, p. 19; L. Leakey, *Southern Kikuyu* II: 814.

[45] Cagnolo, "Akikuyu," p. 206; Kenyatta, *Facing*, pp. 175ff.

ings is evident here). She also claimed that they made it up and forgave each other.[46] Another woman felt that her marriage was saved only by the timely intervention of her mother-in-law. Her husband had already driven off several wives by his ill treatment; when she came her mother-in-law adjured him to treat her better, saying, 'This one is mine. I want to see her here. She is not going anywhere, all right?' But in-laws could also cause problems, as could the demands of parents regarding bridewealth. Esther Ngima reported that her husband would check up on her by visiting his mother before returning home; the mother would tell him lies about her, especially complaining of her failing to help with the farmwork, and then the husband would return home and beat her, a pattern that lasted for years.[47]

Polygyny was a fruitful source of rivalry in some cases; the Kikuyu word for co-wife, *muiru*, derives from the word for jealousy. The hierarchy among wives that affected trading also determined the location of a wife's hut (the first wife's faced the compound entrance), land allocation (a new wife's came from the first wife's allowance), and deference patterns.[48] First wives had advantages but their sons stood to lose out if more children split the inheritance. There is disagreement in the sources over the incidence of polygyny. In 1910 the Routledges claimed that monogamy was usual, as my results from the 1920s and 1930s support, but they also said that it was a result of poverty. When polygyny occurred, they said, two or three wives were usual; only rich men had more--maybe six or seven. Kenyatta said that most heads of household had two wives, and that wives wanted husbands to take another wife to share the workload.[49] The six women among the oldest group who were involved in polygynous marriages were mostly first wives and did not complain about their experiences with polygyny. They said that there was enough land to go around, that they were consulted about taking another wife and expected it, and that they were treated equally, touching on the three key issues involved in polygyny for women. By the time of the survey, however, most of the oldest women disapproved of polygyny, saying it was no longer affordable.

The general impression given by the oldest women about marriage is a good one; it was a productive if unequal partnership in which land was cultivated, children raised, and a hierarchy of respect maintained. There was a sense of security in the preservation of hierarchy and rules, and economic conditions were better. In their view the important thing was to get on with the work, not niggle over details like a husband's infidelity. There may be an element of idealization here. Most of the oldest women (77.8%) were widows and speaking of past conditions in which unpleasantness may have been masked in order to save face and improve memories. Then

---

[46] Interviews 165 Gikomba: 26 Feb. 1988; 167 Gikomba: 23 Feb. 1988. Lindblom, *Akamba*, p. 446, cited a male Kamba viewpoint that concurred in the desirability of maintaining public, non-humiliating, peace.

[47] Interviews 77 Ngara Bean: 12 Nov. 1967; 667 Kangemi: 25 July 1988.

[48] Interview Fisher 14 Oct. 1992.

[49] Routledges, *Prehistoric People*, p. 134; Lindblom, *Akamba*, p. 81; Kenyatta, *Facing*, pp. 169-70; Boyes, *King*, p. 303, gave the same rationale in 1911.

there were also the expectations, which included male dominance expressed in physical abuse and a double standard regarding sexual fidelity. They may have understated the incidence of physical abuse. Lindblom stated unequivocally that husbands had the right to beat their wives, especially if infidelity was suspected, and even detailed forms of torture used by husbands on wives. If his assertion that Kamba women did not like to marry far from home was correct, it may have had to do with looking to their own relatives to protect them from abuse.[50] A woman in her nineties said, "In our times there was a song ... , 'the man beats the drum, tri, tri, tri, he beats and you are moving; I come, dance.'"[51] The complex of meanings here well expresses the marital allegory. Beating and dancing are at once literal, metaphorical, and sexual. Dancing serves both as compulsion and escape. The one constant is the chief instigator of action, the man.

Divorce was not unknown but very rare for the Kikuyu, and common for the Kamba, in Lindblom's view. When it happened it was often a consequence of women running away, as we saw in Chapter III; the anxiety provoked by unruly women among men extended beyond the simple desire to control their wives. Complaints about divorcees collecting bridewealth for their daughters surfaced in the elders' council, along with a suggestion that such an offense be criminalized and the women imprisoned.[52] Perhaps the best summation of marriage was made by the seventy-four-year-old woman whose description of an idyllic marriage cited earlier was accompanied by a more realistic view.

> The best times were when we were young because then we had a lot of love and I do think that love is still there... We stayed without bitterness... In our days there was no time for leisure. You got married, found women in that home. You couldn't eat meat or sugar cane before you were permitted, and a year always passed before you got a child. You never called anyone by name [women were/are called 'mother of so and so']. When our children died we comforted each other and said it was the will of God. How things are today? Well, I don't understand them.[53]

CHANGES IN MARRIAGE, 1940s TO 1980s

Having established a baseline to serve as a departure for discussing change, albeit not a "traditional" one, we need to look at the great changes that have occurred during the pre-independence wars and the post-independence era. There have been fundamental and widespread changes in marriage-related practices, some of which are intimately related to women's trading activities. These changes appeared first among the transitional generation, especially the women in their forties in 1987-88,

---

[50] Lindblom, *Akamba*, pp. 161, 446, 557.

[51] Interview 77 Ngara Bean: 12 Nov. 1987.

[52] Lindblom, *Akamba*, pp. 82, 448; PC/CP 1/4/2 Kikuyu Political Record Book II DC Kiambu 31 Mar. 1914; Reel 85 minutes Kiambu LNC 12-13 Aug. 1941.

[53] Interview 185 Gikomba: 2 Mar. 1988.

and then become cataclysmic among the younger women. They have clear roots in economic factors and have produced an extremely contradictory situation for women in which both autonomy and coercion have strong meaning.

Choice of Spouse

Among the forty-four women in their twenties to fifties in the small sample there was a steady diminution by age group in the number of arranged marriages and an increase in consensual marriages. If for the oldest women 40% of the marriages were arranged by themselves and their prospective spouses, among the women in their fifties 68.2% were, with parental consultation following that agreement. With women in their forties 70.1% of the marriages were made by mutual consent, but in only half were parents consulted about it. All of the marriages of women in their twenties and thirties were made by mutual consent with half consulting with parents afterward. As might be expected, this change was accompanied by a steady rise in the numbers of couples who were lovers before any marital formalities occurred, from 58.8% for women in their fifties (30.8% for those sixty and over) to 100% for those in their twenties and thirties. At the same time the number of women pregnant before any formalities occurred went from 21.4% for women sixty and over to 81.8% for women twenty to thirty-nine. The biggest shift in all of these aspects came among the women in their fifties, who married in the 1940s or 1950s. For instance, the age at marriage dropped from nineteen for the oldest women to 17.9 for women in their fifties and then rose again to 18.2 for women in their forties and to 19.4 for the youngest women.[54] But the age at first conception dropped steadily--from 20.5 for the oldest women to 18.4 for the youngest, indicating the increasing tendency to have children without being married.

In this change it was clear that women's mobility had increased. While the oldest women usually first encountered their future husbands either as children growing up or at customary dances, in the younger groups the places they first met became more varied and public: on the road, at markets, schools, plantations, parties, friends' houses, and even detention camps. Although for the whole sample the most common method of first acquaintance with future spouses was growing up together, only a third of the youngest women met their future spouses around their homes (only one grew up with her future husband). Nonetheless, in the small sample there was only one marriage that occurred across ethnicities--a Kikuyu woman married to a Kamba man, not a departure from customary bounds, especially since the woman was from Kirinyaga, which had extensive long-standing trade links with Ukambani.

---

[54] Boyes, *King*, p. 304, claimed in 1911 that men married at around age twenty-one and women at age eighteen.

Reduction in Marital Formalities

A logical accompaniment to the decline in arranged marriages was a decline in bridewealth and generally in the formalities accompanying marriage. In the oldest group the only marriages without separate bridewealth were leviratic, for which the initial bridewealth stood. The marriages of women in their fifties and forties were mostly accompanied by payment of bridewealth (88.9% and 81.2% respectively), but the consensual unions of women in their twenties and thirties often did not include it (41.7% did not have it). When bridewealth was given among the oldest group the husband's parents usually paid it; in the youngest group husbands usually paid it themselves. The oldest women's bridewealth was more varied, often including not only the usual goats and/or cows but also various items like blankets. The marriages of women in their fifties and forties showed the beginning of a decline in formalities and more emphasis on the payments as well as monetization. While only 16.7% of the oldest women's bridewealth involved a monetary component, 57% of those of women in their forties and fifties did, with substantially higher amounts: for the oldest the average was Sh.220, for those in their fifties Sh.1073, and those in their forties, Sh.2333. For those married in the late 1960s or after, the amount averaged Sh.2667, but of course fewer marriages included it.

Another change regarding bridewealth concerned when it was paid--the oldest women reported that in 83.3% of their marriages it was paid completely before the arrival of children. This percentage declined to 68.7% for women in their fifties, 38.5% for those in their forties, and 28.6% for those in their twenties and thirties. Younger women often referred to it being paid by both themselves and their husbands; in a few cases the wife even took it to her parents by herself, a radical departure from older approved methods of payment.

Summing up the changes as they appear in the statistics, three stages are represented in the formalities regarding marriage: 1) those married before World War II were most likely to have had arranged marriages with payment of bridewealth by the husband's parents; 2) those married in the 1940s, 1950s and early 1960s had more varied arrangements with mutual consent marriages for the most part, accompanied by parental approval and bridewealth paid by the husband (in 57.1% of marriages where it was paid) or his parents (33.7%); 3) those married after independence always made mutual consent marriages and sometimes never consulted their parents about it, with monetary bridewealth supplied less frequently by husbands and themselves, usually completing its payment after the birth of children. These are large changes; how do the results from such a small survey hold up against the written historical record and the participants' views?

Kitching noted that by the late 1930s the terms of trade had turned against pastoralists in favor of Kikuyu agriculturalists. Kiambu overgrazing helped to monetize bridewealth and inflate it further.[55] There were many complaints in the 1940s from elders about loss of control over young men who secured wage work to pay their own bridewealth, or eloped with women when they could not raise it.[56] A fifty-two-year-old woman in the small sample was kidnapped by friends of her future husband and forced to marry in the 1940s; he was orphaned and could not raise the sum.[57] Kitching argued that by the 1950s livestock production was subordinate to agricultural production and women's labor power therefore central, hence the rise in the amount of bridewealth. An adjunct to this process was women's loss of control over decisionmaking about the disposal of agricultural surpluses and the securing of women to the household by higher bridewealth. Kershaw linked this loss of control to European land seizures, which diminished the amount of "discretionary land" that husbands gave wives to increase the wives' marketable surpluses.[58] This interpretation has validity in the 1940s and 1950s, when bridewealth was normally paid, some coercion used on occasion, and divorce still uncommon. The kidnapping victim described above said of her 1956 marriage,

> At that time girls used to be forced to marry... I could not run away because once a girl spent a night at a man's place she could not go back home. She could not be accepted by the society. She would be called a *gicokio* [divorcee]. Even at that time a girl could not stand on the road to talk with a man.[59]

The Emergency only added to the coercion exacerbated by high bridewealth and the poverty of many men. A woman described how her husband, a Homeguard, acquired his third wife, "During that war girls had a problem of where to stay. They lacked refuge and so could easily be seduced by men. When she got children, well ..."[60] Marriages that in the statistics appear to be by mutual consent were sometimes the lesser of two evils and not really a free choice by the women. In 1956 a girl got pregnant after intercourse with a boy with whom she had grown up. "I was pregnant and scared because I had disappointed my parents. He persuaded me to spend the night when I had never spent a night out. I was scared of facing my parents the next day so I didn't go back." His older brother then went to her parents to tell them that their "two-legged goat" was with him and bridewealth was arranged.[61]

By the 1950s Christianity had had several effects on marriage. One was to eliminate the customary Kikuyu or Kamba ceremonies and add a church wedding,

---

[55] Kitching, *Class*, pp. 222-23. See also KNA Microfilm Reel 85, minutes Kiambu LNC 15-16 July 1935.

[56] Native Affairs Dept. AR 1946-47: 2; Thomas, *Politics*, p. 58; DC/KBU 1/40 Kiambu AR 1949: 3; Reel 85 minutes Kiambu LNC 2-3 Dec. 1942, 25-26 Mar. 1943; MAA 6/38 minutes Native Affairs Committee 4, 26 Aug. 1948, Appendix II by H. E. Lambert.

[57] Interview 663 Kangemi: 28 July 1988.

[58] Kitching, *Class*, pp. 239-40; interview Kershaw: 4 Aug. 1994.

[59] Interview 663 Kangemi: 28 July 1988.

[60] Interview 175 Gikomba: 1 Mar. 1988.

[61] Interview 453 Wangige: 6 June 1988.

but not always. A couple sometimes had a customary ceremonial feast, and then converted later, "renewing" the marriage with a church ceremony. The most famous recent case of this sort concerned David Githanga Kinyanjui, son and successor to Kinyanjui wa Gathirimu. In the 1930s under pressure from relatives he took a second wife, Hannah Wanjiru, which caused him to be expelled from the Presbyterian church. In 1988, twenty-three years after the death of his first wife, he reconciled with the church and renewed his wedding vows in an elaborate ceremony with his second/only wife; Wanjiru was seventy-five and he 103. The bride was perhaps justifiably smug, saying, "I am happy for all the people who have come to see me get the certificate... Elizabeth Gachoki had him when he was a young man, but I praise God for giving him to me when he is an old man."[62] In the small sample the only women who had had church weddings were in their forties and fifties. Like Mrs. Githanga, some converts aspired to a Christian marriage in order to secure their position in monogamous marriage.

The age group of the forties was the first to exhibit a dominant pattern of payment of bridewealth after the birth of children, the women helping with that payment. Why would women want to cement a marriage in such a fashion, which contradicts Kitching's and Hirschon's interpretations of bridewealth as an oppressive institution for women? Hirschon felt that bridewealth, especially high bridewealth, exposed women to violence and forced marriages by men who could not afford it.[63] The situation in the 1950s, in particular, lends weight to Hirschon's argument, although the problem was not caused by bridewealth but by the overthrowing of lineage controls at several levels, which allowed some men to coerce women more directly. Women were more likely to see bridewealth as a form of security which legitimized not only their children but the women's access to land and their sons' inheritance.[64] Bridewealth conferred respectability and legitimacy on the marriage, legality in effect. Thus, they made every effort to see that it was paid; it became a de facto tax on marriage paid to their parents in installments over the first few years of the marriage. "We paid it," they said; if the husband could not, "I paid it." In 1950 at the tenth meeting of the Native Affairs Committee the subject of bridewealth inflation was raised yet again, but the members concurred that it was not as "burning" an issue as previously and that customs were changing conforming to no hard and fast

---

[62] *Daily Nation* 10 July 1988: 1-2; see also Davison and Women, *Voices*, p. 132. The bride was dressed in white and the ceremony attended by three great-great-great grandchildren of the couple, among the many who packed a small church at Waithaka.

[63] Kitching, *Class*, pp. 239-40; Hirschon, "Property," p. 14.

[64] Mackenzie, "Woman," p. 68, stressed the importance of bridewealth for securing women's land rights, while Silberschmidt, "Weaker Sex?," p. 250, found some young Kisii wives also paying their own bridewealth to insure access to their husbands' land. Kershaw, however, stated that women were more interested in securing rights to their own children by doing so (interview 4 Aug. 1994).

rules.[65] The new latitude was one of the factors that allowed some of the excesses of men toward women during the Emergency; again we see "mutual consent" as more like partial constraint for women. Rebecca at age fifteen was tricked into marrying her loyalist husband; he got her out of an internment camp by signing for her as his wife at the DC's office.

> He was not like my age-mate. He was like my father. My father's age-mates looked like that. But since he was using force, and the power of the Crown, then what was I to do? ... I was far too young to imagine [sex]; it was real suffering because I ... couldn't imagine being with someone like him. In fact, going to bed with him was a nightmare. But I persevered as it was a time of problems. If one was not in a secure place there was the danger of being killed by Mau Mau. So people looked for security wherever they could.

Another woman's family had severe financial problems so her husband staged a mock kidnapping to avoid her being given for higher bridewealth.[66]

By the late 1950s Kershaw noted that there was often no ceremony before the couple became co-resident, and that the couple began paying bridewealth when the first child was born, with *kindo* [damages for premarital pregnancy] added on. Hake noted an increase in elopement in the 1950s and 1960s. Old men took young wives as old age insurance, often women who had already borne an illegitimate child. Women in their fifties and forties showed the highest age differences from their spouses, husbands averaging 9.3 years older for women in their fifties and 8.2 years for women in their forties. Monogamy was becoming an ideal through Christian influence, especially among wealthy aspirants to high status. Both Leakey and Kershaw (Sluter) complained of bridewealth becoming brideprice when parents sold daughters. A few women used increased mobility to force marriages to impecunious bridegrooms, but that very poverty sometimes killed the marriages.[67] The plan could backfire; one woman became pregnant by her lover and was then forced to marry a wealthy man "so that my mother could have enough property to pay my brother's bridewealth... After my husband finished paying the bridewealth he was well aware that I was stuck with him because my home was very poor, so he started maltreating me."[68]

Marriage in Time of War: Cracks in the Facade

The coercive element was clear in marriage relations among women whose marriages began in the 1940s, 1950s and early 1960s. Women in their forties and

---

[65] This body included six African members out of fifteen, Provincial Commissioners, and the Chief Native Commissioner. MAA 6/38 minutes Native Affairs Committee 5 Oct. 1950.

[66] Interviews 112 Ngara Bean: 23 Nov. 1987; 244 Gikomba: 25 Mar. 1988.

[67] Sluter, "Report," pp. 37-41; Hake, *Metropolis*, pp. 65-66; Carlebach, *Prostitution*, p. 1, said that young prostitutes in Nairobi in 1960 often were married girls who had fled undesirable husbands. Interview 128 Ngara Bean: 10 Dec. 1987.

[68] Interview 149 Gikomba: 26 Apr. 1988. Her father was dead and her relatives could not return the bridewealth to allow her to divorce him.

fifties reported the highest incidence of verbal and/or physical abuse--in half or more of marriages. The average marriage rating for women in their fifties was 3.3, for women in their forties, 2.6, and the percentage of marriages ending in divorce increased precipitously from 11.1% for women in their fifties to 43.7% for women in their forties. Fisher claimed that in 1950 divorce was very rare and difficult to obtain, and that separations were more usual in which the man was supposed to give the woman land to work elsewhere and support the children. But by 1959 the Kiambu ADC Law Panel was debating liberalizing customs accompanying divorce to allow women to remarry and get child custody because of the many changes that were occurring.[69]

Among women in the middle group, those in their forties and fifties, there was less idealization of marriage than with the elderly women and most were still married at the time of the interview (73.5%). The women in their fifties were philosophical about marital conflicts; their marriages had lasted 30.6 years on the average and they had often tolerated a great deal of infidelity and abuse. They used a proverb to describe the situation, "Axes in the same basket must knock together," which presents an informative contrast to one cited in *Muigwithania* in 1928, "Two people cannot dwell together in a house unless there is harmony between them," a prescription for women to be docile.[70] Fisher described the 1950s ideal wife [Kikuyu=*ngatha*] as knowing

> how to cook well and always [having] food for her husband and visitors to the homestead. She keeps her hut clean and tidy and the courtyard well swept. She is a good cultivator and knows how to store crops. She diligently tends the goats and sheep (i.e., those allotted to her 'house'). She looks well after her children. She has zeal for work and takes firewood and water to her husband's hut in the evening. She comes quickly when her husband calls her. She knows how to dispense hospitality and takes good care of all things of the homestead when her husband goes on a journey.

There was no analogous word for an ideal husband indicating that women, not men, were defined by their relationship to men, their performance as wives.[71]

But the increasing landlessness and the crisis of the Emergency with the large-scale arbitrary removals of population placed severe strains on many people; women could not always remain in the background where the welfare of their families was concerned, especially if the husband was away working or fighting. Men frequently failed to send remittances. Kershaw stated that the most important consequence for

[69] Fisher, *Anatomy*, pp. 15, 214. No one in the small sample had been given land to work elsewhere by a husband. Kenyatta, *Facing*, p. 176, also said that divorce was rare. LG 3/2701 minutes Kiambu ADC Law Panel: 20 Oct. 1959.

[70] Interview 561 Kawangware: 23 June 1988; DC/MKS 10B 3/1 *Muig.* (Gathano 1928): 10.

[71] Fisher, *Anatomy*, p. 6; interview 14 Oct. 1992. This value is also evident in L. Leakey's description of advice given to newlyweds (*Southern Kikuyu* II: 786-88), in which men were told about taboos on sexual behavior and women about proper behavior toward husbands and in-laws.

women of the Emergency was their increasing reliance on each other for survival in the absence of the men, especially in the form of multigenerational female households. Some married women and young widows prostituted themselves to support their children. In Nairobi harassment and evictions made life tenuous, while in Kiambu conditions were equally unsettled.[72] The impact on marriage seems to have been that women stayed with their husbands for the most part, even though they were sometimes quite unhappy. They mainly held to the old ideals; they expected and tolerated beatings and infidelity. They tolerated lack of support, additional wives taken without their consent, and general unpleasantness on occasion for the greater good of raising their children and working the land. But some of the fights were epic. A woman who had had another man's child before her marriage responded, when asked if her husband had ever complained about that, "Talk about that? Then I would talk about all the other women he had brought later who were living off my sweat. Then he would threaten to send me away with my children and I would tell him that I was as firm and as permanent there as an orange tree, that kind of talk."[73]

They married because it was what you did. "At that time I was young and could not be realistic. I thought that all that mattered was having a husband." This woman discovered later that her husband was not only abusive but had no land. She stayed with him anyway. When asked if she liked him, she said,

A. "Why not?"
Q. "Why?"
A. "Could I stay with him otherwise?"
Q. "That only?"
A. "Look, he is not helping me, where do I take him? I am not helping him, where does he take me?"
Q. "Do you trust him?"
A. "Do I have a choice?"
Q. "But he abused you."
A. "That must happen."[74]

Her feeling of having no recourse was supported by a widespread lack of intervention by relatives when couples were having problems reported by women fifties and younger. Another woman's first husband died after five years of marriage, at which point she married an older man on her elder sister's advice, thinking she needed a husband. He began abusing her in the second week of the marriage, but she stayed with him for eighteen years.[75] Most women cited duty-related reasons for liking their husbands--"because he is my husband," "because the Bible says we must love our

---

[72] Fisher, *Anatomy*, p. 89; interview Kershaw 4 Aug. 1994; Sluter, "Report," pp. 38-39; Wilson, *Sphinx*, p. 129.

[73] Interview 175 Gikomba: 1 Mar. 1988.

[74] Interview 209 Gikomba: 14 Mar. 1988.

[75] Interview 215 Gikomba: 18 Mar. 1988.

husbands." One of the older women had developed a protective cynicism, but she was unusual; "A good husband loves his wife and does not go around doing this or that, but I am telling you, in this world you will not find even three or four like that. It's the truth!"[76] Most were wholly committed to the old ideals of marriage and motherhood, although even some of the most convinced occasionally demonstrated doubts, like this woman. "Being married is good because a girl needs to settle in a home. When we did not have children we did not have many problems. But it is good to have children, so those days are better, despite the problems... I am happy now that I have my own children."[77]

There were women, however, including almost half of those in their fifties, whose marital relationships rated 5s or 4s. They praised their husbands for their cooperativeness, consideration, patience, and consultative mode of management. They liked the fact that the husbands came home promptly after work (my research assistant editorialized that such men were considered to be bewitched), that they did not drink, abuse them, or run around with other women, which they claimed most men did. They felt that one should not pay too close attention to a husband's behavior, which was bound to disturb a wife, and simply judge him based on the fulfillment of his home obligations.[78] A Wangige woman expressed this philosophy nicely, "Even if my husband had had girlfriends, I would not have been bothered by it because I was only concerned about what we were doing at home. I would only have disliked it if it affected the work at home or he was being unduly extravagant on drink."[79]

A similar attitude characteristic of male dominant societies acknowledged husbands' rights to dominate wives even at their most amiable moments. One woman with a marriage rating of 5 was pleased that her husband was involved in her decision to be interviewed. When she asked him if it was all right he said yes, and then he nagged her about getting dressed promptly in the morning in order to be on time for our appointment.[80] Husbandly consideration was not expected behavior. One wife attributed her husband's unusually considerate behavior to the fact that she came from a wealthy family. Several women rated their marriages good based on how well they obeyed their husbands. One said, "My marriage has always been good because I was never taken back to my parents for discipline." Parents, the refuge for maltreated wives in many societies, were not supposed to side with daughters in marital disputes but reinforce the husband's authority. Another said, "If I made a mistake he came and told me that 'you have done this and that wrong' and I said, 'O.K.,

---

[76] Interview 588 Kawangware: 20 June 1988.

[77] Interview 561 Kawangware: 23 June 1988.

[78] One woman when asked if her husband had girlfriends, said, "That every man has. Follow yours and he will lead you to one." Interview S4 Shauri Moyo: 24 Aug. 1988.

[79] Interview 175 Gikomba: 1 Mar. 1988.

[80] Interview 465 Wangige: 1 June 1988.

I will not do it again.'" Perhaps the best epitaph on marriage among the last generation to accept the old system wholeheartedly was a fifty-four year old's statement
about her husband, "I liked my husband because he was part of me, but he did not
know what that is. He used to beat me but since we had children he was part of
me."[81] Whatever the negatives, women in their fifties felt they should love and obey
their husbands.

Women fifty and over were not usually happy about polygyny--60% of those
aged sixty and over and 78.9% of those in their fifties disapproved of it, the usual
reasons being economic, not wishing to split the husband's support with another
wife, and jealousy and quarreling between wives. But respectively 30% and 21.1%
of these women felt it was good, citing the necessity if the first wife was childless or
the superiority of the husband taking a second wife to his running around with many
women as the most common reasons. Only one woman mentioned wives helping
each other as a reason for approval, and several talked about the importance of meeting husbands' needs for sex and other domestic services. Older women's attitudes
regarding husbands having girlfriends were similar; a small minority approved, and
that only dimly, often mentioning that it was impossible to stop anyway. Several
women in their fifties and older disapproved of the way that younger women snooped
into their husbands' affairs as inappropriate behavior, saying that wives should not
listen when people came to them with tales of their husbands' infidelity, which they
should tolerate. A sixty year old said, epigrammatic for the generational differences
in expectations of marriages, "I have never been close to a man. After the children
we go different ways. This disease of following your husband is very bad because it
drives you crazy."[82]

But the women married in the late 1950s and 1960s, those in their forties,
exhibited different attitudes and behaviors, so much so that they can be dubbed a
transitional generation. Accompanying their skyrocketing divorce rate was low tolerance for polygyny and husbands' infidelity. Only 7.1% of those in their forties tolerated polygyny, and none girlfriends. Women in their forties and younger were more
concerned about detrimental effects on their relationships with their husbands of
polygyny and girlfriends, although all age groups worried most about economic
problems arising from the husband's involvement with other women, whether as
wives or as girlfriends. Some of the older women were quite cognizant of this shift
in attitudes. A woman forced into trade to support her sixty-two-year-old husband,
who had three wives and many children, said, "We used to say, when one had a co-
wife that was good. If you got ill she would look after you and your child. She
would cook for you, but you people don't want that, and the way your husbands have

---

[81] Interviews 808 Kiambu Town: 17 Oct. 1988; 65 Ngara Bean: 28 Oct. 1987; S4 Shauri Moyo: 24
Aug. 1988; 215 Gikomba: 18 Mar. 1988.

[82] Interview 82 Ngara Bean: 9 Nov. 1987.

become bad ... !"[83] For women in their forties or younger polygyny had become grounds for divorce; it figured in the divorces of 26% of the women, even though the incidence and intensity of polygyny were dropping rapidly. Among the marriages of the oldest women 42.8% were polygynous; the corresponding figure for women in their fifties was 27.8%, forties 31.3%, and thirty-nine and younger 19.2%. The husbands of the oldest women averaged 1.57 wives simultaneously which shrank to 1.18 for those of the youngest women with steadily diminishing numbers in between.

It is not only in the incidence of divorce and polygyny that younger women are most distinguished from older women; they were also not as willing to tolerate abuse from their husbands or partners. Abuse was the second most common reason for divorce after nonsupport/desertion (polygyny was third). The increasing lack of tolerance for polygyny can be attributed to a worsening economic situation--nonsupport went from being a factor in the dissolution of the marriages of over a third of the women in their forties to over half of those of women in their thirties and twenties. But the unwillingness to tolerate abuse is less closely linked to economic factors. Lack of independent resources often forced women to tolerate abuse from husbands who supported the family. Women in their fifties and over were more likely to expect abuse and explain it on the grounds of wives cooking or doing laundry improperly.[84] Regardless of economics younger women were not willing to give in to abuse regularly, especially the youngest women, in whose marriages the incidence of abuse was lower than among those in their forties and fifties (36.4% for verbal abuse and 45.4% for physical abuse for women thirty-nine or younger compared to 50% for both for women in their forties, and 55.5% for verbal and 50% for physical for women in their fifties), but the divorce rate was highest among younger women.

Despite the differences exhibited by younger women beginning with women in their forties, there still was a certain level of continuity in attitudes and practices involved with the marital relationship, especially among those in their forties. A Kamba woman aged forty-nine said, "It's your generation that knows how to question husbands; our generation doesn't know how to do that. We only know how to keep quiet."[85] Many stressed obedience to husbands as desirable and the paramount importance of pleasing them with a clean house, good cooking, and so on. The good housewifery aspect of marriage has assumed more importance through home economics classes and church training. Women still seemed to like or love their husbands more out of a sense of family commitment than due to infatuation or prizing his individual qualities. A typical response was, "I love my husband because he is the father of my children and I trust him because I have nowhere else to go. That's my life commitment."[86] Qualities prized in a husband included generosity in support, cooperativeness and consultation, lack of abuse and fidelity. Interestingly, the duty

---

[83] Interview 59 Ngara Bean: 26 Oct. 1987.

[84] Interview 561 Kawangware: 23 June 1988.

[85] Interview 253 Gikomba: 8 Apr. 1988.

[86] Interview 253 Gikomba: 8 Apr. 1988.

aspect involved in liking a husband was *least* important for the women sixties and over and most important for those who were younger. This mechanistic view fostered by biblical teachings cited by some women was being undermined by harsh economic realities for younger women and by a desire by some women for a more companionate marriage. A few younger women had a concept of more egalitarian marriage. One forty year old said, when asked if she trusted her husband, "I cannot entertain thoughts that he would go out with other women. If I find myself getting such an idea, I remember also that he could think about me the same way here in Nairobi, called the city of prostitutes, and if he did, I couldn't trade, could I?"[87] She had obviously decided that mutual trust, and mutual space, were needed, a far cry from the attitude of older women that they were not to know or question their husbands' actions regarding other women; her interpretation of trust as overwhelmingly involved with marital fidelity also differentiates her from them. The oldest women most trusted husbands who treated them politely and never mentioned fidelity in this regard.

MARRIAGE/INDEPENDENCE: THE YOUNGEST WOMEN

If the women in their forties exhibited some strong breaks from the past regarding marital institutions, they also in some cases maintained a facade of older attitudes. One forty-seven year old who eventually divorced her husband because of nonsupport and polygyny said,

> You see, I had no choice but to like him because he was the father of my children. And if I did not tell him that I did, he would not support my children. Even after beating me, I would run away and go home but still come back because my parents were not helping me support the children.[88]

But younger women were no longer willing to maintain even a facade in many cases, especially if the husband failed to support them. Polygyny has become the object of open attack in public fora like newspapers and seminars, with younger women and their supporters opposing it and men more often supporting it, citing the fallacious premise that polygyny is a solution to the "demographic imbalance of the sexes" (because men usually marry younger women the supply of wives always seems to be unlimited and husbands scarce). Religious reasons pro and con were cited, with some men promoting the goal of legitimizing the status of men's mistresses as a consideration. Women and their male sympathizers tended rather to stress the evil of elderly men marrying young women for social security in old age and as a form of conspicuous consumption. Xenophobic reactions were aired as citizens complained about monogamous church weddings as foreign to local cultures, one man mentioning the irrelevance of the wheat-based wedding cake as compared to Kikuyu dishes

---

[87] Interview 94 Ngara Bean: 24 Nov. 1987.

[88] Interview No.112 Ngara Bean: 23 Nov. 1987. It is the economic vulnerability of women that clearly influences such behavior, leading men to accuse women of being golddiggers.

like *njahe*.[89] The debate begun in the 1920s by adamant missionaries who refused to baptize polygynous men still rages. However, most researchers agree with the results here showing that the incidence of polygyny in Kenya has dropped sharply, mainly due to economic factors. Younger women are increasingly militant about opposing it. In 1988 there was a rash of interrupted church weddings in Nairobi when women married by customary law objected to their husbands marrying again; the photographs sometimes included woebegone children of the earlier union dragged along to make a point.[90]

We have already seen that the youngest women--those in their twenties and thirties who married after independence--have the highest incidence of divorce (63.6% of marriages ended in divorce) and low tolerance for husbands' infidelity and polygyny. None of them had marriages arranged by their parents and all were lovers before they became wives. Elopement was the most common form of marriage and most were pregnant before any ceremony or bridewealth was arranged or paid.[91] The average age at first conception (18.4 years) was lowest among all age groups in the sample, but their average age at marriage was highest (19.4). Mainly due to their high divorce rate, their average marriage rating was lowest at 2.1. Their husbands were closer in age to themselves than those of women in their forties and fifties at an average of 6.1 years older, and their abuse rate intermediate between those of the oldest and transitional generations.

The older system functioned well for the oldest women; for the transitional women it was undermined while they tried to maintain a facade of normalcy and used own payment of bridewealth and Christian teachings (see below) to reinforce or modify aspects of the old system. But the grim reality of some of their marriages may have encouraged the youngest women to discard the old system and utilize their elders' experiences rather than their words to evolve a new one with different rules. One of the older values that has been retained is that maturity for women is still achieved upon bearing a child. Davison claimed that women used pregnancy to try to force marriage, while men used it to determine if women were fertile,[92] but some women clearly do not want the hassles involved in marriage, which still carries with it a host of patriarchal assumptions and laws, and less economic security than formerly. Only by not marrying do women have undisputed rights to their own children. In 1980 Wainaina described an increasing divorce rate and opposition to

---

[89] *Standard* 22 Aug. 1988: 12; *Daily Nation* 19 Dec. 1987: 3; 19 Feb. 1988: 3; 10 Dec. 1987; 23 Aug. 1988.

[90] *Standard* 29 July 1988: 2; 15 Aug. 1988; *Daily Nation* 7 Aug. 1988: 3; Glazier, *Land*, p. 121; Maas, *Women's Groups*, pp. 41-42; Central Bureau of Statistics, *Women in Kenya*, Report (July 1978), p. 8; Nzomo and Staudt, "Political Machinery," p. 9.

[91] Silberschmidt, "Men," p. 246, found that elopement was also common in Kisii in the late 1980s.

[92] For men marriage indicated maturity according to L. Leakey (*Southern Kikuyu* II: 782), while Kabwegyere, "Determinants," p. 205, found in the mid-1970s that rural Kamba women's maturity was also proved by fertility. Davison and Women, *Voices*, p. 206.

marriage among young people. "One of the ways in which younger people have chosen to express their opposition to marriage, at least in the form in which it is presently practiced, has been not to marry. Instead, they simply live together."[93]

The Abolition of Formalities

In the matter of formalities there are again class differences. For high socioeconomic status couples an elaborate church wedding has become mandatory,[94] but most traders do not fall into this category. The youngest women reported that bridewealth was not paid at all in over half of the unions, the giving of soft drinks and/or beer being a popular substitute.[95] In only one case was a feast held and no one had had a church wedding. The highly variable methods used to indicate a union make it impossible to describe one dominant pattern. These results accord with those of Ferraro in the 1970s--reduction in the ceremonial aspects of marriage and a rising divorce rate, but his estimate of the average amount of bridewealth at Ksh.1,835 between 1966 and 1970 is lower than average for the youngest women here, Ksh.2667, indicating continuing inflation.[96] Wambeu attributed the popularity of elopement, the most common way of making a marriage among the youngest women in my sample, to the high cost of bridewealth, while noting the decline in the communal aspects of marriage and the tendency for husbands to pay bridewealth themselves. He also noted, and other records confirm, that unions made without bridewealth were still not recognized as legal marriages by the courts, causing a high illegitimacy rate for children. In 1969 an all-male Parliament made paternity suits illegal.[97] But women's objections to patriarchal marriage forms sometimes take the form of strenuous opposition to bridewealth, which in their view commodifies women and may lose them their children in case of divorce. A single mother with three children, a part-time nursery schoolteacher with ambitions to go into business at Mwea, told Davison that bridewealth was, "a stupidity. It makes it seem like a girl is nothing but an object if a man must pay for me because then he would feel he has complete control over me and can do what he wants, even beating me if he feels like it! To me, that tradition is meaningless in today's world."[98]

---

[93] Wainaina, "Divorce," pp. 2, 40-41.

[94] Sometimes brutal bargaining over bridewealth accompanies the occasion. M.N. Kamavuria, "This ugly practice must go," *Kenya Times* 29 Feb. 1988.

[95] This bears an uncanny resemblance to the results of 1970s research with the urban Ga in Accra, Ghana, where marriage formalities among young people had been reduced to a "door-knocking fee" in the form of a gift of drink to the bride's parents. Robertson, *Bowl*, p. 181.

[96] Davison and Women, *Voices*, p. 205, described as typical the woman joining the man with no ceremony when she got pregnant. Ferraro, "Patterns," pp. 105-108.

[97] Wambeu, "Customary Marriage," pp. 34-37; DC/KBU 1/51 Kiambu AR 1966: 3; Glazier, *Land*, p. 127; Werlin, *Governing*, p. 120.

[98] Davison and Women, *Voices*, p. 196.

Love and Marriage? Relationships in the 1970s and 1980s

Class differences also prevail in determining expectations regarding marital relationships. Elite Kenyan women are more influenced by Western-dominated media images and often by Christian teachings, which include ideas of romance in choosing a partner and a companionate (not necessarily egalitarian) marital relationship. But such ideas fit uneasily into a Kenyan context, as N. Wangari, the woman author of this letter to the *Daily Nation* eloquently described.

> The concept of marrying out of love was introduced to us not very long ago by Westerners. The hard fact is that [it] hasn't worked even for them. It is common knowledge that divorce and unhappy marriages are more rampant in Western countries... Not that there is anything wrong with love, but most of us don't understand it. What we think is love usually turns out to be physical attraction or merely sexual ambition. Hence when we marry out of this 'falling in love' we later discover that we overlooked some very important aspects of our partners that are crucial in the practical mechanics of a marriage... Here, in comes bitterness, frustration, resentment and more often than not a broken relationship.[99]

Romantic ideals have also percolated through less affluent sectors of society. A disillusioned twenty-seven-year-old trader whose marriage fell apart leaving her impoverished with six children to support was interviewed by a *Nation* reporter. She said, regarding her marriage vows, "Till death do us part! Whose death? Or is it the death of love?" Another twenty-seven year old in my sample whose marriage had suffered the same fate, turned irascible when asked how it was that she had married her husband in the first place. "Aha! It just happened. How the hell do people fall in love? Don't you know?" Married couples still do not normally socialize together at any level in society, whatever the application of romantic ideals.[100]

A glance at Nairobi popular fiction, novels by a woman and two men, plus a collection of short stories by a man, suggests a lack of faith in Western-style love and marriage. The happy ending in one involved the heroine's reunion with her illegitimate son. In another, which most closely approximated U.S. supermarket fare, the happy ending entailed marriage between a rich Nairobi Indian businessman and an aspiring African businesswoman; the latter had lost interest in her handsome but unreliable African suitor. There was no romantic ending in Kahiga's story of a short-term liaison between two jetset Kenyans broken off when the woman chose independence and returned to her career in the U.S.[101] A collection of stories by Gakaara, more concerned with didactic moralizing than romance, put the lessons of the folktales into modern dress. Common themes presented are that: men lie to women about romance in order to get sex; women are often foolish; Nairobi is "the city where devils dwell, where evils abound, where the young and the unwary sink into

---

[99] *Daily Nation* 8 Mar. 1988: 7.

[100] *Daily Nation* 27 Jan. 1988: 11; interview 123 Nyamakima: 18 Dec. 1987; Oloo and Cone, *Kenya Women*, p. 37.

[101] Ruheni, *Minister's Daughter*; Ngurukie, *Substitute*; Kahiga, *Girl*.

the eternal mud of sin." Disapproval of unwed pregnancy is evident, especially if no marriage eventuated. Women are supposed to dress modestly, work hard, and be charitable Christians.[102] There is a pervasive suspicion of sexuality, and romance is equated with lust, as noted by N. Wangari. Kahiga's jetset woman sums up the situation regarding modern marriage with acuity. When proposed to she says, "We can't talk about it now, not in a moving car, and on a bumpy road." When they make love her lover feels, "we were a couple of lost creatures, no longer sure about right and wrong."[103]

Changes have exaggerated the contradictions affecting women, but not always in ways that benefit women, and sometimes to their detriment. If more flexibility is present, there are also fewer safeguards. Attitudes and expectations still strongly favor male dominance. Wives' labor and loyalty are still most prized by husbands.[104] In the 1970s Thadani summed up the conflicting expectations of women in Kenya, "On the one hand, in their relations with men, women are expected to be deferential, passive and subordinate. On the other hand, in their own sphere, women are hardworking, productive, autonomous, and less dependent on the evaluation of men."[105] Male dominant beliefs have been enhanced and transmitted by Western influence. Many misogynist diatribes in the newspapers are in letters that cite biblical sources, inveighing against women becoming priests or women's equality, a trend that might be strengthened by increasing incursions of North American Christian fundamentalist missionaries. Even male defenders of women's equality cite purportedly immutable biological differences as a justification for the gender division of labor ("there must be different roles owing to the pervasive physical and spiritual differences"). One scholar referred to men now "owning" their wives, after making claims for equality.[106]

The result of such attitudes and the economic underprivileging of women is that women are undervalued and sometimes scapegoated. In Central Province a 1970s study found that 39% of female and 27.5% of male infants were malnourished, suggesting preferential feeding of male infants.[107] In 1988 a group of mourners attacked an elderly woman at a funeral because they suspected her of witchcraft, poisoning a male university student. Her son held them off with a machete.[108] The demonizing of women, then, represents a change that is taking place; the construc-

---

[102] Gakaara, *Market Literature*; Ruheni, *Daughter*, p. 140.

[103] Kahiga, *Girl*, pp. 63, 60.

[104] Browne, "Kawangware," pp. 174-75; L. Leakey, *Southern Kikuyu* II: 741. Waciuma, *Mweru, Feather*, resuscitated in children's books the didactic folktales which justify violence against women.

[105] Thadani, "Forgotten Factor," p. 95.

[106] *Daily Nation* 17, 23 Aug., 26 Feb. 1988; Ndeti, *Akamba Life*, p. 66.

[107] *Women in Kenya*, p. 19. Women in my small survey resolutely claimed for the most part that they had no sex preference in children.

[108] *Nation* 1 Aug. 1988: 3; see also 10 July 1988: 9.

tion of female gender has moved from women being the foolish pawns of men, for good or for evil, to their being active perpetrators of evil.

The situation regarding violence against women is perhaps most symptomatic of the weaknesses of women's position. Wamalwa's excellent study of male violence against women in Kenya was based on 116 cases reported in the *Nation* from 1976 to 1985. Among them 29.3% involved assaults by husbands on wives, 31.9% men assaulting a female relative, 11.2% causing her grievous harm, and 17.2% murdering her. Seventy percent were rural and 30% urban. The sentences ranged from a reprimand to six years in jail. In a 1968 Parliamentary debate wifebeating was defended and a bill outlawing it roundly defeated, meaning that women now must bring individual suits against men which, through fear and lack of resources, women are not likely to do. Public response to such cases was normally to blame the victim, a reaction also common in the U.S.[109]

Many younger traders can read. The constant newspaper stories of violence against women must have an intimidating effect. One of the most horrific concerned Jackson Kaguai, a bar owner who, because his wife of fifteen years, Piah Njoki, had borne only six daughters, carried out a successful plot with his neighbors to gouge out her eyes in 1983. After five years in jail, he resumed his life at Kirinyaga farming eleven acres and tending 1000 coffee trees (he was not a poor man). But the judge had awarded Njoki Ksh.900,000 in damages, which might have meant loss of his property to her. So he wanted a reconciliation. Four churches organized a prayer meeting at which Kaguai claimed Satan had made him do it and repented his actions. His sisters joined in his plea and the local assistant chief said that the government "was keen to see that couples lived in peace as only united family units could build a strong nation." Njoki had meanwhile gotten training to teach Braille and resumed her life.[110] Thus, a sadistic batterer was able to rally the support of family, church and state to plead his case. The most famous cases of violence against women, of course, were the mass rape of seventy-one secondary schoolgirls by their male classmates which resulted in the death of nineteen of them at St. Kizito secondary school in Meru and the rape of twenty schoolgirls by bandits at Hawinga Girls High School in Siaya.[111]

But even for those who do not normally read newspapers, their own experiences and the stories from friends and co-workers must have a similar effect. Many women had stories of beatings. One said, "Abuse, that happens every day ... He beats me and I hide, stay away from home."[112] Another woman left her husband, but not until after he had knocked out many of her teeth.

---

[109] Wamalwa, "Violence," pp. 6-8, 10-12.

[110] *Nation* 4 Mar., 28 Sept. 1988.

[111] *Weekly Review* 9 Aug. 1991: 12-13. The St. Kizito principal and female deputy principal trivialized the incident; she said, "The boys never meant any harm against the girls. They just wanted to rape." *Herald-Tribune* 30 July 1991: 1-2. The school has now been closed. *Standard* 19 Jan. 1993.

[112] Interview 241 Gikomba: 31 Mar. 1988.

> When he came home and felt it was time for war he would beat me, chasing me
> around. He never used to beat me in one spot, so I was always on the run. I think
> God is the one who gave me rest because of my prayers. He told me to leave him.
> So even though now I am renting a house, I don't feel that I have problems.[113]

The markets were sometimes a refuge from maltreatment. Although wifebeating is
expected behavior, severe abuse is not.[114]

Levinson's cross-cultural study of wifebeating found that it was associated
most with women's economic dependence on husbands, forced social change, and
polygyny being permitted. The single most important associated characteristic, however, was men's absolute authority in domestic decision-making.[115] In 1977 Abbott
and Arcury found that predominant characteristics of Kikuyu male-female relations
were distrust, dictum and confrontation, a far cry from the satisfying interchanges
reported by my oldest informants. Beatings were often associated with drunkenness
of husbands; some women expected them every time the husband got drunk. The
immediate justifications used by the men were usually the wife's failure to perform a
domestic chore to his satisfaction, adultery accusations, associating with unapproved
female friends, or simply any annoyance. One woman in her thirties said that one of
the worst incidents occurred when her husband publicly called her a witch because
she would not give him money to go and buy drinks for his girlfriend, and then beat
her. She left him and went home to her parents, refusing to return unless he quit
beating her. That stopped the problem.[116]

In all age groups women did not feel that the beatings were justified, called the
husbands' justifications excuses, but then used rationalizations of their own. A
woman in her fifties said, "A husband must bark in his own house," shrugging it
off.[117] A woman in her thirties indicated the continuing prevalence of the wifebeating
syndrome in the context of two early morning scenarios.

> There was no time I was ever happy in my marriage. At times he would come
> home at 2 or 3 A.M. and wake me up by pounding on the door. When I opened the
> door for him, without a word he would just start beating me. Or it could be during
> the daytime or evening. He would just look at me and say, 'You are committing
> adultery!' and then start beating me. So the days God planned for us to be together
> passed. I didn't know what to do. We divorced.

When asked what a good wife should do, she illustrated methods she thought might
have helped her to avoid the beatings, giving the impression that her own behavior
was at fault.

---

[113] Interview 847 Karuri: 13 Oct. 1988.

[114] Browne, "Kawangware," pp. 315, 246, claimed in 1983 that wifebeating was increasing dramatically along with monogamy.

[115] Levinson, *Family Violence*, pp. 58, 64, 71.

[116] Abbott and Arcury, "Continuity," pp. 339-41; interview 108 Ngara Bean: 18 Nov. 1987.

[117] Interview 561 Kawangware: 23 June 1988.

A good wife should obey her husband according to his likes. If he comes home at midnight, she should open the door whether he is drunk or not. If he has fallen, she should undress and bathe him and show him she is not harboring any bad feelings due to his lateness. She should not shout, 'Where were you all this time??!' Rather she should say sweetly, 'Where did you sleep my dear? Here I was all alone missing you.' That way he will feel happy ... He realizes you love him even if he comes late because he's helping you and providing for all your needs.[118]

Given that her husband provided neither preliminaries to beatings nor adequate support, this scenario loses probity and assumes sadness.

Overall, women have lost most benefits of the old system: age bringing control over the labor of daughters-in-law, protection from abusive husbands by lineage members, deference toward elders, secure access to land through secure marriage. Transitional generations tried to shore up marriage by paying their own bridewealth on occasion or using Christianity, and stuck to the old ideals despite manifest evidence that they were becoming dysfunctional. Now the resources of their bodies remain: their fertility and their sexuality, with which to confirm links with men that may secure survival economically. So they turn to romantic love as an ideal in some cases, but it usually does not work. Faced with increasingly stringent economic conditions, men are trying to shed dependency burdens rather than increase them but still want the services women provide. More commonly, women seek help from elements identified by Levinson as militating against wifebeating: women's work groups, divorce, and independent socioeconomic resources.[119]

The expectations concerning marriage have changed; women want more egalitarian decisionmaking and socializing with faithful non-abusive husbands. The practices have changed drastically in everything from premarital pregnancy to divorce, putting women at a severe structural disadvantage.[120] This section has illuminated the increase in coercion of women by men, a path undoubtedly smoothed by the late-nineteenth-century commodification of women and the inflation of bridewealth from the 1920s on. The crises of the wars largely terminated any protection women got from their own lineages, while the increase in violence against women is the most overt expression of the extreme contradictions in their position.

The Economics of Marriage and Divorce

The economic autonomy of women traders is not the opposite end of a continuum with violence against women at the other end. Rather, some of the same forces

---

[118] Interview 114 Nyamakima: 7 Jan. 1988. A woman at Mutira said (Davison and Women, *Voices*, p. 100), "When a wife is beaten it is because she has not made her husband happy, so she tries to mend her ways."

[119] Levinson, *Violence*, pp. 58, 71.

[120] "Image of African Women Report" of a conference of Kenyan women in the mid-1970s concluded that women were commodified by bridewealth, always owned by a man, and never a full member of a lineage (Pala, Awori, and Krystal, *Participation*, pp. 203-204).

that produced the violence have also contributed to that autonomy. Here the factors connected to marriage that facilitated women's economic autonomy are explored, while positive aspects arising out of it are analyzed in Chapter VII. If marriage has experienced a revolution of rising expectations to some extent, the bottom line in marriage is still the economic aspect. Men and women still view the provider aspect of men's roles as key to concepts of masculinity.[121] For these women marriage was above all a search for economic security. It will probably remain so until or unless women's economic disabilities are remedied and men's misbehavior not predicated upon the economic coercion of women. Nonsupport from husbands was the primary reason for divorce in all age groups, and those divorces, with two exceptions not involving nonsupport, took place after 1963. The economics of marriage and divorce in the post-independence period has played a critical role in motivating women's trade.

It is very clear that, whatever their feelings toward their husbands, many women found divorce necessary for the survival of themselves and their children. A twenty-nine-year-old woman expressed it well.

> I like my husband; I have no other even though we are separated. The children are his. They have refused to accept another father. I trust him because he likes me; he even comes here and asks me to go home with him. I ask him, 'Go and starve there?' Then he tells me that he will support me, so I tell him to go and support the children. If I see that he is supporting them, then I will go . . . ; meantime I have to keep my space here.[122]

Nonsupport was a factor in over 70% of the divorces (N=17) reported by women in the small sample (the next most common was abuse at 47%), and the primary one discussed at length by the women. In the large sample there were sixty-four divorces whose causes were given, of which 79.7% were said to have been sought by women. Of these 76.5% were due to lack of support. Nonsupport was associated with polygyny sometimes and landlessness often. In two cases Kikuyu women left their husbands when they lost or sold their land. Silberfein has identified the same association of divorce, landlessness and nonsupport among Kamba families.[123] When women were asked if they had suffered any negative consequences from the loss of a husband through divorce or death, they invariably answered by citing poverty, although many also grieved for deceased husbands. The exceptions were a few abuse survivors who rejoiced in the relieving of that oppression. Significantly, however, the vast majority of women did not remarry, citing tradition as a justification.[124]

---

[121] Browne, "Kawangware," p. 258. Cohen and Odhiambo, *Siaya*, p. 98, stated that Luo women also commonly "evaluate men through an aesthetic of labour."

[122] Interview 260 Gikomba: 5 Apr. 1988.

[123] Silberfein, *Change*, pp. 112-13.

[124] This contrasts sharply with the serial monogamy dominant among coastal West African women, and helps to reduce Kenyan women's fertility/ dependency burden.

Aside from poverty for women, there have been other consequences of the increasing fragility of marriage. One has been to focus women upon supporting their children rather than serving husbands; getting school fees is a primary goal. Another has been change in residential patterns toward a two- or three-generation, female-headed household in Nairobi and in the countryside.[125] In rural areas not only do men leave home to work, sometimes permanently when land disappears and marriages fall apart, but also ablebodied women in their thirties to fifties leave home to trade, often for weeks at a time. Their children and their mothers, left at home, must care for each other. In town many men live singly or in small groups in rented rooms. Groups of women traders share poor lodgings and makeshift sleeping space. For those who are permanently urbanized three generation families may develop, but usually for the more prosperous since lodgings are expensive and crowded. If a grandmother or an eldest daughter is able to look after them, women prefer to leave children in rural areas.

In Chapter V we saw that trade is a survival strategy for most women, adopted in the face of lack of better alternatives. The relationship of divorce and widowhood to entry into trade for women is evident when comparing the marital status of traders in the large sample (N=1016) to that of the Nairobi population aged fifteen and over, shown in Table VI.1. Clearly, women who were divorced or widowed were more likely to be trading, while male traders were more likely to be single and less likely to be married than the general population.[126]

The relationship of family support burdens to trade is also manifest in the dependency statistics. The mean average number of persons supported by women in the large sample (N=683) was 5.5 compared to 4.9 for the men (N=330).[127] The male

VI.1. Marital Status by Gender of Traders in 16 Nairobi Markets, 1987-1988 (T), and of Nairobi Population Aged 15 and Over (N)

Marital Status:	Never Married		Married at Present		Divorced/ Separated		Widowed/ Widowered		Total	
	T	N	T	N	T	N	T	N	T	N
% of:										
Women	19.1	35.7	53.7	57.4	13.8	3.7	13.4	3.2	100	100
Men	41.7	38.6	57.4	60.3	0.9	0.8	0.0	0.3	100	100

Source for the Nairobi population: *Kenya Census, 1979*, Vol. 3: 24, 26.

---

[125] Kershaw, interview 4 Aug. 1994, in the 1950s and Browne, "Kawangware," p. 317, in 1983 found this to be a growing trend.

[126] McCormick, "Manufacturing," p. 169, also found a disproportionate number of widows and divorcees among Nairobi women entrepreneurs.

[127] Njiro, "Labour Force Participation," p. 68, found that Kenyan women in general have more dependents than men do.

statistic, however, was inflated by the fact that some men claimed that their wives were not helping at all when the children were living with the wives on a farm and being fed by them, at least, while receiving help from those being interviewed in the form of remittances. Here the construction of women's work in farming and feeding children as extensions of housework and of no value, which defines cash as the only means of support worth mentioning, comes into play.

A look at the occupations of spouses who were reported not to be helping with support validates this contention. Since women do most of the agricultural labor, especially when a husband is away in town, it can safely be assumed that most of the wives reported to be non-supporters are probably at least supplying some food to the family. The same cannot be said for non-supporter husbands or ex-husbands who were farmers, however. Since it was humiliating for women to admit that the children's father was not helping (several widows even claimed that their husbands were helping!), women tended to overestimate their help if anything and minimize any degree of estrangement. Therefore, when women said that men were not helping, I tended to believe them. One woman, franker than most, said that her husband was farming. When asked if he was actually doing farmwork, she said that no, he was "supervising," and then, "You know, that's what men do." She later said that he was elderly and disabled and not able to do any work. "Supervising" was clearly a euphemism for not helping, couched in male dominant terms. The 26.2% of male non-supporters who were farmers were probably not helping to any significant extent. The number of male non-supporters who had skilled white-collar, artisanal or service occupations is more noteworthy: 49.6%. Like the women who were listed as housewives, they were mostly urban residents.

The marital status of non-supporters is equally illuminating. Women could count on more help from husbands than from lovers or ex-husbands; 80.5% of husbands helped, but respectively 98.1% and 95.3% of lovers or ex-husbands who were fathers of children did not help support them. The importance of marriage beyond the concern of legitimizing the children is evident.

We also asked respondents for whom they were providing most of the support or part of the support. This question yielded the results shown in Table VI.3 broken

VI.2. Occupations of Non-Supporting Spouses/Ex-spouses of Traders*

Occupa-tion:	Trade/commerce	Farmer/fisher	White collar	Skilled/service	Military/guard	Day labor	House-wife	Unem-ployed	Other
% of: Wives (N=49)	4.1	71.4	2.0	0.0	0.0	0.0	20.4	2.0	0.0
Husbands (N=145)	11.7	26.2	11.7	31.0	4.8	4.8	0.0	7.6	2.1

*Definition of marriage used here includes common-law unions.

down by age and sex of the respondent. Only 13.9% of the whole sample listed a spouse among those being supported, 29.3% of the men and 6.5% of the women. However, wives who were being supported were usually listed as sharing in their own support, whereas husbands who were being supported were not; they were mostly elderly or disabled living on farms. Women did not complain about having to support these men; when alcoholism was involved, however, they often divorced the husband, who was likely to be abusive as well as a non-supporter. Women's role in supporting elderly husbands made taking a younger wife a survival strategy for a man; in the small sample husbands were on the average seven years older than wives.

The age-specific data show that women generally began supporting dependents at a younger age than men, reflecting both a younger age at marriage and unmarried motherhood. Children were by far the largest category of persons supported. Men in the large sample who had never married reported supporting no children of their own. The few men who reported divorces had remarried and, if they had custody of children by a previous marriage, their second or subsequent wives were caring for them. Child custody usually went to mothers, despite the law upholding paternal custody (most divorces were not taken to court and if bridewealth had not been paid men had no rights to the children). The responsibility of a husband's lineage to support the children of a deceased male member seems to have disappeared along with leviratic marriage. Co-residence was a critical factor in support; children not living with a male parent were highly unlikely to be supported by him, whatever the status of the union that produced them. There were, however, a few cases in which mothers supported sons and daughters living away from home by paying their rent, especially sons, whose right to live in a separate residence was widely recognized. Grown daughters were more likely to live with the mother if unmarried.

A prime survival strategy involved sharing the burden of support; both sexes reported sharing support for far more people than they provided with most of the support. The next most important category of persons supported after children for both women and men was members of their family of origin: mothers, fathers, sisters and brothers. Interestingly, women were also supporting significant numbers of relatives by marriage, usually their husbands' mothers and sisters, and sometimes their

VI.3. Mean Average Number of Dependents by Traders' Age, Gender (N=985)

Age group:	15-19		20-29		30-39		40-49		50-59		60-69		70+	
Gender:	F	M	F	M	F	M	F	M	F	M	F	M	F	M
Average by amount of support:														
Most	.4	0	.6	.3	1.8	1.1	1.9	1.7	2.3	4.1	1.9	3.8	.7	4.0
Partial	2.5	3.3	3.3	4.4	4.7	4.4	4.2	6.0	3.5	5.4	5.0	4.5	4.0	8.0
Total	2.9	3.3	3.9	4.7	6.5	5.5	6.1	7.7	5.8	9.5	6.9	8.3	4.7	12.0

co-wives' children. Men reported supporting a much narrower range of relatives. They shared support for more of their siblings than women did, but they supported far fewer of their relatives by marriage and only one grandchild, compared to the ninety-five grandchildren supported by women. Women provided most of the support for 27.9% of their dependents, while men provided it for only 15.2% of their dependents.

The overall differences in the dependency burden are clear, then. Women traders are providing more support for more people than men traders, more of whom are younger with no dependents. Women began younger and peaked earlier in their support pattern, but men, while reporting more dependents in their older years, do less support altogether. There were few men traders in their sixties or above but many women. The usual minuscule earnings of the elderly women traders contrasted sharply with those of the older men, who were likely to be proprietors of the few businesses of some scale, long-time urban residents, and sometimes governors of the markets. The elderly women were more often recent urban immigrants whose rural destitution forced them to remove themselves from burdening their children. There were also a few well-established women traders who fit more into the male profile mentioned above, but most of them were younger--in their forties and fifties and still physically strong enough for an active trading life. One woman said, "Your profits depend on the strength of your back." The time they must put in trading militates against such women farming themselves, while prosperous men have wives who farm for them. A case of woman-marriage, in which an older woman trader took a young wife, had to do not only with a mother of daughters seeking to secure a male heir for her deceased husband, but also with her need to secure labor for her husband's land, as her daughters were either married and farming their husbands' land or helping her trade. But woman-marriage was not an option exercised by many (only two instances in the large sample). Man-marriage was the usual strategy adopted.

For some the strategy worked. They were able to achieve a solid marriage with sharing of property; the latter is quite unusual in the Kenyan context but clearly pursued in some Christian communities, as Nyokabi's history demonstrates.

Nyokabi, a tall imposing woman, lived and worked at Wangige, an area rapidly succumbing to the expansion of Nairobi. She and her husband married when Nyokabi was sixteen and pregnant with their only child, a daughter. Unusually for a woman of fifty-nine, Nyokabi had gone to Standard 4, her husband to Standard 6, in the mission school at Wangige founded by Canon Leakey. Both Nyokabi and her husband were devout churchgoers and Nyokabi was an active member of the Anglican Mothers' Union. Nyokabi attributed some of her husband's steady qualities to his Christian devoutness. She noted proudly that, unlike his cohorts, he never stayed out drinking beer and running around with women. This devotion, however, did not prevent him from taking a second wife when Nyokabi proved to be subfecund, a move she approved. In 1986 her co-wife deserted them, leaving six children needing support. They also had supported four of her husband's elder brother's children when his wife died during the Emergency. But Nyokabi and her husband did not find this support as onerous a burden as it might have been because they had had time to get established economically before taking it on.

Cooperation among family members served this family very well. Nyokabi and her husband began with four acres of land he inherited, on which they grew coffee and market garden crops, while Nyokabi traded and belonged to two women's groups. They prospered and built a three-roomed house for rental purposes, while purchasing a total of seventeen more acres of land in four locations. In 1988 as members of a savings association made up of his patrilineal relatives they embarked on construction of an eight room house in order to get more rental income. Their own house was built of stone and timber with a metal roof, unlike the usual mud and wattle construction for poorer people. Although Nyokabi was selling bananas, dried staples, and milk from their cow two days a week at Wangige Market, it was clear that more income came from their joint landholdings. He used hired labor to farm cash crops. They had managed to send their daughter to Form 4; at age forty-three she was married with children and self-sufficient as a primary teacher. The four nieces and nephews had enough training to secure jobs and were living independently. Nyokabi's eldest stepdaughter had attended Standard 8 and was the mother of twins. The eldest stepson had also gone to Form 4 and was in training to be a welder. The other four stepchildren were in school in grades appropriate to their ages. Nyokabi reported that she and her husband shared money impartially, giving cash to each other at need, and that she was very happy with her husband's support. They shared ownership of the land that was purchased. "We are united," she said.[128]

The most economically secure women were those with employed husbands who helped, like the 80% of the married women in the large sample. Women therefore place a high priority on achieving marriage, hence paying their own bridewealth on occasion, but the goal is difficult to achieve for many women. In the large sample 45.6% of the women traders did not have husbands, while 6.5% had husbands who were dependents themselves, as we have seen. An additional 2.6% of the women had husbands who were not helping to support their families, yielding a total of 54.7% of 686 women who could not count on husbands for support, nor did they get substantial help from other relatives, who were struggling with their own burdens.[129]

---

[128] Interviews 450 Wangige: 16, 25 May 1988.

[129] In 1969 McVicar, "Twilight," p. 90, found that wealth variations among rural Kikuyu families were associated primarily with land and labor inputs rather than urban remittances, and that extended family connections were not important in this regard.

Most traders, then, are forced to be self-reliant. Indeed, they pride themselves on it, which came out in many conversations about support.

A number of examples show the force of women's belief in self-sufficiency. A ninety-four-year-old Kamba woman who eked out a meager living hawking said, "I don't get anything from my children and I don't like to take anything from anybody, unless one of these women here gives me rice to go and cook. No, I have never spent a night under somebody else's roof." A forty-three year old said, when asked from whom she would get money if she needed it, "There is no one whom I can ask. I would just use my mind. I come and sell something here so that I can get the Ksh.100 but I can't go get it from anyone."[130] Sturdy independence was an ideal for many women, expressed succinctly by a fifty-four year old at Kawangware. When asked if there was anyone who should be helping her, she replied, "I don't get any assistance and I also don't want that assistance. Everybody has his or her own problems." Hannah, a thirty-five-year-old woman who was having a difficult time paying school fees for her two children, with an alcoholic husband as an extra liability, said that getting help from her childless elder sister, a wholesaler and landowner, would be difficult; "she might say that if we just waste our money on my husband, we shouldn't bother her. You know, it's not usual for Kikuyus to support others..." Another said, "When I get old, I will just go home and work on that farm. I won't rely on anybody." She had access to fifteen acres and so looked forward to being self-reliant.[131] The strongest statement about self-reliance came from a successful bean trader at Kiambu Town Market.

> I have four children. The boy became a thug and joined a band; he started drinking beer which I don't like because if I joined hands with him he would wreck my business... Whatever money he gets let him help himself. Each of the girls has her husband, so they should use their brains to support themselves. I won't ask them to help me and in return, I won't help them.[132]

Self-reliance also is evident in the sources of starting capital for businesses, as shown in Table VI.4, which compares men and women traders (N=1063 businesses from the large sample in which cash was used).[133] Men got significantly more help from fathers or father's side relatives and from parents, but less help from their mother's side than women did. Women got less help from their mother's side, sisters and female friends than men got from their male connections, probably because of superior male access to cash. Women got help from some sources not tapped by men: lovers, children (mostly sons), and rotating savings associations, and relied

---

[130] Interviews 77 Ngara Bean: 11 Nov. 1987; 142 Gikomba: 15 Jan. 1988.

[131] Interviews 559 Kawangware: 22 June 1988; 108 Ngara Bean: 18 Nov. 1987; 253 Gikomba: 8 Apr. 1988.

[132] Interview 808 Kiambu Town: 19 Oct. 1988.

[133] Pala Okeyo's results, "Women," p. 339, were significantly different for her sample of 84 Luo fish or agricultural produce traders: 57.1% got capital from relatives, and 42.9% from selling their own produce or wages.

VI.4. Sources of Starting Capital by Gender, 1987-1988

Gender:	Women	Men
Source:		
Self	54.1%	66.1%
Spouse	19.6	.1
Father or father's		
side relative	2.4	11.3
Mother or mother's		
side relative	4.1	3.0
Parents (unspec.)	.5	2.1
Brother	2.7	5.9
Sister	1.3	1.7
Child	1.2	0.0
Same sex friend	4.4	6.9
Opposite sex friend	1.4	0.0
Credit/loan (non-		
lated source)	2.1	1.4
Rotating savings asso.	1.4	0.0
Other	4.5	1.5
Total	99.7	100.0

more on credit. Neither men nor women relied a lot on credit, however, for starting capital; both were most likely to finance their own startups, whether using their savings or homegrown produce (women used their own produce for starting capital in 12.1% of businesses compared to 4.1% of men's).[134]

If many women made economic independence a matter of pride, reluctant to accept help even from their children, many also interpreted their own economic responsibilities broadly. One of the women at Githega said, "Children don't ask their fathers for food, do they? They ask their mothers. The responsibility is hers." Many women go further than this basic view, however. A forty-five-year-old woman at Gikomba explained, "You see, in Ukambani when a girl gets married, they don't bother about you any more. My brothers could help me support my children, but you see I am married; I have to look after my own."[135] But this woman was helping her brothers whenever they came to Nairobi and viewed that as part of her responsibilities.

Although many women carried out their patrilocal responsibilities by helping their affinal relatives, that help was often not reciprocated. One forty-seven-year-old widow said that her husband's mother and brothers were not helping her, and, "out of the realization that they will never help, if I had problems I would never go to anybody." While making claims on no one, she claimed responsibility herself, saying

---

[134] This finding is supported by those of Aboagye, *Informal Sector*, pp. 12-23. Freeman, *City*, p. 112, noted that many Nairobi women urban farmers used their own produce for entry into trade.

[135] Interviews E Githega: 12 July 1988; 149 Gikomba: 26 Apr. 1988.

that her daughter "can work and get money to clothe her children, but I am responsible all the same."[136] One of the most extreme cases in which women claimed responsibility for supporting grandchildren was that of Njoki, a forty-seven-year-old dried staples wholesaler with eleven dependents, including two grandchildren fathered by two of her unmarried sons. The mother of one of these brought her daughter to Rachel Njoki asking that she care for her. Another of Njoki's sons refused to marry the mother of his son but, "he went there and found that the child was going to die because the mother didn't care for him." So he brought him for Njoki to look after. Njoki's nineteen-year-old daughter Muthoni was pregnant, which was going to add another dependant, while another unmarried twenty-eight-year-old daughter had two children and was trading in the same market. Njoki said, "Muthoni does try but she doesn't really know the value of children like I do because she's also still a child. So it's my responsibility."[137]

In contrast to Njoki, who was separated from her husband but eagerly accepted added dependents to be supported from a thriving urban wholesale business, some women found the dependency burden so overwhelming that they contemplated suicide. Wangui at age forty-six was trying to support four daughters aged twenty down to twelve on a small rural retail dried staples business. She said her husband had divorced her because of her conversion to Christianity (some men strongly resisted the efforts of wives to reform their behavior encouraged by Christianity).

> If my daughters had children I would accept them. I pray to God to help my children so that we can help each other. I pray Him every day so that He can change my husband's heart and he comes back to me. I pray God also to help my daughters get husbands and they stay together. And I always pray God for these children not to have children to add to my burden. I don't think I can manage an extra burden.[138]

Worries about child support clearly were a strong influence in a number of reported suicides by women, although abuse from husbands was also important.[139]

By the time women began to trade at age thirty or so they were already likely to have four or five children to support. They started in order to meet family needs like school fees, rather than because they saw it as a career they might enjoy. Some women came to enjoy trade, but that was not their primary reason for doing it. Many said that they would do any other work if it was more profitable, showing a low commitment to trade as an occupation. Trade, then, was a strategy more than a commitment for most women traders, albeit one that absorbed most of their time. In contrast, many men began trading when unmarried, indicating the presence of many wage jobseekers in the markets (they and a few elderly women were the only persons

---

[136] Interview 133 Nyamakima: 15 Dec. 1987.

[137] Interview 112 Ngara Bean: 23 Nov. 1987.

[138] Interview 847 Karuri: 13 Oct. 1988.

[139] *Daily Nation* 20 July, 27 Aug. 1988.

in the sample with no dependents). Young men often helped their parents support their siblings.

Despite the necessity for women to trade, control over the profits of that trade was still a prime subject for dispute in the era after independence. In 1976 Abbott found among a rural Kikuyu sample that the control of surplus [?] subsistence crops and egg sales, as well as discipline and support of children were the usual sources of conflict in marriages.[140] In the 1980s the conflicts continued; some escalated. In Nyeri in October 1988 a fifty-year-old man was clubbed to death by family members enraged at his appropriation of the profits from selling potatoes at the market; in Kirinyaga in June a woman tried to poison her husband as a result of a quarrel over finances including her opening a secret bank account. At Gikomba a man stormed into the market upset about his wife leaving home in Kitui to come to Nairobi to trade, ranted at her and ended by destroying her shoes, a symbolic gesture if ever there was one. Some of the husbands--about 8%--of women in the small sample objected to their wives trading, but most approved of it. Some even devised it as a strategy to support their families, the husbands remaining in the rural areas. Several husbands withdrew their opposition to wives trading when that trade became the family's sole support.[141]

A number of businesses were jointly operated by husbands and wives. In fact, family businesses were more likely to be run by couples than by any other combination of relatives, but these comprised less than 1% of the businesses surveyed in the large sample. Marris and Somerset in 1971 found that male entrepreneurs considered wives to be the most secure guardians of family interests and businesses,[142] perhaps because of their subordination: their economic dependence, their obligation to put the husbands' interests before that of their own relatives, and their unpaid labor obligations to their husbands. In my samples husbands helped wives with their businesses by supplying capital when needed (we have already seen that husbands were the largest source of starting capital for women aside from their own savings), by paying for training, and by helping wives make contributions to rotating savings associations. In one case a woman began by helping in her husband's business, her husband giving her an allowance out of the profits; she then progressed to keeping the profits to buy more stock, giving the husband loans on occasion.[143] Husbands could also be a business liability, however, apart from simply being dependents on occasion. One man borrowed Ksh.6000 from his wife to buy stock for his shop and wasted it, so she refused any further loans. A male trader at Ngara got his starting

---

[140] Abbott, "Full-Time Farmers," p. 168.

[141] *Standard* 18 Oct. and 24 June 1988; interviews 241 Gikomba: 31 Mar. 1988; 149 Gikomba: 26 Apr. 1988; 667 Kangemi: 25 July 1988.

[142] Marris and Somerset, *African Businessmen*, pp. 119-23, 150.

[143] Interviews 808 Kiambu Town: 19 Oct. 1988; K14 Kariakor: 1 Mar. 1988; 514 Wangige: 30 May 1988; 297 Gikomba: 1 Apr. 1988.

capital mainly from his wife's sales of coffee and tea; he did not repay her because, "the farm is mine, the wife is mine, so I don't have to give her anything."[144]

The figures on repayment of capital are illuminating with regard to the practice of community of property in marriage. The large sample provided information about repayment of capital in 465 businesses when relatives or friends gave or lent it. Parents more often expected sons to repay capital than daughters, but not by much (39.2% versus 30.1%). Friends of the same sex as the trader usually expected repayment. Wives did not expect husbands to repay them, but 6.6% of husbands expected repayment from wives. The fact that husbands usually did not expect repayment is misleading to some extent; the provision of capital was an extension of the husbands' obligations to support the family and sometimes substituted for the allocation of land; the women's profits were supposed to go for family support. Whereas husbands were free to spend as they pleased on entertainment and other personal purposes, wives who spent on their own wants were regarded with suspicion.[145] The usual emblem of an extravagant wife was a new dress. Older women talked about how in the old days appearing in a new dress was likely to lead to charges of adultery even more than of extravagance, because men were supposed to provide clothing for their wives. Anything not provided by the husband was therefore suspect. But since wives' earnings were seen as family earnings, husbands felt that they had a right to them, even if they had not provided any capital, a logical extension of viewing the wife herself as property. Monsted found a similar phenomenon in the Rift Valley, where husbands were bearing a "very limited" share of the costs of socializing and caring for children; wives, even of wealthy farmers, sometimes lived in poverty as a result.[146]

This situation is inherently unequal because wives' earnings are treated as community property but husbands' earnings are not. The presumption is that what is hers is his but not vice versa. Any time a husband contributed capital to a business, whether expecting repayment or not, he could demand the profits from it. But because women had few resources and also little choice if the husband wanted them to trade, they accepted such demands. Women, asked if they had ever loaned money to their husbands, said reprovingly that one did not *loan* money to husbands, one gave it. Most had. Wives often wanted joint ownership and use of resources with their husbands, who were more likely to have assets, but husbands sometimes used exclusive ownership of a small business as a means to perpetuate economic control over a wife and children.[147] Nyokabi was an example of a successful strategist in this regard. But husbands who had acquired assets often resisted sharing them. Women,

---

[144] Interviews 108 Ngara Bean: 18 Nov. 1987; 33 Ngara: 19 Oct. 1987.

[145] Browne, "Kawangware," pp. 150, 169; Monsted, "Division," pp. 301-305; Stichter, "Women," pp. 148-51, found the same phenomenon among middle-class Nairobi couples in the 1980s.

[146] Monsted, "Division," pp. 301, 312.

[147] Browne, "Kawangware," p. 155.

therefore, are in a highly conflictual position, halfway between being property themselves and independence. This was the situation faced by most Euro-American women until the late nineteenth century, when laws allowing married women to own property were enacted, and the twentieth century when communal property laws gave spouses a claim on each other's property. In Kenya the largest obstacle to moving toward communal property is the interest of men's lineages in their property,[148] so that it is difficult for women to maintain a partially secured right to inheritance, much less fight the household-level battles necessary to achieve more economic security. The laws, in any case, apply mainly to those who have the resources to secure a favorable decision in the courts.

Meanwhile, women are not usually exercising the option of expanding their trade by employing their children or other relatives in their businesses. The businesses were overwhelmingly one-person operations. Very few women were in trade with their relatives; most preferred that their children get educated for better-paying occupations. Children, in particular, acted as a brake on their businesses; businesses shrank when pillaged of capital to pay school fees. One woman described her sole effort at wholesaling as a failure because her grown daughter gave birth while the woman was on a buying trip and the grain had to be used to feed the family.[149] Unlike in the past when women were more likely to sell their own produce, many landless or near-landless traders now rely completely on purchasing their trading stock, so that capital is crucial. When capital goes for family needs they go bankrupt. Their family fortunes, then, are critical for the fortunes of the women's businesses.

As one response to this situation many women traders are trying to reduce their dependency burden by having fewer children.[150] In this respect they form a leading contingent of Kenyan women mostly responsible for the welfare of their families who are highly motivated to control their fertility due to their poverty. The small sample survey included a knowledge, attitudes and practices (KAP) survey regarding contraception, which yielded strong indicators of attempts to control fertility among these women. The number of children ever borne per woman with completed fertility declined from 8.2 for women in their sixties and over, to 6.9 for women in their fifties, to 6.2 for women in their forties.[151] Women in their thirties or younger averaged 4.3 children and most were satisfied with the number of children they already had (only one in her twenties wanted more). Urban fertility rates in

---

[148] Stamp, "Burying."

[149] Interview 215 Gikomba: 18 Mar. 1988.

[150] Nelson, "'Selling,'" p. 298, found that there was a positive correlation between successful entrepreneurship for women and barrenness.

[151] For Africa Kenya, as well as Botswana and Zimbabwe, have relatively low infant mortality rates, high levels of education and high use of contraceptives, such that fertility began dropping in the late 1980s from 7.1 in 1978-85 to 6.5 in 1985-88. Demographic and World Health Surveys, *World Conference Report*, p. 6; Caldwell et al., "Fertility Decline," p. 212.

Kenya, as elsewhere, are normally lower than rural ones. The ideal number of children women felt that a woman under present conditions should have declined steadily from 4.2 for women in their fifties and over, to 3.6 for those in their forties, to 2.7 for those thirty-nine or younger. Women now can be more confident that the children they have will survive, whereas half used to die.[152] Use of methods to hinder fertility rose from 20.7% of women fifty and over to 68.7% of those in their forties, to 72.7% of those in their thirties and younger, with the oldest women having used postpartum abstention and women in their fifties and younger surgical or medical contraceptive methods. The reasons given for using contraception were invariably economic; most women who were dissatisfied with the number of children they had felt that they had too many to support adequately. These results contrast sharply with the recorded increases through the mid-1980s in the Kenyan population growth rate.[153]

The reasons for declining fertility in this population are both economic and social. In the large sample when marital status was cross-tabulated with number of children, divorced or separated women always had significantly fewer children than married women in all age groups. Also, women who had never married had fewer children than divorced women (most women aged twenty-four and over who had never married had at least one child). As women got older the fertility differences according to marital status grew higher, so that women of completed fertility aged forty-five to fifty-five (N=162) exhibited the strongest differences: never-married women in that age group had had 3.3 children on the average, divorced women 4.2, and married women 6.2.[154] While never-married Kenyan women demonstrate higher fertility than their counterparts in many countries, the correlation of divorce with lower fertility is consonant with results from other countries indicating the positive effect of long-term stable unions on fertility.

These traders, then, are actively trying to lower their fertility; many had strong feelings about contraception and were counselling their daughters to use it. The strength of their convictions led to many digressions from the questionnaire and discussions about the effectiveness of methods. The story of Serafina illustrates a common problem, however.

---

[152] A 1970 survey of middle-class residents of Nairobi housing estates found that husbands were more likely than wives to feel that it was women's duty to bear as many children as possible. Martin, "Family Planning." McCormick, "Enterprise," p. 86.

[153] Faruqee, "Fertility," p. 30, found that births per woman in Nairobi rose from 5.6 in 1969 to 6.1 in 1977-78. Lestaeghe and others have attributed increasing fertility in Kenya to the decline in postpartum abstention from sex and therefore closer child spacing. A diminution in polygyny is usually felt to increase fertility and decrease child spacing. *Situation Analysis* II: 7; Lesthaeghe, "Introduction," p. 11; Lesthaeghe and Eelens, "Components," p. 90.

[154] A study that also showed declining fertility in Kenya (from 7.7 births per woman in 1984 to 6.7 in 1989) offered the null explanation that the decline was due to an increase in use of contraceptives, which ignored the long availability of contraceptives in Kenya along with failure to use them, and the socioeconomic reasons affecting their use. *Kenya Demographic and Health Survey*, p. xix.

Serafina, a tall striking forty-two year old, had both financial and physical problems after the birth of her sixth child and began using birth control pills without telling her husband. She needed to get her husband's consent to use contraceptives or have an abortion or tubal ligation, but her doctor, like some others, was willing to help her evade the rules.[155] Serafina's husband discovered the pills in her bedding while she was away trading in Nairobi and got furious with her, accusing her of practicing prostitution, a common assumption associated with contraceptive use. He then threw the pills down the latrine and told her never to use them again. She bore three more children, which weakened her health considerably. After the birth of the last child the doctor, afraid that further childbearing would kill her, tricked her husband into signing the permission for her to have a tubal ligation.[156] When Serafina's husband discovered the trick he again got angry and threatened to take another wife. In other matters, however, he was notably cooperative, feeding the children in her absence and doing a strong portion of the agricultural labor.[157]

He illustrated a changing gender division of labor in agriculture fostered by women's trade and male unemployment, wherein men were taking a stronger role in agricultural labor and even assuming some domestic responsibilities. While quite a few women noted the former, the latter was rare.[158]

The economics of marriage are complex, then, and changing. The older cooperative household has become less common with the rise in landlessness since independence, but it is not being replaced by cooperation of relatives in trade. Women's search for security has taken several forms when their marriages have collapsed: trade, lovers, farming rented land, using contraception. Regarding marriage they have attempted to shore up their position by paying bridewealth, urging Christianity, seeking romantic love and joint property, and taking over husbands' businesses on occasion. If the strategies used are innovative, they are also products of real hardship.

Conclusion

The dramatic changes that have occurred in marriage among Nairobi traders are common among twentieth-century impoverished populations: from

---

[155] Some women reported that doctors refused even to consider giving them a tubal ligation unless they had already had six children, and the Kenyan family planning program routinely refuses service to unwed girls under eighteen. Caldwell et al., "Fertility Decline," p. 217.

[156] Superfecundity was a cause of women's death reported by some women. One trader, who had used birth control herself and borne only two children, found her family's improving fortunes reversed because her sister died after giving birth to her fourteenth child. The impoverished husband could neither nurture nor support them so she adopted them.

[157] Interview 72 Ngara Bean: 20 Nov. 1987.

[158] A finding confirmed by Stichter, "Women," p. 138.

marriages arranged by relatives to individual choice of spouse; from elaborate formalities linking two lineages to small tokens of celebration signaling common-law marriages; and from stable marriages characterized by hierarchical cooperation to unstable love matches with little economic security. Inflation in bridewealth beginning in the early decades of the century led to occasional kidnapping of women by poor men and forced marriage of girls by poor parents to wealthy men. But these changes are not evenly paced; the dispossession and tumults of the 1950s and 1960s were clearly crucial in accelerating changes that progressed even more rapidly in the 1970s and 1980s. In this process these women traders, like many women worldwide, have become subject to large contradictions, between the coercion of physical abuse and the independence of single urban living, and between economic autonomy and vulnerability. The transitional generations saw attempts to secure access to land and respectability when women sometimes contributed to their own bridewealth, but increasing landlessness has reduced the usefulness of that tactic. While economic and social autonomy has allowed a few to prosper beyond previous bounds, it also left many with narrower family ties and therefore more dependent on husbands or their own efforts. Economic coercion has subjected women to violence from men. Not only women's labor, but also women's bodies are seen as male property. Thus, the struggle over women's profits is also a struggle over their bodies; both are contested terrain. Many women, having seen the limitations or disadvantages of "cooperation" with men, or having been forced to do without it, are making the best of segregation and testing boundaries everywhere--getting custody of children, pushing into new territory in business, and asserting control over their own bodies by rejecting abusers and restricting their own fertility. The rest of this history explores changes in methods by which women organized themselves to achieve a measure of security for themselves and their children.

VII

Organizing:
Women and Collective Action, 1920 to 1990

Those who take counsel together do not perish.[1]

The history presented to this point has delineated how individual women have faced collective problems. These problems are related to landlessness, crops grown and traded, control over trade profits and labor, marriage, and dependency burdens. Nairobi women traders, disproportionately single, divorced or widowed, have suffered greatly from discrimination in access to critical resources, everything from land and education to fertilizer. A few women cried when telling of terrible experiences they had endured, of husbands' beatings, of poverty and starvation, of the deaths of children or beloved husbands, of imprisonment or internment by the British under the Emergency or by the government in the 1980s for selling illegally, of backbreaking labor for little pay on the plantations of the wealthy, or of prostitution undertaken to feed their children. More laughed, danced, and persevered in the face of overwhelming odds. In the end, they refused to see themselves as victims; they dried their tears, picked up their heavy baskets of produce, and trudged off, determined to overcome and carry out their activities so essential to the survival of Kenyans.

These voices seemed most self-confident and optimistic when women organized themselves to meet their problems. For most of this history women have attempted collective solutions to meet their obligations and change the behavior of those who incurred their disapproval by going against women's collective interests. We have already seen that women fought and are fighting at the household level to control their fertility, their businesses, their mobility, the conditions of their marriages, and the crops they grew/grow.[2] But one of the best ways to contest jurisdiction over their bodies and their labor is to organize collectively. This chapter traces changes in the ways women have organized themselves from the 1920s to 1990. Just as men's collective efforts to control women shifted in plane from women's sexuality/fertility to attempts at economic independence, women's collective efforts have moved from a more specific form of gerontocratic organization concerned with producing properly socialized adults and controlling sexuality to a more class-based

---

[1] DC/MKS 10B/3/1 *Muig.* (Gathano 1928): 3.

[2] These struggles mirror those described by Mackenzie, "Woman," p. 68, in Murang'a, "Conflict over land and labour within the household emerges as individual men attempt to exert control over both, exercising proprietary rights that had not previously existed, and women counter in an attempt to maintain budgetary autonomy and their ability to sustain household reproduction."

women's solidarity involved with promoting women's economic activities. This transition involved women's solidary groups moving away from female initiation, with its associated clitoridectomy, but retaining and transforming collective labor, *ngwatio*.[3] Part of this struggle emerged out of women's trading experiences in Nairobi, which may have influenced the many well-organized, large-scale rural women's protests that took place from the 1920s through the 1940s. Also included here is the continuing history of resistance to controls on the staples trade and of hawker protests after independence. This chapter begins by describing the transition from older forms of women's organizations to the late colonial and post-independence formation of rotating savings associations, continues with an overview of the control barriers faced by women traders from the 1960s to 1990, and ends by analyzing efforts by market-based organizations to counter the controls and persecution. A motif crossing several sections concerns changes in images of traders among the ruling class that accompanied class formation. Overall, gender segregation became more entrenched as a principle of socioeconomic organization pervading most levels, but especially effective among the underclass, where it both prevented and enabled solidarity depending on the venue.

Women's Organizations to the 1920s
So God helped me and these women taught me.[4]

The old form of women's organization centered around their age-sets (*mariika*) and solidarity induced by their common initiation ritual and solidified by participation in groups doing communal labor, *ngwatio*. Part of the initiation ritual was genital mutilation in the form of clitoridectomy. This practice, which Westerners from missionaries to feminists have found shocking (see Chapter III), has absorbed much of the energy of modern scholars who have encountered it. It has been voyeuristically sensationalized in Western mass media, while its cultural context and local processes that are diminishing it have been ignored. The explanations given for its persistence have related to blind tradition, naked patriarchal power, or a type of false consciousness. But its persistence in central Kenya is most closely connected to its function as part of initiation rites; so is its diminution. Senior women's authority was reinforced by initiation and its abandonment has ambivalent implications for women. Gerontocratic organization for women was extremely important and reluctantly surrendered. At the same time, the meanings of clitoridectomy have been further complicated by some Kenyan men, who as unwitting enforcers of the views of some Western feminist crusaders, have transposed clitoridectomy into an unambiguous symbol of

---

[3] Stamp, "Mothers," has also made this argument in an article which magnificently lays out the contemporary relevance of old forms, while not based in historical data. Nor does it consider genital mutilation.

[4] Interview 71 Ngara Bean: 1 Dec. 1987.

female subordination.[5] Here I will argue that diminution in the practice of clitoridectomy is most related to transformations in the ways women organize themselves.

Initiation (Kikuyu=*irua*) has often been viewed as the most important old Kikuyu custom and also was universally practiced by the Kamba.[6] Boys and girls underwent a series of ceremonies which had the ultimate aim of initiating them into adulthood. Before initiation they were not supposed to have sexual intercourse or marry. Sex with an uninitiated person was regarded as polluting, requiring a purification rite to expunge it.[7] Boys were circumcised during initiation, which usually took place when they were sixteen to eighteen. Girls had the clitoris and sometimes the labia removed, depending on the prevailing custom in the geographic locale where the operation was performed; they underwent initiation before the onset of menstruation at the first appearance of breasts between the ages of ten and fifteen.[8] Girls' initiation ceremonies were held annually, but boys' usually took place more rarely with more fanfare. Each group chose its own name, so that the best method of ascertaining the age of older Kikuyu is to ask the name of their *riika* (Kamba women often claimed there were no names). These names often reflected new or strange events that year, a plague of insects, a new dance, the arrival of the first airplane. Whereas girls' age-sets usually had local names, boys' drew participants from a wider area and had wider application. The rites might have taken place together or separately.[9] It is possible that one effect of the smaller scale and more restricted area of the girls' groups was to heighten solidarity.

An extremely important part of initiation was the knowledge imparted to the initiates by their elders. It involved traditions, laws, manners, the duties of adults, ideas of appropriate behavior regarding sexual intercourse, in particular, childrearing, and generally any knowledge necessary to function as a successful adult in Kikuyu or Kamba society. Part of the Kikuyu knowledge imparted at initiation concerned socially permissible forms of petting called *ng'weko*, much disapproved of in mis-

---

[5] This process seems to have begun with the construction of the nationalist woman by Kenyatta. Shaw, *Colonial Inscriptions*, p. 71, described accurately the symbolism of the mutilations at initiation as follows. Circumcision and clitoridectomy "have always been about the *historical production of gendered bodies*, removing the female covering--the foreskin--from men and the phallic clitoris from women, marking bodies for the roles they will play." However, the stress in her analysis on the physical aspects of initiation common to most feminist literature is lopsided in privileging only one aspect of *irua* for attention, while it has multiple meanings. A more detailed version of this section appeared in Robertson, "Grassroots."

[6] Kenyatta, *Facing*, p. 128; Muriuki, *History*, p. 119; Kabwegyere, "Determinants," p. 215. Lindblom, *Akamba*, pp. 79, 574, referred to it only in passing but described male initiation in detail.

[7] Kenyatta, *Facing*, p. 127.

[8] In Meru and Embu more radical operations were performed. PC/CENT 2/1/4 minutes Kiambu LNC 20-21 Feb. 1929; PC/CP 4/1/2 Kikuyu Province AR 1930: 26; 1931: 4; Native Affairs Dept. AR 1928: 7. Kenyatta, *Facing*, pp. 130-31; Boyes, *King*, p. 304; Routledges, *Prehistoric People*, p. 24.

[9] White, *Comforts*, pp. 155-57; Tate, "Native Law," pp. 285-90.

sionary circles, as were the dances associated with initiation.[10] Such interactions contradicted some women's statements about the desirability of the separation of the genders before marriage. In the dances athleticism was prized; there was also a footrace whose winners were to be leaders-for-life of their age sets.[11] Girls approaching puberty were given privileged treatment, such as food containing *njahe*. They and the boys were told that they were supposed to prove themselves by showing courage in maintaining silence during the operation, despite the fact that the operator, not a close relative, was supposed to look terrifying. The pain endured at excision was to prepare a girl for that at childbirth. A respected woman elder acted as a girl's sponsor and held her during the operation. Afterward initiates were supposed to be well cared for along with their mates. Their collective healing process helped to solidify lifelong friendships. A Mutira woman said, "The pain we shared kept us together from that day."[12] The symbolic rebirth of the person as an adult in possession of new knowledge, as well as a sense of triumph over a physical test, must have imparted feelings of empowerment to at least some of the female initiates. Thus, as Moore stated regarding the Endo in Western Kenya, the initiation rites helped women by "affirming and reinforcing female identity, sexuality, and solidarity," and, one might add, senior women's authority.[13]

The missionaries' attack on clitoridectomy was rooted not just in moral indignation (after all, it was also practiced in Europe in some quarters)[14] but also in fear of the overthrow of British rule. The memoranda that circulated among missionaries and administrators, ostensibly about "female circumcision," as it was called, often said more about the Kikuyu Central Association and the political threat that it represented. In his well-known demand that his (male) Kikuyu mission teachers not have their daughters excised, the Reverend Arthur also insisted upon a declaration that they were not members of the KCA. He was convinced that female excision would have died out had the KCA not made it an issue. Scott, the Director of Education, said that Arthur "had completely underestimated the depth of spiritual feeling among the Kikuyu in regard to female circumcision."[15]

The clitoridectomy controversy clearly had different meanings for different participants.[16] Missionaries, scholars, and administrators disagreed about

---

[10] Kenyatta, *Facing*, pp. 130-41; PC/CP 8/1/1 Rev. John Arthur, Church of Scotland Mission Kiambu, to Director of Education, Nairobi 16 Jan. 1930.

[11] Kenyatta, *Facing*, pp. 135-36.

[12] Davison and Women, *Voices*, pp. 42, 22. Another stated, "One must buy maturity with pain."

[13] Moore, *Space*, p. 172.

[14] Harcourt, "Gender," pp. 66-68.

[15] PC/CP 8/1/1 memo. Director of Education Nairobi to Colonial Secretary Nairobi 18 Jan. 1930: 1, 10. Welbourn, *Rebels*, stressed political motivations for the KCA's crusade. If violence against women was a big issue, then it is strange that missionaries did not also take on publicly the custom of a new male initiate raping a married woman as part of the ritual. Lawren, "Masai," p. 579.

[16] For a more extensive discussion of the controversy see Murray, "Controversy"; Sandgren, "Kikuyu"; Waruiru, "Initiation"; L. Leakey, "Problem"; Pedersen, "Bodies."

clitoridectomy, Leakey serving as an apologist for it at one point.[17] Administrators first saw initiation as a labor issue and objected to workers being absent or laid up for months because of the rites, but they soon were forced to deal with it as a moral and political issue, which, for the sake of peace, they generally ducked. They often classified clitoridectomy as a merely cosmetic operation along with earpiercing, hairplastering, (with mud), and the extraction and filing of teeth. Under pressure from the administration some LNCs passed resolutions either limiting the extent of the operation or forbidding it entirely, but they were not enforced.[18] Some missionary-educated young men split with young militants like the contributors to *Muigwithania*.

Although the implications of excision for the women were more intimate and profound, they are scarcely represented in the public record. Women's thoughts on the subject were not collected by researchers in a position to do so. Two women wrote to *Muigwithania*, both concerned about girls running away to Nairobi to become prostitutes. One associated that outcome with girls' going away to school, that is, escaping their parents' supervision and, by implication, being uninitiated because in a mission school, while the other attributed it to the fact that uninitiated girls were scorned by their families and potential mothers-in-law. Both abased themselves thoroughly, Wanjiru wa Kinyua saying that she had never heard of *Muigwithania* "containing the utterance of a woman," and that she was nervous about writing at all since she was a woman and "bought." She was afraid of what they might do to her if they did not want letters sent by women since "we have no power apart from you." The other was less shy and pleaded that her letter be published even though "a woman has no right to speak before men."[19]

Did women through their age-sets have power apart from men, which Wanjiru wa Kinyua denied so firmly? The answer is, yes, but that "apart from" is the correct term to describe it as they had very little power *over* men. Some of the functions of the age-sets legitimized and perpetuated patriarchal values, while others defined women's sphere and forbade male entry.[20] The perpetuation of clitoridectomy as an exclusively female ceremony did both. There was a transfer of values stressing male dominance in the form of service and cosmetic alterations done to please men (for instance, scarification of the pubis done to heighten male sexual pleasure).[21]

---

[17] L. Leakey, "Problem," pp. 277-82.

[18] PC/CP 7/1/2 ADC Nyeri to DC Nyeri 16 Sept. 1920; Acting PC Nyeri to Chief Native Commissioner Nairobi 27 May 1920. Much of the essential correspondence is in PC/CP 8/1/1 for 1928-30. See also DC/KBU 1/22 Kiambu AR 1929: 2; PC/CENT 2/1/4 minutes Kiambu LNC ? Sept. 1925; 9 Feb., 14 July 1926.

[19] DC/MKS 10B/13/1 *Muig.* II, 1 (June 1929): 10; I, 12 (May 1929): 7.

[20] Lindblom, *Akamba*, p. 94, in one of his few references to clitoridectomy said that *ukate* (Kikamba=clitoris) was a women's word and that there were traces of a special language for women having to do with avoidances and respect.

[21] A related custom decreed that a mother should be beaten on the day her eldest child was initiated. Davison and Women, *Voices*, pp. 148-49. Kenyatta. *Facing*, p. 139.

But there were also functions which provided strong reinforcement of female solidarity among age-sets and an introduction to, and respect for, a hierarchy of women in which the senior age grades wielded significant authority. Muriuki, Middleton and Kershaw all described the hierarchy of women's age grades; advancement from one to another required not only progressive age but payments to the women elders and brought increasing status and privileges. The highest grade, not achieved by everyone, was the council of women elders called variously *kiama kia aka* or *ndundu ya atomia*. It condemned and ostracized transgressors such as men who assaulted women. Respect for the elders was an essential teaching in the *irua* ceremony; if a girl's sponsor was supposed to provide lasting friendship and help to the girl, the girl was supposed to obey her unquestioningly, hide nothing from her, and deny her nothing.[22] The *kiama kia aka* decided when girls were to be initiated, punished immoral behavior, provided ceremonial food, and perhaps most important, arranged *ngwatio*, cooperative agricultural work parties. Contradicting Shaw's supposition that women's authority over food distribution allowed them (as with the Iroquois women's councils) to have a strong influence over declarations of war, Presley called the councils "invisible" in corporate lineage public affairs with no say regarding warfare, territorial expansion, or the maintenance and regulation of the legal system. Some women elders had important roles in land transfer ceremonies and purification rituals, but menstruation taboos kept women out of many ceremonies. Lindblom minimized the importance of women's authority over men by saying, "in many things [women] have their own rules to observe, which are respected by the men, even though they do not attach much importance to them," after his discussion of the Kamba version of *guturamira ng'ania*, discussed below.[23]

H. E. Lambert gave an elaborate description of the women's councils activities. They dealt with "purely domestic affairs," he said, such as agricultural matters like food crops, rainfall and land use, and the discipline and regulation of the social life of girls and women or other offenders. They punished men who maltreated women by levying fines to be paid in gourds, cooking pots or millet beer, by their wives' withdrawal of services, ostracism, or, if the offense was very bad, a curse placed by baring their private parts toward the object of the curse and hurling genital insults, accompanied by other anti-social behavior. This phenomenon, called *guturamira ng'ania* in Kikuyu, was used by Mary Muthoni Nyanjiru and her cohorts in the 1922 Thuku demonstration described in Chapter I and suggests the paradoxical nature of women's power, that avoidance and sexual taboos could be reversed to confer power on those who are normally regarded as inferior.[24] The meaning of the act, however, rested on the reference to women's reproductive power, that men would be betraying

---

[22] Muriuki, *History*, p. 122; Middleton and Kershaw, "Central Tribes," pp. 33-34; Maas, *Women's Groups*, p. 54; Davison and Women, *Voices*, p. 43; Kenyatta, *Facing*, p. 138.

[23] Clark, "Land"; Shaw, *Colonial Inscriptions*, pp. 42ff. Curiously, Shaw considers *ngwatio* mainly as a male phenomenon. Presley, *Kikuyu Women*, pp. 27-28; Lindblom, *Akamba*, p. 180.

[24] Lambert, *Institutions*, pp. 95-100; Wipper, "Kikuyu Women."

the source who gave them life if they continued to misbehave. Some of the "purely domestic matters" like marriage negotiations, which according to an informant initiated in 1940 were a chief subject of women's age-set meetings, had important political consequences for lineage relations.[25] It is clear, then, that some women could exercise some power in groups into the 1940s, and that initiation provided girls with an induction into how to exercise authority independent of men, or in limited cases, over men.

The Transition

The intermediate period of the 1930s through 1950s began the decline of the importance of initiation and age-sets as the basis for women's solidary groups and the elaboration of *ngwatio* into different more specialized forms in which the basis of solidarity became economic.[26] Women's groups were transformed by the catalyst of the continuing struggle over women's labor, widely requisitioned by government chiefs for forced labor on British-mandated land conservation measures. Kamba and Kikuyu women's preeminent ritual and economic responsibility for the land established their right to activism where the health of the crops was involved.[27] Lambert's interest in the groups was piqued by a number of incidents he observed in Meru; thousands of women from Abothuguchi marched on their administrative station to protest improper burials, which they felt had caused the crops to fail in 1934. In 1938 a number of Ndia women went to Nairobi to object to forced labor on erosion control measures, and over 2000 Kamba women did the same to protest forced destocking of cattle; in 1939 Igembe women looted a shop whose Asian owner was not felt to be giving fair prices for their produce. Tigania women forced an old man to give them a sacrificial sheep in compensation for his son's committing a murder that they believed caused the fields to go barren.[28] The effort to free Harry Thuku in 1922 was only one of a number of protests or strikes over labor issues between 1912 and the 1950s, which included protesting terracing work in Murang'a in 1947-48 and 1951, cattle dipping and rinderpest inoculations in 1951, and plague-related deroofing of huts in 1941.[29] All of this activity was well organized, drawing women from many villages, and most involved over a thousand women. Poor women tended to

---

[25] Interview 581 Kawangware: 14 June 1988.

[26] Stamp, "Groups," p. 27.

[27] Lindblom, *Akamba*, p. 180; Shaw, *Colonial Inscriptions*, p. 29.

[28] Lambert, *Institutions*, p. 100; Native Affairs Dept. AR 1938: 14. The anti-erosion control protest was by wives of Nairobi sweepers. Wisner, "Man-Made Famine," p. 12; ARC (MAA) 2/3/1VIA Nairobi AR 1938: 12-13.

[29] Maas, *Groups*, p. 57; African Affairs Dept. AR 1951: 34-35; 1948: ARC (MAA) 2/3/8III Central Province AR 1941: 2; Presley, "Transformation"; Wipper, "Kikuyu Women." Igembe women were in the habit of attending *barazas* en masse: PC/CP 1/1/2 Hemsted, "Short History," p. 24.

participate more because the burden of forced labor fell more heavily upon them.[30] As with the Igbo Women's War, such large-scale protests were not purely spontaneous, especially given the distances traversed by the demonstrators and their numbers.

The issues which roused these women to action were economic and intimately concerned with their labor, agricultural wellbeing and trade. The exploitative burden of colonialism in Kenya fell heavily on women, who, in addition to an increased agricultural workload at home, did much of the forced labor on roads and farms while their authority structures were either ignored or disrespected by British administrators and missionaries. Because women more often than men remained in the villages those structures could nevertheless endure. That the realm of work was the first to produce protests of any magnitude and that women organized those protests is logical. That they were organized by the *kiama kia aka*, as Lambert assumed, is suggested by evidence showing the continuation of women's groups in the period from 1930 to the 1950s. Njau and Mulaki have several histories of elderly Meru, Kikuyu and Kamba women leaders with roots in such groups, and a Mutira woman spoke of being initiated into the *kiama*, which played a role in organizing coffeepickers' protests. The *kiama kia aka* played a role in selecting girls to go to Githunguri Independent School in the late 1940s.[31] Fisher described the continuance of *ngwatio* work parties in 1950.[32]

But the 1950s Emergency restrictions drove initiation underground. Excision became a test of loyalty to the LFA; it and all associated male or female ceremonies were banned by the government. There are mixed indicators of the effectiveness of this ban in the 1950s, but afterwards initiation persisted including clitoridectomy.[33] In Nairobi clitoridectomy was still carried out regularly in the early 1960s; most young prostitutes had had it. Initiation was practiced by squatters in new areas until independence in 1963, while in 1974 informants gave Stamp accounts of continuing activity by the *kiama kia aka*.[34] Clitoridectomy continues now, though much diminished in importance; most germane here, it is independent of belonging to the newer type of women's groups. Among 199 women and their daughters in the small sample 61.4% had been excised, but these included all of the women aged fifty and over, 77.4% of the women aged thirty to forty-nine, and only 39% of those aged fifteen to twenty-nine. In the critical age group of ten to fourteen, only 20% had been

---

[30] Lonsdale, "Depression," p. 127.

[31] Njau and Mulaki, *Women Heroes*, pp. 18-25, 42-49, 67-75; Davison and Women, *Voices*, p. 55; Presley, *Kikuyu Women*, pp. 100-101, 181-82.

[32] Fisher, *Anatomy*, p. 208.

[33] Davison and Women, *Voices*, p. 44; CS 1/14/33 minutes Kiambu ADC 16-17 Nov. 1954: 4; DC/KBU 1/40 Kiambu AR 1949: 4; Fisher, *Anatomy*, p. 15; Reel 85 minutes Kiambu LNC 12-13 Aug. 1941: 8; LG 3/2700 minutes Kiambu ADC 18-19 Feb. 1957; African Affairs Dept. AR 1952: 27; Interviews 72 Ngara Bean: 20 Nov. 1987; 728 Gitaru: 17 Aug. 1988.

[34] Davison and Women, *Voices*, p. 44; Carlebach, *Juvenile Prostitution*, pp. 9, 19; Kanogo, *Squatters*, pp. 77-78; Stamp, "Mothers," p. 75.

initiated. Since several of these were going to have it done, according to their mothers, the final statistic for that age cohort might be more like 25%. Kabwegyere's 1970s' rural Kamba sample, drawn from areas from which most of the Kamba traders in my sample came (Kaungundo, Mitaboni, Masii, Mwala), showed a similar diminution in the practice.[35]

Women's reasons for dropping the practice generally fell into three categories: 1) clitoridectomy and the associated ceremonies were seen as being uncivilized and counter to the Bible; 2) it was no longer the style and difficult to find operators to do it; 3) it was expensive and undesirable for health reasons. Significantly, only one woman cited its illegality (President Moi outlawed it in 1982 after fourteen girls in one district died from associated infections).[36] Several women said that they were not going to impose on their daughters something that they themselves had objected to but had had to have done. One of these said that she was bitter because she was not allowed to go to school in 1954 because she had been excised and that it was "a foolish tradition." Another said, "that was darkness."[37] The women who had had it done or were going to have it done to their daughters often did so at the insistence of a mother or mother-in-law. There were a number of families in which the oldest daughters had been excised but the youngest escaped it because the grandmother had died by the time they were of age to be initiated.[38] The grandmothers were clearly trying to perpetuate gerontocratic authority.

If among the Kikuyu and Kamba the practice of clitoridectomy is diminishing sharply,[39] membership in contemporary women's groups is rising and has emerged seamlessly from the older versions. The transitional period of the late 1940s and 1950s saw the modification of women's groups for new purposes using *ngwatio* as the base. One factor in such organization was the increased involvement of women in trade after World War II documented in Chapter IV. During the 1940s new forms of economic organization including egg marketing cooperatives were formed by Kiambu women for the Nairobi trade.[40] Monsted mentioned "women's clubs" formed among the "middle peasantry" in the late 1940s.[41] These development-oriented women's groups were in existence in Kiambu after World War II and were independent of government involvement. The age-set groups were shifting their

---

[35] Kabwegyere, "Determinants," p. 215.

[36] Rasna Warah, "Kenyan Men Say No to Female Circumcision," *Viva* Sept. 1987: 15, said that men objected to women's lack of enjoyment of sex if excised.

[37] Interviews 731 Gitaru: 24 Aug. 1988; 244 Gikomba: 25 Mar. 1988; 61 Ngara Bean: 27 Oct. 1987.

[38] Interviews 843 Karuri: 17 Oct. 1988; 561 Kawangware: 23 June 1988; 133 Nyamakima 15 Dec. 1987; 865 Kiambu 4 Nov. 1988.

[39] A 1985 report, however, found that the practice is still common among Kisii, Maasai, Somali and Boran women. Warah, "Men," p. 15.

[40] They were so efficient that they could trace the owner of any bad eggs and fine her. If that happened three times she was expelled permanently. Interview Mwaura: 4 Mar. 1988.

[41] Monsted, "Women's Groups," p. 1.

concerns from sexual politics to economics and developing new occupation-related bases for membership. If the foundation for this proliferation was laid by the age-sets, communal labor was its method of perpetuation.

Also in the late 1940s there was a growing organizational effort by a few European women who taught African women spinning and weaving. In the 1950s their efforts were turned to political purposes when the colonial administration, cognizant of the possibilities of such groups for cementing government loyalty under the Emergency, promoted the foundation of Maendeleo ya Wanawake (Kiswahili=Progress for Women). The rationale for this action was explained most thoroughly in the 1954 Department of Agriculture *Annual Report*, which bears forcible reminders of experiments with "liberating" Soviet Central Asian women conducted in the 1920s, efforts with the ultimate purpose of controlling the hearts and minds of both women and men.[42] The Report proposed a solution to the "problem" of motivating male Africans to work.

> It is believed that the most promising focal point for attack [!] is the women and the home. It is the woman who must be educated to want a better home and a better life for her children. A man needs encouragement and pressure for sustained effort and the most potent driving force is woman. [British] women agricultural officers are unsatisfactory employees in many ways; they get married, they need escorts. African women agricultural instructors are employed in large numbers and they perform a most useful function in our approach to the true tillers of the soil, the women, but some more subtle approach, possibly through the medium of Women Social Welfare Workers seems desirable. This approach is being used to a limited extent but the aim merits the employment of selected, well-educated African women whose object should be to create in their particular parish a body of women who will not be content with their present lot.[43]

This not so thinly veiled "domestication of women," as Barbara Rogers put it,[44] was to be applied to African women farmers and carried out by the wives of low level British administrators; home economics skills were to be taught. Also noteworthy here is the elimination of British women's eligibility to be agricultural officers on the grounds of marital status and the threat of male assault. A few "selected, well-educated" African women were seen as either less vulnerable to perils or less important to protect, and to be appointed as welfare workers, thus undermining the status of African women as agricultural instructors, and aiming women toward the home. African women farmers were most attracted by agriculture extension lectures. Their popularity commonly drew audiences of two or three hundred women, who sometimes traveled long distances to attend. Counterinsurgency activities also included

---

[42] Massell, *Surrogate Proletariat*.

[43] Agri 4/116 Dept. of Agriculture AR 1954: 3-4.

[44] Rogers, *Domestication*.

encouragement of the founding of the Kawangware Women's Egg Co-operative in 1956, which fostered women's solidarity among Kikuyu landowning families.[45]

The first Maendeleo ya Wanawake club was set up at Thogoto in Kiambu in 1951. Although its strength was mainly in rural areas it was also an urban effort; the first Nairobi group met at Pumwani Community Center in August 1954. Membership grew rapidly to begin with; one incentive to belong was remission from five or six days of forced labor out of ten required per month. Some members served as government informers. In the 1950s membership reached its highest level at 4,280 in Kiambu in 1956. Once the government got the LFA insurgency under control they no longer felt the need to support such efforts; in 1958 all funds were withdrawn from community development in Kiambu, and British women, in particular, were dismissed. The dependence on European leadership made the groups fragile; once the political and economic benefits of belonging disappeared, women dropped their membership.[46]

Into a New Mode: the 1960s to 1990

After independence women's groups developed new functions and proliferated. Maendeleo ya Wanawake weakened, but the beginnings of rotating savings groups are evident. Between 1963 and 1965 there were five dominant women's groups in Central Province and Ukambani called, significantly, Nyakinyua Mabati groups, or Women Elders' Roofing groups. They practiced keeping their savings in a tontine arrangement, sang and danced for political leaders, and had as one goal buying metal roofing (Kiswahili=*mabati*) for members.[47] These are clearly the prototypes for the present-day groups.

The early 1970s was a period of great expansion. In 1976 nationally there were 1300 groups with a membership of over 150,000. By 1984 these numbers had quadrupled to 16,500 groups with a membership of 630,000, and by early 1988 they had more than doubled again to 23,000 groups with 1,400,000 members. Maendeleo ya Wanawake in 1985 had 8000 branches with 300,000 members. In 1987 it was taken over by the ruling party, KANU. All along its chief emphasis was on women as homemakers. The more politically militant National Council of Women of Kenya (NCWK) began in 1964 as an umbrella group for women's organizations and

---

[45] The Jeanes School at Kabete had been promoting agricultural education since the 1920s, although very minimally for women. DAO/KBU 1/1/36 Kiambu District Monthly Report June 1955; Commissioner for Community Development Nairobi to Director of Agriculture Nairobi 24 Feb. 1959; Chitere, "Self-Help Movement," p. 53; Browne, "Kawangware," pp. 47-48; interview 27 June 1994; Werlin, *Governing*, p. 125, claimed that ICDC loans to small businesses in Kenya were given preferentially to Kikuyu, which may have been part of the counterinsurgency benefits to loyalists.

[46] DC/KBU 1/42 Kiambu AR 1951: 27; NCC AR 1954: 59. Some have mistakenly found the origins of modern women's groups solely in Maendeleo ya Wanawake, Chitere, "Movement," pp. 54-55, 59; Thomas, *Politics*, p. 44; Monsted, "Groups," p. 2; DC/KBU 1/46 Kiambu AR 1958: 8; 1/45 Kiambu AR 1955: 24; Kiambu AR 1956: 9.

[47] Chitere, "Movement," pp. 59-60.

demanded legislative change under the leadership of Dr. Wangari Maathai between 1975 and 1987.[48]

But the national organizations are more likely to be a preferred venue for elite women; women traders have their own sex-segregated organizations. Most are based on the rotating savings principle, also popular among West African traders, but the resemblance is limited. Unlike in West Africa, these associations were not usually family- or neighborhood-based, but rather composed of co-workers, whom traders saw as their most important recourse for help in a crisis.[49] Many of the associations were targeted in purpose; the pooled money was intended to buy land to be worked cooperatively by members, to buy roofing for members' houses (so common is this goal that all such associations are sometimes called roofing societies), to buy water tanks, home equipment, grade cattle, poultry, pigs or goats, or to do handicrafts like basketry.[50] Some rural women's groups sold their labor at piecework rates rather than work without pay for their husbands. In 1978 most of the women's groups in Kiambu, in contrast to those in Murang'a and Machakos, were involved in commercial activities.[51] In the large sample in 1987-88 personal needs like paying for funerals were in the minority (astonishingly, paying school fees was not even mentioned) in uses for the funds, and women did not talk about investment in business as a goal of these associations, although one said that her two rotating savings associations provided loans to members at 20% interest.[52] Of course, when not targeted, which most were not, women could use the money as they wished. Some women in the large sample (3.6%) belonged to *harambee* (self-help) groups, which usually do communal labor such as building schools; *harambee* groups tended to be mixed sex in membership and oriented toward communal labor and school fees, often associated with political support.[53] More women (14.2%) belonged to church groups, which performed a variety of functions, some of which were economic.

Kenyan women have made cooperation in groups their own preeminent method of self-help, for which they have received international attention.[54] Among traders men control the formal hawkers' associations; women have their own sphere. They rely more than men on rotating savings associations; 56.6% of the women in the large sample belonged compared to 22% of the men. Moreover, women belonged to more groups than men did, an average of 1.1 apiece compared to .4 for

---

[48] Nzomo, "Impact," pp. 10-11. Maendeleo ya Wanawake withdrew from the NCWK in 1981 and rivalries split (elite) women's energies.

[49] Maas, *Groups*, p. 31, said that women from one family did not usually do communal agricultural labor in 1986.

[50] Monsted, *Groups*, p. 30; MA 12/52 Kiambu AR 1971: 46; MA 12/80 Kiambu AR 1979: 66.

[51] Kongstad and Monsted, *Family*, p. 91; Monsted, "Groups," p. 26.

[52] Interview S18 Shauri Moyo: 25 Mar. 1988.

[53] Holmquist, "Class Structure"; Keller, "Harambee!"; Barkan, "Rise."

[54] Stephen Buckley, "A New Force Rising," *Washington Post* National Weekly Edition, 20-26 Mar. 1995: 17.

men. Male associations tended to be less numerous, narrower in focus, and somewhat larger in membership, averaging thirty persons compared to twenty-three persons for women's. The dues were larger; those who belonged paid an average of
Ksh.413 per month to their associations compared to Ksh.342 for women. The priority women gave to such associations is obvious in ratios comparing mean average
earnings for female and male traders to the amount they paid in dues. The ratio for
women was 121 compared to 734 for men, indicating that many women found them
to be an essential strategy in mitigating their poverty, and therefore took a higher proportion of their earnings to invest in them. Traders' profits varied inversely with the
amount they put into savings associations, chiefly because women earned less than
men and invested more. However, savings were often not invested in businesses,
possibly because of their very fragility, especially when illegality was involved.

The accomplishments of such women's groups were often formidable. In
1971 the 367 women's groups in Kiambu, with a total membership of 18,350,
improved 5600 houses, bought 900 cattle and 8800 water tanks, cultivated 30,000
acres, and earned Ksh.812,000.[55] A Kamba women's group in Kitui, Kauwi
Muungano Women's Cooperative, was the largest employer in the small town of
Kabati with 120 employees, and had in one year installed 104 water tanks, built 193
two room houses and a number of ventilated latrines. Attendees at a 1990 Habitat
for Humanity conference in Nairobi were stunned by descriptions given by three
Kenyan women of their unassisted community building efforts.[56] Among the traders
surveyed, one women's group bought a house and built another one to get rental
income. A group of beansellers built five small rental houses and a house called
Nyakinyua House at Starehe, which they used for lodging when in town, and for daycare. Some dried staples sellers were doing rotating selling, putting tins of maize or
beans instead of money into a common fund. Another group based at Kangemi Market had set up a tailoring business. Some women widened their options by belonging
to both urban and rural groups. For instance, a woman at Kariakor was part of a bas-
ketmaking cooperative there but also belonged to a group that owned a sawmill at her
rural home in Masii.[57] Perhaps no one symbolizes better the smooth transition from
old to new than the 1970s groups in Kiambu observed by Stamp. About 20% of
women belonged to groups which carried on old age-set functions like *matega* gifts
for weddings, and help for funerals and childbirth, but they also had started a small
shoe factory, did *ngwatio*, and purchased a town plot to develop as rental property.[58]
But traders particularly needed women's groups to facilitate evasion of the many

---

[55] MA 12/52 Kiambu AR 1971: 40.

[56] Kinuthia, "Women Groups," p. 53; Katumba, "Kenya," p. 56.

[57] Interviews 175 Gikomba: 1 Mar. 1988; 215 Gikomba: 18 Mar. 1988; 233 Gikomba: 15 Mar.
1988; head, Mwereri Women's Group, Kangemi: 21 July 1988; K16 Kariakor: 2 Mar. 1988. Traders were
undoubtedly involved in the women's groups at Eastleigh and Kamukunji mentioned by Opinya, who were
building blocs of flats. Opinya, "Population Pressure," p. 123.

[58] Stamp, "Groups," p. 40.

oppressive regulations to which they were subjected, so that the groups could not concentrate only on positive development efforts.

Controls on the Staples Trade, 1963 to 1990

The necessity of participating in an underground economy heightened the usefulness of women's groups after independence for combatting or evading government measures taken against dried staples, as will be shown here after consideration of the persistence of those controls. The Kenya Ministry of Agriculture continued the commitment to maize at the expense of other crops, despite growing evidence of breakdown of the price control system and of soil depletion that no longer allowed a profitable crop, especially by the 1980s.[59] Some Kamba traders, in particular, were refugees from soil exhaustion induced by maize overproduction, although some were also renewing production by diversifying into raising crops suited to dry conditions such as coriander, chickpeas and mung beans. Protective price and marketing policies continued while large African producers replaced some of the European farmers; few Kenyan ministers of state are without their showplace farms. Between 1946 and 1972 seven commissions of inquiry recommended reduction of state involvement in marketing, but it was not implemented. African producer cooperatives often had trouble marketing their produce in the face of continuing price controls and other impediments. Despite criticism, price controls continued on maize and beans and profited large maize producers with great disparities in relation to uncontrolled retail bean prices.[60] After independence the situation worsened; the control price ratio for beans to maize was 1.59:1 compared to 2.16:1 for the retail price ratio, an even greater discrepancy. Illicit marketing continued.[61] A drastic shortfall in maize supplies in 1965-66, which provoked a commission of enquiry, was blamed on illegal export of maize to Uganda, abolition of the maize reserve or its export to Japan, endless bureaucratic confusion in buying and importing large quantities of maize from the U.S., problems with a crooked New Orleans firm, a chief minister hiring his wife as his secretary, and even Hurricane Betsy, which sank boats on the Mississippi River.[62] No substantive effort was made to change the system.

Jones' study of the maize control system in the late 1960s systematically refuted the rationale for government support of statutory marketing boards. His chief criticism of the system focussed on the monopolistic tendencies created by a dual export/domestic trade system wherein the export trade controlled by the Maize and

---

[59] Ironically, the overpricing and consequent overproduction of maize earned kudos from some political scientists, who attributed Kenya's economic health compared to other African countries to its self-sufficiency in maize. Leonard, *Successes*, p. 2; Lofchie, *Policy Factor*, p. 160.

[60] Haugerud, "Food Production," p. 65; Dept. of Agriculture AR 1964 I: 73; 1966 I: 65-6. LG 3/2704 minutes Kiambu County Council Trade and Markets Sub-Committee 5 Feb. 1964; Maize Commission of Inquiry Report 1966: 45, 51.

[61] Clayton cited in Cone and Lipscomb, *History*, p. 90.

[62] Maize Commission of Enquiry Report 1966: 45, 51, 60ff., 71, 78, 131.

Produce Board (MPB) "seriously hampered" the private sector domestic trade and prevented the evolution of an efficient redistributive system to supply the country. Official prices of foodstuffs were not reliable because of the tonnage moved in illegal transactions. He documented continued overpricing of maize and underpricing of beans by the MPB. Small farmers who grew maize were less likely to sell at control price because they got less profit on it than large farmers by a significant margin (10%), while farmers who grew beans had little incentive to sell at control prices. Certain varieties, Canadian Wonder, for example, were especially underpriced and therefore undersold to the MPB. He particularly criticized the impact of the system on small wholesalers, who were discriminated against because Europeans and Africans feared that Asians would dominate that level of the trade. In 1967 the MPB reduced the minimum amount it would sell to traders from 140 bags of maize to five, a measure aimed at eliminating the necessity for middlepersons and the dependence of African retail traders on Asian wholesalers. Prepayment in full was still required, however, at a minimum cost of K£13.25, thus helping small wholesalers but not small retail traders, whose capital investment would not normally stretch to that amount.[63]

The price of beans, however, was less stringently controlled even though also constrained by centralized marketing.[64] Beginning with the efforts to drive out mixed beans in the mid-1930s, and continuing with the efforts to promote export beans, different kinds of beans had different control prices, but *njahe*, because only Kikuyu ate them, and *njugu*, because few were grown in Central Province, were not regulated by the 1960s.[65] With the lifting of population movement restrictions, small traders could with impunity ignore controls since small amounts (up to twenty-five kilos, or slightly over a quarter of a bag) could always be moved and sold anywhere without a permit; up to five bags could be sold within their district of production.[66]

In the mid-1960s Alvis and Temu estimated that 90% of maize production was disposed of in consumption, barter and illegal sales, and there is no reason to believe that the small proportion of staple crops sold to the MPB changed considerably in the 1970s or 1980s. Rather than relaxing controls, the number of bags traders were allowed to move without a permit was reduced to two in the 1970s.[67] But selling maize to the Produce Board was difficult. Schmidt in 1979 itemized a long list of problems: lack of MPB agents in many districts; failure to standardize measures; poor circulation of information on prices; limited storage capacity and long waits at the MPB depot inducing bribery so sellers could jump the queue; bribery of police at

[63] Jones, *Marketing*, pp. 3, 224-225, 230-231.

[64] Alvis and Temu, "Marketing," pp. 3-5.

[65] Dept. of Agriculture AR 1963 I: 83, 73; Central Province Marketing Board Second AR 1960-1: 4.

[66] Agr 4/70 Memo. No. 23 Manager Central Province Marketing Board 17 Jan. 1961.

[67] Alvis and Temu, "Marketing," pp. 3-5; Heyer, "System," pp. 316, 320, 323; Schmidt, "Effectiveness," p. 159; Musyoki, "Spatial Structure," p. 178.

road checkpoints to let produce through; and limited drying capacity. Heyer in 1976 levied more systemic charges including: failure to supply areas with shortages (just the problem the system was intended to avoid); mismanagement of imports and exports; inefficiency in the pricing system; extensive evasion of the legal marketing system; high cost of the marketing system; and a monopolistic milling system. Prices of maize were set too low in areas where its production was economical and too high where it was a marginal crop, thus discouraging its production where it did well and encouraging soil depletion in areas poorly adapted to its cultivation. The high cost of the system she attributed largely to police harassment of staples traders. Along with other experts who looked at the system, both Schmidt and Heyer recommended complete and immediate decontrol.[68] The reduction in the number of large European-owned farms, as well as the high sustained population growth that made more production go for subsistence, may also have helped to reduce the amount of maize sold at control prices.

By the mid-1970s the defects of a system that was breaking down were very evident, especially as regards beans. Sales to the MPB had become "negligible," less than 1% of production, while movement restrictions led to extreme regional price differences that furthered the illegal trade and the profits of middlepersons. Schonherr and Mbugua could find no one with clear responsibility for, or methods of, establishing price policy.[69] No effort was made by the MPB to gather knowledge about price and supply conditions or to even out supplies. Hesselmark concluded that illegal sales had grown even larger and "created a vested interest in keeping the controls with large scale institutionalized evasion." He described the Nairobi wholesale trade by the MPB as the sole redistributive beneficiary of the system in which "a handful of commodity dealers" bought all of the beans sold by the Board for resale to urban retailers to the neglect of rural areas, which were forced to depend on uneven local supplies. He noted that in the 1975-76 drought in Kitui bean prices rose to Sh.350 per bag but remained at Sh.150 in Meru, while traders paid off the MPB officers so that they could move beans illegally. The bean market was, in his estimation, "completely chaotic and needs drastic measures to reach an acceptable level of effectiveness." He recommended that the MPB establish adjustable minimum prices to farmers, facilitate the movement of beans from one area to another rather than have the police harass those with small loads (large ones escaped by bribery), and pay particular attention to rural needs and traders.[70] At the same time the maize market was suffering similar erratic fluctuations but retail prices generally stayed below control levels. In 1976 Kenyatta, under pressure from big producers, abruptly raised maize prices by 23%; there was a glut and the price had to be put back to its previous level,

---

[68] Schmidt, "Effectiveness," pp. 164-78; Heyer, "Marketing," pp. 320-27.

[69] Schmidt and Mbugua, "Aspects," pp. 6-9; Schonherr and Mbugua, "Bean Production," pp. 47, 58.

[70] Hesselmark, "Marketing," pp. pp. 5-6, 8, 12-15, 28, 32-42. Unlike many analysts, Hesselmark was not irrevocably committed to free trade, giving his critique more weight.

leading to shortages in 1979-80. Temporary decontrol in 1977-78 caused a price slump. Nairobi maize prices, due to more dependence on officially marketed maize, tended to be slightly above control price.[71] In the meantime the staff list for the Kiambu District administration, a unit about equivalent in size to a U.S. county, had grown to fill thirty-two pages of the annual report in 1977, many of whom were concerned with enforcing unenforceable regulations.[72]

The arbitrariness, sporadicity, and unevenness of the controls, as well as the cumbersomeness of the bureaucracy, made the staples trade a highly risky business. Enforcement was erratic and bureaucracy sluggish to aid those at the lower levels in pursuing trade. For example, in 1980 Mrs. Teresia Wanjiru, a wholesaler, wished to move 300 bags of beans from Moi's Bridge to the Naivasha area, but was not registered as a Rift Valley transporter. Her request to register and move the produce went to the highest levels and became the subject of discussion between the Permanent Secretary of the Ministry of Agriculture and the Acting Managing Director of the Produce Board, the former alleging, "When we discussed this issue lastly, we agreed that the Government is not in a position to finance the entire movement of grains within the Republic and that the private sector has a role to play." The Managing Director, despite repeated intercessions by the Permanent Secretary, had not given the requisite permission. In 1981 Mrs. Margaret Wachike had a truckload of eighty-three bags of beans confiscated at Loitokitok by the divisional agriculture officer although she possessed a permit.[73] Therefore, with or without a permit, even well connected traders were on their own when faced with local enforcers and could not expect any rectifying action from the central government. The impact on traders of these conditions of intermittent interference in prices, movement, and supply was to penalize large investment and long-term commitment. Reinvestment of profits in a business that could be wiped out by a single uncompensated confiscation of produce was not popular. Farmers and traders were more likely to look to wages and education investment for help.[74]

The 1980 and 1984 droughts not only brought agricultural depression in many areas and the flight of many women farmers into Nairobi petty trade, but also a healthier underground economy. Official maize and bean prices in 1980 were a sixth to an eighth of unofficial ones, the Board finally not being able to keep maize control prices above street prices. The official permit-free movement limit was reduced further to one bag, with the renamed National Cereals and Produce Board serving as the only legal buyer of beans in quantities of over ten bags (900 kilos). Produce inspection became rudimentary. The function of "produce inspectors" in rural markets in

---

[71] Leonard, *Successes*, p. 211; Schmidt, "Effectiveness," pp. 176-78; Mukui, "Impact," pp. 68-70.

[72] MA 12/70 Kiambu AR 1977: 87-119.

[73] Ministry of Agriculture File Bean 1/Vol.II Permanent Secretary Ministry of Agricullture to Acting Managing Director National Cereals and Produce Board 25 Sept. 1980; General Manager Highland Seed Co. to Director of Agriculture 25 July 1981.

[74] Haugerud, "Food Production," p. 69.

1988 was to collect fees per bag for sale, not look at the quality of the produce. The NCPB had difficulty insuring that farmers were paid promptly for their produce, exacerbating an already seriously troubled system.[75]

In the face of such massive problems the government began making noises about decontrol in the 1974 Development Plan and subsequent public announcements, but reform came slowly. In 1980 maize prices were set at 24% *below* import parity levels, but by 1986 they were almost at parity, following the recommendations of a Ministry of Agriculture Sessional Paper.[76] In January 1988 the Minister of Finance announced that by the terms of an aid contract signed with the European Economic Community the NCPB would be restructured to introduce private sector participation "gradually" into maize marketing, while infrastructural inputs like storage depots, railroad rolling stock, and agricultural machinery would be provided by the EEC. The program was to be implemented over three years "to boost food security and make the cereals marketing system more effective." Although much was made of the Ksh.1,365 million (approximately $76,000,000) worth of inputs to be made available to Kenya immediately under the agreement, no specific goals regarding privatization were set and nothing further was said about the details other than that the NCPB was to lose its monopoly.[77] It was not clear how wide an impact limited reforms would have.

By the end of 1988 few changes had occurred. In July 1988 beans were no longer on the control price list and control prices were regarded as floor prices guaranteed to producers, above which they could sell legally. A trader buying below that price, however, committed an infraction, meaning that maize continued to be a privileged crop for large producers, but the bean market was normalizing. Although by law farmers were supposed to sell beans to the Board, only movement control was being enforced and any amount could be sold locally. Evasion of a ban on importation of beans from Tanzania was routine as Tanzanians sought the more highly valued Kenyan currency while Kenyans avoided any controls.[78] Random extortionate police harassment continued on a wide scale in both urban and rural areas. In late 1991 under pressure from international donors, President Moi legalized opposition parties and scheduled multiparty elections. In October 1992 perhaps as a political ploy in the face of regional shortages and coming elections, the government clamped down on liberalized movement of grain, placing the NCPB back in control. The

[75] MA 12/80 Kiambu AR 1980: 23-24; Haugerud, "Food Production," p. 65; Lofchie, *Factor*, p. 167; fieldnotes Karuri Market 29 Aug. 1988; Schluter, "Constraints," p. 78.

[76] Smith, "Overview," p. 135; Central Bureau of Statistics, *Situation Analysis* II: 30n.; Leonard, *Successes*, pp. 211-13.

[77] *Daily Nation* 26 Jan. 1988: 10.

[78] Interviews Were, Head Crop Production Officer Ministry of Agriculture: 13 July 1988; Odok, Crop Production Officer: 13 July 1988.

effect was to put private grain millers out of business.[79] In February 1993 under renewed pressure from lenders, the government at least paid lip service to complete removal of controls over grain movement, milling, and prices, to reorganization of NCPB management, and to privatization of buying. Simeon Nyachae, the Minister for Agriculture, Supplies and Marketing, made pronouncements to the effect that all these reforms, called the Cereal Sector Reform Program, would be hastened. But at the same time controls were to be kept on buying maize in order to achieve a suffi-cient stock for food security and the NCPB was to maintain its role as a "regulator of grain marketing" by setting ceiling prices.[80] In 1993, three days before the arrival of an IMF team to ascertain Kenya's compliance with the agreement, Nyachae backed down on maize marketing reforms, although foreign exchange restrictions were removed, in essence devaluing the shilling radically.[81] Nowhere in all of this was concern demonstrated for diversifying staples. However, the 1996 complete deregu-lation of dried staples prices increased bean prices considerably and may result in their increased cultivation, signaling a new era beyond the scope of this study.[82]

In response to controls in the 1970s and 1980s women traders found organiza-tion essential and used it in everything from their agricultural activities (varying their crops almost instantaneously to take advantage of prices) to their trade.[83] Dried sta-ple wholesalers were in the habit of traveling by night and delivering before day-break in order to avoid police harassment. Collective buying was used as a risk-reducing measure intended to speed up transactions. Setting prices helped to insure a steady profit; the ostracism incurred by breaking agreed prices could lose a trader her selling space and reinforced solidarity. Women formed assembly lines in which ille-gally acquired staples were repackaged as official government supplies, and adjusted their buying times, in particular, to the exigencies of night travel for wholesalers. Because produce *movement* was taxed, and due to other transport difficulties, most was sold locally by its producers, meaning that redistribution into areas of shortage was not fostered by the market, and the marketing chain was shortened, restricting the profits of middlepersons.[84]

---

[79] H. Awori, "Kenya: FORD Accuses Government of Politicking with Food," Internet communica-tion 2 Dec. 1992.

[80] *Weekly Review* (Nairobi) 26 Feb. 1993: 26-27. Simeon Nyachae was one of the case studies used by Leonard, *Successes,* to praise the abilities of top-level Kenyan administrators.

[81] "Bold Steps Towards Liberalization," *Weekly Review* (Nairobi) 26 Feb. 1993: 26-27; "Moving in-to Private Hands," *Weekly Review* 26 Feb. 1993: 25-26.

[82] Pers. comm. Ongugo 29 Apr. 1997.

[83] Pala Okeyo, "Women," p. 340, said that Luo grain traders usually worked in groups of two to six, which regulated wholesale and retail prices, guaranteed fair trade to group members, and helped each oth-er by exchanging labor and defending against police persecution. Schmidt and Mbugua, "Aspects," p. 9; Bates, *Markets,* p. 87.

[84] Interview 259 Gikomba: 18 Apr. 1988; Casley and Marchant, "Smallholder Marketing," p. 27; Central Bureau of Statistics Integrated Rural Survey 1977-78: 125; Jones, *Marketing,* p. 215.

The widespread evasion of controls and the corruption they engendered caused some to liken the post-independence situation to the colonial one. Under both regimes corruption existed on a large scale; its efflorescence coincided with the imposition of price controls. But after independence it was in a sense democratized. Colonial officers, especially those with close settler links, knew that applying the rules would ultimately enrich them, as was the intention of such a system, British rule would be maintained and those loyal to the government would be rewarded with power and wealth.[85] Africanization brought a system that could yield profits to those involved in enforcing it only by milking it at each level. Those at the bottom, the police and produce inspectors, had nothing to gain in the long run by passing profits along up the ladder; their services would be needed by whoever was in power. The government was not providing those in the lower classes with significant evidence of benefits accruing to them in particular, or even regular pay. It was a question rather of rearrangement of scarce resources within the underclass. It is, however, perhaps fairer to focus upon efficiency rather than corruption. The differences between Ghana, Nigeria and Kenya in this regard were that in West Africa contravention of price controls involved less violence and more routine payment of bribes so that the underground economy performed the function of redistributing scarce produce, while in Kenya a higher level of efficiency prevailed bringing greater disruption of trade. The system might have functioned better had it been either completely efficient or completely corrupt.

Regarding the role of the traders and farmers in contravening regulations, it is very clear that controls were aimed at privileging both large producers and large wholesalers in the case of maize, in particular, while the bean market was distorted by the Board as the market for such exports as cocoa was by marketing boards in West Africa, taxing small peasant producers to fund government purposes other than benefits for farmers or traders involved with beans. Such controls criminalized the profitmaking of those who sought fair market prices for their produce. As controls widened, so did their evasion until the primary energies of local agriculture officers were devoted to enforcement at the expense of development efforts. For an extractive colonial economy the controls were a logical attempt to profit white settlers; for an independent African government they were an expensive and disastrous mistake that undermined the health of both trade and agriculture. Both governments ignored the vital need of consumers for dried staples, and of small producers and traders to make a profit, in favor of playing public games for private gain with the economy.

Post-independence Hawker Policy: Accommodation, 1965-1980

If rural staples traders had to cope with produce movement controls, urban women's groups were faced not only with trade impediments but also with difficult

---

[85] Although frowned upon at times by the administration, there appears to have been widespread intermarriage between administrators and settlers as time went on, and a merging of the interests of the two groups to some extent.

living arrangements exacerbated by systematic demolitions. Urban controls on hawking experienced a contradictory evolution after independence. In the second half of the 1960s and the 1970s Kenya's independent government retreated from populism, which seems in retrospect to have been a manipulatory diversion designed to gain political support from traders but was clearly not a commitment once KANU's rule was assured. Male traders' associations like the Nairobi Hawkers and Traders Association used the plight of women traders to try to gain advantage with the government, while the government used the unlicensed traders' plight equally cynically to gain power and allowed them no real say in government as well.[86] The problem for the Kenyan government became re-establishing order over traders without the insulating distance from the population that allowed the colonial government the use of force majeure. They used instead the available politically acceptable means, KANU male youth brigade members called youthwingers. In May 1964 140 of them carried out Operation Clean Up of squatter and hawker areas. The police also continued trying to control the "problem," and in 1966 over 3000 people were charged with illegal hawking, while again they resisted arrest and stoned the inspectors.[87] In the mid-1960s McVicar interviewed a divorced elderly Kikuyu woman trader who had been in Nairobi since 1938 and was having difficulties with police persecution, which she claimed was worse than under colonial rule.

> I have never had any permanent employment. I have always been selling maize gruel and maize and beans. But now this government is giving us a lot of trouble. I don't have a license and I have been arrested three times. Last month I was in Langata Prison because I didn't have Shs.100 to pay the fine ... an old woman like me! [Then she became angry--standing up and shouting] I'm not stealing! I've done nothing wrong! Where do you think I could get a hundred shillings?! ... I wish I had a license. That would cost about Shs.40 for three months, but before you get one you have to pay poll tax for three months [Ksh.12]. That's a lot of money, but I guess I'll have to get one someday. But at the same time, I'm afraid that I would get involved with paying taxes. I don't think I'm over the right age yet. If I tell them I'm too old to pay taxes they would just say, 'So you're old, you should stay at home.' It's too bad--in the old days people like me didn't need a license. Things have changed so much--I was never arrested before.[88]

Lest this seem too much like a reprise of the situation immediately before independence, the deliberations of the NCC Hawkers and Licensing Sub-Committee of 26 September 1966 sound quite different. The Town Clerk asked what was to be done about the peddling of a large variety of commodities not covered by the bylaws

---

[86] JA/LG 5/1 petition from Mincing Lane Stallholders Association to Town Clerk, 23 Nov. 1959, p. 1: "some of the traders here are husbandless mothers with a number of children to look after and educate, with this occupation the only likely source of their livelyhood [sic]." Robertson, "Traders," deals with this material in more detail.

[87] Werlin, "Hawkers," p. 203.

[88] McVicar, "Twilight," pp. 209-11. Unlicensed vendors other than (male) bottle and scrap metal sellers were being persecuted.

(reconstituted in 1963-64). A resolution was passed allowing traders to employ assistants and a debate took place over permitting them to erect shelters in the new open air markets (OAMs). One member requested that licenses be given to two women hawkers at Gikomba; the Town Clerk agreed if they moved to another location. The Town Clerk in 1967 surveyed 150 unlicensed women hawkers who were selling house to house and said that they should be encouraged to go into OAMs. In February 1966 the Director of Social Services and Housing allocated a number of trading pitches at Doonholm Market to destitute persons rent free for a month. At the end of the month most paid the rent; the two who could not had the debt written off.[89] This hands-on approach indicated a change from the punitive tone of the late colonial phase.

Africanization of government personnel brought more mention of women traders in official documents, but the contradictions in the policies show the government's own complex divisions and class hierarchies. On the one hand, there was a set of rules that continued the British tradition and discriminated against the poor, in particular, rules concerned both with competition offered by hawkers to shops, and with presenting a shiny, prestigious, newly minted image to the world of a well-run African nation, for Nairobi what Freeman called the "city beautiful ethos." On the other, there was the plea for compassion for women traders from members of official bodies conversant with the realities on the street, a plea notably absent from colonial officials' discourse. Thus, on 22 February 1967 a member of the NCC Finance Committee responded negatively to the rule that applicants for hawkers' licenses had to present a receipt showing that they had paid the Graduated Personal Tax, saying that unemployed illiterate women suffered hardship from it and did not know how to apply for exemption.[90]

Meanwhile, class differentiation was evident when the allocation of trading plots in Kiambu became more restrictive. Whereas previously most applications were granted, beginning in mid-1964 the number of applications grew sharply, and stricter criteria were used to award them including trade experience, financial ability to build on the plot (traders were allowed seventy-two months to build in stone or had to forfeit the plot), and status as a Kiambu taxpayer. Groups of people or companies were to apply. In 1964-65 only 21.2% of the applications were granted (149), of which 15.4% went to women. Included among these was an application from twenty women to operate a fuel and charcoal dump. Women were making some progress, since they constituted only 11.8% of the total applicant pool but 15.4% of the licensees. Politics assumed a more important role in plot allocation at Kiambu Town

---

[89] LG 3/3155 minutes NCC Hawkers and Licensing Sub-Committee 26 Sept. 1966; Social Services and Housing Committee 7 Mar. 1966; NCC 27/10 minutes General Purposes Committee 9 June 1967.

[90] Freeman, *City*, p. 21; LG 3/3156 minutes 22 Feb. 1967.

market from 1973, when the Council began using a ballot system to allocate market plots.[91]

In Nairobi the police campaigns against hawkers had as a primary object confining them to designated OAMs. The decision to set up city-owned OAMs was first made in 1963, when three were established, and four more were proposed in 1966. The other most significant development of the 1970s and 1980s, in particular, was the growth of large illegal outdoor markets, the two largest in 1988 being Gikomba and Korogocho at Kariobangi in eastern suburban Nairobi. The chief struggle of hawkers with the authorities after independence was not over establishing markets, of which there were plenty (over thirty legal ones by 1988 in Nairobi), but rather over building permanent stalls in legal or illegal outdoor markets, which was not allowed, and over the continual explosion of new illegal trade sites.[92] To some extent the NCC followed hawkers around providing new OAMs. In a few new public housing areas like Dandora the enclosed markets provided were not used significantly due to poor siting and the cost of stall rental and licenses. OAMs were located in African areas only, as the de jure segregation of colonial times gave way to de facto segregation, meaning that hawking in central city locations was severely restricted to those selling curios, flowers, pictures, and shoeshines, a situation that, if one includes newspapers and books, endured to at least 1990. The vast majority of such hawkers were and are male.[93]

Throughout the late 1960s and 1970s the debate over restrictions on hawking continued in various NCC committees, as did arrests of hawkers. The steady pressure of growing unemployment and the concentration of the mostly male unemployed (at least 50,000) in Nairobi helped to restrain those who would be strongly repressive, but also provoked calls for colonial-style restriction of movement into Nairobi. The "hawker problem" was increasingly conflated with the poverty and unemployment problem; on 8 November 1968 the NCC General Purposes Committee recommended that the whole hawker issue be referred to the Unemployment

---

[91] LG 3/2705 minutes Kiambu County Council Trade and Markets Committee 7, 13, 22 May 1964; Kiambu County Council 20, 22 Apr., 8-11 May 1964; 21-28 Apr., 8-10 May 1965; MA 12/57 Kiambu AR 1973: 27. Between August 1960 and February 1964 12.5% of trading plots were allocated to Kiambu women, 58 out of 519. LG 3/2702- 2704 minutes Kiambu ADC Trade and Markets Committee 30 Aug., 28 June, 18 Nov. 1960; 23 May, 25 July, 20, 31 Oct. 1961; 8 Feb., 25 July 1962; 1 May 1963; 5 Feb. 1964.

[92] LG 3/3155 minutes NCC 7 Feb. 1966; LG 3/3156 minutes NCC 9 Jan., 10 July, 13 Oct. 1967; 7 Feb. 1969: 1588; 8 Jan. 1975.

[93] LG 3/3154 minutes NCC General Purposes Committee 15 May 1965. The central city boundaries were (and are) Haile Sellassie Avenue, Uhuru Highway, Grogan/Kirinyaga Road, and Racecourse Road. LG 3/3155 minutes NCC Social Services and Housing Committee 12 Sept. 1966. Minutes NCC 26 July 1971: 243. Even shoeshiners, however, were arrested in 1976 in an effort to clear the town of "undesirables"; Mukui noted that "before the policemen were back from lunch the 'industry' was back in full swing, taken over by the friends of those arrested." Mukui, "Anatomy," p. 142.

Sub-Committee.[94] In September 1970 the Nairobi Town Clerk in a report stated, "It was not ... easy to assert at present that many hawkers would automatically graduate into big businessmen and it would appear that the majority were likely to remain in that form of trade for years to come." He recommended that more OAMs be established to give traders selling space on which they would be allowed to build permanent structures. If followed, the recommendation would have been a significant victory in the turf war for the traders. At the same time he noted that corruption was causing more hawkers' licenses to be issued than the 1500 that were officially allocated, and that the "championship of unscrupulous politicians" was preventing the "determined" control of hawkers.[95] The contradictory aspects of hawker policy were due partly to continued police raids seemingly to extract bribes in contravention of official NCC policy.[96] Controlling hawkers had become a matter of controlling corruption in city government (2200 licenses were issued, 700 over the quota, in 1970), a difficulty encountered by many governments.

In the 1970s, not only were more OAMs established, but accommodations were made in the number of licenses issued and in the method of allocation. When it was discovered that 2,222 had been issued in 1971, it was recommended that that number be adopted as the limit. A lottery system was implemented to improve fairness in stall allocation at the new OAMs.[97] Perhaps the high water mark of liberal policy was a report prepared by the Nairobi Town Clerk John Mbogua in 1975 recommending, among other things, that 10,000 hawkers' licenses be issued. None of his recommendations was adopted, however, although the number of licenses issued was set at 5000 in 1977 and remained there until 1987. At the same time, police harassment of women traders and customers continued, forming a dark undertow beneath the liberal rhetoric. Even relatively prosperous kiosk owners were susceptible to arbitrary government action in the 1975 closures due to a cholera outbreak. One woman, disgusted with repeated harassment, abandoned her four children and her license in the Licensing Superintendent's office. When she returned to claim it later the license had been reallocated to someone else (what about the children?!).[98]

In the late 1960s and 1970s policy had changed considerably from the previous situation, then. Images of traders also shifted, reflecting class consolidation. The

---

[94] Onstad, "Life," p. 236; LG 3/3156 minutes NCC General Purposes Committee 7 Apr. 1967; 4 Sept. 1970.

[95] Minutes NCC General Purposes Committee 4 Sept. 1970; Hake, *African Metropolis*, p. 180.

[96] Elkan, Ryan and Mukui, "Economics," p. 253. This situation bears a strong resemblance to that in Zaire, described by Schatzberg, *Dialectics*, p. 56, as an aspect of the "state as bandit." "Gendarmes use their parcels of power to extract what they can from those in contextually inferior positions in the class hierarchy ... [by extorting] illegal fines from unlucky citizens who fall into their hands."

[97] Minutes NCC General Purposes Committee 5 Mar. 1971; Social Services Committee 28 Sept. 1973, 28 Feb. 1974.

[98] Onstad, "Life," pp. 246-48; Mitullah, "Hawking," p. 78; minutes NCC General Purposes Committee 4 Nov. 1977; Social Services and Housing Committee 2 July 1975, 2 May 1979; Mukui, "Anatomy," p. 138; NCC 7/8/14 Licensing Superintendent to Deputy Town Clerk 18 June 1973.

issue of women trading changed from embodying men's concern over controlling women's sexuality/fertility to a concern about the alleviation of poverty, with women accurately being viewed as the poorest of the poor by male hawkers and researchers.[99] Compared to the 1940s and 1950s, the stated goal of the authorities changed from stopping hawking completely to controlling and facilitating its orderly expansion in legal locations, from authoritarian eradication to benevolent supervision. The latter, however, was undermined by the NCC's apparent inability or unwillingness to control the activities of their police, who kept up a sporadic campaign of harassment of both licensed and unlicensed traders, and even of customers, especially women. The association in the minds of the upper classes of hawking with poverty and unemployment placed persecution of hawkers in the same category as demolition of squatter slum housing, which also continued in the 1970s.[100] If these efforts with regard to hawkers were less major than previously or subsequently, they still caused misery and indicated acute contradictions in government policy. Corruption only accentuated economic differentiation among traders; the better-off could bribe the harassers or obtain licenses more easily, while affluent businesspeople could obtain loans to improve their businesses, but not poor people. The 1966 Vagrancy Act included colonial-style provisions requiring repatriation to rural areas and was mainly applied to women; periodic roundups of women on the street at night circumscribed traders' activities.[101]

"Just getting something to eat": the 1980s and the Second Hawker War

The 1980s saw a renewal of autocratic government with a vested interest in Nairobi property, and consequently more repression, which produced a highly conflictual situation since the worsening economy made urban trading an absolute necessity for a growing number of traders, especially women and unemployed young men. The urban trading activities of older women were increasingly viewed as a legitimate survival activity, but urban traders became embroiled in a renewed hawker war of unprecedented magnitude that culminated in the 1990 destruction of many illegal markets in Nairobi. Unlike in the first hawker war, the male hawkers were at a disadvantage in that their organizations were either defunct or far less active than they had been. They were also the target of a government campaign to destroy them, as when two District Officers tried to dissolve or take over the two largest hawkers' organizations in 1988.[102] A national identity card system that began in 1978 helped the government to control the population, which became a primary goal once the calmly

---

[99] Mukui, "Anatomy," pp. 134, 138, 143. The changing images of women traders are explored more thoroughly in Robertson, "Traders."

[100] Hake, *Metropolis*, pp. 159ff.; Etherton, *Mathare Valley*.

[101] In 1975 ICDC loans to small enterprises stopped but joint ventures with foreign capital and parastatal banks continued on a large scale. Kaplinsky, "Accumulation," p. 100; Imikai, "Legal Framework," p. 97; Gutto, "Status of Women," p. 50; Cummings, "Migration," p. 156.

[102] Onstad, "Life," pp. 221-23; *Daily Nation* 12 July 1988.

autocratic rule of Kenyatta devolved into the fearful grabbing at control of Moi, exacerbated by the coup attempt of 1982. Once again the markets, dominated by Kikuyu traders, were viewed as seats of disaffection and sedition, and hawkers as an unruly population needing repression. This was not an undifferentiated campaign since gender considerations determined to some extent the fate of traders. The ongoing struggle is over the use of space in Nairobi's old African center of population on the north side of the Nairobi River. The upper classes, who want the land for profitable undertakings, especially the political elite, are winning.

The 1980s did not begin with the declaration of a hawker war. President Moi assumed office peacefully in 1978 at Kenyatta's death and seemed bent on pursuing the same erratic course of his predecessor's government: arrests and demolitions, not always sanctioned by the NCC, combined with an effort to help some traders. To some he was a defender of the common people (Kiswahili=*wananchi*), more sympathetic than Kenyatta, who dismissed the poor as *ragai* (lazy or useless). This help, however, translated the 1972 ILO Report recommendations into gendered applications. The chief new aspect of positive government policy regarding hawkers concerned measures taken to help *jua kali* (Kiswahili=hot/fierce sun), artisans forced by poverty to work in the open air. Although women traders are more often without sheltered space and in the sun, the term *jua kali* has been applied only to male manufacturers, with occasional gestures toward the garment industry. Small manufacturers such as metalworkers, carpenters, and shoemakers were entirely male. In 1988 McCormick found in a survey of Nairobi manufacturers that only the garment industry had a significant proportion of female owners, and that none of the male-owned businesses had any female artisanal employees or trainees, a finding borne out by my surveys.[103] By conventional economic definitions those who manufacture are more productive than those who simply sell. The state, responding to ILO Report recommendations, chose to privilege them as recipients of permanent workspace. The Kenyan Development Plan for 1979 to 1983 included provisions for building space, investment advice, loans, extension services, marketing facilities, and preferential treatment in governmental purchasing programs. The 1982-83 Report on Unemployment stated that manufacturers only formed 14.8% of informal sector workers in 1977 and 16.4% in 1982, compared to the over 70% in trade, but recommended that the former be given training at village polytechnical schools.[104] The only attention paid specifically to women was to point out a need for home economics courses for restaurant workers (presumably men wanted tasty food prepared by sanitary methods). Police harassment of sellers was supposed to stop. In the mid-1980s President Moi saw to it that neat metal sheds were built for such artisans at Kamukunji across the river from Gikomba. In 1987 a Small Scale Enterprises Unit was established

---

[103] Gray et al., *Entrepreneurship*; Himbara, *Capitalists*, p. 93; McCormick, "Enterprise," p. 149.
[104] Kenya Report on Unemployment 1982/83: 27, 212-16, 259.

within the Ministry of National Planning and Development that emphasized helping manufacturers.[105]

Although the ILO considered retail sellers to be a worthy part of the informal sector, the brunt of the second hawker war fell upon them, most of them women traders, who still have more difficulties getting permanent selling space or pursuing legal trade. For instance, in May 1980 among a sample of ninety-four stall allocations by the NCC General Purposes Committee Hawkers' Licensing Sub-Committee, 36.2% went to women.[106] This represents a significant improvement over earlier statistics but is still far from proportionate to their representation among the whole trading population.

The fortunes of the large dried staples trading population at Gikomba Market are emblematic of the situation for most women traders. Unlike most of Gikomba, the dried staples area was the object of repeated attacks by NCC police. In July 1988 the women, who had assurances from the District Officer and the local chief that they could build without molestation, constructed a handsome set of open sheds with metal roofs and posts to shelter themselves and their goods from the elements. This construction immeasurably bettered the whole appearance of the market. The women neatly arranged their open bags of staples on platforms beneath the sheds. It was a prime example of the positive virtues of following the Kenyan government slogan, *harambee,* self-help (translated by the cynical as "help yourself"). In mid-August the NCC police came and without warning demolished the whole, purposefully destroying pieces of metal roofing to prevent its reuse. A trader at Gikomba was bewildered at the arbitrary strictures of the authorities.

> Here we had built shelters against the sun and the rain, but they've been demolished. That's why we are suffering. At first [the chief] told us to demolish them. Then he told us to move down there to the vegetable sellers' place [by the Nairobi River]. The vegetable people had nowhere to go, but he told us to go and squeeze in. We refused and went to the member of Parliament for this area, Maina Wanjigi; he told us to stay. After that the chief told us that we should not construct anything; we should stay in the sun. I don't know why, and I don't know much.[107]

The permanent, often more flimsy, structures erected by other sellers were left unmolested; this differentiation in treatment had occurred repeatedly. In November the

---

[105] Noormohamed, "Development Strategy," p. 188; *Situation Analysis* II: 46; Macharia, "Slum Clearance," pp. 230-31; Stren et al., "Coping," p. 179; McCormick, "Enterprise," pp. 78-79; Macharia, "Slum Clearance," pp. 230, 234; Mitullah, "Hawking," pp. 73, 75; *Daily Nation* 12 July 1988. A 1987 IDS Consultancy Report (No.16, pp. 159-63) by Ng'ethe and Wahome justified supporting only manufacturers because of the heterogeneity of the trading population defying the possibility of a comprehensive program to help them, and went on to assert that manufacturers "have a less transitory stake in the informal sector" because they invest in permanent structures (ignoring that small traders' structures get torn down by the police routinely), and that they have more growth potential, despite their own data showing that the scale of the traders' businesses was as large as that of the manufacturers.

[106] Minutes 9 May 1980.

[107] Interview 214 Gikomba: 16 Mar. 1988.

women composed a praise song for President Moi and sent a delegation to ask him for permanent selling space, an effective route to success for those whose support is perceived as being important.[108] They did not succeed. While poor rural women's self-help efforts are lauded as promoting development, poor urban women have had their activities disrupted and their painfully earned infrastructure destroyed.

In 1988 the major battle over turf again involved central city areas. A Mathare Valley protection scheme reputedly existed involving payments to KANU youth-wingers of Ksh.5 per month to secure freedom from NCC harassment of traders, but poor women selling on the streets in the central city had no protection. In December 1987 there were at least four raids by plainclothes police on a group of streetside staple sellers, who suggested that the police wanted their confiscated goods for Christmas, while nearby storeowners encouraged the raids to discourage competition. One trader said that in 1986 the adjacent storekeepers had each paid Ksh.1000 to have them removed and that sometimes the police came six times a day. Several of the more established market stallholders complained about competition from hawkers, one man calling them prostitutes.[109]

A broader view of the impact of police harassment on traders comes from Mitullah's 1988 survey of 425 street traders, who gave the following reasons for not having licenses: ignorance of licensing procedures (55%); failure of attempts to get one (13.1%); illegal sites or activities making licensing impossible (15.6%); not affordable (12.6%). They reported the incidence of police harassment as occurring daily or weekly for 54.2%, monthly for 24.4%, and occasionally for 21.3%, while 68.4% said that the harassment was because they were unlicensed (in my large sample most could not afford the average amount paid for licenses annually of Ksh.1096). In 94.9% of the cases the harassment was by the NCC police, 3.5% by KANU youth-wingers. The consequences for most traders of the harassment were that they had their commodities confiscated, but 8.2% were convicted of trading offenses, 4.5% paid bribes, and 2.7% had their structures demolished. Mitullah claimed that there were about 25,000 hawkers who were always at war with the authorities.[110] A rice-seller said that she had been caught three times by the police with illegal rice from Mwea. The first two times the police confiscated the rice but then sold it for her and gave her the money because they were sympathetic about her need to pay her son's school fees. The third time was not the charm; the rice was confiscated and she gave up on it. A woman pineapple seller resorted to hiring a man to grab the pineapples and run if the police appeared.[111] At one location a group of street sellers were raided so often that half of them disappeared within a week, only the younger, hardier, more desperate ones remaining. Dried staples sellers are caught in a legal impasse in

---

[108] Interviews 241 Gikomba: 31 Mar., 22 Aug. 1988.

[109] Interviews 142: 7 Jan. 1988; S23 Shauri Moyo: 28 Mar. 1988; 54 Ngara: 23 Oct. 1987.

[110] Mitullah, "Hawking," pp. 15, 56-60, 72-73.

[111] Interviews 82: 2 Nov. 1987; 516 Wangige: 2 June 1988.

which feeding Nairobi efficiently is least considered. The Deputy Town Clerk in 1988 said that they fell into a "funny" category and could not be licensed under the bylaws as vegetable sellers, that the Gikomba sellers contravened the rule that sellers were not to be within 440 yards of a roadway, and that various pressures--from politicians, business owners, the mass of the unemployed--made for a balancing of interests between "inside" legal and "outside" illegal traders.[112]

The climax of a steadily mounting anti-hawker campaign came in October 1990, when all of the central city illegal markets were destroyed. Divisions within the government and public discourse were evident in the events leading up to the destruction. In February 1988 the chairman of the NCC toured Gikomba promising better garbage disposal, while in June 1990 the Minister of Local Government ordered no more squatter settlement or hawker demolitions. The government-owned *Nation* ran a feature article on unemployment on 10 October 1990 six days before the massive destruction, while the NCC planned to open five new OAMs for hawkers.[113] However, on 11 October 1990 at Machakos Bus Depot 300 NCC police took on hawkers with teargas and batons and were met with active resistance including stonethrowing from residents of an adjacent estate, hawker-constructed barricades, a bonfire lit to disrupt traffic (successfully), and fisticuffs. Most business in the central city stopped and the situation was not gotten "under control" until late in the day, when armed groups of NCC police still patrolled, presumably to stop the few shabbily dressed "crafty hawkers" who were trying to sell vegetables and fruit on the streets to homeward-bound workers. On 16 October Gikomba was bulldozed and other illegal markets destroyed.[114] The impact of the destruction was major; traders roamed seeking temporary places to sell. It seemed that illegal selling was no longer an option for most and the days had returned when the goal of government was to annihilate trading as an option for indigent urbanites. Increasingly only the relatively wealthy could trade; traders themselves showed economic, gendered divisions. A successful male trader in 1988 told Onstad, "The genuine trader is in a shop. The hawkers we see now, they are not in business; they are just getting something to eat."[115]

The ferocity of this attack was clearly linked to political causes. In Nairobi in July 1990 there were demonstrations centering in congested areas near or on the site of some illegal and legal markets (Kamukunji and Kawangware, for instance). These became riots when the demonstrators were attacked by the police and achieved international notice since they involved supporters of a multiparty political system, whose

---

[112] Interview Njora 2 Nov. 1988.

[113] *Daily Nation* 15 Feb. 1988, 16 June 1990, 2, 10, 16 Oct. 1990.

[114] *Daily Nation* 12, 17 Oct. 1990.

[115] Onstad, "Life," p. 283.

leaders had been imprisoned.[116] Macharia analyzed recent massive slum demolitions carried out in Nairobi from an ethnopolitical point of view, pointing out that the destruction of predominantly Kikuyu residential areas at Kamukunji (Muoroto) and Kibagare, which were heavily involved in the multiparty movement, has resulted in the displacement of over 40,000 people. Wanjigi protested the demolitions, calling it another Operation Anvil, which cost him his position as MP and his membership in KANU.[117]

Small-scale traders epitomize the dispossessed in Nairobi, the growing number of those whose plight involves taking desperate measures to survive in a tough urban world. The specter of the dispossessed organizing was distinctly unsettling to those in power. On 12 October 1990 President Moi was quoted as stating that "bad elements" had infiltrated the Kenya Hawkers' Association and gathered stones to use "against my officers." Dissident politician Koigi wa Wamwere was arrested and accused of organizing illegal hawkers and matatu drivers, and promoting a "defiant culture."[118]

What of the women traders in this crisis? The news photos showed exclusively male hawkers battling police in October 1990. In the attack some men fought; the majority of traders fled, trying to save as much of their property as possible. One woman cried as a bulldozer took down her stall, for which she had just paid Ksh.10,000 to the market committee.[119] Several women said that bankruptcy was the result of such attacks, and, on occasion, physical harm. The situation was worsening, not just at Gikomba. A pregnant woman was seriously injured in a stampede of people waiting to get forms to apply for NCC kiosks. Attempts to organize a queue failed and a barred door was also broken in the rush, while officials extended the deadline for handing out forms, giving out more than planned. Some of the kiosks were mobile and cost approximately Ksh.15,000; others were stationary at a cost of Ksh.10,000.[120] Women sellers had particular difficulty raising capital to obtain NCC-allocated stalls, which cost Ksh.16,000 (or approximately $940) in 1988, plus an unspecified amount in bribery (at least five years of an average Kenyan's income).[121] Esther Wanjiru Kamau, the subject of a *Daily Nation* article, had her kiosk home demolished without warning. She was getting by--doing casual labor in the chief's office and selling greens and other foodstuffs from the kiosk--for which she had been paying an annual rent of Ksh.450 to the Ministry of Works. In an accompanying

---

[116] *Weekly Review* 13 July 1990.

[117] Macharia, "Slum Clearance," pp. 230-31; Stren et al., "Coping," p. 179.

[118] *Daily Nation* 12 Oct. 1990.

[119] Pers. comm. JNT: 5 Nov. 1990; *Daily Nation* 17 Oct. 1990.

[120] *Daily Nation* 27 Jan., 16 Feb. 1988.

[121] Minutes NCC Education and Social Services Committee 5 Aug. 1988: 90.

photo she was glumly sitting on the wreckage with her ten children and a grandchild, all of whom she was supporting.[122]

In response to such persecution the marketwomen used collective action. The older illegal markets were often tightly organized. In large markets this organization was usually by commodity, meaning that dried staples was the only commodity for which a woman was likely to be elected to represent the group on the market governing committee. The market committee assigned selling space, collected rent or sometimes an initial large fee for the use of the space, settled disputes and made rules about what could be sold in the market (at Gikomba, for instance, no marijuana or alcoholic drinks were allowed). They hired guards to patrol at night and dealt with rodent removal.[123] The commodity groups set prices, bought collectively and settled disputes. In order to interview sellers I had to get permission from elected commodity representatives; one day I was embroiled in a tense discussion for over an hour explaining our activities to three influential male partners in a used clothing business who ran that section of a market. Since selling their commodity was illegal, they were afraid that I was a government representative or a journalist out to profit from them without giving them any profit. Presentation of a presidential research permit and consultation brought only grudging assent to our activities, to which they had no objection. They could have prevented us from interviewing in that section. Collective protection is an important function of the commodity group leaders.

Some traders formed multiethnic dance groups, which performed at political rallies and ceremonies, including for President Moi. They were exclusively female and devoted to raising female solidarity as well as cash to carry out such projects as rental housing, daycare and communal lodgings. An unplanned vacation from interviewing resulted one day when virtually all of the ablebodied sellers at a small market emerged swaying and singing in a long line. They were practicing for their next performance and shut down the market to do so. Such groups had names and reputations to uphold, and were paid for their efforts, in one case Ksh.1350 banked collectively by the forty members.[124] Some were also commodity selling groups.

There were, then, many organizations to which marketwomen belonged, the rotating savings associations being most important in terms of membership. Most were apolitical and concerned mainly with development issues. However, the potential for political militance was present among the urban market-based associations, in particular, which were organizing to defend their interests when it became evident that market space (legal or illegal) was politically allocated. They recognized that "political insecurity is now a major variable in Nairobi's small business

---

[122] *Daily Nation* 27 Aug. 1988.

[123] Interview 175 Gikomba: 1 Mar. 1988.

[124] Interview 167 Gikomba: 18 Feb. 1988; 233 Gikomba: 15 Mar. 1988.

environment."[125] The immediate response of the women whose stalls were destroyed in 1988 was to seek the use of political influence--a patron to protect them. Thomas noted in 1985 that there was growing pressure on these groups to contribute money for political purposes; they were being forced into politics.[126] Even itinerant hawkers were organizing. In March 1989 over 300 women hawkers, typically aged thirty or more and the sole support of their families, marched to the Nairobi Provincial Commissioner's Office to protest "constant harassment by the askaris [Kiswahili=police]." Upon being denied entrance to the PC's office and that of the Director of the City Inspectorate, they blocked the County Hall entrance until the Director came out to talk to them. He agreed to issue all of them hawkers' licenses, but at a rate which they refused as too high. One woman shouted, "We sell our vegetables from estate to estate and we make too little income to meet the licence fee!" Photos accompanying the article showed women, some aged in their sixties and seventies, with arms raised militantly.[127] In early 1992 a group of elderly Kikuyu mothers of political prisoners (including Koigi wa Wamwere) took refuge in Nairobi Cathedral after a Uhuru Park protest that included *guturamira ng'ania* and a hunger strike was attacked by police. In support the hawkers at Gikomba and Machakos Bus Stop instigated a boycott that became a riot.[128]

If women are often the primary victims in class-based gendered oppression, they also form a key part of the increasingly militant poor. They are using their formidable collective energy to try to mitigate their situation; how long they will persist in peaceable protests in the face of blatant betrayal of their interests is a question.

Conclusion

Contemporary central Kenyan women's organizations have deeper roots than is often supposed. Women have transformed age-sets into work-based rotating savings associations and market associations of various kinds. In this process of transformation initiation rites are disappearing, along with the associated clitoridectomy and gerontocratic authority. The leaders of the market-based organizations are usually not elderly women, but rather women whose competence is widely recognized, some in their late twenties or early thirties. Knowledge, which used to come from experience, now comes more from education; literate skills are highly prized. Elderly women traders are more often in the category of near-beggars and not particularly venerated by the others. The prime leadership positions are usually elective and held by women in their forties who are active traders. Those positions are not hereditary and malfeasance could bring removal from office. Success in trade is a desirable characteristic for a leader, but not absolutely necessary, since having an amiable per-

---

[125] McCormick, *Manufacturing*, p. 77.

[126] Thomas, *Politics*, p. 180.

[127] *Kenya Times* 15 Mar. 1989. Some of the women were from an illegal central city market.

[128] *Standard* 5 Mar. 1992: 1.

sonality and/or street smarts is also rewarded. Sometimes sheer toughness is the most prized characteristic, especially in illegal markets.

Among Nairobi marketwomen, then, the gerontocratic aspects of female leadership have fallen by the way as they have elsewhere in Kenyan society. If initiation ceremonies had strong elements of induction into gerontocratic authority, they also entail the formation of solidary age-sets, peer groups whose linkages are now reinforced by urban occupational solidarity. A rotating savings association may name its business Nyakinyua Enterprises after the authority-bearing female age-set, but in the markets survival skills, not age, count the most. And, the shared experience of an underclass whose survival may be assured by cooperation and flexibility is more important than ascribed characteristics in generating solidarity. The economic basis of solidarity is most important. Most women traders in 1987-88 relied for help on neighbors (at home or in the market) who traded, rather than on their families, perhaps because they had problems recruiting labor in trade as in farming. Their peers were most reliable; they helped in many ways: watching commodities, giving loans, subbing during necessary absences, conveying necessary information, and preventing or minimizing damage caused by police raids. In essence, the transgenerational family and locational linkages emphasized at initiation have diminished in favor of stronger peer links.

Nonetheless, most female traders were resolutely individualistic in their preferences. They had one-woman businesses and did not want either friends or family members as partners.[129] They wanted their daughters and daughters-in-law not to be corrupted by Nairobi and to stay at home in rural areas with their young children. Friends might not be trustworthy, as stated by this woman who defined the limits of informal network help, "I sell alone; I don't like partners because we might not trust each other. All I can do is if someone is sick or with a child out of school, I can transport for her, sell for her and deduct my transport costs so that she can have children back in school."[130] The older women tried to maintain the age distinctions by keeping the young women at home, but the junior women tried to escape the burden of agricultural labor in order to trade in town. One woman said that if her daughter came to sell at Gikomba, "she can go over there [gesturing toward the other side of the market] to trade so she won't compete with me." With increasing landlessness this may change with the formation of more multi-generational urban female-headed households who cooperate in trade. Both continuity and change are evident, then, in forms of women's solidarity and its limits, which are sometimes rooted in the emergent class-based nature of the women's organizations.

The struggle for Nairobi continues with valuable central city property as a chief battleground. Commensurate with its almost two million population, Nairobi's

---

[129] Male small business owners at Kibera had even fewer family partnerships than women did. Parker and Dondo, "Kibera," p. 21.

[130] Interview 82 Ngara Bean: 9 Nov. 1987.

complexities have increasingly drawn in surrounding areas. The conflicting interests represented in the struggle are not confined to Kenya. The fundamental role of capitalism is seen in the persecutions of traders even when most are men as in India or Hong Kong.[131] In Nigeria, Peru and Ghana campaigns against illegal trading by women in the 1970s and 1980s had clear class implications, as in Kenya.[132]

Gender ideology operated in this situation as a means of isolating a group regarded as other, but who were viewed by the upper classes as undesirable for reasons other than simply being women. In Kenya in recent years we have seen more implicit than explicit sexism with regard to women traders; many of their troubles related directly to their position as the most disadvantaged of the group. Now the symbolic others for those in power are the poor, whether imaged as beggars, thieves, or seditious troublemakers. As Kenyan society has become more stratified it is logical that the visualization of the "other" by the upper classes has become more class-bound, whereas gender crosscuts class. Gender discrimination has become subordinated to the perceived necessity of controlling the threatening mass of the poor and has taken different forms, such as denying women selling space and access to trading capital/loans. A subsidiary explanation for the reduction in the gendered aspects of the images of traders may be that more *poor* hawkers now are young male school leavers, whereas from the 1920s to the 1960s they were overwhelmingly female.[133] Male traders would be seen as posing more of an active political threat than women traders, who have only recently begun organizing politically and whose dual residence in many cases inhibits that organization. However, even though these women are busy fulfilling their mandatory economic obligations, with the increasing market demolitions the women are finding that organizing politically is the only way to survive and are channeling more energy into this strategy.[134] Thus, gender segregation has now become an assumption rather than a contested area in some ways, with a segregated gender division of labor translated into traders' organizations as well as a stratified labor market. Women traders are discriminated against mainly through access to critical resources and are imaged mainly as poor.

After independence the new government drew on colonialist-introduced techniques to control trade and traders when it was expedient to do so, not only perpetuating maize control but also vagrancy laws and antihawker, antisquatter policies. If occasional humanitarian concerns and perceptions of possible economic benefit diminished the persecution in the 1970s, they never stopped it. Indeed, the oppressiveness of the system in which the police are struggling from an underprivileged

---

[131] Lessinger, "Trader"; Smart, "Hawking."

[132] Eames, "Women," pp. 87-88; Babb, "Field," p. 17; Robertson, "Death."

[133] Interview Haldane, World Bank, 25 Mar. 1991. She was employed from 1967 to 1973 in Nairobi by the National Council of Churches of Kenya allocating loans to small traders.

[134] House-Midamba, "Gender," described the increasing political activism of Kenyan women in the 1990s with information about NCWK, the Green Belt Movement, and the impact of the KANU takeover on Maendeleo ya Wanawake.

position to carry out the wishes of the ruling class is intensified by its divisive effects. Government persecution of traders or squatters in effect supplements the pay of police, who have demonstrated against irregular pay.[135] Cooper has described the situation well.

> Harassing squatters, beer brewers and prostitutes underlined the hegemony of the dominant class, whose orderly ways were made to appear legitimate, while the 'illegitimacy' of lower-class life was rubbed in by the humiliation of police raids. Such an urban policy might also preclude other forms of control, cooptation and legitimacy, and make more difficult the development of a hierarchy of privileges and incentives that would encourage a differentiated and "respectable" working class instead of a threatening urban mass.[136]

With government authoritarian tendencies exacerbated, immediate political considerations outweigh the necessity not only to provide employment but also to feed Nairobi. Such a policy seems bound to bring trouble. Harming the distributive system penalizes both traders and the general populace by undermining a cheap urban food supply.[137] Criminalizing many survival-oriented strategies of an underclass makes it inevitable that they will break the law, and "seek by noncompliance to influence the state" to change things. They have become adept at employing what Scott called "everyday forms of resistance" to defend themselves and their livelihoods against the depredations of various arms of the state.[138] Most traders have, as Onstad put it, "joined a burgeoning lower class empire with its separate housing estates, wage labour force, and systems of stratification."[139] For lack of other opportunities more and more educated young men and women are joining the ranks of the traders and adding literate talents to increasingly vociferous political efforts. More political ructions have already resulted. It seems unlikely, given its current record, that the Kenyan government will adopt policies to ameliorate matters for traders and squatters, whose persecution often is simultaneous in keeping with its class nature. In March 1991 a new squatter settlement demolition campaign began in Nairobi; the incidence of "brutal" demolitions was increasing in a systematic campaign involving not only demolitions, but also police beating and mugging the inhabitants. The reasons? Developers wanted the land, especially around wealthy suburbs, and those in

---

[135] *Daily Nation* 12 Dec. 1987: 1. They are, in any case, woefully underpaid. The situation resembles the pre-1930 tribute exaction by chiefly retainers, who were not paid a wage. Tignor, "Colonial Chiefs," p. 349.

[136] Cooper, "Introduction, p. 8.

[137] Freeman, *City,* pp. 115ff., protested police actions such as crop destruction taken against Nairobi urban farmers and stressed their importance in feeding the population. He ignored the class interests involved, however (the upper classes can afford to buy maize and big maize producers prefer that the poor buy it rather than grow it), in saying that all that would be required to solve the problem would be a change in attitude on the part of the government. Similarly, rather than supply cheap clothing to the growing number of indigent in the U.S., K-Mart policies include burning unsold clothing.

[138] Smith, "Introduction," p. 69; Scott, "Resistance," pp. 7, 9.

[139] "Life," pp. 250-51.

power feared the poor as a political threat. Such policies encourage riots and efforts to overthrow the government. There may be political limits to the privileging of wealth, especially where most people are poor.[140] In 1989 the 300 women traders who protested did not succeed in gaining their ends, but they will try again in double the numbers. The wellbeing of their families depends on them. Next time they may succeed. Much of Gikomba was flattened early in 1987. It was rebuilt then and after the 1988 destruction. It will continue to be rebuilt. If trouble showed them the way, these women helped each other to overcome their troubles.

VII.1 A Leader Among Women

---

[140] A massive effort to gentrify the riverine area downtown is underway, which plans no doubt will ultimately include the Gikomba site. The Shabbir Center is to be "an ultra-modern complex that will combine residential and business facilities to transform the area that was a massive shanty town ten years ago." *Daily Nation* 25 Jan. 1988: 11-12.

VIII

Trouble Showed the Way[1]
Conclusion: Empowerment?

If it is not appropriate for women, it is not appropriate.[2]

A 1987 incident on a Nairobi *matatu* indicated a direction of change in self-esteem among urban women. The *Daily Nation* article describing it was ostensibly about the career of a musician, Julius Kang'ethe (a.k.a. By-law), who failed to find a job when he first came to Nairobi in 1979 and hawked at Machakos Bus Stop while he composed his first song, "a prayer to God asking for help for jobless young men." He then went on to compose another song called "Ithe wa Kiune" (Kikuyu=Father of Calamity), which prescribed severely deferential behavior for married women and justified abuse by husbands if wives were not deferential enough. A *matatu* driver annoyed many of his women passengers by repeatedly playing it until most of the women on the bus demanded that he stop and let them off, whereupon they "accused those who were left behind of being half-women who enjoy hearing and seeing their lot being ridiculed by male chauvinists."[3] This incident invites comparison with Mary Muthoni Nyanjiru's exhortations at the Thuku demonstration in 1922, and indicates a fundamental change that urbanization, along with women's growing involvement in trade, has encouraged. Whereas Mary urged men on to do their duty and take action, these women were pushing other women to join in a protest action intended to boost their self-esteem. To protest male dominance was seen as incumbent upon women; not to do so as insufficiently womanly. The resonances here are both with the precolonial gender system and its checks on male abuse fostered through the *ndundu ya atomia* and with new forms of gender relations in which male abuse is countered by a female solidarity engendered by urban solidary groups and peer efforts.

The signs of women's empowerment in terms of self-esteem are everywhere, but especially with those women who have achieved some material success. As with Wambui in Chapter V, suicide is no longer the only way out if men do not meet their

---

[1] Many women in Nairobi gave this answer when asked why they had started trading.

[2] Slogan of Women's Appropriate Technology Workshop sponsored by the Kenya Women's Bureau and NGOs, Aug. 1988. *Women's Standard* 23 Aug. 1988: 12.

[3] *Daily Nation* 19 Dec. 1987. Another male-composed popular song, "Mumunya" (Kiswahili=Suck), accused Nairobi women of being golddiggers, provoking a response by two Kikuyu women singers, "Mumunya Part II," saying that men should blame themselves for encouraging women to exploit them by bragging about money and being foolish about beautiful women. *Daily Nation* 19 June 1988: 14.

obligations. Kinyanjui's granddaughter, pregnant by a man who refused to marry her but self-supporting in a good job, in 1980 took as her model a wealthy real estate owner at Kawangware, who had made her fortune as a prostitute, taken a wife since she herself was sterile, and paid off the lover she chose for her wife. "Everything she has is hers," she said. "No man can kick her off. My grandfather used to take land from women who had no men with them when he was chief but no one can do that to me, not in this our New Kenya... I swear by this soil [land bought by her with money given by her uncle], I will die first." Wambui Waiyaki Otieno, notable daughter of a prominent Kikuyu clan, challenged resurrected "customary law" and male dominance in seeking to bury her husband in Nairobi rather than with his Luo kin.[4] Women, objectified and segregated physically and economically by colonial and neo-colonial rule, have worked creatively to overcome the obstacles posed by their reification.

The air is full of women's mutual exhortations. Mumbi Gakuo declared women's independence.

> Women should not pressurise men to marry them because by so doing, the men may marry them under conditions which only suit them. Women should express their ability to take care of themselves and their children without men partners. Even though it was not originally out of their own choice, women who have been left by husbands either through death or divorce, or who have never been married at all, have been able to look after their children very well, and in most cases more successfully than those whose marriage partners are alive.[5]

In constructing her feminist nationalist heroine Micere Mugo rebelled against both gender as constructed in folktales and Western stereotypes, "The women in our society must reject the role of the sacrificial lamb, ... must rebel against imprisonment in the kitchen, since this has come to mean repression and denigration."[6] A woman farmer told Mackenzie a story about the daughters of Muumbi, who saved men from famine by inventing agriculture. The leader of the Gikomba dried staples sellers told us that trading has made women feel better about themselves and their abilities because they no longer have to depend solely on their husbands and can be self-reliant; they are no longer exploited by men; and they can help build their homes if they have husbands. Trade, she said, has replaced farming because the farms are no longer productive.[7] Women's growing involvement in urban trade has clearly played a role in boosting their self-esteem, but the phenomenon affects more women than traders and more realms than self-esteem.[8] Trouble showed them the way to Nairobi.

---

[4] Browne, "Kawangware," pp. 294-98; Stamp, "Burying Otieno."

[5] Gakuo, "Kenyan Women," p. 378.

[6] Mugo, "Role of Woman," p. 218.

[7] Mackenzie, "Local Initiatives," p. 397n.1; interview 241 Gikomba: 25 May 1994.

[8] For a fine post-modern analysis of how Moroccan women's new involvement in trade is giving women a voice see Kapchan, *Gender*. It has limited analysis of the material realities of their work, however.

This study has described and analyzed first a truncation of Kikuyu women's precolonial involvement in long-distance trade accompanied by a diminution of cross-ethnic contact when colonialists furthered the construction of segregated "tribal" ethnicities in the Reserves. At the same time, however, there was an intensifying of women's involvement in trade in the Nairobi area, which entailed the abandonment of precolonial complementarity between the genders in the organization of trade with the increasing segregation of women's and men's trade in scale and organization. Nonetheless, some women's trade has now overcome these limitations by replicating or surpassing not only the scope of their own precolonial trade but also men's post-independence accomplishments. It was therefore necessary to redefine the Nairobi area to include an expanding hinterland that supplies both its food and its traders. While I have paid most attention here to the increasing involvement of Kiambu and Ukambani in feeding Nairobi, any future study would need to look at western and southern Kenya. If Kikuyu and Kamba women traders dominate the produce trade in and around Nairobi, Kikuyu women also now exercise most influence in the Rift Valley and Western Province, with significant trade to Mombasa, while Luo women trade fish to Nairobi and control the trade to sugar growing schemes and tea plantations in Kericho. Luhya women from Kakamega are expanding their vegetable trade into Nandi, Trans-Nzoia and Uasin Gishu. Kongstad and Monsted, who conducted research in the expanding areas of women's trade, called it the "normal business of women in the more intensely cultivated areas."[9]

The most intense struggle by traders was in Nairobi, which has a population that is rapidly becoming urban in both residence and orientation. If I have emphasized here the rural connections of many traders, the obverse has also been evident in the statistics; most Nairobi traders (over 80%) have become part of a permanent urban population.[10] Most women migrants to Nairobi now are seeking their own or their families' economic advancement, not simply joining their husbands, which used to be the case. If landlessness/divorce/widowhood made many of them "reluctant urbanites," to use Browne's term, there are a number of advantages accruing to such women out of urban residence, the kind that make them ever more willing to concentrate their energies in the urban sphere.[11] In 1977 Weisner and Abbott found that stress indicators were higher for rural than urban Kikuyu women. Why? They had "all of the work and much of the ultimate responsibility for its successful completion, but without the commensurate autonomy in other domestic spheres enjoyed by the urban Kikuyu women ... [or] adequate material and labor supports," especially

[9] Kongstad and Monsted, *Family*, pp. 120, 107.

[10] Adagala and Bifani, *Self-Employed Women*, p. 9; Mitullah, "Hawking," p. 17; Weisner and Abbott, "Women," p. 426.

[11] *Situation Analysis* I: 22; Olenja, "Patterns," pp. 13-17. The most stunning statistic concerning landlessness is that between 1976 and 1979 in Central Province households without land increased from 10.3% to 21.8%. Ministry of Economic Planning and Development *Integrated Rural Surveys: 1976-79*, p. 89; Browne, "Kawangware," p. 304.

since their children were in school, which cost money and deprived them of child labor. Suburban women like Nyokabi, who had access to land, rental, and trade profits, were in the best position but not numerous.[12] But urban women were more often free of obligations to men, more self-reliant, and independent of kin relations in general, advantages which helped to offset their shaky economic situation and the lack of a publicly validated and valued role as independent market women. Ross and Thadani in 1979-80 studied urban working-class women, who were more likely to have neighborhood-based, pan-ethnic friendship networks than either their male cohorts or upper-class women, and who were mobilizing politically through those networks.[13] The women traders form a core group in that mobilization.

Urban market traders are also increasingly committed to trade in that it is their sole method of earning a living, which differentiates them not only from many rural traders but also from the wealthier entrepreneurs who may establish market-based businesses but are seldom there selling themselves.[14] With further erosion of the rural economy for small producers we can expect that the straddling aspect of women traders' roles will decline, which will make them more financially vulnerable but perhaps also more willing to invest in (and expand) their businesses and urban real estate holdings. After all, only a very few traders managed to acquire land of their own. Landlessness among women, along with the increase in female-headed households, make them the prototypical urban residents of the future; most of the women in the large sample (63.1%) did not have the option of moving back to a rural area when they retire because they had no access to land. Even many of the rural resident women had no access to land (42.3%), meaning that they also relied essentially on trade for income.[15]

We are looking, then, at a cup half-empty or half-full. Although increasing involvement in urban trade has undoubtedly raised women's autonomy and self-esteem, it is also a manifestation of greater destitution and sometimes desperation; the generally low profits involved, although essential for family survival, are usually not enough for the women traders either to raise their class status or expand the scale of their businesses. Moreover, urban small-scale businesses were reaching saturation point in terms of generating employment in the late 1980s, generating fewer jobs and damaged by higher competition and deteriorating conditions. As Barnes stated, "Small-scale commerce ... makes important contributions to [women's] sense of self-reliance and individual identity, but it rarely leads to total economic

---

[12] A similar point is made by Engel, *Fields*, Ch.7, regarding the impact of late-nineteenth-century Russian urbanization.

[13] Weisner and Abbott, "Women," pp. 428-33; Ross and Thadani, "Participation," p. 330.

[14] The chief example of this phenomenon among the samples were women owners of garment industry shops at Gikomba.

[15] Trenchard, "Women's Work," p. 167, found in five rural African case studies an increasing reliance on small-scale trade to meet subsistence needs.

independence."[16] But many women traders are perforce independent of men and male earnings. Resting the argument at the self-esteem level of trade's functions for women would be woefully inadequate.

Women's Labor, the Economy, the State and Gendered Class Formation

The findings of this study have direct theoretical and practical implications for our analysis of gender, the economy, the state and the relationship of all these to class formation. What do the results here say about my original premise, that control over women's labor forms a fundamental basis for male domination, and what implications does that level of control have for women's empowerment? In this study control over women's labor was indeed a central area of conflict; struggles over trade profits, marriage forms, women's domestic labor in childrearing and bearing and otherwise, crops grown and traded, and such necessities for women to conduct trade as mobility, pervade the history of women's trade over the twentieth century. That trade changed from its episodic precolonial barter form to an urban supply network beginning before World War I, to a locally contested wider more gender-differentiated form in the interwar period, to a highly contested often illegal system during the wars of 1940 to 1963, and to a Kenya-wide food supply system differentiated between and within genders after independence, in which women dominate the lower echelons and have assumed responsibility for much small and mid-size wholesaling. In the latter stage the level of government persecution rose, largely due to political considerations, but from about 1940 to the present control over a growing rambunctious Nairobi small trader population and their trade has been a primary interest of government. That that control has now taken on ethnic aspects once again with government interest in suppressing Kikuyu dissidence only increases the resemblance to the Emergency.[17] The changing construction of gender, and of the poor, which are linked for urban women, has played a role in the state persecution of traders.

Control over women traders' economic functions, their labor within and without the household, was and is seen as necessary by those who would control the state, but such control has increasingly been subsumed into class considerations as an autocratic government seeks to maintain its hegemony, using the rhetoric of ethnicity for foreign consumption. In response to efforts at control, women are fighting battles from the household to the societal level. Unlike in Accra to the 1970s, where solidarity among women traders was undermined by declining female gerontocratic authority and increasing class divisions that accompanied the widened capitalist economy, in Nairobi women's solidarity is picking up strength and developing political organization, perhaps because of a more efficient education system, a stronger cultural heritage of peer group solidarity, and government persecution, which reduces opportunities for differentiation or betterment among women traders. At the same time gender stratification among traders, in which some of the more prosperous

---

[16] Zeleza, "Labour System," p. 354; Barnes, "Women," p. 263.

[17] Macharia, "Slum Clearance."

adopt strategies of cooperation and pooling of resources with husbands, is emblematic of the wider society with its male-dominated elite. Gender segregation is particularly characteristic of the underclass, where class-specific household disruptions caused by poverty help siphon women and men in different directions, where they do not help each other as much as they could. Thus, gender segregation among the underclass serves the purposes of the dominant classes as a divide-and-conquer tactic that reduces the likelihood of the most exploited organizing to rectify matters.

Regarding the economy, women did/do not work to create their own leisure time and their work has for some time not shielded them from the capitalist economy; it has become instead integral to capital formation. The difference is that mercantile capitalism made Kinyanjui a profit based on the labor of his forty-nine wives, whereas now women's waged and unwaged labor feeds directly into generating profits at every level from flower harvesting for multinational corporations to selling dried beans in order to refinance a husband's business or feed children, the bearing of which responsibility allows men to earn and invest more. Households and women are neither stagnant sites of immutable reproductive activity nor unproductive victims of colonialist capitalist exploitation.[18] Women's labor is not only productive in contributing to their own (and others') profits, but also manifest evidence that this is a peasantry that was "captured" some time ago by the world capitalist economy (this capturing never more evident than in their increasing trade activities), and is trying valiantly to survive that incorporation. The problem of economic development is not that people continue their precapitalist activities, but rather "the struggle over how society will be reorganized to take advantage of [a capitalist mode of production]."[19] For men the cup was half full because sufficient male dominance based on control of women's labor was already in place when colonialism was imposed that only adjustments were required; for women the cup of capitalism is already half empty and their survival depends upon the struggle to reapportion labor and earnings more equitably within a world system that seeks ever more efficiently to expropriate them, while denying that there was anything there to expropriate in the first place.

It is clear that the limited capital formation among the micro-entrepreneurs forming Nairobi's market population does not provide a strong basis for business expansion, and yet it is solidly rooted in local supply and demand. Only if Kenya were to become completely dependent on imported staples would that stop. But government policies are in many ways hostile to the expansion of women-owned businesses. Enlightened self-interest might at least mandate consideration of the maintenance of government stability through an assured food supply and dictate efforts

---

[18] Gerry and Birkbeck, "Petty Commodity Producers," p. 134, noted that petty commodity production is essential to neocolonial capitalism because it provides cheap food and goods to keep down the cost of labor and inflate the value of elite earnings; maintains a reserve army of labor; provides opportunities for more earnings for independent men; and its businesses provide a market for capitalist products. Scott, *Gender*, p. 103.

[19] Leo, *Land and Class*, p. 71.

similar to those of the British to form a stable petty bourgeoisie. If there was a genuine commitment to a realistic and growing economy whose aim is to benefit most of the people, the central position of women's trade could be factored into the GNP, economic planning, and laws that aim at bettering the economic and social welfare of the Kenyan population as a whole. But the rising ethnopolitics of a comprador state suppresses any such efforts and absorbs funds that might be used for the public welfare.

Meanwhile, if trade helped to generate self-confidence and goals of political empowerment for women, it also fostered women's property rights by giving some independent resources to acquire property. The relatively strong property rights of patrilineal coastal West African women may have come from a centuries-old involvement in trade. The undermining of that trade by present conditions is in turn undermining their property rights, given their lack of resources to defend those rights. Any consideration of the origins or the future of the law should not be based solely on some abstract structural formulation like the black box of "tradition," but on the changing situation of its manipulators, including economics.

Concerning the state, both the findings regarding women's trade and state persecution should lead to a rethinking of theories of various kinds. At the macro-level they demonstrate the incompleteness of adopting with Bourdieu and Gramsci a definition of power that "operates less through force than by subtly shaping the contexts in which people negotiate the definition of events."[20] This definition is more useful for middle-class women, who feel the batons of the police less often and the subjection to male dominant ideology more prominently. The traders do bear, and try to negotiate their way out of, significant burdens imposed by male dominance, but many are also exposed daily to considerable levels of state force. To them the vagaries of the dominant state ideology described here and the divisions within the ruling classes matter little. It is the reality of the streets that imposes devastating insecurities on their lives. That reality is leading them to revoke any "spontaneous" consent they may have given to the dominant classes to provide leadership.[21]

If the evidence of persecution suggests caution about overreliance on abstract definitions of power, the findings regarding women's trade raise questions concerning that "uncaptured peasantry" that Leys and Hyden would have impeding Kenya's development. Leys seems to have been unduly influenced by the postindependence land redistribution that divided up large estates in some cases and temporarily increased rural farmers' landholdings, while Hyden seems to have resuscitated a Chayanovesque division in which peasants belong to a noncapitalist mode of production where they do not work for economic advantage and their rural residence somehow protects them from the incursions of capitalism. This may have been true to

---

[20] Bledsoe, "School Fees," p. 284; Gramsci, *Prison Notebooks*, pp. 12-13; Bourdieu, *Outline*.

[21] Fatton, "Gender," pp. 52-54, claimed that African male-dominated ruling classes do not possess hegemonic authority, in any case, which lack prevents the state from taking into account the interests of women and the lower classes.

some extent for precolonial African men whose political ambitions, however, were furthered by the labor of women. Hyden's "economy of affection" rests at base on the problematic construction of the undifferentiated household.[22] Similarly, Mamdani suggested that peasants did not organize to resist worker demands for cheap labor and high wages because workers and peasants were one class in that workers' wages were subsidized by family labor, an explanation that masks gender differences.[23] This explanation ignores that rural and urban women of peasant origin have organized, and continue to organize, to influence the source of the problem, the extractive state.

Then there is the theoretical and actual problem presented by gender when defining the class position of small-scale traders and the role of the state in gendered class formation. In this case gender differentiation/discrimination divides traders into a hierarchical structure. In analyzing the position of groups within petty commodity production with regard to the relations of production gender is a salient category, though still largely unrecognized within the materialist literature. Wealthy older male traders/employers are at the top of a hierarchy in the category Gerry and Birkbeck called "lumpen-capitalists,"[24] with possibilities for their children and themselves to maintain or raise their class position. They own a proportion of the means of production (land, shops, tools), control their own and others' labor, the productive process, and are sole appropriators of the surplus generated by their businesses, which they may reinvest in the business. Few women fit into this category; more are at the middle level, where they own the tools of their trade (infrastructure, equipment), and dispose of their own labor, but their profits are expropriated by family demands, often conditioned by male dominance. In contrast, men at the middle level are more likely to be artisans possessing a skill as a critical resource, as well as the tools of their trade, and also the preferential treatment government and NGOs give to manufacturing.

At the lower level are many women proprietors of micro-enterprises in subsistence trade, itinerant hawkers, and women and men who are proletarianized in that they work for tiny wages, produce baskets or pound maize for entrepreneurs on a piecework basis, or take dried staples on credit to sell for others. They neither own the means of production nor control their own labor. But again, even these men may keep their own profits, if any, while women's profits are expropriated from above and below. Moreover, the eligibility of many young men for skilled jobs in the wage sector boosts their chances of obtaining capital or supporting themselves, while women's family responsibilities and lower education levels reduce theirs. Petty commodity production, then, is problematized by considerations of gender, which adds

---

[22] Goran Hyden, *Beyond Ujamaa*; Leys, *Underdevelopment*. For an excellent critique of Hyden that delineates his "masculinist" construction of entrepreneurship see Scott, *Gender*, pp. 50-68.

[23] Lecture cited in Leonard, *Successes*, p. 74.

[24] Gerry and Birkbeck, "Petty Commodity Producer," pp. 136-40.

substance to an already highly contradictory situation and status. But gender is neither a prior nor a pristine category and is constructed in part through changing relationship to the means of production. This particular intersection of labor and business history is fraught with contradictions that have been exacerbated by the increased incorporation of Kenya into an industrialized world capitalist economy and do not succumb easily to undifferentiated class analysis.

The contradictions become overwhelming when the role of state persecution of traders is considered. For women, in particular, such persecution encourages investment in children's education for wage jobs, or in real estate (for the better off), and discourages reinvestment of profits or employment of relatives to expand businesses. By increasing the cost of doing business it damages support for cheap provisioning of workers, and therefore for low wages, and helps to undermine the position of small-scale trade within the economy. It therefore contributes both to steady inflation in the amount of education needed to obtain wage jobs and to an increase in the number of traders whose lesser education disqualifies them in that race, mainly women. Heightened competition lowers profits, while the growing discontent of the educated underemployed and the overemployed undereducated contributes to political activism and volatility. Women's position in the relations of production, persecution by the state and by men, and their cultural history of solidary groups related to their labor generate solidarity, which contributes to militance. Thus, the positions of both the small traders and the state are undermined by their own actions taken in the face of mutual threats.

Change in this situation seems unlikely because the state is an extractive control mechanism dominated by a hegemonic class that enriches itself in the best neo-colonial tradition. The middle peasantry so beloved of Cowen, those "small-scale [male] farmers who rely almost exclusively on household labour," and who were prospering,[25] are now being undermined by encroachments of every kind from above and the escape of household labor from below when children go (expensively) to school and women refuse to turn over their coffee and trade profits to them. These are the hazards of theorizing as if women are non-existent, invisible, or without volition, and of drawing general models from historically specific locations. The paradox regarding women's labor in both food production and trade, now that food crops are cash crops, is that "capitalist penetration has simultaneously both depended on women's food providing role and undermined it, until the whole system is now in danger of collapse."[26] The seeming contradiction in the state's roles of ensuring capitalist accumulation while maintaining social control is resolved by the dependence of accumulation on controlling women's labor. As Lovett noted, women's urban migration represents a fundamental challenge to patriarchal accumulation and also threatens the preservation of men's land rights. But the current situation in Kenya for

---

[25] Cowen and Kinyanjui, "Problems," p. 65; Cowen, "Commodity Production," p. 141.

[26] Editors' introduction to Trenchard, "Women's Work," p. 153.

many women resembles the consequences for Indian women lacemakers of incorporation into the world capitalist economy, which include the expropriation not only of
women's surplus labor but also of their necessary labor, the point at which survival is
jeopardized.[27]

Kongstad and Monsted described Kenyan households as being "held together
by ... patriarchal organization" but divided by their members' "increasingly being
exposed to quite different relations with the market," mirroring the differentiation
within small-scale trade.[28] Male dominance within households is weakening as marriages disintegrate under the impact of a peripheral capitalist economy with very few
social welfare provisions. Wealthy households may prosper and be more stable, but
for the poor conditions are worsening. Women's unpaid labor is not infinitely elastic
and their reproductive capacity may collapse due to ill health and poor nutrition for
themselves and their families. Allison noted much evidence of hypertension among
African women "caused primarily by heavy work burdens and conflicting
demands."[29] Structural Adjustment Programs (SAPs) mandate reduction in the costs
to the state of pensions, maternity leave and healthcare programs and shift them to
the private sector, meaning women, a procedure approved of by most economists,
whose accounting does not include unpaid labor.[30] The decline in indicators of family wellbeing like resources, health, and diet, and increase in domestic violence make
this scenario operative for Kenya.

Some of the contradictions which appear to be undermining the cheap labor
and provisioning of the working classes supplied by petty commodity production can
be explained by a primary aim of maintaining male dominance, as when inefficient
men are employed or promoted over efficient women. Many women are challenging
high population growth by controlling their own fertility, which might advance their
individual and class interests, but men often oppose that control and promote the
treatment of people as disposable commodities that the growth encourages. The
maintenance of male dominance keeps the cost of reproduction of the labor force
among subordinate classes low. The colonial state gave African men new tools like
Western education and skills that boosted their position relative to women, while
sanctioning the eradication of women's authority structures and customary rights to
resources; the postcolonial state continues these policies while using arbitrary author-

---

[27] Lovett, "Gender Relations," pp. 25-29; Mies, *Lacemakers*.

[28] Kongstad and Monsted, *Family*, p. 23. The implications for theories of class of men's and wom-
en's different relationships to the means of production are dealt with by Robertson and Berger, introduction to *Women and Class*. See also Robertson, *Bowl*, Conclusion.

[29] Barnes, "Women," p. 257, described the continuing necessity of labor control for African political success. "The more one is able to use the services, labor, or support of others, the more one is able to
accumulate wealth and invest it in the kinds of social and material items that make participation in community affairs possible," which women have more difficulties in achieving. Allison, "Alternative," p. 142.

[30] Elson, "Structural Adjustment," pp. 67-72.

ity to maintain an unbalancing sense of insecurity among its subjects.[31] The colonial and neocolonial state, then, has played a major role in gendering class formation and facilitating male control over women's labor.

Solutions?

Ultimately this study has analyzed the gender economics that make sexual politics possible. If ideology legitimates, perpetuates and is created by socioeconomic structure, economics pushes changes in the ideological realm, as shown here with respect to women's urban roles and controls over traders. The dominant discourse has shifted to a class-biased analysis similar to that of right-wing Americans in the welfare debate; the poor are by definition lazy and dishonest. Poor women are bad mothers and immoral, at best helpless victims of foolishness.[32] Whatever the realities of seventy-hour weeks, failed contraceptive efforts, and injurious official policies, this view legitimizes the punitive persecution of slum demolitions and hawker raids. The 1972 ILO Report assumed that remedying the "pejorative view" of the nature of the informal sector would also fix the punitive policies.[33] But colonial and postcolonial statist ideology was/is functional for maintaining upper-class dominance. Part of the problem with British colonial policies toward African traders was the false assumption that the Kikuyu had never traded, but why did the early contact knowledge of those like Lugard disappear with later administrators? The purposeful ignorance of African trade activities, as well as negative views of poor people and the invisibility of women's labor now, were and are necessary to justify the superexploitation of the labor of poor people that enriches the upper classes. An immoral act is committed more easily if the pain it causes is made invisible by denial of the humanity of those harmed by it. Only if severe disruption of the economy and/or uncontrollable political eruptions result, caused by the policies and the persecution, will enlightened self-interest force a change in policy. Even then, the government would have to get control over their enforcers by paying and policing them, a difficult prospect by now. It will be interesting to see if the massive noncompliance with the laws that has developed out of economic necessity will force the government to implement positive changes.[34] Not only economic but also political necessity dictate the advisability of change.

---

[31] Parpart and Staudt, introduction to *Women*, pp. 6, 12; Schatzberg, *Dialectics*, p. 70; Stamp, "Groups," pp. 39-40, analyzed the situation succinctly, "male control of female productive and reproductive labor is more important to national politics than overall economic productivity or women's reproductive health."

[32] Similarly, U.S. right-wing ideology justifies the abolition of social welfare measures by utilizing racism and sexism to stereotype all poor people as poor black single mothers, whereas most poor people are (and always have been) white. Such stereotyping also has utility for encouraging poor whites to hide their poverty rather than organize to overcome it in conjunction with blacks.

[33] ILO, *Employment and Incomes*, pp. 5-6.

[34] Scott, "Everyday Forms," pp. 14-15, has given examples of rural resistance which accomplished this.

Moreover, neither Kenyan society nor the economy should endure the continuing costs of gender segregation. The lessons of colonialism and neocolonialism, that it is fine not to put resources into families and the collective good, and that life is a zero-sum game in which if women gain men will lose, need to be unlearned. All will gain if the divisive effects of male dominance, colonialism and neocolonialism, and class formation can be overcome by attention to collective interests. Indeed, to pursue policies for the public good independent of World Bank prescriptions will require unity. A new internationalism is needed that acknowledges the necessity for, and takes responsibility for, reconstructing gender roles in an egalitarian mode, while forswearing the excesses of class formation. We all have to ask ourselves, what is the economy for? Most of us would not answer, to enrich the already privileged.

What sorts of changes might benefit women traders? We need to look at the possibilities for empowerment of women coming out of their involvement in trade. These are connected to profits as well as self-esteem, since it was noticeable that good profits bore a positive relationship to self-esteem. Profits are intimately linked to the persecution of traders. In the late 1980s relatively well-established Kenyan garment industry entrepreneurs, including many women, found that because of the high risks involved it was safer to keep businesses small and flexible.[35] A substantial part of that risk for most traders is connected to the illegality of many of their activities. Because of the persecution we do not know what the possibilities are for profits and economic development for the same reason that we do not know what Cuba's economy would be like without the U.S. boycott. The playing field is not level, especially for women traders since male dominance imposes additional burdens in terms of domestic labor obligations, support of dependents, forced loans, and scale and type of businesses (exclusion from most manufacturing, for instance). Many women cannot make a profit by staying within the law and therefore must constantly be prepared to cut and run, metaphorically or physically. De Soto itemized the costs of illegality as follows: bribes, fines, protection money, confiscation of goods, high interest rates on scarce capital (moneylenders), reliance on word of mouth advertisement only, and little infrastructure. Good law, he said, "guarantees and facilitates the efficiency of the economic and social activities it regulates and a bad law ... disrupts or totally prevents it... Good law should create incentives to seize economic and social opportunities and facilitate specialization and interdependence of individuals and resources."[36]

It is, of course, nice to have the laws on one's side, but de Soto's reliance on law to solve the problems of developing countries resembles the old "free market economy" solution, which ignores the vested interests served by the restrictions on lower-class enterprises. SAPs, which aim at repaying large bank debts, further the removal of laws concerning worker safety, environmental protection, minimum

---

[35] McCormick, "Enterprise," p. 236.

[36] De Soto, *Other Path*, pp. 152-54, 158, 161, 182, 185.

wage, union protection, import tariffs, and anything else which inhibits cheap exports. Susan George used the analogy of a war to describe the consequences of SAPs, wherein the battles are between police and rioters protesting their effects.[37] Nor does it further women traders' cause to view the underground economy as crime-as-a-business with profitability enhanced by its very illegality.[38] Crime is a tough world for those with multiple dependents; women traders' crimes enhance their vulnerability and that of their children, and lower their profits.

Still, in the hopes of realizing the positive energy and benefits derived for everyone from working together, we need to look at the changes that are happening and that might benefit women traders. The households of women traders may be in the vanguard in this respect. In conjugal households the following changes are coming, if not voluntarily, then forced by necessity.

1. The gender division of labor is shifting so that men are doing more farm labor on their own farms, especially in the absence of women who are trading, and occasionally more domestic chores, although that is rare. Necessity is forcing changes toward more meaningful cooperation for those who understand its benefits. However, more often the domestic work falls on elder daughters, whose schooling therefore suffers.
2. Consensual decisionmaking is becoming more common as women supply more of the households' cash income, a phenomenon with worldwide resonances. Failure to do so is more likely to result in conflict and divorce, especially if male autocracy inhibits women's abilities to feed their children (as in the sale of land, refusal of permission to trade or work off-farm, or seizure of women's profits for non-family needs).
3. Segregated and/or expropriative expenditure still impoverishes the family when men remove land or capital from women's farming or trading activities to invest in businesses or private wants.[39]
4. Reduction or elimination of bridewealth has reduced lineage interests in preserving marriage and increased the mutability of conjugal households.

In female-headed households the following changes are underway.

1. Trade, or other paid work, is an absolute necessity.
2. Segmentation is common with middle-aged women (thirties to fifties) in town and children and elderly women on farms, remittances and visits being paid whenever possible. Land rights will lapse with the death of the oldest woman unless they have purchased land.

---

[37] Beulink, "Women," p. 91; Sen and Grown, *Development*, p. 54; Shiva, "Development," p. 86.

[38] Ryan, "Illegal Activities," p. 22.

[39] The withdrawal of capital by men (or women) from agriculture lowers labor productivity in that sector. Kitching, *Class*, p. 199.

3.   Permanent urban residence is becoming more common with all generations together or co-resident peers, sometimes with their children.
4.   Urban real estate is becoming the investment of choice as a result of urban residence, a trend that began with the early twentieth-century urban pioneers, but farmland is still highly desired.
5.   Men are increasingly peripheral in their contributions and sometimes kept out deliberately lest they try to coopt profits. When they make contributions it is usually as sons rather than as fathers, lovers or brothers.

The government could, but probably will not, help women to deal with the disadvantageous aspects of their household situation by allowing paternity suits and enforcing child support by men; supporting women's full rights to make economic and social decisions independent of men in everything from reproductive decisions to credit arrangements; rewarding investment in food production; and pushing women's rights to land over those of husbands' male agnates.

At present the best-case scenario for helping small-scale enterprises is represented by articles on opposing pages of the *Daily Nation*. A story headlined "It's Lucy's turn to smile! Road accident left her crippled but she has been helped to start a thriving business in the city," described the harrowing history of Lucy Wanjiru, a twenty-nine-year-old unmarried mother of one child, who established a successful tourist curio business in a city center market, despite confinement to a wheelchair. The necessary training and capital was supplied by Undugu Society, one of the few NGOs that attempts, albeit on a small scale, to provide help in getting started for the smallest of entrepreneurs. With little education, Lucy had trouble keeping accounts so the training was necessary. She was thinking of hiring an assistant due to her modest success. "The Limuru artisan on a creative path" detailed the history of James Kiongo Rugunya, a thirty-five-year-old artisan who worked as a technician for Brooke Bond for nine years before setting up his own metal fabrication business, for which he invented a number of new appropriate technology machines for such tasks as steel rolling. His education came from the Rift Valley Technical School and his business employed ten assistants, all male.[40]

These stories convey not only the most positive common conflicting images of female and male entrepreneurs (needy victim versus clever entrepreneur)[41] but also the conflicting realities they face, with implications for the necessity of gender-specific solutions to their problems. Lucy and Florence (in Chapter V) both got help because of especially exigeant circumstances involving physical disabilities; that help was not aimed at all those in their category. James began from a relatively

---

[40] *Daily Nation* 22 July 1988: 13-14. For a perceptive analysis of Undugu Society and of the Green Belt Movement founded by Dr. Wangari Maathai see Ndegwa, *Two Faces*, pp. 81-108.

[41] Another headline to a story detailing the exploitation of Kariakor Market *ciondo* makers at the hands of middlepersons made this view more explicit: "Helpless victims of exploitation," while conveying the women's competent efforts to better their position with the aid of the Kenya Women Finance Trust, a women's self-help banking organization. *Daily Nation* 8 June 1988: 13.

privileged position with a technical education and lots of experience in wage work (his family circumstances are not mentioned so we do not know how many dependents he had). Undugu Society, according to the article, had undertaken systematic training of *jua kali*, but no such program aimed at women traders was mentioned. They have yet to be the targeted group of any government or NGO development program in Kenya to the best of my knowledge; efforts to uncover widely available programs that could supply small traders with loans in 1987-88 were fruitless.

What, then, could be done to help women traders? Consultation with the women revealed overwhelming concern about obtaining loans, hence my search for any available facilities. The meagerness of the offerings placed this need at the top of our list.

1. Provide low cost loans and credit; the establishment of private sector Grameen Bank-type facilities in which groups of traders could secure ever increasing loans based on proved performance seems eminently suited to their situation.
2. Stop police harassment and other violence against women.
3. Provide security of tenure in selling space, an issue intimately connected to elimination of police harassment. City planning needs to incorporate affordable selling space for even the smallest traders, while markets could have condominium characteristics (as Gikomba's illegal area already does).[42]
4. Incorporate women's groups into participatory planning for marketing and its infrastructure, which would avoid such disasters as empty markets and failed loan programs (women tend to have better repayment records than men do).
5. Simplify regulations, eliminate licensing in some areas, and reinvest market fees in infrastructure.
6. Provide appropriate participant-controlled training in accounting and managerial skills, budgeting and basic literacy, if needed. Incorporate women without harassment into training and apprenticeship programs aimed at all forms of manufacturing and provide them with technical skills, while teaching men appropriate domestic skills to promote a reformed gender division of labor.
7. Protect traders from predatory criminals (including corrupt officials) who use the traders' illegality to extort bribes or steal with impunity. Decriminalize activities like transporting goods across borders.
8. Legalize illegal markets and improve infrastructure at existing markets, especially sanitation and shelters, or let traders build their own. Vacant markets might be used if no fees were charged for their use, and maintained by traders' organizations.
9. Stop demolition of low-cost self-help housing unless better housing has already been provided for all of its residents.[43]

---

[42] Bromley, "Small," p. 333.

[43] ILO, *Employment*, p. 1045, identified the necessity for informal sector business to depend on low-cost housing.

The persecution of traders must be stopped by enforcement of laws beneficial to them, not by particular, easily rescinded or denied, dispensations. The Gikomba staples sellers have operated under occasional permissions. It might seem that if they had permanent permission to occupy their selling site and sheds to protect themselves and their goods, their problems would be solved as they would no longer be subjected to the same police actions street sellers incur. But street sellers also need help and that limited advance would not benefit all traders. The measures above should help all women traders both as individuals and as groups. More specific recommendations I leave to the experts, the traders involved in all kinds of small-scale endeavors.[44]

In 1987 USAID sponsored a development workshop for small businesses in a town outside Nairobi. One woman participant was expected but sixteen arrived. None spoke English and none of the workshop staff spoke their language, but translation was arranged. In effect, the women carried the vote and focused the group on obtaining *posho* mills.[45] Women's and men's small-scale trade has high utility for Kenya. It processes, bulks, recycles, and distributes most food products at affordable prices to the majority of the population. Traders assume credit risks for customers, supply convenient neighborhood shopping, provide entrepreneurial training, employment and income for many young persons with little education, substitute labor for capital in a situation of scarce capital and abundant labor, and provide canteen facilities for low-income workers in every neighborhood.[46] It should therefore not be necessary for women's groups to force accomplishment of the goals listed above, but it may be. One can only hope that through the murk of rhetoric and control the government can perceive the desirability of meeting the socioeconomic needs of the population with positive measures aimed at securing the welfare of traders, farmers, children, and families. Nothing is more important than food.

In this respect Lonsdale's Anglican compromise between determinism and free will regarding the nature of the state gives room for hope.

> The state itself [is] a complex form of social process--derived in part from but not simply reduced to the necessities of its mode of production--in which neither all-healing function, nor autonomous will, nor canny instrumental conspiracy can be more than partial, contested, and fleeting aspects of a system of domination which is always subject to stress and forever incomplete.[47]

Efforts at control that are too strong bring an irrationality of power and create anarchy with their widespread contravention. Governments *are* limited in power, especially when taxes come mostly from the poor. Bromley noted,

---

[44] Kenya NGO Organizing Committee, Reports of 1985 Workshops, "Women and Credit," pp. 16-17; "Income Generation," pp. 13-17; Mwagiru and Ouko, "Women and Development," p. 258.

[45] "Small Towns' Development," p. 16.

[46] Robertson, "Death," p. 477.

[47] "States," p. 146.

the poor have greater moral justification for breaking the laws and norms of society than the rich. The poor did not make the laws ... that they are expected [to obey], and they can legitimately claim that their ... poverty combined with the presence of wealth and conspicuous consumption around them, lead them to break these laws and norms.[48]

Looking at the heroic struggles of these traders, both legal and illegal, it is easy to mire oneself at the individual level, but we need to keep in mind Abu-Lughod's prescription, "We respect everyday resistance not just by arguing for the dignity or heroism of the resistors but by letting their practices teach us about the complex interworkings of historically changing structures of power," among which male dominance is entwined with most.[49]

* * * * *

The transformations described in this study embody evidence of women's empowerment in terms of self-esteem and political awakening. These women are both aware of class privilege and ready to take it on in order to secure their survival.[50] They are also increasingly aware of male privilege and of the environment. Women's empowerment in Kenya is a true grassroots effort that includes as a fundamental part of the agenda an environmental movement. For women protecting the environment was and is a labor control issue. Tree nurseries began as a government-mandated chiefs' effort, using women's labor, an echo of the forced labor used for colonial terracing. Mwethya women's groups in Ukambani now are doing soil conservation on their land and withdrawing their labor from the chiefs' purview, causing another struggle for control.[51]

Dr. Wangari Maathai's career as an environmentalist began before she became head of the National Council of Women of Kenya, and a fearless opponent of the government's more arbitrary efforts. Before she drew international attention by protesting the construction of a government building in Nairobi's Uhuru Park, she won the first Better World Award in 1986 and the UN Environment Program's Global 500 Award. In 1993 she took a visiting team of journalists to the worst-affected areas of government-sponsored "ethnic clashes," which urged Kalenjin to attack others in the Rift Valley. Her efforts included forming a resettlement committee to raise funds for the refugees and the dissemination of pamphlets to inform the public of what was happening in western Kenya. In response, President Moi severely reprimanded her and blamed her for fomenting "tribal" clashes. One of his adherents in Parliament threatened to excise Wangari forcibly "according to the Kalenjin tradition," thus illustrating the redefinition of clitoridectomy as an instrument for male

---

[48] Bromley, "Working," p. 165.

[49] Abu-Lughod, "Romance," p. 332.

[50] Interview 17 Ngara: 15 Oct. 1987.

[51] Pers. comm. Nyamweru 24 Sept. 1993.

dominance. The president of the NCWK, Lilian Mwaura, then entered into this new clitoridectomy controversy by calling the MP's threat, "primitive and irresponsible in an era when Kenyans are fighting to eliminate the harmful traditional practices like female genital mutilation... [They] need to be sensitized so that they ... learn to respect the anatomy of women."[52] The assumptions that Maathai had not been excised and that clitoridectomy would produce mental and political subordination are clear, while its use as code for assassination translates it to a wider political level.

The world in all its aspects is now the forum for Kenyan women's politics. Organized attacks by boys or men on schoolgirls, as at St. Kizito and Hawinga, have led to an increasingly unified women's movement concerned about women's strategic interests. The Kenyan women's movement is unusual for its cross-class solidarity in which elite women defend and educate the poor for independence.[53] It is also distinguished by its connection to the environment. Whether urban or rural, women are trying to cope with what Shiva has called the "paradox and crisis of development," that

> arises from the mistaken identification of culturally perceived poverty with real material poverty, and the mistaken identification of the growth of commodity production as better satisfaction of basic needs. In actual fact, there is less water, less fertile soil, less genetic wealth as a result of the development process. Since these natural resources are the basis of nature's economy and women's survival economy, their scarcity is impoverishing women and marginalised peoples in an unprecedented manner.[54]

These traders operate within the market economy often with the quadrupled awareness of producers/farmers and traders, as well as of gender and class. From their awareness and experiences they are seeking to expand, reclaim and regenerate what is theirs, but what is theirs is the world. In the natural world certain seeds were believed to embody a fundamental female quality lost with all the other losses of colonialism. These women, however, refused to accept that loss as irrevocable, transformed their involvement with beans and trade, and ultimately are attempting control over many aspects of their lives. This study delineated that transformation--of women's relation to crops, trade, marriage, and their bodies. Sharing their pain at initiation evolved into helping each other with all the problems that women face. Other women showed them the way through their troubles. Their best resources are each other. In the end the story is not of dispossession but of reclamation, not so much in material terms, but in ways that position women to attempt material repossession. African women, as the Ngubane song which began this book illustrates, are constructed and construct themselves in terms of their labor, and are

---

[52] Maathai, *Green Belt Movement*; Topouzi, "Kenya Women," p. 44; Awori, "Women Attack," 11 Mar. 1993.

[53] Stamp, "Mothers"; Jahava, "Nyandarua Women," p. 20.

[54] Shiva, *Staying Alive*, p. 13.

using that labor to reconstruct their world. The displacement of *njahe* and of women has ultimately brought re-placement, the recentering of women, who are re-visioning and revising a future in which categories have lost rigidity and assumed a flexibility amenable to change.

VIII.1 Grandmother and Granddaughter at a Thatching Party, 1950

BIBLIOGRAPHY OF WORKS CITED

Abbreviations

CIAT = Centro International para la Agricultura Tropicale (Cali, Colombia)
IAS   = Institute of African Studies, University of Nairobi
IDS   = Institute of Development Studies, University of Nairobi
KNA   = Kenya National Archives, Nairobi

BOOKS AND ARTICLES

Aaronovitch, S., and K. Aaronovitch. *Crisis in Kenya.* London: Lawrence and Wishart, 1947.

Abbott, Susan. "Full Time Farmers and Week-End Wives: An Analysis of Altering Conjugal Roles." *Jl. of Marriage and the Family* 38 (February 1976): 165-74.

Abbott, Susan, and Thomas Arcury. "Continuity with Tradition: Male and Female in Gikuyu Culture." *Youth and Society* 8, 4 (1977): 329-58.

Aboagye, A. A. *Informal Sector Employment in Kenya.* Addis Ababa: ILO, 1985.

Abu-Lughod, Lila. "The Romance of Resistance: Tracing Transformations of Power through Bedouin Women." In Sanday and Goodenough, 313-37.

Adagala, Kavetsa, and Patricia Bifani. *Self-Employed Women in the Peri-urban Setting: Petty Traders in Nairobi.* Nairobi: Derika Associates, 1985.

Adagala, Kavetsa, and Wanjiku Mukabi Kabira, eds. *Kenyan Oral Narratives.* Nairobi: Heinemann, 1985.

Adams, M. W. and G. B. Martin, "Genetic Structure of Bean Landraces in Malawi." In Gepts, *Genetic,* 347-60.

Ahlberg, Beth Maria. *Women, Sexuality, and the Changing Social Order: The Impact of Government Policies on Reproductive Behavior in Kenya.* Philadelphia: Gordon and Breach, 1991.

Akare, Thomas. *Twilight Woman.* Nairobi: Heinemann Spear Books, 1988.

Allison, Caroline. "What Alternative for Women in Africa?" In Ndegwa, Mureithi, and Green, 135-152.

Allman, Jean. "Adultery and the State in Asante: Reflections on Gender, Class and Power from 1800 to 1950." In *The Cloth of Many-Colored Silks.* Ed. J. O. Hunwick and N. Lawler. Evanston: Northwestern University Press, 1997.

Alvis, V., and P. Temu. "The Marketing of Selected Food Crops in Kenya, Comprising Maize, Beans, English Potatoes, and Bananas." IDS Discussion Paper No. 39B (1966).

Ambler, Charles H. *Kenyan Communities in the Age of Imperialism: The Central Region in the Late Nineteenth Century.* New Haven: Yale University Press, 1988.

Ames, Philip. "Migration, Urban Poverty, and the Housing Market: the Nairobi Case." In Eades, 249-68.

Anderson, David. "Depression, Dust Bowl, Demography, and Drought: The Colonial State and Soil Conservation in East Africa during the 1930s." *African Affairs* 83 (July 1984): 321-43.

Anderson, David, and David Throup. "Africans and Agricultural Production in Colonial Kenya: The Myth of the War as a Watershed." *Jl. of African History* 26, 4 (1985): 327-45.

Anker, Richard, and James Knowles. *Population Growth, Employment and Economic-Demographic Interaction in Kenya: Bachue-Kenya.* NY: St. Martin's/ILO, 1983.

Arens, William, ed. *A Century of Change in Eastern Africa.* Paris: Mouton, 1976.

Arkell-Hardwick, A. *An Ivory Trader in North Kenya.* London: Longmans, Green, 1903.

Auckland, A. K. "Soya Bean Improvement in East Africa." In Van Schoonhoven and Voyseat (see Gepts and Debouck), 130-54.

Awori, Horace. "Women Attack Government Over Gender Insensitivity." Interpress Service. 11 Mar. 1993.

Babb, Florence E. "From the Field to the Cooking Pot: Economic Crisis and the Threat to Marketers in Peru." In Clark, *Traders*, 17-40.

Barkan, Joel D. "The Rise and Fall of a Governance Realm in Kenya." In *Governance and Politics in Africa.* Ed. G. Hyden and M. Bratton. Boulder: Lynne Rienner, 1992. 167-93.

Barkan, Joel D., and John J. Okumu, eds. *Politics and Public Policy in Kenya and Tanzania.* NY: Praeger, 1979.

Barnes, Carolyn. "Differentiation by Sex among Small-Scale Farming Households in Kenya." *Rural Africana* 15-16 (Winter-Spring 1983): 41-63.

Barnes, Sandra T. "Women, Property and Power." In Sanday and Goodenough, 255-80.

Barnett, Donald L., and Karari Njama. *Mau Mau From Within.* London: MacGibbon and Kee, 1966.

Barra, G. *1000 Kikuyu Proverbs.* Nairobi: Kenya Literature Bureau, 1960.

Bates, Robert H. "The Agrarian Origins of Mau Mau: A Structural Account." *Agricultural History* 61 (1987): 1-28.

_____. *Markets and States in Tropical Africa: The Political Basis of Agricultural Policies.* Berkeley: University of California Press, 1981.

Beckman, Bjorn. "Imperialism and Capitalist Transformation: Critique of a Kenyan Debate." *Review of African Political Economy* 19 (1980): 48-62.

Beech, Mervyn W. H. "Suicide amongst the A-Kikuyu of East Africa." *Man* 29-30 (1913): 56-57.

Beecher, L. J. *The Kikuyu.* Nairobi: Ndia KUU, 1944.

Benson, T. G., ed. *Kikuyu-English Dictionary.* Oxford: Clarendon, 1964.

Berman, Bruce, and John Lonsdale. *Unhappy Valley: Conflict in Kenya and Africa.* Book 2, *Violence and Ethnicity.* London: James Currey, 1992.

Beulink, Anne-Marie. "Women and the Debt Crisis." *Development* 1 (1989): 88-94.

Bienefeld, Manfred. "Dependency Theory and the Political Economy of Africa's Crisis." *Review of African Political Economy* 43 (1988): 68-87.

Blackburne-Maze, C. I. *Journal of My African Travels.* Maidstone: W.E. Thorpe and Son, 1913.

Blakeslee, H. Virginia. *Beyond the Kikuyu Curtain.* Chicago: Moody, 1956.

Bledsoe, Caroline. "School Fees and the Marriage Process for Mende Girls in Sierra Leone." In Sanday and Goodenough, 283-309.

Blumberg, Rae Lesser. "Income under Female versus Male Control." In *Gender, Family, and Economy.* Ed. R. L. Blumberg. Newbury Park: Sage, 1991. 97-127.

Bohannan, Paul, and George Dalton. *Markets in Africa.* Evanston: Northwestern University Press, 1962.

Bourdieu, Pierre. *Outline of a Theory of Practice.* Trans. Richard Nice. Cambridge: Cambridge University Press, 1977.

Boyes, John. *King of the Wa-Kikuyu.* 1911; London: Frank Cass, 1968.

Brett, E. A. *Colonialism and Underdevelopment in East Africa.* Nairobi: Heinemann, 1973.

Brockway, Lucile H. *Science and Colonial Expansion: The Role of the British Royal Botanic Gardens.* NY: Academic Press, 1979.

Bromley, Ray. "Introduction. The Urban Informal Sector: Why Is It Worth Discussion?" *World Development* 6, 9/10 (1978): 1033-39.

‗‗‗‗‗‗‗. "Small May Be Beautiful, But It Takes More Than Beauty to Ensure Success." In Bromley, 321-41.

‗‗‗‗‗‗‗. "Working the Streets: Survival Strategy, Necessity, or Unavoidable Evil?" In *Making a Living in the City.* Forthcoming. 161-82.

‗‗‗‗‗‗‗, ed. *Planning for Small Enterprises in Third World Cities.* NY: Pergamon, 1985.

Bromley, Ray, and C. Gerry, eds. *Casual Work and Poverty in Third World Cities.* NY: J. Wiley, 1979.

Brown, L. H. *A National Cash Crops Policy for Kenya.* Parts I-II. Nairobi: Government Printer, 1963.

Brown, Wendy. "Finding the Woman in the State." *Feminist Studies* 18, 1 (Spring, 1992): 7-34.

Browne, Dallas LaSalle. "Kawangware: Urbanization by Absorption Identity and Social Change in Nairobi." University of Illinois Dept. of Anthropology Ph.D. diss., 1983.

Bryceson, Deborah. *Food Insecurity and the Social Division of Labour in Tanzania, 1919-85.* NY: St. Martin's, 1990.

‗‗‗‗‗‗‗. *Liberalizing Tanzania's Food Trade.* London: James Currey, 1993.

Bujra, Janet M. "Ethnicity and Religion: A Case-Study from Pumwani Nairobi." IAS Disc. Paper No. 13 (Oct. 1970).

‗‗‗‗‗‗‗. "Women Entrepreneurs of Early Nairobi." *Canadian Jl. of African Studies* 9, 2 (1979): 220-49.

Bunker, Stephen G. *Peasants against the State.* Urbana: University of Illinois Press, 1987.

Butterfield, Cynthia. "Women and the Modern Wage Sector: A Study of Female Participation in Commercial Banks and Finance Companies in Nairobi." IDS Disc. Paper No.256 (1977).

Cagnolo, Fr. C. *The Akikuyu, Their Customs, Traditions and Folklore.* Nyeri, Kenya: Mission Printing School, 1933.

Caldwell, John C., ed. *The Persistence of High Fertility.* Canberra: Australian National University, 1977.

Caldwell, John C., I. O. Orubiloye, and Pat Caldwell. "Fertility Decline in Africa: A New Type of Transition?" *Population and Development Review* 18, 2 (June 1992): 211-42.

Caplan, Patricia. "Cognatic Descent, Islamic Law and Women's Property on the East African Coast." In Hirschon, 23-43.

‗‗‗‗‗‗‗, ed. *The Cultural Construction of Sexuality.* London: Tavistock, 1987.

Carlebach, Julius. *Juvenile Prostitution in Nairobi.* Kampala: East African Inst. of Social Research Applied Research Unit East Africa Studies No. 16 (1962).

Casley, D.J., and T.J. Marchant. "Smallholder Marketing in Kenya." UNDP/FAO Project Wkg. Document. Nairobi: Government of Kenya, Central Bureau of Statistics, 1979.

Chanler, William Astor. *Through Jungle and Desert: Travels in Eastern Africa.* London: MacMillan and Co., 1896.

Chege, Michael. "A Tale of Two Slums: Electoral Politics in Mathare and Dagoretti." *Review of African Political Economy* 20 (1980): 74-88.

Child, Frank C. "Entrepreneurship, Management and Labor in a Society in Transition." IDS Wkg. Paper No. 128 (1973).

Child, Frank C., and Mary E. Kempe, eds. *Small-Scale Enterprise.* IDS Occas. Paper No. 6 (1973).

Chitere, Preston O. "The Women's Self-Help Movement in Kenya: A Historical Perspective, 1940-80." *Transafrican Jl. of History* 17 (1988): 50-68.

Christian, Barbara. "The Race for Theory." *Feminist Studies* 14, 1 (Spring, 1988): 67-79.

Church of Scotland. *Memorandum Prepared by the Kikuyu Mission Council on Female Circumcision.* KNA, 1931.

Ciancanelli, Penelope. "Exchange, Reproduction, and Sex Subordination among the Kikuyu of East Africa." *Review of Radical Political Economy* 12, 2 (Summer 1980): 25-36.

City Council of Nairobi. *Nairobi City in the Sun.* Nairobi: East African Printers [c. 1963].

Cixous, Helene. "The Laugh of the Medusa." In *New French Feminisms.* Ed. E. Marks and I. de Courtrivon. NY: Schocken, 1981. 245-64.

Clark, Carolyn. "Land and Food, Women and Power in Nineteenth Century Kikuyu." *Africa* 50, 4 (1980): 357-70.

Clark, Gracia. "Money, Sex, and Cooking: Manipulation of the Paid/Unpaid Boundary by Asante Market Women." In *The Social Economy of Consumption.* Ed. H. J. Ruiz and B. S. Orlove. Lanham: University Press of America, 1989.

_____. *Onions Are My Husband: Survival and Accumulation by West African Market Women.* Chicago: University of Chicago Press, 1994.

_____, ed. *Traders versus the State: Anthropological Approaches to Unofficial Economies.* Boulder: Westview, 1988.

Clark, Mari H. "Woman-headed Households and Poverty: Insights from Kenya." *Signs* 10, 2 (1984): 338-54.

Cohen, David William, and E. S. Atieno Odhiambo. *Siaya. The Historical Anthropology of an African Landscape.* London: J. Currey, 1989.

Colburn, Forrest D., ed. *Everyday Forms of Peasant Resistance.* London: M. E. Sharpe, 1989.

Coldham, Simon. "Land Control in Kenya." *Jl. of African Law* 22 (1978): 63-77.

Collier, Paul, and Deepak Lal. *Labour and Poverty in Kenya, 1900-1980.* Oxford: Clarendon, 1986.

Cone, L. Winston, and J. F. Lipscomb, ed. *The History of Kenyan Agriculture.* Nairobi: University Press of Africa, 1972.

Coontz, Stephanie, and Peta Henderson. "Property Forms, Political Power, and Female Labor in the Origins of Class and State Societies." In Coontz and Henderson, 108-55.

Coontz, Stephanie, and Peta Henderson, eds. *Women's Work, Men's Property: The Origins of Gender and Class.* London: Verso, 1986.

Cooper, Frederick. *On the African Waterfront: Urban Disorder and the Transformation of Work in Colonial Mombasa.* New Haven: Yale University Press, 1987.

_____, ed. *Struggle for the City: Migrant Labor, Capital and the State in Urban Africa.* Beverly Hills: Sage, 1983.

Court, David, and Dharam P. Ghai, eds. *Education, Society, and Development: New Perspectives from Kenya.* Nairobi: Oxford University Press, 1974.

Cowen, Michael. "Commodity Production in Kenya's Central Province." In Heyer, Roberts, and Williams, 121-42.

Cowen, Michael, and K. Kinyanjui. "Some Problems of Capital and Class in Kenya." IDS Occas. Paper No.26 (Nov. 1977).

Cowen, Michael, and N. Westcott. "British Imperial Economic Policy during the War." In Killingray and Rathbone, 20-67.

Crosby, Alfred W. *The Columbian Exchange: Biological and Cultural Consequences of 1492.* Westport: Greenwood, 1972.

_____. *Ecological Imperialism: The Biological Expansion of Europe, 900-1900.* Cambridge: Cambridge University Press, 1986.

Cummings, Robert J. "Migration and National Development: The Kenya Example." In *African Migration and National Development.* Ed. B. Lindsay. University Park: Pennsylvania State University Press, 1985. 148-69.

Daily Nation. Nairobi. 1987-1993.

Dalgety's Market Newsletter. Royal Show Edition, 1961. KNA.

Davidson, B. R., and R. J. Yates. "Relationship Between Population and Potential Arable Land in the African Reserves and the European Highlands." *East African Economics Review* 6, 2 (Dec. 1959): 133-38.

Davison, Jean. "Who Owns What? Land Registration and Tensions in Gender Relations of Production in Kenya." In *Agriculture, Women and Land.* Ed. J. Davison. Boulder: Westview, 1988. 157-76.

Davison, Jean and the Women of Mutira. *Voices from Mutira: Lives of Rural Gikuyu Women.* Boulder: Lynne Rienner, 1989.

Dawson, Marc H. "Socioeconomic Change and Disease: Smallpox in Colonial Kenya, 1880-1920." In *The Social Basis of Health and Healing in Africa.* Ed. S. Feierman and J. M. Janzen. Berkeley: University of California Press, 1992. 90-103.

de Beauvoir, Simone. *The Second Sex.* NY: Vintage, 1989.

Delaney, J., M. J. Lupton, and E. Toth. *The Curse.* NY: Dutton, 1976.

Demographic and World Health Surveys. *World Conference Report.* Dec. 1991.

De Soto, Hernando. *The Other Path: The Invisible Revolution in the Third World.* NY: Harper and Row, 1989.

Dickerman, Carol Wilson. "Africans in Nairobi During the Emergency: Social and Economic Changes, 1952-60." University of Wisconsin Dept. of History M.A. thesis, 1985.

Dondo, C. Aleke, et al. *Mobilization of the Informal Sector for Kenya's Development.* Vol. I, *Informal Sector Workshops: An Executive Summary.* Nairobi: Fredrich Ebert Foundation/National Council for Science and Technology, 1986.

Duchen, Claire. *Feminism in France: From May '68 to Mitterand.* London: Routledge and Kegan Paul, 1986.

Dundas, K. R. "Notes on the Origin and History of the Kikuyu and Dorobo Tribes." *Man* 75-76 (1908): 136-39.

Eades, Jeremy, ed. *Migrant Workers and the Social Order.* NY: Tavistock, 1987.

Eames, Elizabeth A. "Why the Women Went to War: Women and Wealth in Ondo Town, Southwestern Nigeria," In Clark, *Traders,* 81-97.

Eisenstein, Zillah. *The Color of Gender: Reimaging Democracy.* Berkeley: University of California Press, 1994.

Elkan, Walter. "Is a Proletariat Emerging in Nairobi?" *Economic Development and Cultural Change* 24 (1976): 695-706.

_____, T. C. I. Ryan, and J. T. Mukui. "The Economics of Shoe Shining in Nairobi." *African Affairs* 81, 323 (1982): 247-56.

Elson, Diane. "How is Structural Adjustment Affecting Women?" *Development* 1 (1989): 67-74.

Emecheta, Buchi. *The Joys of Motherhood.* NY: Braziller, 1969.

Engel, Barbara Alpern. *Between the Fields and the City.* Cambridge: Cambridge University Press, 1994.

Engels, Friedrich. *The Condition of the Working Class in England.* Chicago: Academy, 1984.

_____. *The Origin of the Family, Private Property and the State.* NY: International Publishers, 1972.

Etherton, David. *Mathare Valley: A Case Study of Uncontrolled Settlement in Nairobi.* Nairobi: University of Nairobi Housing Research and Development Unit, 1976.

Faruqee, Rashid. "Fertility and Its Trend in Kenya." *Rural Africana* 14 (Fall 1982): 25-48.

Fatton, Robert, Jr. "Gender, Class and State in Africa." In Parpart and Staudt, 47-66.

Feierman, Steven. *The Shambaa Kingdom.* Madison: University of Wisconsin Press, 1974.

Ferguson Anne E., and Susan L. Sprecher. "Component Breeding: A Strategy for Bean Improvement in Eastern Africa and Other Regions Where Beans Are Grown as Mixtures." Paper Presented at Bean/Cowpea CRSP, Sept. 1989.

_____. "Women and Plant Genetic Diversity: The Case of Beans in the Central Region of Malawi." Paper Presented Bean/Cowpea CRSP, AAA Meeting, Chicago, Nov. 1987.

Ferraro, Gary. "Changing Patterns of Bridewealth Among the Kikuyu of East Africa." In Arens, 101-13.

_____. "Tradition or Transition? Rural and Urban Kinsmen in East Africa." *Urban Anthropology* 2, 2 (1973): 214-31.

Fisher, Jeanne. *The Anatomy of Kikuyu Domesticity and Husbandry.* London: Dept. of Technical Cooperation, [c.1953].

Folbre, Nancy. "Socialism, Feminist and Scientific." In *Beyond Economic Man, Feminist Theory and Economics.* Ed. M. A. Ferber and J. A. Nelson. Chicago: University of Chicago Press, 1993. 94-110.

Freeman, Carla. "Colonialism and the Formation of Gender Hierarchies in Kenya." *Critique of Anthropology* 7, 3 (1987-88): 33-50.

Freeman, Donald B. *A City of Farmers: Informal Urban Agriculture in the Open Spaces of Nairobi, Kenya.* Montreal: McGill/Queen's University Press, 1991.

Furedi, Frank. "The African Crowd in Nairobi: Popular Movements and Elite Politics." In *Third World Urbanization.* Ed. J. Abu-Lughod and R. Hay, Jr. NY: Methuen, 1977. 225-40.

_____. "The Kikuyu Squatter in the Rift Valley: 1918-1929." Paper presented at the Annual Conference of the Historical Association of Kenya, 1972. KNA.

_____. "The Social Composition of the Mau Mau Movement in the White Highlands." *Jl. of Peasant Studies* 1, 4 (July 1974): 486-505.

Gakaara wa Njau. *A Kikuyu Market Literature.* Trans. Patrick R. Bennett. *Ba Shiru* Supp. 1 (1983). Madison: University of Wisconsin Dept. of African Languages and Literature.

Gakuo, Mumbi. "The Kenyan Women and Situation and Strategies for Improvement." *Women's Studies International Forum* 8, 4 (1985): 373-79.

Gepts, Paul. "Biochemical Evidence Bearing on the Domestication of Phaseolus (Fabaceae) Beans." *Economic Botany* 44, 3rd Supplement (1990): 28-38.

_____, ed. *Genetic Resources of Phaseolus Beans.* Dordrecht: Klusser Academic Publishers, 1988.

Gepts, Paul, and F. A. Bliss. "Dissemination Pathways of Common Bean (Phaseolus vulgaris, Fabaceae) Deduced from Phaseolin Electrophoretic Variability II: Europe and Africa." *Economic Botany* 42, 1 (1988): 86-104.

Gepts, Paul, and Daniel Debouck. "Origin, Domestication, and Evolution of the Common Bean (Phaseolus vulgaris L)." In *Common Beans: Research for Crop Improvement.* Ed. A. Van Schoonhoven and O. Voysest. Oxford: CAB International/CIAT, 1991. 7-53.

Gerry, Chris, and Chris Birkbeck. "The Petty Commodity Producer in Third World Cities: Petit-Bourgeois or 'Disguised' Proletarian?" In *The Petty Bourgeoisie.* Ed. F. Bechhofer and B. Elliott. London: Macmillan, 1981. 182-200.

Gladwin, Christina, ed. *Structural Adjustment and African Women Farmers.* Gainesville: University Press of Florida, 1991.

Glazer, Nona Y. "Questioning Eclectic Practice in Curriculum Change: A Marxist Perspective." *Signs* 12, 2 (1987): 293-304.

Glazier, Jack. *Land and the Uses of Tradition among the Mbeere of Kenya.* Lanham: University Press of America, 1985.

Gordon, David. *Decolonization and the State in Kenya.* Boulder: Westview, 1986.

Gramsci, Antonio. *Prison Notebooks.* Trans. J. A. Buttigigi and A. Callari. NY: Columbia University Press, 1992.

Gray, Kenneth R., William Cooley, Jesse Lutabingwa, Bertha Mutai-Kaimenyi, and L. A. Oyugi. *Entrepreneurship in Micro-Enterprises, A Strategic Analysis of Manufacturing Industries in Kenya.* Lanham: University Press of America, 1996.

Greenway, P. J. "Origins of Some East African Food Plants." *East African Agricultural Jl.* 10, 1 (July 1944): 34-39; 2 (Oct. 1944): 115-19; 3 (Jan. 1945): 177-80; 11, 1 (July 1945): 56-63.

Grisley, William. "Observations on the Economics of Bean Seed Issues in Africa." Paper, Nov. 1989.

Gulliver, P. H. *Social Control in an African Society.* Boston: Boston University Press, 1963.

Gutto, S. B. O. "Legal Constraints on Female Participation in the Economy." University of Nairobi LL.B. diss., 1975.

_____. "The Status of Women in Kenya: A Study of Paternalism, Inequality, and Underprivilege." IDS Disc. Paper No. 235 (Apr. 1976).

Guy, Jeff. "Analysing Pre-Capitalist Societies in Southern Africa." *Jl. of Southern African Studies* 14, 1 (Oct. 1987): 18-37.

Guyer, Jane. "The Raw, the Cooked and the Half-Baked: A Note on the Division of Labor by Sex." Boston University African Studies Center Wkg. Paper No. 48 (1981).

_____, ed. *Feeding African Cities.* Bloomington: Indiana University Press, 1987.

Hake, Andrew. *African Metropolis, Nairobi's Self-Help City.* NY: St. Martin's, 1977.

Halleman, Dorothy M., and W. T. W. Morgan. "The City of Nairobi." In Morgan, 98-120.

Hansen, Karen Tranberg. "Dealing with Used Clothing: *Salaula* and the Construction of Identity in Zambia's Third Republic." *Public Culture* 6 (1994): 503-23.

Harcourt, Wendy. "Gender, Culture, and Reproduction: North and South." *Development* 2/3 (1988): 66-71.

Harris, Olivia, and Kate Young. "Conceptualizing Women," *Critique of Anthropology* 3, 9-10 (1977): 101-30.

Harrison, Regina. *Signs, Songs, and Memory in the Andes: Translating Quechua Language and Culture.* Austin: University of Texas Press, 1989.

Haugerud, Angelique. "Food Production and Rural Differentiation in the Kenya Highlands." In *Food and Farm Current Debates and Policies.* Ed. C. Gladwin and K. Truman. Lanham: University Press of America/Society for Economic Anthropology, 1989. 59-83.

Hay, Margaret Jean. "Luo Market Women, 1930-1945: The Limits on Accumulation." Paper presented at Berkshire Women's History Conference, June 1987.

Heinrich, Fritz. *The Marketing of Fruit and Vegetables in Kenya.* Preliminary Report, Nairobi, 1973. KNA.

Hemsted, R.W. (DC Kiambu) *A Short History of the Kikuyu Province, 1911-1927.* 1929. KNA, PC/CP 1/1/2.

Herskovits, Melville J. Preface to Bohannan and Dalton, vii-xvi.

Hesselmark, Olof. "The Marketing of Maize and Beans in Kenya: A Proposal for Improved Effectiveness." IDS Wkg. Paper No. 300 (1977).

Hetherington, Penelope. "Generational Change and Class Formation in Kenya: the Kamore Family." *Australian Jl. of Politics and History* 36, 1 (1990): 51-61.

Heyer, Judith. "Agricultural Development Policy in Kenya from the Colonial Period to 1975." In Heyer, Roberts, and Williams, 90-120.

_____. "The Marketing System." In Heyer, Maitha, and Senga, 313-63.

Heyer, Judith, J.K. Maitha, and W.M. Senga, eds. *Agricultural Development in Kenya.* Nairobi: Oxford University Press, 1976.

Heyer, Judith, Pepe Roberts, and Gavin Williams, eds. *Rural Development in Tropical Africa.* NY: St. Martin's, 1981.

Hidalgo, Rigoberto, Leonard Song, and Paul Gepts. *The Cultivated Species of Phaseolus.* Cali, Colombia: CIAT, 1986.

Hill, Mervyn F. *Cream Country.* Nairobi: Kenya Cooperative Creameries, 1956.

Himbara, David. *Kenyan Capitalists, the State, and Development.* Boulder: Lynne Rienner, 1994.

Hirschon, Rene. "Property, Power, and Gender Relations." Introduction to Hirschon, 1-22.

_____, ed. *Women and Property--Women as Property.* NY: St. Martin's, 1984.

Hobley, C. W. *Kenya: From Chartered Company to Crown Colony.* London: H. F. and G. Witherby, 1929.

Holmquist, Frank. "Class Structure, Peasant Participation, and Rural Self-Help." In Barkan and Okumu, 129-53.

Hoorweg, Jan, and Rudo Niemeyer. "Classification of Foods among the Kikuyu." University of Nairobi/University of Leiden (Netherlands) Bureau of Educational Research, African Studies Center, Nutrition Intervention Research Project Report No.7 (1978).

House, William J. "Nairobi's Informal Sector: An Exploratory Study." In Killick, 357-68.

House-Midamba, Bessie. "Gender, Democratization, and Associational Life in Kenya." *Africa Today* 43, 3 (July-Sept. 1996): 289-305.

Humphrey, N. *The Kikuyu Lands* (Kenya Colony). Nairobi: Government Printer, 1945.

_____. "The Relationship of Population to the Land in South Nyeri." In Humphrey, 1-15.

_____. "Thoughts on the Foundations of Future Prosperity in the Kikuyu Lands." In Humphrey, 17-60.

Huxley, Elspeth. *The Mottled Lizard.* NY: Penguin, 1962.

_____. *Red Strangers.* London: Chatto and Windus, 1955.

Hyden, Goran. *Beyond Ujamaa in Tanzania: Underdevelopment and an Uncaptured Peasantry.* Berkeley: University of California Press, 1980.

Imikai, Ichirou. "The Legal Framework for Small-Scale Enterprise Development with Special Reference to the Licensing System." In Child and Kempe, 88-99.

International Labour Office. *Employment, Income, and Equality: A Strategy for Increasing Productive Employment in Kenya.* Geneva: ILO, 1974.

_____. *Employment, Incomes and Equality. Report of the U.N. Development Programme and ILO.* Geneva: ILO, 1972.

Itote, Waruhiu. *Mau Mau in Action.* Nairobi: Transafrica, 1979.

Jackson, Sir Frederick. *Early Days in East Africa.* 1930; London: Dawson of Pall Mall, 1969.

Jackson, Kennell A., Jr. "An Ethnohistorical Study of the Oral Traditions of the Akamba of Kenya." University of California-Los Angeles Dept. of History Ph.D. diss., 1972.

_____. "The Family Entity and Famine Among the Nineteenth Century Akamba of Kenya: Social Responses to Environmental Stress." *Jl. of Family History* 1, 2 (Winter 1976): 192-216.

Jahava, Walter. "Nyandarua Women Leaders Learn Better Management." *Daily Nation.* 11 Mar. 1988: 20.

Jones, William O. *Marketing Staple Food Crops in Tropical Africa.* Ithaca: Cornell University Press, 1972.

Juma, Calestous. *The Gene Hunters: Biotechnology and the Scramble for Seeds.* Princeton: Princeton University Press, 1989.

Kabira, Wanjiku Mukabi, and Karega wa Mutahi. *Gikuyu Oral Literature.* Nairobi: Heinemann, 1988.

_____. "Storytellers and the Environment." In Khasiani. 67-74.

Kabwegyere, Tarsis. "Determinants of Fertility: A Discussion of Change in the Family among the Akamba of Kenya." In Caldwell, 189-221.

Kahiga, Samuel. *The Girl from Abroad.* Nairobi: Heinemann, 1974.

Kamau, Lucy Jayne. "Semipublic, Private and Hidden Rooms: Symbolic Aspects of Domestic Space in Urban Kenya." *African Urban Studies* N.S. 3 (Winter 1978-79): 105-15.

Kanogo, Tabitha M.J. "Kikuyu Women and the Politics of Protest: Mau Mau." In *Images of Women in Peace and War, Cross-Cultural and Historical Perspectives.* Ed. S. MacDonald, Pat Holden and S. Ardener. Madison: University of Wisconsin Press, 1987. 78-99.

_____. *Squatters and the Roots of Mau Mau.* Nairobi: Heinemann, 1988.

_____. "Women and environment in history." In Khasiani, 7-18.

Kanyeihamba, G.W., and J.P.W.B. McAuslan, eds. *Urban Legal Problems in Eastern Africa.* Uppsala: Scandinavian Inst. of African Studies, 1978.

Kapchan, Deborah A. *Gender on the Market: Moroccan Women and the Revoicing of Tradition.* Philadelphia: University of Pennsylvania Press, 1996.

Kaplan, Lawrence, and Lucille N. Kaplan. "Phaseolus in Archeology." In Gepts, 125-42.

Kaplinsky, Rafael. "Capitalist Accumulation in the Periphery--The Kenyan Case Re-examined." *Review of African Polical Economy* 17 (1980): 83-105.

Katumba, Rebecca. "Kenya." In *The Power to Change, Women in the Third World Redefine Their Environment.* Ed. Women's Feature Service. London: Zed, 1993. 52-65.

Kayongo-Male, Diane. "Urban Squatters in Nairobi and Policies for Improving on Their Condition." In Kanyeihamba and McAuslan, 85-103.

Kayongo-Male, Diane, and Parveen Walji. "The Value of Children in Rural Areas: Parents' Perceptions and Actual Labour Contributions of Children in Selected Areas of Kenya." In Mati and Buigutt, 66-74.

Keller, Edmond J. "Harambee! Educational Policy, Inequality, and the Political Economy of Rural Community Self-Help in Kenya." *Jl. of African Studies* 4 (1977): 86-106.

Kenya (East African) Standard. Nairobi.

Kenya Times. Nairobi. 1987-1988

Kenyatta, Jomo. *Facing Mount Kenya: The Tribal Life of the Gikuyu.* 1938; NY: Vintage, 1965.

_____. *My People of Kikuyu.* Nairobi: Oxford University Press, 1966.

Kershaw, Greet. "The Changing Roles of Men and Women in the Kikuyu Family by Socioeconomic Strata." *Rural Africana* 29 (1975-76): 173-94.

Kershaw, Gretha. "The Land Is the People: A Study of Kikuyu Social Organization in Historical Perspective." University of Chicago Dept. of Anthropology Ph.D. diss., 1972.

_____. *Mau Mau from Below.* Oxford: J. Currey, 1997.

Keyter, C. F. *Maize Control in Southern Rhodesia, 1931-1941: The African Contribution to White Survival.* Salisbury: Central African Historical Association, 1978.

Khasiani, Shanyisa A., ed. *Groundwork. African Women as Environmental Managers.* Nairobi: African Centre for Technology Studies, 1992.

Khasiani, Shanyisa A., and E.I. Njiro, eds. *The Women's Movement in Kenya.* Nairobi: AAWORD, 1993.

Killick, Tony, ed. *Papers on the Kenyan Economy.* London: Heinemann, 1981.

Killingray D., and R. Rathbone, eds. *Africa and the Second World War.* NY: St. Martin's, 1986.

Kimani, S. M. "The Structure of Land Ownership in Nairobi." *Canadian Jl. of African Studies* 6, 3 (1972): 379-402.

King, Kenneth. *The African Artisan, Education and the Informal Sector in Kenya.* London: Heinemann, 1977.

_____. "Petty Production in Nairobi: The Social Context of Skill Acquisition and Occupational Differentiation." In Bromley and Gerry, 217-28.

Kinuthia, Cecilia. "Women Groups in Kenya with Special Reference to Housing and Community Development." In Khasiani and Njiro, 39-58.

Kinyanjui, Alex R. "A Biography of Paramount Chief Kinyanjui wa Gathirimu (1865-1929)." University of Nairobi Dept. of History B.A. diss., 1975.

Kitching, Gavin. *Class and Economic Change in Kenya: The Making of an African Petite Bourgeoisie, 1905-1970.* New Haven: Yale University Press, 1980.

Kjekshus, Helge. *Ecology Control and Economic Development in East African History: The Case of Tanganyika, 1850-1950.* Berkeley: University of California Press, 1977.

Klein, Martin S. "African Trade in Kenya." Report for Ministry of Commerce and Industry. KNA, MCI 6/1385.

Kloppenburg, Jack Ralph, Jr. *First the Seed: The Political Economy of Plant Biotechnology, 1492-2000.* Cambridge: Cambridge University Press, 1988.

Kneerim, Jill. *Village Women Organize: The Mbeere Bus Service.* Seeds, 1980.

Kongstad, Per, and Mette Monsted. *Family, Labour and Trade in Western Kenya.* Uppsala: Scandinavian Inst. of African Studies, 1980.

Kuczynski, R. R. *Demographic Survey of the British Colonial Empire.* Vol. II. London: Geoffrey Cumberledge, 1949.

Kusterer, Ken. "The Imminent Demise of Patriarchy." In Tinker, 239-55.

Lambert, H. E. *Kikuyu Social and Political Institutions.* London: Oxford University Press, 1956.

Lamphear, John. "The Kamba and the Northern Mrima Coast." In *Precolonial African Trade.* Ed. R. Gray and D. Birmingham. London: Oxford University Press, 1970. 75-86.

Lawren, William L. "Masai and Kikuyu: An Historical Analysis of Culture Transmission." *Jl. of African History* 9, 4 (1968): 571-83.

Leacock, Eleanor. *Myths of Male Dominance.* NY: Monthly Review, 1981.

Leakey, C. L. A. "Factors Affecting Increased Production and Marketing of Food Crops in Uganda." *Jl. of Rural Development* 4 (1972): 1-20.

————. "The Improvement of Beans in East Africa." Paper.

————. "Report to H.J.Heinz on Potential Problems for a Supply of Pea Beans from Ethiopia, Kenya, Tanzania and South Africa." 7 Feb. 1974.

Leakey, L. S. B. "The Economics of Kikuyu Tribal Life." *East African Economics Review* 3, 1 (1956): 165-80.

————. *Kenya Contrasts and Problems.* 1937; Cambridge, MA: Schenkman, 1966.

————. "The Kikuyu Problem of the Initiation of Girls." *Jl. of the Royal Anthropological Inst.* 61 (1931): 277-85.

————. *The Southern Kikuyu before 1903.* Vols. I-III. NY: Academic Press, 1977.

Leitner, Kerstin. *Workers, Trade Unions and Peripheral Capitalism in Kenya after Independence.* Frankfurt am Main: Peter Lang, 1977.

Lee-Smith, Diana. "Urban Management in Nairobi: A Case Study of the Matatu Mode of Public Transport." In *African Cities in Crisis.* Ed. R. E. Stren and R. R. White. Boulder: Westview, 1989. 276-304.

Leo, Christopher. *Land and Class in Kenya.* Toronto: University of Toronto Press, 1984.

Leonard, David K. *African Successes: Four Public Managers of Kenyan Rural Development.* Berkeley: University of California Press, 1991.

Lerner, Gerda. *The Creation of Patriarchy.* NY: Oxford University Press, 1986.

————. "Women and Slavery." *Slavery and Abolition* 4, 3 (Dec. 1983): 173-98.

Lesthaeghe, Ron J., ed. *Reproduction and Social Organization in Sub-Saharan Africa.* Berkeley: University of California Press, 1989.

Lesthaeghe, Ron J., and Frank Eelens. "The Components of Sub-Saharan Reproductive Regimes and Their Social and Cultural Determinants: Empirical Evidence." In Lesthaeghe, 60-121.

Levinson, David. *Family Violence in Cross-Cultural Perspective.* London: Sage, 1989.

Levi-Strauss, Claude. *The Raw and the Cooked.* NY: Harper and Row, 1969.

Leys, Colin. "African Capitalists and Development: Theoretical Questions." In *African Capitalists in African Development.* Ed. B.J. Berman and C. Leys. Boulder: Lynne Rienner, 1994. 11-38.

————. "Capital Accumulation, Class Formation, and Dependency: The Significance of the Kenyan Case." *Socialist Register* (1978): 241-66.

————. *Underdevelopment in Kenya: The Political Economy of Neo-Colonialism.* London: Heinemann, 1975.

Leys, Norman. *Kenya.* 1924; London: Frank Cass, 1973.

Likimani, Muthoni. *Passbook Number F. 47927 Women and Mau Mau in Kenya.* London: MacMillan Publishers, 1985.

Lindblom, Gerhard. *The Akamba in British East Africa.* Uppsala: Archive d'Etudes Orientales Vol. 17, 1920.

Livingstone, Ian. *Rural Development, Employment and Incomes in Kenya.* ILO Report for Jobs and Skills Programme for Africa. Addis Ababa: ILO, 1981.

Lofchie, Michael F. *The Policy Factor: Agricultural Performance in Kenya and Tanzania.* Nairobi: Heinemann, 1989.

Lonsdale, John. "The Depression and the Second World War in the Transformation of Kenya." In Killingray and Rathbone. 97-142.

————. "Explanations of the Mau Mau Revolt." In *Resistance and Ideology in Settler Societies.* Ed. T. Lodge. Johannesburg: Ravan Press, 1986. 168-78.

————. "Mau Maus of the Mind: Making Mau Mau and Remaking Kenya." *Jl. of African History* 31 (1990): 393-421.

————. "States and Social Processes in Africa: A Historiographical Survey." *African Studies Review* 24, 2/3 (June-Sept. 1981): 139-225.

Lovett, Margot. "Gender Relations, Class Formation, and the Colonial State in Africa." In Parpart and Staudt, 23-46.

Lugard, F.D. *The Rise of Our East African Empire.* London: Wm. Blackwood, 1893. In *East African Explorers.* Ed. C. Richards and J. Place. Nairobi: Oxford University Press, 1967.

Maas, Maria. *Women's Groups in Kiambu, Kenya.* Leiden, The Netherlands: African Studies Center Research Report No. 26 (1986).

Maathai, Wangari. *The Green Belt Movement.* Nairobi: Environment Liaison Centre International, 1988.

MacCormack, Carol and Marilyn Strathern, eds. *Nature, Culture and Gender.* Cambridge: Cambridge University Press, 1980.

MacDonald, J. R. L. *Soldiering and Surveying in British East Africa, 1891-1894.* London: Edward Arnold, 1897.

Macharia, Kinuthia. "Integrating Youth in the Informal Sector: Lessons from Nairobi and Harare." In *Urban Management and Urban Violence in Africa.* Ed. I. O. Albert, J. Adisa, T. Agbola, and G. Herault. Ibadan: IFRA, 1994. 161-69.

————. "Slum Clearance and the Informal Economy in Nairobi." *Jl. of Modern African Studies* 30, 2 (1992): 221-36.

Mackenzie, Fiona. "Gender and Land Rights in Murang'a District, Kenya." *Jl. of Peasant Studies* 17, 4 (July 1990): 609-43.

_____. "Local Initiatives and National Policy: Gender and Agricultural Change in Murang'a District, Kenya." *Canadian Jl. of African Studies* 20, 3 (1986): 377-401.

_____. "Without a Woman There Is No Land: Marriage and Land Rights in Smallholder Agriculture, Kenya." *Resources for Feminist Research* 19, 3-4 (1990): 68-74.

Mackinder, H. J. *The First Ascent of Mount Kenya.* Ed. K. M. Barbour. Athens: Ohio University Press, 1991.

Maloba, Wunyabari. *Mau Mau and Kenya.* Bloomington: Indiana University Press, 1993.

Manasseh, Jane Mwangi. "Problems of Planning and Management within the Nairobi City Council." University of Nairobi Dept. of Urban Planning M.A. thesis, 1975.

Manley, Michael. *Marketing in Kenya.* U.S. Dept. of Commerce, Overseas Business Report (1977).

Maritim, L. H. K. "Analysis of Produce Flows to Wakulima Wholesale Market, Nairobi." University of Nairobi Dept. of Agricultural Economics, Agriculture Economics Studies No. 3 (1977).

Market Research East Africa, Ltd. *African Income in Nairobi.* 1959.

Marris, Peter. "The Social Barriers to African Entrepreneurship." IDS Disc. Paper No. 61 (1968).

Marris, Peter, and Anthony Somerset. *African Businessmen: A Study of Entrepreneurship and Development in Kenya.* London: Routledge and Kegan Paul, 1971.

Martin, Walter T. "Family Planning Attitudes and Knowledge: A Study of African Families in Nairobi." 1970. Paper in Africana Collection, University of Nairobi Library.

Massell, Gregory. *The Surrogate Proletariat.* Princeton: Princeton University Press, 1974.

Matheson, J. K., and E. W. Bovill, eds. *East African Agriculture.* London: Oxford University Press, 1950.

Mathu, George W. "Gikuyu Marriage: Beliefs and Practices." IDS Disc. Paper No. 17 (1971).

Mati, J. K. G. and K. A. Buigutt, eds. *Population Growth and Its Relevance to Socio-Economic Development: Proceedings of the First Annual Symposium of the Kenya National Academy for Advancement of Arts and Sciences.* Nairobi, 1980.

Maxon, R. M. *John Ainsworth and the Making of Kenya.* Lanham: University Press of America, 1980.

Mazumdar, Vina. "Education and Rural Women: Toward an Alternative Perspective." In Rao, 13-27.

Mbilinyi, Marjorie. "'City' and 'Countryside' in Colonial Tanganyika," *Economic and Political Weekly* 20, 43 (26 Oct. 1985): WS-88-WS-96.

_____. "'This is an Unforgettable Business': Colonial State Intervention in Urban Tanzania." In Parpart and Staudt, 111-29.

Mbithi, Philip M., and Fred E. Chege. "Linkage between Agriculture and Rural Small-Scale Enterprises." In Child and Kempe, 33-50.

McCormick, Dorothy. "Small Manufacturing Enterprise in Nairobi: Golden Opportunity or Dead End?" Johns Hopkins University Dept. of Economics Ph.D. diss. 1988.

_____. *Manufacturing in Miniature: Small Scale Production and Development.* Baltimore: Johns Hopkins University Press, 1992.

McGee, T. G. "Mass Markets: Little Markets. Some Preliminary Thoughts on the Growth of Consumption and Its Relationship to Urbanization: A Case Study of Malaysia." In Plattner, 205-33.

McVicar, K. G. "Twilight of an East African Slum: Pumwani and the Evolution of African Settlement in Nairobi." University of California-Los Angeles Dept. of Geography Ph.D. diss., 1969.

Memon, P. A. "The Spatial Dynamics of Trade and Urban Development in Kenya During the Early Colonial Period up to 1915." IDS Wkg. Paper No. 78 (1973).

Michigan State University Bean/Cowpea Collaborative Research Program. *Annual Report* (1983); *Research Highlights* I, 4 (1984): 1.

Middleton, John, and G. Kershaw. "The Central Tribes of the North-eastern Bantu." In *Ethnographic Survey of Africa: East Central Africa.* Ed. D. Forde. London: International African Inst., 1965. 11-67.

Mies, Maria. *The Lacemakers of Narsapur.* London: Zed, 1986.

Miracle, Marvin P. "An Economic Appraisal of Kenya's Maize Control." *East African Economics Review* 6, 2 (1959): 117-25.

————. "Economic Change Among the Kikuyu, 1895 to 1905." IDS Wkg. Paper No. 158 (1974).

————. *Maize in Tropical Africa.* Madison: University of Wisconsin Press, 1966.

————. "Myths About the Behavior of Kikuyu Labourers in the Early Colonial Period." IDS Wkg. Paper No. 157 (1974).

Mitullah, Winnie V. "Hawking as a Survival Strategy for the Urban Poor: The Case of Nairobi." Report submitted to the Ford Foundation-Nairobi, May 1990.

————. "Hawking as a Survival Strategy for the Urban Poor in Nairobi: The Case of Women." *Environment and Urbanization* 3, 2 (Oct. 1991): 13-22

Moghadam, Valentine M. "Introduction: Women and Identity Politics in Theoretical and Comparative Perspective." In *Identity Politics and Women.* Ed. V. M. Moghadam. Boulder: Westview, 1994. 3-26.

Mohanty, Chandra. "Under Western Eyes: Feminist Scholarship and Colonial Discourses." *Feminist Review* 30 (Autumn 1986): 61-88.

Molyneux, Maxine. "Mobilization without Emancipation? Women's Interests, the State, and Revolution in Nicaragua." *Feminist Studies* 11, 2 (1985): 227-54.

Momsen, Janet Henshall, and Janet G. Townsend, eds. *Geography of Gender in the Third World.* London: Hutchinson/SUNY, 1987.

Monsted, Mette. "The Changing Division of Labour within Rural Families in Kenya." In Caldwell, 259-312.

————, Mette. "Women's Groups in Rural Kenya and Their Role in Development." Center for Development Research Paper A.78.2, 1978.

Moock, Joyce Lewinger, ed. *Understanding Africa's Rural Households and Farming Systems.* Boulder: Westview, 1986.

Moore, Henrietta L. *Space, Text and Gender.* Cambridge: Cambridge University Press, 1986.

Moore, Henrietta L., and Megan Vaughan. *Cutting Down Trees: Gender, Nutrition, and Agricultural Change in the Northern Province of Zambia, 1890-1990.* London: James Currey, 1994.

Morgan, W. T. W. "Kikuyu and Kamba: The Tribal Background." In Morgan, 57-66.

————, ed. *Nairobi: City and Region.* Nairobi: Oxford University Press, 1967.

Morrison, Toni. *Sula.* NY: Knopf, 1977.

Moser, Caroline O. "Informal Sector or Petty Commodity Production: Dualism or Dependence in Urban Development." *World Development* 6, 9-10 (1978): 1041-64.

————. *The Settler Economies.* Cambridge: Cambridge University Press, 1983.

Mugo, Micere. "The Role of Woman in the Struggle for Freedom." In Pala, Awori, and Krystal, 210-19.

Mukaru-Ng'ang'a, D. "A Political History of Murang'a District, 1900-1970. A Study of Society and Politics." University of Nairobi Dept. of History M.A. thesis, 1978.

Mukui, J. T. "Anatomy of the Urban Informal Sector: A Study of Food Kiosks and Shoeblacks." In Westley, 119-45.

————. "The Impact of Price Controls on Inflation and the Distribution of Real Income in Kenya." In Mukui, 48-78.

————, ed. *Price and Marketing Controls in Kenya.* IDS Occas. Paper No. 32 (1979).

Mungai, Evelyn, and Joy Awori. *Kenya Women Reflections.* Nairobi: Lear, 1983.

Munro, J. Forbes. *Colonial Rule and the Kamba: Social Change in the Kenya Highlands, 1889-1939.* Oxford: Clarendon, 1975.

Muriuki, Godfrey. *The History of the Kikuyu, 1500-1900.* Nairobi: Oxford University Press, 1974.

Murray, Jocelyn Margaret. "The Kikuyu Female Circumcision Controversy, with Special Reference to the C.M.S.'s Sphere of Influence.'" University of California-Los Angeles Dept. of History Ph.D. diss., 1974.

Musyoki, Agnes Koki. "The Spatial Structure of Internal Trade in Staple Foodstuffs in Machakos District, Kenya." Howard University Dept. of African Studies Ph.D. diss., 1986.

Muwonge, Joe Wamala. "Urban Policy and Patterns of Low-Income Settlement in Nairobi, Kenya." *Population and Development Review* 6 (1980): 595-613.

Mwagiru, Wanjiku and Riria Ouko. "Women and Development." In *Kenya, an Official Handbook.* Nairobi: Ministry of Information and Broadcasting, 1988. 246-59.

Mwangi, Rose. *Kikuyu Folktales.* Nairobi: Kenya Literature Bureau, 1982.

Ndegwa, P., L. P. Mureithi, and R. H. Green, eds. *Development Options for Africa in the 1980s and Beyond.* Nairobi: Oxford University Press/Society for International Development, 1985.

Ndegwa, Stephen N. *The Two Faces of Civil Society.* West Hartford, CT: Kumarian Press, 1996.

Ndeti, K. *Elements of Akamba Life.* Nairobi: East African Publishing House, 1972.

Nelson, Nici. "Female Centered Families: Changing Patterns of Marriage and Family Among Buzaa Brewers of Mathare Valley." *African Urban Studies* N.S. 3 (Winter 1978-79): 85-103.

————. "How Women and Men Get By: The Sexual Division of Labour in the Informal Sector of a Nairobi Squatter Settlement." In Bromley and Gerry, 283-302.

————. "'Selling her Kiosk': Kikuyu Notions of Sexuality and Sex for Sale in Mathare Valley, Kenya." In Caplan, 217-39.

————. " Women Must Help Each Other': The Operation of Personal Networks Among Buzaa Brewers in Mathare Valley, Kenya." In *Women United, Women Divided.* Ed. P. Caplan and J. Bujra. Bloomington: Indiana University Press, 1979. 77-98.

Ng'ethe, Njuguna, and James G. Wahome. "The Rural Informal Sector in Kenya: Report of a Survey in Nyeri, Uasin Gishu, and Siaya Districts." IDS Consultancy Report No. 16 (1987).

Ngugi, James. *The River Between.* London: Heinemann, 1965.

Ngugi wa Thiong'o. *Devil on the Cross.* London: Heinemann, 1982.

————. *Moving the Centre: The Struggle for Cultural Freedoms.* Nairobi: EAEP, 1993.

Ngumo, Dunstan. "Trade during the Pre-Colonial Time in Nyeri District." University of Nairobi Dept. of History B.A. diss., 1972.

Ngurukie, Pat Wambui. *I Will Be Your Substitute.* Nairobi: Kenya Literature Bureau, 1984.

Nimpuno-Parente, Paula. "The Struggle for Shelter: Women in a Site and Service Project in Nairobi, Kenya." In *Women, Human Settlements, and Housing.* Ed. C. O. Moser and L. Peake. London: Tavistock, 1987. 70-87.

Njau, Rebecca, and Gideon Mulaki. *Kenya Women Heroes and Their Mystical Power.* Nairobi: Rich Publications, 1984.

Njiro, Esther I. "Labour Force Participation and the Women's Movement." In Khasiani and Njiro, 59-76.

Njoroge, Wambui. "Oh, What Milestones These?" In *Whispering Land: An Anthology of Stories by African Women.* Ed. Karen Himmelstrand. Stockholm: SIDA, 1985.

Njugunah, S. K., A. M. M. Ndegwa, H. A. van Rheenen, and D. M. Mukunya. "Bean Production in Kenya." Ottawa: International Development Research Center Publication, [c. 1976].

Njururi, Ngumbi. *Tales from Mount Kenya.* Nairobi: Transafrica, 1975.

Noormohamed, Sidik Osman. "Development Strategy for the Informal Sector: The Kenyan Experience." Paper presented at the Society for International Development. Mar. 1983. Also in Ndegwa, Mureithi, and Green, 186-93.

Nzomo, Maria. "The Impact of the Women's Decade on Policies, Programs, and Empowerment of Women in Kenya." *Issue* 17, 2 (1989): 9-17.

Nzomo, Maria, and Kathleen Staudt. "Man-Made Political Machinery in Kenya: Political Space for Women." In *Women and Politics Worldwide.* Ed. Naima Choudhury and Barbara Nelson. New Haven: Yale University Press, 1994.

Obudho, R. A. *Nairobi, Kenya: A Bibliographic Survey.* Monticello: Vance Bibliographies Public Admin. Series P-1398, 1982.

_____. *Urbanization in Kenya.* Lanham: University Press of America, 1983.

Ogilvie, G. C. W. *The Housing of Africans in the Urban Areas of Kenya.* Nairobi: Kenya Information Office, 1946. KNA.

Okoth-Ogendo, H. W. "Data Collection on the Urban Informal Sector." In Westley, 79-84.

Olenja, C. K. "Patterns and Trends of Migration in Nairobi up to 1978." IAS Occas. Paper No. 141 (June 1980).

Oloo, Celina, and Virginia Cone. *Kenya Women Look Ahead.* Nairobi: East African Literature Bureau, 1965.

Ominde, S. H. "Population Distribution and Urbanization." In Ominde, *Population,* 54-67.

_____, ed. *Population and Development in Kenya.* Nairobi: Heinemann, 1984.

Onstad, Eric. "Age Mates: Petty Traders and Wage Laborers in Nairobi, 1899-1960." Seminar paper, University of Nairobi Dept. of History, 1988.

_____. "Street Life: A History of Nairobi's Petty Traders and their Organizations, 1899-1975." University of Nairobi Dept. of History M.A. thesis, 1990.

Opinya, Nicholas O. "Population Pressure on Urban Housing: The Case of Nairobi, Kenya." University of Nairobi Dept. of Population Studies M.A. thesis, 1982.

Orr, J. B. and J. L. Gilks. *The Physique and Health of Two African Tribes.* London: British Medical Research Council, 1931.

Ortner, Sherry B. "Is Female to Male as Nature Is to Culture?" In *Women, Culture and Society.* Ed. M. Z. Rosaldo and L. Lamphere. Stanford: Stanford University Press, 1974. 67-87.

_____. "The Virgin and the State." In *Gender in Cross- Cultural Perspective,* ed. C. B. Brettell and C. F. Sargent. Englewood Cliffs, NJ: Prentice-Hall, 1993. 257-68.

Pala Okeyo, Achola. "Women in the Household Economy: Managing Multiple Roles." *Studies in Family Planning* 10, 11-12 (Nov.-Dec. 1979): 337-43.

Pala Okeyo, Achola, Thelma Awori, and Abigail Krystal, eds. *The Participation of Women in Kenya Society.* Nairobi: Kenya Literature Bureau, 1978.

Parker, Joan, and C. Aleke Dondo. "Kenya: Kibera's Small Enterprise Sector Baseline Survey Report." GEMINI Wkg. Paper No. 17 (April 1991).

Parker, Mary. "Political and Social Aspects of the Development of Municipal Government in Kenya, with Special Reference to Nairobi." Great Britain Colonial Office. N.d. [c.1949].

Parpart, Jane L., and Kathleen A. Staudt, eds. *Women and the State in Africa.* Boulder: Lynne Rienner, 1989.

Pedersen, Susan. "National Bodies, Unspeakable Acts: The Sexual Politics of Colonial Policy-making." *Jl. of Modern History* 63 (Dec. 1991): 647-80.

Perham, Margery. *East African Journey: Kenya and Tanganyika, 1929-30.* London: Faber and Faber, 1976.

Philip, C. R. "Nutrition in Kenya: Notes on the State of Nutrition of African Children." *East African Medical Jl.* 20 (1943): 227-34.

Porter, Philip W. *Food and Development in the Semi-Arid Zone of East Africa.* Syracuse University Maxwell School of Citizenship and Public Affairs Foreign and Comparative Studies/African Series 32 (1979).

Presley, Cora Ann. *Kikuyu Women, the Mau Mau Rebellion, and Social Change in Kenya.* Boulder: Westview, 1992.

_____. "The Transformation of Kikuyu Women and Their Nationalism." Stanford University Dept. of History Ph.D. diss., 1986.

_____. "Women, the Media and Mau Mau: Putting the 'Spin' on Women Rebels." Paper presented African Studies Association conference, Boston, 1993.

Procter, R. A. W. "The Kikuyu Market and Kikuyu Diet." *Kenya Medical Jl.* 3 (1926): 15-22.

Radford, William J. "Report on Bubonic Plague in Nairobi, April-May 1902." Report for Ministry of Health. KNA, MOH 1/6019.

Ramphele, Mamphela. "Women and Rural Development: The Debate About Appropriate Strategies." *SAGE, A Scholarly Jl. on Black Women* 7, 1 (Summer 1990): 9-12.

Rempel, Henry. *Rural-Urban Labor Migration and Urban Unemployment in Kenya.* Laxenburg, Austria: International Inst. for Applied Systems Analysis, 1981.

Robertson, Claire C. "Black, White, and Red All Over: Beans, Women and Agriculture Imperialism in Twentieth Century Kenya." *Agricultural History* 71, 3 (1997).

_____. "The Death of Makola and Other Tragedies". *Canadian Jl. of African Studies* 17, 3 (1983): 469-95.

_____. "Gender and Trade Relations in Central Kenya in the Late Nineteenth Century." *International Jl. of African Historical Studies.* Forthcoming.

_____. "Grassroots in Kenya: Women, Genital Mutilation and Collective Action, 1920-1990." *Signs* 21, 3 (Spring 1996): 615-42.

_____. *Sharing the Same Bowl.* Ann Arbor: University of Michigan Press, 1990.

_____. "Trade, Gender, and Poverty in the Nairobi Area." In *EnGendering Wealth and Well-Being.* Ed. R. L. Blumberg and C. A. Rakowski. Boulder: Westview, 1995. 65-87.

_____. "Traders and Urban Struggle: Ideology and the Creation of a Militant Female Underclass." *Jl. of Women's History* 4, 3 (Winter 1993): 9-42.

_____. "Transitions in Kenyan Patriarchy: Attempts to Control Women Traders in the Nairobi Area, 1920 to 1963." In *Courtyards, Markets, City Streets: Urban Women in Africa*. Ed. K. Sheldon. Boulder: Westview 1996.

Robertson, Claire C., and Iris Berger, eds. *Women and Class in Africa*. NY: Holmes and Meier, 1986.

Robertson, Claire C., and Jeanne Fisher. "Contested Terrain: The Political Economy of Markets in the Nairobi Area, 1880-1960." Forthcoming.

Robertson, Claire C., and Martin A. Klein, eds. *Women and Slavery in Africa*. Madison: University of Wisconsin Press, 1983.

Rogers, Barbara. *The Domestication of Women*. NY: St. Martin's, 1979.

Rogers, Peter. "The British and the Kikuyu 1890-1905: A Reassessment." *Jl. of African History* 20, 2 (1979): 255-69.

Rosberg, Carl, and John Nottingham. *The Myth of Mau Mau*. NY: Praeger, 1966.

Roscoe, John. *Twenty-Five Years in East Africa*. 1921; NY: Negro University Press, 1969.

Ross, Marc H. *Grass Roots in an African City: Political Behavior in Nairobi*. Cambridge: MIT Press, 1975.

Ross, Marc H., and Veena Thadani. "Participation, Sex and Social Class." *Jl. of Comparative Politics* 12 (1979-80): 323-34.

Ross, W. McGregor. *Kenya from Within*. 1927; London: Frank Cass, 1968.

Routledge, W. S., and K. P. *With a Prehistoric People: The Akikuyu of British East Africa*. London: Edward Arnold, 1910.

Ruheni, Mwangi. *The Minister's Daughter*. Nairobi: Heinemann, 1975.

Rutten, M. M. E. M. *Selling Wealth to Buy Poverty*. Saarbrucken: Verlag Breitenbach, 1992.

Ryan, T. C. I. "Illegal Activities in Frustration of Controls: Theoretical Considerations." In Mukui, 21-36.

Sacks, Karen. *Sisters and Wives*. Westport, CT: Greenwood, 1979.

Sanday, P. R., and R. G. Goodenough, eds. *Beyond the Second Sex: New Directions in the Anthropology of Gender*. Philadelphia: University of Pennsylvania Press, 1990.

Sandgren, David P. "The Kikuyu, Christianity and the African Inland Mission." University of Wisconsin Dept. of History Ph.D. diss., 1976.

_____. "Twentieth Century Religious and Political Divisions among the Kikuyu of Kenya." *African Studies Review* 25, 2-3 (June-Sept.): 195-207.

Sandstrom, Alan R. *Corn Is in Our Blood. Culture and Ethnic Identity in a Contemporary Aztec Indian Village*. Norman: University of Oklahoma Press, 1991.

Schatzberg, Michael G. *The Dialectics of Oppression in Zaire*. Bloomington: Indiana University Press, 1988.

Schluter, Michael. "Constraints on Kenya's Food and Beverage Exports." IDS/International Food Policy Research Inst. Occas. Paper No. 43 (1984).

Schmidt, Elizabeth. *Peasant Traders and Wives: Shona Women in the History of Zimbabwe 1870-1939*. Portsmouth, NH: Heinemann, 1992.

Schmidt, G., and E. S. Mbugua. "Aspects of Marketing Effectiveness for Selected Food Crops in Kenya: Proposals for Further Research." IDS Wkg. Paper No. 287 (1976).

Schmidt, Guenter. "Effectiveness of Maize Marketing Controls in Kenya." In Mukui, 158-80.

Schonherr, Siegfried, and Erastus S. Mbugua. "Bean Production in Kenya's Central and Eastern Provinces." IDS Occas. Paper No. 23 (1976).

Scott, Catherine V. *Gender and Development: Rethinking Modernization and Development Theory.* Boulder: Lynne Rienner, 1995.

Scott, James C. "Everyday Forms of Resistance." In Colburn, 3-33.

Scott, Joan W. "Gender: A Useful Category of Historical Analysis." In *Women's Studies International.* Ed. Aruna Rao. NY: Feminist Press, 1991. 13-37.

Sen, Gita, and Caren Grown. *Development, Crises and Alternative Visions: Third World Women's Perspectives.* Norway: Development Alternatives with Women for a New Era (DAWN), 1985.

Shaw, Carolyn Martin. *Colonial Inscriptions: Race, Sex and Class in Kenya.* Minneapolis: University of Minnesota Press, 1995.

Shiva, Vandana. "Development: The New Colonialism." *Development* 1 (1989): 84-87.

————. *Staying Alive.* London: Zed, 1989.

Silberfein, Marilyn. *Rural Change in Machakos, Kenya.* Lanham: University Press of America, 1989.

Silberschmidt, Margrethe. "Have Men Become the Weaker Sex? Changing Life Situations in Kisii District, Kenya." *Jl. of Modern African Studies* 30, 2 (1992): 237-53.

Sluter, Greet. "Confidential Report on Migrant Labour and Connected Matters in Four Villages in the Kiambu Reserve of Kenya" [c.1958]. KNA.

"Small Towns' Development." *Housing and Urban Development Digest* 5, Special Issue (April 1987). Nairobi: USAID Regional Housing and Urban Development Office for East and Southern Africa.

Smart, James. *A Jubilee History of Nairobi 1900-1950* [c. 1951]. KNA.

Smart, Josephine. "How to Survive in Illegal Street Hawking in Hong Kong." In Clark, *Traders*, 99-138.

Smith, L. D. "An Overview of Agricultural Development Policy." In Heyer, Maitha, and Senga, 111-85.

Smith, M. Estellie, ed. *Perspectives on the Informal Economy.* Lanham: University Press of America/Society for Economic Anthropology, 1990.

Sorenson, Anne Marie. "Consequences and Potentials of Contract Farming for Women: The Case of Smallholder Tea Production among the Kipsigis in Kenya." University of Nairobi Dept. of Sociology Seminar Paper No. 58 (Oct. 1988).

Sorrenson, M. P. K. *Origins of European Settlement in Kenya.* Nairobi: Oxford University Press, 1968.

Spencer, John. *The Kenya African Union.* London: KPI Ltd., 1985.

Stamp, Patricia. "Burying Otieno: The Politics of Gender and Ethnicity in Kenya." *Signs* 16, 4 (Summer 1991): 808-45.

————. "Kikuyu Women's Self-Help Groups: Toward an Understanding of the Relationship between Sex-Gender Systems and Modes of Production in Africa." In Robertson and Berger, 27-46.

————. "Mothers of Invention: Women's Agency in the Kenyan State." In *Provoking Agents: Gender and Theory in Practice.* Ed. J. K. Gardiner. Urbana: University of Illinois Press, 1995. 69-92.

Stichter, Sharon. *Migrant Labour in Kenya: Capitalism and African Response, 1895-1975.* London: Longman, 1982.

————. "Women and the Family: The Impact of Capitalist Development in Kenya." In *The Political Economy of Kenya.* Ed. M. G. Schatzberg. NY: Praeger, 1987. 137-60.

————. "Women and the Labor Force in Kenya, 1895-1964." IDS Disc. Paper No. 258 (1977).

Strayer, Robert W. *The Making of Mission Communities in East Africa, Anglicans and Africans in Colonial Kenya, 1875-1935*. London: Heinemann, 1978.

Stren, Richard E. "Urban Policy." In Barkan and Okumu, 179-208.

Stren, Richard E., Mohamed Halfani, and Joyce Malombe. "Coping with Urbanization and Urban Policy." In *Beyond Capitalism vs. Socialism in Kenya and Tanzania*. Ed. J. D. Barkan. Boulder: Lynne Rienner, 1994. 175-200.

Suttie, J. M. "A Review of Crop Introduction in Kenya and a Check List of Crops." *East African Agricultural and Forestry Jl.* 35, 4 (1970): 372-85.

Swainson, Nicola. *The Development of Corporate Capitalism in Kenya, 1918-1977*. Berkeley: University of California Press, 1980.

Swynnerton, R. J. M. *A Plan to Intensify the Development of African Agriculture in Kenya*. Kenya Colony and Protectorate, Dept. of Agriculture. Nairobi: Government Printer, 1954.

Tate, H. R. "The Native Law of the Southern Gikuyu of British East Africa." *Jl. of African Society* 9 (1910): 233-54; 10 (1911): 285-97.

Taylor, D. R. F. "Changing Food Habits in Kikuyuland." *Canadian Jl. of African Studies* 4, 3 (1970): 333-49.

Thadani, Veena. "The Forgotten Factor in Social Change: The Case of Women in Nairobi, Kenya." Bryn Mawr College Dept. of Political Science Ph.D. diss., 1976.

_____. "Social Relations and Geographic Mobility: Male and Female Migration in Kenya." Center for Policy Studies, Wkg. Paper No. 85 (1982).

Thomas, Barbara P. *Politics, Participation, and Poverty: Development Through Self-Help in Kenya*. Boulder: Westview, 1985.

Thomas-Slayter, Barbara, and Dianne Rocheleau. *Gender, Environment, and Development in Kenya*. Boulder, CO: Lynne Rienner, 1995.

Thomson, Joseph. *Through Masai Land*. London: Sampson, Low, Marston, Searle & Remington, 1887.

Throup, David W. *Economic and Social Origins of Mau Mau*. Nairobi: Heinemann, 1988.

Thuku, Harry, with Kenneth King. *Harry Thuku: An Autobiography*. Nairobi: Oxford University Press, 1970.

Tignor, Robert L. "Colonial Chiefs in Chiefless Societies." *Jl. of Modern African Studies* 9, 3 (1971): 339-59.

_____. *The Colonial Transformation of Kenya: The Kamba, Kikuyu and Masai from 1900 to 1939*. Princeton: Princeton University Press, 1976.

Tinker, Irene, ed. *Persistent Inequalities: Women and World Development*. NY: Oxford University Press, 1990.

Tiwari, R. C. "Some Aspects of the Social Geography of Nairobi, Kenya." *African Urban Notes* 7, 1 (Winter 1972): 36-61.

Topouzi, Daphne. "Kenya Women Fight Deforestation." *Africa Recovery* 4, 3-4 (Oct.-Dec. 1990): 44.

Trench, Charles Chevenix. *Men Who Ruled Kenya*. London: Radcliffe, 1993.

Trenchard, Esther. "Rural Women's Work in Sub-Saharan Africa and the Implications for Nutrition." In Momsen and Townsend, 154-72.

Truth, Sojourner. "Ain't I a Woman?" In *Feminism The Essential Historical Writings*. Ed. M. Schneir. 93-95.

van Rheenen, H. A. "Diversity of Food Beans in Kenya." *Economic Botany* 33, 4 (1979): 448-54.

Van Zwanenberg, R. M. A. *Colonial Capitalism and Labour in Kenya, 1919-1939.* Nairobi: East African Literature Bureau, 1975.

_____. "History and Theory of Urban Poverty in Nairobi: The Problem of Slum Development." IDS Disc. Paper No. 139 (1975). *Jl. of Eastern African Research and Development* 2 (1972): 167-203.

Van Zwanenberg, R. M. A., and Anne King. *An Economic History of Kenya and Uganda, 1800-1970.* London: MacMillan, 1975.

Voss, Joachim. "Farmer Management of Varietal Bean Mixtures in Central Africa: Implications for a Technology Development Strategy." Paper presented to Farmers and Food Systems Conference, Lima, Peru. Sept. 1988.

Waciuma, Charity. *Daughter of Mumbi.* Nairobi: East African Publishing House, 1969.

_____. *The Golden Feather.* Nairobi: East Africa Publishing House, 1966.

_____. *Mweru, the Ostrich Girl.* Lagos: African Universities Press, 1966.

Wainaina, J. N. "Divorce and Its Impact on Society in Kenya." University of Nairobi LL.B. diss., 1980.

Wakefield, T. "Routes of Native Caravans from the Coast to the Interior of Eastern Africa." *Jl. of Royal Geographical Society* 40 (1870): 303-28.

Wamalwa, Betty. "Violence against Wives and the Law in Kenya." Paper presented at the Women, Law, and Development Seminar, Mombasa, Nov. 1987.

Wambeu, D. N. "Kikuyu Customary Marriage with Particular Reference to Elopement." University of Nairobi LL.B. diss., 1979.

"Wangu wa Makeri: Portrait of a Great African Queen." n.d. KNA.

Waruiru, Christopher. "The Female Initiation Controversy at C.S.M. *Tumutumu*, 1912-1937." University of Nairobi Dept. of History B.A. diss., 1971.

Weekly Review. Nairobi. 1987-1994.

Weiner, Annette. "Stability in Banana Leaves: Colonization and Women in Kiriwina, Trobriand Islands." In *Women and Colonization.* Ed. Mona Etienne and Eleanor Leacock. NY: Praeger, 1980. 270-93.

Weisner, Thomas. "Kariobangi: The Case History of a Squatter Resettlement Scheme in Kenya." In Arens, 77-99.

_____. "The Structure of Sociability: Urban Migration and Urban-Rural Ties in Kenya." *Urban Anthropology* 5, 2 (1976): 199-223.

Weisner, Thomas, and Susan Abbott. "Women, Modernity and Stress: Three Contrasting Contexts for Change in East Africa." *Jl. of Anthropological Research* 33 (1977): 421-51.

Welbourn, F. B. *East African Rebels: A Study of Some Independent Churches.* London: SCM, 1961.

Werlin, Herbert H. *Governing an African City, A Study of Nairobi.* NY: Africana, 1974.

_____. "The Hawkers of Nairobi: The Politics of the Informal Sector." In Obudho, *Urbanization and Development Planning*, 194-214.

Westley, Sidney B., ed. *The Informal Sector in Kenya. Papers Presented at a Workshop at IDS, Nov., 1976.* Nairobi: IDS, 1977.

White, L., W. Thornton, L. Silberman, and P. R. Anderson. *Nairobi: Master Plan for a Colonial Capital.* London: Government Stationers, 1948.

White, Luise. "Bodily Fluids and Usufruct: Controlling Property in Nairobi, 1917-1939." *Canadian Jl. of African Studies* 24, 3 (1990): 418-39.

_____. *The Comforts of Home: Prostitution in Colonial Nairobi.* Chicago: University of Chicago Press, 1990.

_____. "Separating the Men from the Boys: Colonial Constructions of Gender, Sexuality, and Terrorism in Central Kenya, 1939-1959." Paper prepared for Wenner-Gren Foundation for Anthropological Research International Symposium, "Tensions of Empire: Colonial Control and Visions of Rule," Nov. 1988. *International Jl. of African Historical Studies* 23, 1 (1990): 1-25.

_____. "Vice and Vagrants: Prostitution, Housing, and Casual Labor in Nairobi in the mid-1930s." In *Labour, Law, and Crime: Historical Perspectives.* Ed. D. Hay. London: Tavistock, 1987. 202-27.

Wilson, Elizabeth. *The Sphinx in the City: Urban Life, the Control of Disorder, and Women.* Berkeley: University of California Press, 1991.

Winter, K. J. *Subjects of Slavery, Agents of Change.* Athens: University of Georgia Press, 1992.

Wipper, Audrey. "Kikuyu Women and the Harry Thuku Riot: Some Uniformities of Female Militancy." *Africa* 58, 4 (1989): 300-37.

Wisner, Ben. "Man-Made Famine in Eastern Kenya: The Interrelationship of Environment and Development." University of Sussex Inst. of Development Studies Disc. Paper No. 96 (July 1976).

Wolff, Richard D. *Britain and Kenya, 1870-1930.* Nairobi: Transafrica Publishers, 1974.

Wood, L. J. "Market Origins and Development in East Africa." Makerere University Dept. of Geography Occas. Paper No. 57 (1974).

Worboys, Michael. "The Discovery of Colonial Malnutrition between the Wars." In *Imperial Medicine and Indigenous Societies.* Ed. D. Arnold. Manchester: Manchester University Press, 1988. 208-25.

Wright, Marcia. *Strategies of Slaves and Women.* NY: Lilian Barber, 1993.

Zeleza, Tiyambe. "The Labour System in Independent Kenya." In *An Economic History of Kenya.* Ed. W. R. Ochieng and R. M. Maxon. Nairobi: East African Educational Publications, 1992. 347-69.

_____. "Women and the Labour Process in Kenya Since Independence." *Transafrican Jl. of History* 17 (1988): 69-107.

GOVERNMENT DOCUMENTS

Call numbers listed are for Kenya National Archives, Ministry of Agriculture Bean files located there, or Nairobi City Council (NCC) files. Authored works are listed by author above.

KENYA, GOVERNMENT OF

Districts/Provinces

Central Province

> *Annual Reports.* 1938; ARC(MAA) 2/3/1 VIA. 1940-42, 1947, 1949-51, 1953-54; ARC(MAA) 2/3/8 II-IV, 2/3/36 VI-VII.
>
> Provincial Commissioner.
>
> Census and Vital Statistics. 1919-28; PC/CP 8/3/1.
>
> Female Circumcision. 1920; PC/CP 7/1/2.
>
> Female Circumcision. 1928-30; PC/CP 8/1/1.
>
> Forced Marriage of African Girls. 1936-40; PC/CP 19/1.

General Policy Native Affairs. 1925-27; PC/CP 6/4/5.

Native Areas, General Policy. 1922; PC/CP 6/4/4.

Natives in Reserves Other Than Their Own. 1921-27; PC/CP 16/1/1.

Report on Labour. 1914-15; PC/CP 4/2/1.

A Short History of Kikuyu Province (1911-1927). 1929; PC/CP 1/1/2.

Statistics of Native Populations. 1935; PC/CP 8/3/10-11.

Trading Centres. 1961-63; LG 3/2438.

Dagoretti District

Annual Reports. 1912-18; DC/KBU 1/4-5, 9-11.

Handing Over Reports. 1912-14; DC/KBU 1/4-5.

Sub-District Report. 1928; DC/KBU 1/21.

Fort Hall District (Murang'a)

African District Council Minutes. 1954-56; CS 1/14/63.

Annual Reports. 1939; PC/CP 4/4/1. 1940; ARC(MAA) 2/3/8 II.

Kiambu District

African District Council Minutes. 1953-56; CS 1/14/33. 1957-58, 1960-65; LG 3/2700-05.

Annual Reports. 1907-12, 1914-17; DC/KBU 1/1, 3, 7-9. 1922-34, 1936-62, 1964, 1966-67; DC/KBU 1/15, 17-52. 1968-80; MA 12/42-80.

County Council Minutes. 1962-65; LG 3/2704-5.

Handing Over Reports. 1927-28, 1930-31; DC/KBU 1/20, 22-24.

Local Native Council Minutes. 1925-34; PC/CENT 2/1/4. 1944-50; PC/CENTRAL 2/1/13. 1957-68; LG 3/2700-01.

Local Native Council Resolutions. Microfilm Reel 85.

Nairobi County Council Kiambu District Commission and Road Board Minutes. LG 1/57.

Quarterly Reports. April-June 1911, Jan.-March 1912; DC/KBU 1/3.

Kikuyu District

Annual Reports. 1909-10; PC/CP 4/2/1. 1917-21; DC/KBU 1/11,12,14. 1920-21, 1923-33; PC/CP 4/1/2.

Political Record Book, Part II. 1912-13; PC/CP 1/4/2.

Machakos District

Muigwithania, Kikuyu Newspaper (translations). DC/MKS 10B/13/1.

Meru District

Annual Reports. 1939; PC/CP 4/4/1.

Nairobi District

Annual Reports. 1909-10, 1914-15; PC/CP 4/2/1. 1910-11; DC/MKS 1/4/1. 1912-13, 1913-14, 1939-47; PC/CP 4/4/1-3. 1942; ARC(MAA) 2/3/8. 1945; MNAO ARC(MAA) 2/3/36.

Political Record Book. 1899-1915; DC/CP 1/8/1.

Nairobi Extra Provincial District

　　Annual Reports. 1954-62; AA 13/1/8/9.

Nairobi Municipality

　　Annual Reports. 1914-15; PC/CP 4/2/1.

　　Municipality. 1939; LG 3/3207.

　　Nairobi Township. 1909; PC/CP 4/2/1.

　　Native/African Advisory Council Minutes. 1944-46; CS 1/14/11. 1954-56; CS 1/14/85. 1957-59;
　　　　LG 3/2825. 1932, 1944-45, 1954-55; NCC 27/10.

Thika District

　　Annual Reports. 1938; ARC(MAA) 2/3/1 VIA.

Ukamba Province

　　Annual Reports. 1906-15, 1915-21; PC/CP 4/2/1, 2. 1916-21; DC/KBU 1/10-14.

　　Handing Over Reports. 1919-20; DC/KBU 1/13.

MINISTRIES/DEPARTMENTS

　　African/Native Affairs, Ministry of

　　　　Annual Reports. 1923-28, 1930-36, 1938-51; no call numbers given.

　　　　Associations - Kikuyu. MAA 9/835.

　　　　Central Commodity Distribution Board. 1949-51; MAA 8/58.

　　　　Complaints and Petitions by Natives. MAA 9/904.

　　　　Criminal Jurisdiction: Witchcraft Cases. 1946-50; MAA 7/835.

　　　　Handing Over Report of Chief Native Commissioner, 1934-53. MAA 8/53.

　　　　Intelligence and Security. 1948-50, press cuttings; MAA 8/102.

　　　　Intelligence Report. ARC (MAA) 2/3/16 IV.

　　　　Internal Security and Defence, Crime and Incident Report. 1960; MAA 9/1022.

　　　　Legislation - Credit to Africans (Control) Ordinance. 1941-57; MAA 9/959.

　　　　Maize Control. 1947-51; MAA 8/143.

　　　　Ministry of African Affairs. MAA 8/22.

　　　　Monthly Court Returns, Kiambu. 1958-59; MAA 2/24.

　　　　Monthly Court Returns, Kiambu - Criminal. 1960; MAA 2/26.

　　　　Nairobi Extra-Territorial District Court Returns. July 1960-Jan. 1961; MAA 2/16.

　　　　Nairobi Municipal African/Native Affairs Dept. Annual Reports. 1938; ARC(MAA) 2/3/1
　　　　　　VIA. 1939; no call number. 1940-41; ARC(MAA) 2/3/8. 1950; MAA 7/639.
　　　　　　1952-57; no call numbers.

　　　　Native Affairs Committee Minutes. 1948-52; MAA 6/38.

　　　　Native Marriages - Martin Parr's Report. 1941-42; MAA 10/133.

　　　　Native Tribes and Customs; Marriage of Girls. 1944-50; MAA 7/700.

Policy - Africans in Urban Areas. Ndola Urban Conference, 1958; MAA 9/978.

Policy - Slavery. 1938-58; MAA 7/125.

Policy - Urban Areas - Nairobi. 1945; MAA 7/491.

Royal Commission Report on the Marketing and Distributive System. 1956; MAA 9/993.

Unrest - Effects of Operation Anvil, Nairobi. 1954; MAA 7/756.

Unrest - Masai District. 1945-47; MAA 7/736.

Agriculture, Dept./Ministry of

Agricultural Policy. 1963. ARC/MAWR-3 AGRI 3/156, 3/214.

Annual Reports. 1928, 1930-36, 1941-43, 1945-68; no call numbers given. 1954; Agr 4/116.

Annual Report of the Research Division. 1970.

Bean Files 1/II, 4/XV, 5/VII. (at Ministry of Agriculture)

Central Province

Agricultural Reports. 1936-41, 1951, 1954, 1958, 1961; Agr 4/114-16, 125, 144. 1983; no call number given.

Marketing Board Annual Reports. 1959-63; no call numbers given.

Marketing Board. Agr 4/70.

Coast Province Agricultural Report. 1928; no call number given.

Fort Hall (Murang'a) Agricultural Report. 1936; Agr 4/114.

Kiambu District

District Agricultural Report. 1961; DC/KBU 1/48.

District Agricultural Officers Weekly Reports, Kiambu-Githunguri Division. 1953-57; DAO/KBU 1/1/144.

District Dept. of Agriculture Reports. 1936, 1953, 1957, 1963, 1964; Agr 4/114, 465, 154, 140, 531.

Marketing Monthly Reports. 1956-61; Agr 4/69.

Marketing Officer Safari Report. 1958-59; DAO/KBU 1/1/148.

Kiambu Safari Diaries, Divisional Agricultural Officers. 1935-37; Agr 4/440. 1956-57; Agr 4/207.

Kikuyu District

Agricultural Reports, S. Kikuyu. 1928-29; no call numbers given.

Marketing Kikuyu Province. 1931-50; DAO/KBU 1/1/92.

Seed Issues Kikuyu to Natives. 1932-39; DAO/KBU 1/1/257.

Machakos District Agricultural Report. 1936; Agr 4/114.

Meru Agricultural Reports. 1928; no call number given. 1936; Meru and Embu Agr 4/114.

Miscellaneous Files

Beans. 1933-38; Agr 4/319.

Beans. 1939-41; Agr 4/527.

Beans. 1944-58; Agr 4/239.

Beans, General. 1934-1961; DAO/KBU 1/1/218.

Beans Other Than Seeds. Agr 4/500.

Board of Agriculture Plant Industry, Maize Enquiry Committee. 1935-36; CNC 10/9.

Crop Inspection Report. Agr 4/510.

Defence (Control of Prices) Regulations. 1945, 1949 Amendment.

Inspection Markets. Agr 4/334.

Laws of Kenya: The Price Control Act, Chapter 504. Revised from 1962. 1972.

Maendeleo Clubs. DAO/KBU 1/1/36.

Market Prices. 1942-57; Agr 4/409.

Marketing and Trade Report. 1962; no call number given.

Marketing of Native Produce Ordinance. 1935; Agr 4/493.

Markets. Agr 4/68.

Markets. 1939-44; Agr 4/574.

Markets, Marketing General and Marketing Rules. 1954-61; DAO/KBU 1/1/93.

Monthly Purchase Returns. 1939; Agr 4/496.

Price Controls. Agr 4/71.

Nyanza Agricultural Report, 1928.

Attorney General's Office

Food Control Ordinance. 1929; AG 4/3231, 3233, 3235.

Married Women's Property Act, 1935 Amendment. AG 4/2787.

Native Marriage and Divorce Ordinance. AG 4/2792-93.

Native Marriage Ordinance. 1916-22; AG 4/2789.

Registration of Heathen Marriage. 1922; AG 4/2790.

Status of Native Women-Legislation. AG 4/2791.

Central Bureau of Statistics (also Ministry of Economic Planning and Development)

Census. Volumes II and III. 1979.

Consumer Price Indices in Nairobi. Ministry of Finance and Planning. March 1977.

"Continuity and Change in Metropolitan and Rural Attitudes Towards Family Size and Family Planning in Kenya Between 1966/1967 and 1977/1978." *Social Perspectives* 5, 1 (Dec. 1980): 1-8.

Educational Characteristics and Their Relationship to Fertility for a Selected Area of Kenya. Demographic Wkg. Paper No. 3 (June 1976).

"Infant Feeding Practices in Nairobi, Kenya." *Social Perspectives* 8, 1 (May 1984): 1-5.

Integrated Rural Surveys: 1976-79 Basic Report. Ministry of Economic Planning and Development. February 1982.

Kenya Contraceptive Prevalence Survey, 1984. Ministry of Planning and National Development. Nairobi. May 1986.

Kenya Economic Survey. 1979, 1982, 1987-88.

Market Information Bulletin. Ministry of Economic Planning and Development. 1981-85.

Population Projections for Kenya, 1980-2000. UNICEF. Nairobi: March 1983.

Selected Data on Social Conditions in Kenya. Ministry of Planning and National Development. Dec. 1985.

Statistical Abstract. 1979.

Statistical Abstracts. Economics and Statistics Division, Office of the Minister of State for Constitutional Affairs and Economic Planning. 1962, 1966.

Survey of Distribution. Ministry of Finance and Economic Planning. 1960.

Urban Food Purchasing Survey, Part I. FAO Marketing Development Project. Ministry of Finance and Planning. 1977.

Women in Kenya. July 1978.

Chief Native Commissioner's Office

Native Tribunal Cases

Kiambu and Dagoretti. 1931-52; CNC 10/45.

Kiambu Native Tribunals, Returns. 1952-53; CNC 10/45.

Nairobi. 1935-50; CNC 10/29.

Returns, Criminal Cases, Nairobi. Jan.(?) 1951-52; CNC 10/30.

Native Tribunals Ordinance. 1930; CNC 10/45.

Commerce and Industry, Ministry of

African Traders. 1955; MCI 6/1272.

African Traders Course, Jeanes School, Kabete. First, 1960, English; MCI 6/1303. Third, 1961, Swahili; MCI 6/1311. Fifth, 1961, Swahili; MCI 6/1313. Second, 1962, English; MCI 6/1316.

Kenya Market Profile. Dept. of External Trade, External Trade Authority. Nairobi, April 1980.

Native Marketing Ordinance. 1935-38; MCI 5/1.

Regulation of Hawkers. MCI 6/881.

Trade and Commerce Legislation - Trader's Licensing Ordinance. 1959-61; MCI 6/883.

Working Party on Assistance to African Traders. 1954-55; MCI 6/813.

East African Statistical Dept. (later Central Bureau of Statistics)

[Report on] National Income and Output of the Colony and Protectorate of Kenya. 1949.

The Pattern of Income, Expenditure and Consumption of African Labourers in Nairobi, Oct.-Nov. 1950. 1951.

Reported Employment and Earnings in Kenya. 1960.

Economic Planning and Development, Ministry of

Kiambu District Development Plan 1979-83. Jan. 1980.

Finance and Economic Planning, Ministry of

"The Growth of the Economy, 1954-1962."

Situation Analysis of Children and Women in Kenya. Sections 1-4. Central Bureau of Statistics/UNICEF. 1984.

Health, Ministry of

Outbreak of Plague, Nairobi; 1911 and the Indian Bazaar. MOH 1/6020.

Home Affairs and National Heritage, Ministry of

Kenya Demographic and Health Survey. National Council for Population and Development/Inst. for Resource Development/Macro Systems, Inc. Oct. 1989.

Local Government, Ministry of

Miscellaneous files

Cost of Living Commission Report. 1950; MLG 2/2/119.

Hawker's Licenses. MLG 2/125.

Native Markets in Rural Settled Areas. 1945-53; LG 2/202.

"The Patterns of Income, Expenditure and Consumption of Africans in Nairobi, 1957-58." East African Statistical Dept. MLG 2/2/119.

Report of the Taxation Enquiry Committee. 1947. Called the Plewman Report.

Report on Famine Relief. MLG 2/2/119.

Traders Licensing Ordinance. 1941-62; LG 3/733-34.

Trading Centres. 1955-59; LG 3/2434.

Technical Manual: Markets. Local Authority Development Programme. Oct. 1986.

Nairobi City/Municipal Council (NCC)

African Affairs Dept. 1951; LG 3/3204.

Annual Reports. 1951-52; LG 2/40. 1952-55; no call numbers given. 1956-60; LG 3/2958-59. 1960, 1963-65, 1967; no call numbers given.

Complaints. LG 3/2502.

Control of Public Markets Local Government (Municipalities) Ordinance. 1928; JA/LG 5/1.

East African Protectorate Official Gazette. 1903-22.

Finance Committee Minutes. NCC file.

Food Shops and Stores - Bylaws. 1958-61; LG 3/3046.

Hawkers' By-laws. 1962-64; LG 3/3048.

Housing and Employment of Servants. 1939; NCC 1/201.

Nairobi Municipal Council. 1948-50; LG 2/39.

Nairobi Municipal Council Minutes. 1905-09, 1914-15; NCC file. 1937-41; McMillan Library. 1944-47, 1949, 1951-59; LG 3/3137-49. 1960; McMillan Library. 1961-67; LG 3/3150-56. 1967-88; McMillan Library.

NCC files. 1953-59; NCC 27/10. 1966-71; NCC 7/8/14.

"Report of the Commission of Inquiry into Alleged Corruptions or Other Malpractices in Relation to the Affairs of the Nairobi City Council, Dec. 1955-March 1956." KNA.

"Report on the Incidence of Destitution Among Africans in Urban Areas." 1954. KNA.

Nairobi County Council

African Welfare. Nairobi County Council 1/65.

Nairobi County Council. 1957-62; LG 3/2976.

Nairobi Municipality Verandah Trading By-laws. 1949; LG 2/281.

Planning and National Development

Agricultural and Livestock Data Compendium. 1989.

Treasury, Dept. of

"Domestic Income and Products in Kenya." 1959.

UNITED KINGDOM COLONIAL OFFICE

East Africa Royal Commission Report. 1953-1955.

INTERVIEWS AND PERSONAL COMMUNICATIONS with author (excludes numbered survey informants)

Abwunza, Judith, Researcher. Pers. comm. 10 Jan. 1988.

Askwith, T.G., Municipal Native Affairs Officer, Nairobi, 1945-47, and Patricia Askwith. Interview. Cheltenham. 13 Oct. 1992.

Bliss, Frederick, Professor of Agronomy, University of California-Davis. Pers. comm. 25 June 1992.

Blundell, Sir Michael, Minister of Agriculture 1955-59; 1961-62. Interview. Nairobi. 10 Sept. 1988.

Browne, Dallas L., Researcher. Pers. comm. 27 June 1994.

Chege, Dr. Michael, Ford Foundation Program Officer. Interview. Nairobi. 4 Nov. 1988.

Colchester, Thomas, Municipal Native Affairs Officer, Nairobi, 1940s, and Nancy Colchester. Interview. Aldeburgh. 19 Oct. 1992.

Fisher, Jeanne, Anthropologist. Interview. Cambridge. 14 Oct. 1992.

Gepts, Paul, Professor of Agronomy, University of California-Davis. Pers. comm. 25 June 1992.

Githaiga-Bowman, Wairimu, Researcher. Interview. Nairobi. 21, 27 Jan. 1988.

Githuka, James. Interview. Nairobi. 2 Nov. 1988.

Hake, Andrew, Author, C.M.S. Missionary, and Member, Nairobi City Council, 1960-62, and Jean Hake, Social Worker, Nairobi, 1955-62. Interview. Swinden. 12 Oct. 1992.

Haldane, Donna, World Bank. In Nairobi 1967-73 working for NCCK. Pers. comm. 25 Mar. 1991.

Huxley, Elspeth, Author. Interview. Oaksey. 12 Oct. 1992.

Jobita, Mrs. Margaret, Acting Deputy Director of Social Services and Housing. Interview. Nairobi. 20 Apr. 1988.

Kabuga, J.M., Head, Industrial Crops Division, Ministry of Agriculture. Interview. Nairobi. 19 July 1988.

Kershaw, Greet, Professor of Anthropology, University of California-Berkeley. Pers. comm. 4 Aug. 1994.

Kirkby, Roger, Regional Coordinator, CIAT East African Bean Programme. Interview. Nairobi. 18-19 July 1988.

Leakey, C.L.A., African Bean Breeder and Plant Pathologist. Interviews. Cambridge. 15, 21 Oct. 1992, and 7 June 1993.

Makungo, Paul, Market Inspector #762671, Gikomba Market. Interview. Nairobi. Apr. 1988.

Migunda, J., Operations Director, Government of Kenya National Cereals Produce Board. Interview. Nairobi. 10 Aug. 1988.

Mitullah, Winnie, Sociologist. Interview. Nairobi. 2 Nov. 1988.

Muigai, Matthew W., Acting Markets Superintendent, Kiambu County Council. Interview. Kiambu. 12 Aug. 1988.

Mwaniki, Grace. Pers. comm. 6 Mar. 1988.

Mwaura, Helen, Researcher. Interview. Nairobi. 4 Mar. 1988.

Ndegwa, Stephen, Researcher. Interview. 22 Sept. 1991.

Njora, John, Deputy Town Clerk, Nairobi. Interview. Nairobi. 2 Nov. 1988.

Njugunah, K., Director, Kenya Agricultural Research Inst., Thika. Interview. Thika. 29 Sept. 1988.

Nyamweru, Celia, Professor of Anthropology, St. Lawrence University. Pers. comm. 24 Sept. 1993.

Odok, O., Crop Production Officer, Ministry of Agriculture. Interview. Nairobi. 13 July 1988.

O'Hagan, Desmond, District Commissioner, Nairobi, 1939-40, Ft. Hall, 1945-47. Interview. Kiambu. 8 Nov. 1988.

Ongugo, Paul, Policy Analyst, Kenya Forestry Research Institute. Pers. comm. 29 Apr. 1997.

Palmer, Jean, Coordinator, Evening Programs, Kenya Museum Society. Pers. comm. 26 July 1988.

Voss, Joachim, Anthropologist with CIAT, Rwanda. Interview. Nairobi. 30 July 1988.

Were, M.O., Head of Crop Production, Ministry of Agriculture. Interview. Nairobi. 13 July 1988.

Werlin, Herbert, Researcher. Pers. comm. 24 Mar. 1991.

B.1 Ngara Market, 1987: A Furniture Factory

INDEX

ABOUT THE AUTHOR

Claire Robertson is Associate Professor of History and Women's Studies at The Ohio State University. Her research interests focus mainly on many facets of the history and lives of African women, especially those involved in trade. She is the author of *Sharing the Same Bowl: A Socioeconomic History of Women and Class in Accra, Ghana*, which won the African Studies Association Herskovits Award in 1985. She has also co-edited two books, *Women and Slavery in Africa*, with Martin Klein, and *Women and Class in Africa*, with Iris Berger. She has published in addition a number of articles. She is now developing her interest in women's role in environmental issues and its ethnobotanical aspects, as well as working on a precolonial history of African women.

}